HERE WE STAND

HERE WE STAND

Where Nazarenes Fit in the Religious Marketplace

STAN INGERSOL / WESLEY D. TRACY

BEACON HILL PRESS
OF KANSAS CITY

10   9   8   7   6   5   4

CONTENTS

PART V
THE BELIEVERS' CHURCH TRADITION

PART VI
PENTECOSTAL AND
CHARISMATIC CHURCHES

PART VII
UNITING AND INDEPENDENT CHURCHES
AND ORGANIZATIONS

Campus Crusade for Christ
Promise Keepers
Compassion International
Focus on the Family

PART VIII
THE AMERICAN MELTING POT OF RELIGION

PART IX
NON-CHRISTIAN RELIGIONS

FOREWORD

HERE IS A BOOK THAT IS DESPERATELY NEEDED in Nazarene circles and beyond. The changing face of the Church of the Nazarene, the striking emerging shifts in the larger body of Christendom, and the novel perspectives and attitudes toward religion and faith being advanced throughout our societies clamor for the publication, distribution, and careful reading of this work.

As a consequence of the many positions being promoted, some persons are becoming confused as they have few if any resources to evaluate the validity of the large variety of religious claims being made. In part, this volume has been produced to help obviate this confusion. Whatever one's religious or denominational background, this material is valuable, for it factually and fairly portrays historic Christian faith and practice. It even deals with non-Christian religions whose ideas have been imported within our North American shores from various parts of our rapidly shrinking world.

Nazarenes particularly (and they are the primary audience) will profit from this reading and will be enabled to understand the positions taken by the Church of the Nazarene both in the past and currently. It will help Nazarenes and others to see the new and older denominations and the relationships and differences between them.

I am not aware of another book like this one. Every branch of Christendom that values an informed constituency could well emulate the outstanding work of these authors. Stan Ingersol and Wes Tracy have written to appeal to pastors, scholars, and students and compellingly speak to the questions of people whose children may be involved with cults, those who have neighbors who belong to a strange tradition, or Sunday School teachers who must understand people from various denominational backgrounds. This book speaks directly but warmly to the identity crisis that now seems to plague some parts of our church.

The authors are prepared for this assignment both by the best in technical and professional training and by their lifetime personal backgrounds in the Church of the Nazarene. Their training equips them to seek objectivity in discussing non-Nazarene traditions, and their many years of experience in our denomination help them to appreciate the best in their own Nazarene heritage. They are keenly aware of the strengths and vulnerabilities that have appeared at various times throughout our 100-year history.

The Church of the Nazarene has experienced a 52 percent net growth in the last decade. It is incumbent upon the church to inform these newer Nazarenes, as well as the older ones, of the resources within our tradition to deal with the strong and sometimes appealing voices from many quarters of our post-Christian era. This can be done better when we know who we are. That's what this volume is all about.

Roots are important. They provide security, a network of fellowship, a living tradition, a sense of belonging—desperate needs of our day. These benefits can and must be maintained without succumbing to individualism, subjectivism, sectarianism, exclusivism, legalism, pharisaism—any form of spiritual narrowness or ecclesiastical bureaucracy.

It isn't necessary to become a generic Christian or a disconnected church member in order to overcome the aberrations of denominational loyalty. Admittedly, one's heritage can be exalted inordinately, leading to alienation. But it can also be appreciated and appropriated in ways that provide meaning and joy.

This is not a plea for narrow provincialism—but everybody has to be somewhere. Every believer has to stand on some place, and every Christian needs an enlightened understanding of his or her religious and spiritual backgrounds.

Although Drs. Ingersol and Tracy are aware of the "freckles" on the face of the Church of the Nazarene, they do not find the label "Nazarene" to be confining or detrimental, but fulfilling and satisfying in service to God and others. Furthermore, they have sought to treat other traditions with respect while simultaneously identifying their differences.

A proper understanding of one's personal faith lineage is necessary to avoid degeneration of religious commitment into a private or subjective affair, making one a closet Christian (a concept foreign to the New Testament and Wesleyan faith).

In light of the seeming disenchantment of many with the Church or its structures, the words of Cyprian, one of the Early Church fathers, are poignant: "No man can have God for his Father who will not have the Church for his Mother." This book, prayerfully read, studied, and discussed, will contribute to a greater appreciation for the broader Church of Jesus Christ, for the various branches of Christendom, and certainly for the teachings, practices, and spirit of the Church of the Nazarene.

Here We Stand is must reading for every Nazarene and a valuable guide for non-Nazarenes and would-be Nazarenes as well.

—*John A. Knight*
General Superintendent
Church of the Nazarene

INTRODUCTION

Why This Book Had to Happen

AS I SIT IN MY THIRD-FLOOR STUDY trying to break through writer's block, I gaze out my window. To the southwest is a row of homes and mailboxes, to the north a string of backyards with bikes and firewood, and with tomato stakes waiting for spring, when they'll punctuate tiny suburban gardens.

From where I sit I can see the Presbyterian pastor's dog—tied up, thankfully. Across the street and up two houses lives a family from India—Buddhists, I gather, from brief encounters at the homeowners' association meetings. Three houses north, an African-American family lives out the Baptist faith. Their congregation belongs to the Progressive National Baptist Convention—"the one that Martin Luther King belonged to," the husband explained when my face betrayed my ignorance of the movement.

About a block and a half away lives another African-American family with names as strange to me as a Kwanza celebration. "Islam is the Answer," their bumper stickers proclaim.

Half a block east, the house of the richest family in our neighborhood sits like a solemn sentinel. No one's home at this DINKs (Double Income, No Kids) residence. They drive his and hers Lincolns. Both are executives. They practice their own religion, which seems to be half Unity and half Shirley MacLaine, complete with crystals, I'm told. A Roman Catholic family moved in next door to them; I guess they're Catholic—the statuette by the birdbath looks like the holy virgin.

A quarter of a mile to the southwest on Wornall Road, the new Mormon church lifts its colonial spire. I could see it from here if it weren't for the big hackberry tree and a couple of giant oaks that have held their leaves knee-deep into winter. They put down their roots here long before this became a middle-class suburb. I don't know which of my neighbors are Mormon, but the Mormon church's parking lot was full when I came home from First Church of the Nazarene last Sunday. Just 300 yards from the new Mormon church is the new Pentecostal church. That congregation is frenetically ambitious, out to win the world by coffee break time today.

Two blocks due south, right next to the fire station, stands a Jehovah's Witnesses Kingdom Hall. As I stare out the window, I notice a pair of Jehovah's Witness canvassers on the next street. I recognize them because they hit our house last evening just as we were sitting down to our low-sodium, no-fat casserole. The *Watchtower* they left now sticks up out of the wastebasket beside my desk. These canvassers are now ringing the doorbell at one of the Jewish homes

11

in our subdivision. I would like to hear this conversation—but it looks as if no one is home. Does a Jehovah's Witness caller feel relief or frustration when no one answers the door? They head now for the door of the Asian family that talks about the *I Ching* and yin and yang.

Two Nazarene families live in our neighborhood. We also have a Seventh-Day Adventist preacher, a one-parent ex-Quaker family, and a set of Methodist grandparents whom we met at Jess and Jim's Steak House. Plenty of faith-free neopagans live here too—that's for sure. Many of them are so young that they think a Cadillac, a time-share in Cancún, or a condo in Colorado would satisfy the ache in their hearts.

The same religious diversity persists throughout the metropolitan area. Yesterday's newspaper carried news about local gay and lesbian "faith communities." An ad announced that Elizabeth Clare Prophet would appear at a local luxury hotel. She's the "guru mom" of the Church Universal and Triumphant. For five bucks you could hear her talk about angels and have the opportunity to buy her books and tapes. A sketchy story about a police raid that turned up a houseful of chickens and goats also appeared. Police seemed puzzled, but the animals were probably headed for Santeria sacrifices.

Given the racial and religious diversity of my neighborhood, you would think I lived in New York, Los Angeles, maybe Miami, or San Francisco. But I live in the placid, complacent, conservative Midwest—Kansas City.

So here we are, all jammed up in one housing subdivision called Woodbridge:

Nazarenes and neopagans,
Jews and Jehovah's Witnesses,
Mormons and Methodists,
Baptists and Buddhists,
New Agers and Adventists,
Muslims and Catholics,
Charismatics and Greek Orthodox (the best cooks in the community),
and who knows what other faith families are represented?

We mingle in the restaurants, the service clubs, the Sun Fresh and Hy-Vee supermarkets. We nod on the sidewalks and chat over roses and snow shovels. Our kids gather each morning at the corners to board the same school buses. At school they study, lunch, and mix. They discuss marriage, politics, sex, drugs, rock music, violence, racism, abortion, and sports. From each other they build ideas about the meaning of life.

In school, society, and community affairs, the Christian viewpoint is not predominant, preferred, or even permitted in many cases. Try putting a Christmas crèche in a public school classroom, and see what happens. Knowing who we are and what we believe is more important than ever.

These post-Christian times and cultural realities call Christians to rediscover that what they have in common in Christ can be more important than sectarian differences. We must pull together against common postmodern challenges of pluralism, relativism, and secularism. When I was growing up, the most fun a young Arminian theologue could have was scalping Calvinists. Fifty years ago, trumping Catholics with the King James Version was great Evangelical sport. Today, focusing our energies on such activities is counterproductive. Both the times and the culture call for more enlightened responses.

Isms galore glut today's religious idea market. No age, no world area has ever had to wade through the number of religious options that now confront North Americans. How can young people make responsible choices in such an atmosphere? When and where will they learn how to stand on a firm foundation? In the home? On television? Public schools? At church, maybe—if sound teaching wins out over the consumer church bent on making everyone feel good.

Our children mingle and talk with people pushing every religious notion imaginable. They need to know where we, their parents and grandparents, their mentors and teachers, stand on the things that really matter. They need to know where the anchors are—not so they can argue down a Hindu or a Mormon, but so they'll know the resources of their own Christian tradition.

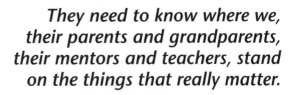 *They need to know where we, their parents and grandparents, their mentors and teachers, stand on the things that really matter.*

You yourself may not know what you need to know about the Christian faith. We have a rich heritage and an adequate theology that speaks with faith and reason and precedent to the social, religious, economic, and spiritual problems that bedevil our times. You need to know that you don't have to figure all these things out from scratch. Your faith has resources, but if you don't know your faith, you're condemned to struggle with reinventing the wheel.

Not that you don't have a worldview or a theology—you do. Beliefs create action, and actions create beliefs (often to justify instinctive conduct). If your belief system was put together in today's pluralistic culture, it may very well be an incoherent collection of impressions, reminiscences, assumptions, unexamined gut-level reactions, inherited truisms ("My mama always said . . ."), and the like. They may be inherently contradictory, irrational, and blatantly unchristian, but you have them, and they guide your life. You need to know the Christian faith so that you can live with the confidence of an informed mind.

You need to know that Christian denominations or churches have predictable strengths and vulnerabilities. Christian groups who stress predestination, or those who emphasize salvation by grace alone to the exclusion of other doctrines, predictably will have problems about the lack of daily holy living among their members. On the other hand, those who stress holy conduct to the point of diminishing grace will predictably face a vulnerability called legalism. Denominations for whom ecstatic spiritual experience becomes all in all will predictably produce a shortage of critical thinking. On the other hand, groups who seem to think that ancient ceremonies produce salvation by the church's authority or those who believe that conversion consists of memorizing a catechism will predictably need to be careful not to trivialize a personal relationship with God.

A Spiritual Home

I love the Church of the Nazarene, vulnerabilities and all. Everywhere I go, I find more to love about this wonderful family of faith. I've had the privilege to teach, preach, or worship with Nazarenes in Jerusalem, Kyiv, New York, London, Denver, Buenos Aires, Manila, Indianapolis, Recife, Miami, San Antonio, Los Angeles, Boston, and Santo Domingo.

I have also been to places like Chillicothe, Cross Roads, Edmond, Beatrice, Clever, Oil City, Kokomo, Rock City, Granby, San Bruno, and Hutchinson. I've even been to Muleshoe and Gnaw Bone—I didn't get to worship there, but the names are too quaint to leave out of a list like this.

My coauthor on this project, Stan Ingersol, could make a similar list of places where he has encountered the Nazarene family. He's a Duke Ph.D. and a lifelong Nazarene. He joined the church at age nine in Ponca City, Oklahoma, and followed his parents to Africa for a seven-year sojourn.

Wherever I go, I run into family, the great Nazarene family who put their arms around the world and create homelike churches. I love the family atmosphere at least as much as our theology and our "get things done" attitude. We are a covenant community of faith. Everywhere you drop in on Nazarenes, you get bright-eyed welcomes and hugs as if you were the last person to show up at a family reunion.

Nazarenes seem to sense that our common faith in Christ, our Wesleyan-Holiness heritage, and our family ties are much more important than our regional and cultural differences.

Another thing I like about our Nazarene family is the way we treasure the past, where our memories were carved out. Yet we're not enslaved to the methods and peculiarities of a world that we have outgrown. Prizing our heritage does not so preoccupy us that we

Everywhere you drop in on Nazarenes, you get bright-eyed welcomes and hugs as if you were the last person to show up at a family reunion.

enter the future shoulder blades first. Rooted in what matters most, we lean into the future, knowing that God shares His creativity with us so that we can help give a Christlike shape to the years that are about to be.

I also like our sense of humor. The Nazarene laugh is distinctive. That's because for the most part we don't take ourselves too seriously. True, now and then you see a grim Nazarene going about with a face that looks like a hatchet dipped in vinegar. But most of us don't fit that description. When we congregate, we laugh at our gaffes and glitches and our bold plans that have nose-dived worse than Orville and Wilbur's first airplane. The ability to laugh at ourselves is a precious gift.

This family of faith has been bound together by shared adversity. It hasn't always been popular to be a Nazarene. For starters, most Nazarenes have come from the ranks of the poor. We know about praying down rent money, putting cardboard soles in shoes, wearing hand-me-down clothes, and making pledges on faith and not on cash reserves.

Further, our doctrines have often been treated with condescending tolerance, even by other Christians. The idea of being pure in heart and life sounds as ludicrous as the Three Stooges to a society fed on neo-Freudian psychology. To the mildly religious and to our Calvinist friends, entire sanctification sounds insufferably arrogant, and sometimes they tell us so.

Nazarene standards of dress and behavior and our resistance to worldly entertainment have drawn caustic comments "knee-deep in snide" from friend and foe alike. Ever been the brunt of "We don't smoke, we don't chew, and we don't go with girls who do"?

True, some of our number have developed the knack of flaunting what we don't do into an art, and all of us get pinched or punched for it. Legalism is one of our predictable vulnerabilities, you know, particularly if our doctrine of sanctification by faith alone gets off center.

But through it all, self-surrender in favor of a Christ-centered life has marked the movement. But that doesn't mean we'll be popular. Holiness was jeered, not cheered, when John Wesley called England to prayerful searching for sanctifying grace. When he and his Methodist lay preachers proclaimed perfect love, they became at once the scandal and the blessing of the nation.

Shared Christian service draws the Nazarene family together. Read the Prison Epistles of Paul, and see what was on his mind as he faced death and eternity. He did not write about the stock market or the Super Bowl. He wrote to old friends with whom he had shared in Christian service. Likewise, Nazarenes have joined hands to establish gospel beachheads in nearly 120 countries.

Shared adversity and shared Christian service have bound us together in loving partnership. Ever notice how camaraderie grows among travelers when hardships strike? Something like that has happened on the Nazarene journey. The adversity and the shared service have welded us closer together than ever.

We made mistakes as an adolescent church. We flirted with legalism more than once. Strange, isn't it, how your strengths often create flip-side vulnerabilities? Our standards of dress and conduct (a strength) also made us vulnerable. Sure enough, some people acted as if keeping the rules is what saves or sanctifies. Only God redeems and purifies. Just being Protestant should teach us that.

Others don't always understand our conduct codes. But we came by them honestly. Our blue-collar origins (that's not negative) caused us to express our social conscience in terms of controlling personal vices. Our working-class roots meant that we didn't know how to broker political influence. But we *could* avoid smoking, drinking, dancing, movie theaters, and the like.

The social conscience of Christians in other social rungs took different forms, though. For example, the middle-class Presbyterians might be expected to think our personal conduct social rules legalistic and trivial. For them, the way to make society more Christian was not through staying out of dance halls, but by changing unjust laws and policies. While Nazarenes were not (in the early years) at home in the halls of power, many Presbyterians were. Their fathers, brothers, and uncles were the corporate presidents, the bankers, the governors, the senators. Compared to putting pressure on a senator to pass a fair labor law, staying out of the pool hall might look trivial. But we are more mature now; our social concerns go beyond (but do not exclude) personal conduct.

In our ecclesiastical adolescence we also flirted with Fundamentalism. While we believe in traditional Christianity, we believe there's something better than the rigid Fundamentalism of our day. We think there is something better than single-issue politics, see-it-my-way-or-else theology, and lowest-common-denominator churchmanship. We prefer the inclusive spirit of our Wesleyan heritage that takes root in the broad Christian traditions and not in sectarian dogmatism. The revival of interest in a full-orbed Wesleyan heritage that marries personal religion and social responsibility has been a defining event in our church.

Another vulnerability arose from one of our strengths. We rightly taught that the Christian is to live above willful sins. But we allowed our challengers to push us so far in the direction of "sinless perfection" that many of our people lost the art of confession. Saved-and-sanctified people do not have to sin, but sometimes they do. The only thing for a Christian to do when he or she wakes up with sin on his or her hands is to confess it to God. Calling it by another name is no good. But some of our people made mistakes here. Even corporate prayers of confession were deleted from the worship services. It's been a hard lesson to learn. But we've discovered that John Wesley knew what he was doing when he advised even the most holy to properly pray the Lord's Prayer, including "Forgive us our trespasses." That does not mean the believer has committed deliberate sins; but all of us are members of a fallen race, and even our best effort leaves us needing the blood of Christ to atone for unwitting errors and failures born of "a thousand infirmities."

We have learned a lot, as any adolescent denomination would. We are now better prepared than ever before. Our doctrine of radical optimism, the cleansing from inner sin, is more needed than ever before. Some say that the Church of the Nazarene was raised up not for the 20th century but for the 21st.

Not everyone can be won by Nazarenes. Not every Christian would make a good Nazarene. But our Wesleyan-Holiness message of the radical optimism of grace is what our world needs most. Few others believe, as we do, that there is almost no limit to the good things that can happen because of the atoning grace of Jesus Christ. Social scientists say that personality is formed by age three, or even sooner. They declare that a bad home or neighborhood marks a person negatively forever, period. We believe, however, in miracles of grace, including the miracle of a pure heart re-created in the image of Christ, available for any believer. Among some of our Protestant friends, it is believed that there is no deliverance from the inner sinfulness of the human heart. Not even the atonement of Jesus, they say, can do that; we must live in a Rom. 7 type of struggle with sin all our lives. But we believe in the miracle of entire sanctification.

They call us Holiness people. That's good. That's another thing I love about Nazarenes. Wherever I hear a Nazarene choir sing, hear a Nazarene pastor preach, visit a Nazarene college chapel service, or enjoy the delights of a Nazarene potluck dinner, I know I am with people who take to heart our Savior's call to holiness. I look at their faces and know they have met the Lord in a saving encounter, that they would not willingly do anything wrong. These are people who grieve when they fail, who make the pursuit and possession of sanctifying grace life's chief priority. No casual sinning, no cheap grace, no glib discipleship here—these are Nazarenes.

Lately I've seen some evidence that some Nazarenes are almost eager to join the ranks of the nearly nameless, almost faceless generic Evangelical movement. This is predictable given the popularity of a sunshiny Evangelicalism that, above all, wants everybody to have a nice time. This is particularly true in light of the pressure on Nazarene churches and pastors to "grow." It's also predictable because the pluralistic religious scene today tends to bless religion, any religion, in such a way that theological distinctives are trivialized or erased.

But to be uncritically "tossed . . . about" by that "wind of doctrine" (Eph. 4:14, KJV) can end in shipwreck. That's one reason that Stan Ingersol and I have spent most of our discretionary time over the

> *The pluralistic religious scene today tends to bless religion, any religion, in such a way that theological distinctives are trivialized or erased.*

last year and a half on this book, which explores the religious idea market so that Nazarenes can know where they stand in relation to other beliefs and religions.

We're not out to hammer our competitors, but rather to teach our people the heart of their own faith tradition and to help them understand some of the 1,500 denominations and religions on the North American scene.

I think I understand the heart of our church. Therefore I may be too quick to make allowances for the clay feet often in evidence. But I appreciate other traditions as well. Many of them do some things well at which we're mediocre. I have studied at a Lutheran university. I have two degrees from a Presbyterian seminary (as well as having graduated from Southern Nazarene University and Nazarene Theological Seminary). But I was never tempted to become a Presbyterian pastor, and the Lutherans were never tempted to invite me into their fellowship.

I've been in a Nazarene church somewhere in the world almost every Sunday since I was three weeks old. My parents named me after John Wesley and took me to the Church of the Nazarene in Howard, Kansas. There they were saved under the preaching of evangelist A. F. Balsimeier. The Nazarene family has nurtured me all my life. I want our church to make the best possible contribution to this post-Christian era. Understanding the religious idea mart is a start.

"You are here," the red arrow read. The Mall of America in Minneapolis, the world's largest shopping mall, they claim. Hundreds of stores, thousands of shoppers. How would I ever find the bookstores? I seek out the directory with the red arrow that reads, "You are here." My wife doesn't need it. She's going to cruise every store anyway. But without a directory, I'm in trouble.

The religious idea market today is a lot like the Mall of America: a spiritual shopper's paradise. In America there are more than 1,500 stores, that is, religions or denominations. Forty percent—some 600—are non-Christian religions. That leaves us with some 900 brands of Christianity. Each one of these religions beckons, "Come bathe in my waters."

What's a spiritual seeker to do? Go to the church with the most handsome preacher, the slickest video, the one that speaks to felt needs, the one that keeps the kids off the street, the one with the most raucous music? How about the one with biblical teachings and sound doctrines?

This book is your directory. It starts with the Church of the Nazarene. Then it proceeds to identify with respect and fairness the chain stores in the religious mall.

"You are here." Here we stand. Here's your directory.

—*Wesley D. Tracy*

Part I

WHO ARE THE NAZARENES?

- They Shared a Dream:
  Launching the Nazarene Movement

- What Nazarenes Believe and Practice

THEY SHARED A DREAM:
LAUNCHING THE NAZARENE MOVEMENT

Historical Background

From roots in the Wesleyan revival in 18th-century England, the Holiness Movement blossomed in America. Wesleyan-Holiness denominations sprang up in every section of the country. Three such denominations and substantial parts of two other groups joined together in 1907 (Chicago) and 1908 (Pilot Point, Texas) to form the Church of the Nazarene.

Key leaders were Phineas F. Bresee, C. B. Jernigan, C. W. Ruth, and H. F. Reynolds, among others.

Core Beliefs

The dream that drew the founders together was a believers' church in the Wesleyan tradition. This was fleshed out with firm beliefs in orthodox Christianity. Traditional doctrines of the inspiration of the Bible; the Holy Trinity; the deity of Christ; and Protestant beliefs in *sola scriptura* (Scripture alone) as the Rule of faith and practice; *sola gratia,* salvation by grace alone; *sola fidei,* faith alone; and the priesthood of all believers marked the new Nazarene denomination.

The Wesleyan doctrine of salvation, particularly entire sanctification, became the foundation for theology, worship, evangelism, nurture, service, and church administration.

The new denomination also stressed education, ordination of women, solidarity with the poor, daily holy living that avoided wicked or worldly practices, and global missionary vision.

The Nazarene founders wanted a believers' church that was rooted firmly *in the Wesleyan tradition.*

1 ～ They Shared a Dream: Launching the Nazarene Movement

Nineteenth-Century America was a hotbed of religious chaos. False prophets slandered one another and prospered. Zany new religions flourished. Flamboyant spellbinders called themselves evangelists and mesmerized the simple with threats and promises that God, they bellowed, had endorsed. "Farmers became theologians, offbeat village youth became bishops, odd girls became prophets."[1] The times produced eccentricities such as Mormonism, Christian Science, and Jehovah's Witnesses.

The Wesleyan-Holiness Movement was not immune to the stresses. Divided by race and region, it floundered at the edge of a sectarian snake pit by the dawn of the 20th century. Yet from this doubtful setting, the Church of the Nazarene arose, rooted in orthodox Christianity and guided by a vision.

The Holiness Movement at a Crossroads

Early in the 19th century Sarah Lankford combined the women's prayer groups of two Methodist churches in New York City to create the Tuesday Meeting for the Promotion of Holiness. That action, coupled with the publication of Boston pastor Timothy Merritt's *Guide to Christian Perfection,* marked the Holiness Movement's advent.

The remarkable career of Phoebe Palmer, Lankford's sister, followed. Leader of the Tuesday Meeting, transatlantic revivalist, cofounder of a mission in New York City's slums, author of several books, and editor of *The Guide to Holiness* (Merritt's old paper), Mrs. Palmer stoked the fires of 19th-century Evangelical piety.

John Inskip, J. A. Wood, and other Methodist clergy initiated a new phase of the movement after the Civil War. The National Camp Meeting Association for the Promotion of Holiness fostered specialized meetings throughout the

---

1. Sydney E. Ahlstrom, *A Religious History of the American People* (London and New Haven, Conn.: Yale University Press, 1972), 475.

United States. But Inskip was dead by 1890, while Wood had retired to California and preached occasionally from Phineas F. Bresee's pulpit.

A democratic spirit pervaded the Holiness Movement. Bishops could control Methodist clergy, but not the laity who led many local, county, and state Holiness associations. Some were headed by women excluded from leadership in other arenas. Independent-minded evangelists defied the Methodist *Discipline* and used a local preacher's license as authority to conduct revivals, even competing with local pastors.

By century's end, the Wesleyan-Holiness Movement included sectarian "come-outers," "put-outers" dismissed from their churches, and Methodist loyalists. The fragmenting Holiness revival posed daunting questions: would anyone—*could* anyone—gather the pieces?

The Nazarene Synthesis

The Pentecostal Church of the Nazarene originated in this milieu as a *believers' church in the Wesleyan tradition.*

Believers' churches have a distinctive way of being the church. They are voluntary fellowships of those who have experienced the regenerating power of divine grace. Their members form a covenant between God and one another and are active in Christian works. They do not allow obvious sin among the clergy and laity to slide but practice church discipline. They give willingly to the poor and follow a simple pattern of worship. And "they center everything on the Word, prayer, and love."[2]

Anabaptists (Mennonites, Amish) pioneered the believers' church during the Reformation, and many groups have adopted it since: Baptists, Quakers, Disciples of Christ, Congregationalists, Church of the Brethren—the list goes on. The parent bodies of the Church of the Nazarene shared the characteristics of believers' churches. So, too, did the united church they created.

To *really* understand the intent of the founders, we must grapple with a fact usually ignored: the majority of late 19th-century Holiness people remained in the Methodist churches while continuing to play a vital role in the Holiness Movement. They supported an extensive system of Holiness camp meetings and schools, including Asbury College, Taylor University, and Asbury Theological Seminary.

What does this fact say about our founders, who stepped aside from Methodism? It says they wanted to put behind them the ongoing argument over the Holiness Movement's methods and theology that raged at the time. They were willing to start over again from nothing in order to remain focused on their primary mission.

It tells us that they wanted sacramental integrity. They rejected Methodism's growing acceptance of the church as a mixed multitude of Christians and "almost Christians." But they equally rejected the notion that independent Holiness missions and prayer circles would suffice.

Why did C. B. Jernigan organize the scattered Holiness bands in Texas into churches? Because their people needed "a place where the sacraments could be

---

2. Donald F. Durnbaugh, *The Believers' Church: The History and Character of Radical Protestantism* (New York: Macmillan Co., 1968), 32-33.

administered." In the independent bands "there was no baptism, no sacraments for her people, and they were called come-outers by the church people."[3]

It was not enough, however, to have a believers' church. The Nazarene founders wanted a believers' church that was rooted firmly *in the Wesleyan tradition,* oriented theologically toward landmark doctrines of original sin, justification and sanctification wrought by grace through faith, and the clear witness of the Spirit to the distinct works of divine grace in believers' lives.

They were not the first. Francis Asbury, founder of American Methodism, had shared the same dream. In 1784 Methodism had an exceedingly small share of the American religious public, but by 1850 it was the largest denomination in America, its growth driven by great engines of revivalism and dedicated circuit-riding preachers. It also was a victim of its own success. It excelled at reaching the unconverted but drew them in faster than it could catechize them into the Wesleyan ethos, and its identity slowly changed.

"What was your *experience* this week?" Generations of Methodist class leaders posed the question weekly to those under their care until the class meeting and its leaders were deemed unimportant and disappeared. But the question really mattered; it was a crystal-clear expression of essential Methodism. The leader was not inquiring about generalized experience, but about a person's present experience of a trustworthy God.

The Nazarene prayer meeting, testimony service, and altar service were among the ways that the concern for personal, vital piety would be communicated to a new generation. The experience of God's transforming grace lay at the heart of the Nazarene movement.

Unity in Holiness

The vision for bringing these impulses together was centered in a union movement with many leaders: Phineas Bresee, C. B. Jernigan, J. B. Chapman, H. F. Reynolds, E. E. Angell, and C. W. Ruth.

Their unflagging efforts united these Holiness denominations and portions of two other groups in a series of steps that culminated in the uniting General Assemblies in Chicago (1907) and Pilot Point, Texas (1908). Other denominations united with them in 1915, including one in Scotland.

What distinguished the united church from others?

1. **Women joined men in its ministry.** Women were eligible for every office in the church. The ordination of women was practiced in the three original parent bodies and occurred at both uniting General Assemblies. It was no secondary issue. Bresee insisted that a ministry inclusive of women is *apostolic,* while one that excludes women from the ministry is not apostolic.[4] The key scripture was Acts 2:16-17. Men and woman share in proclaiming the gospel in the church that moves by the power of the Holy Spirit!

---

3. C. B. Jernigan, *Pioneer Days of the Holiness Movement in the Southwest* (Kansas City: Pentecostal Nazarene Publishing House, 1919), 109, 123.

4. J. B. Chapman, "October Gleanings," *Herald of Holiness,* October 15, 1930, 5; idem, "Dr. Bresee, an Apostolic Leader," *Preacher's Magazine,* December 1938, 2.

"We want places so plain that every board will say welcome to the poorest."

2. The new church stood shoulder to shoulder with the poor and broken. Orphanages in North America and India, homes for unwed mothers, rescue missions for alcoholics—these were visible expressions of inward holiness. "We want places so plain that every board will say welcome to the poorest," Phineas F. Bresee wrote from Los Angeles, while half a continent away tears coursed down Mary Lee Cagle's cheeks as she preached to the prisoners—Black and White alike—in an Arkansas prison.[5] The early Nazarenes listened with their hearts to Jesus' words in Luke 4:18 (KJV): "The Spirit of the Lord is upon me, because he hath anointed me to preach the gospel to the poor." An identification with the Lord's own mission had led Wesley to England's prisons, slums, and mining communities. Now it was the Nazarene founders' concern. Holiness builds a church with a heart for the poor and broken.

3. The early Nazarenes were energized by a vision of worldwide ministry. In 1908 the Nazarenes already ministered in Cape Verde, India, and Japan. They soon did the same in Central America, South America, Africa, and China. Evangelism, education, and compassionate ministries were their characteristic methods. Mission stations, preaching points, Bible women, colporteurs, schools, clinics, hospitals, and printing presses were dedicated to the global spread of the Wesleyan-Holiness revival.

4. The Christian college was regarded as an important ingredient of a Wesleyan-Holiness church. The united denomination started with more colleges than it could support and had to consolidate them. Nazarene communities grew up around these colleges, and some parents uprooted their families to move to these communities so that their children could enjoy the benefits of a Nazarene education.

5. Entire sanctification was central. The uniting core was the idea of a believers' church in which God's grace was real in human lives. Justifying and sanctifying grace were central in the experience and thought of the founders, who knew personally the transforming nature of this grace.

Every other Christian doctrine was somehow related to entire sanctification, and no method could be employed that contradicted it.

Entire sanctification represented a real cleansing—a real grace in this life—that conquers sin. Every other Christian doctrine was somehow related to this one, and no method could be employed that contradicted it. The deep awareness of sin, repentance, the regenerating power of the new birth, life in the Spirit, true eucharistic celebration—all were related to entire sanctification.

---

5. P. F. Bresee, "Editorial: It Is All Right," *Nazarene Messenger,* January 15, 1902, 6.

6. Commitment to righteous living. Early Nazarenes agreed that holy living was an important part of Christian stewardship and witness. They committed themselves daily to avoid the wicked and worldly. How could one be a true disciple and have a lavish, worldly lifestyle? They adopted John Wesley's three rules for the Methodist societies and drew up further rules that guided them through the temptations of the times and brought credit to the church. They agreed to avoid entertainments, personal habits and vices, dress and behavior that would conflict with Christian simplicity. Keeping rules could not save them. But they recognized that ethical conduct is important when it comes to stewardship, discipleship, and witness.

Review and Reflection

1. Identify and define in your own words:
   a. Believers' church

   b. Phoebe Palmer

   c. National Camp Meeting Association

   d. Entire sanctification

   e. Apostolicity and ordination of women

2. Evaluate the role that missions, identification with the poor, and Nazarene colleges had in the development of the Nazarene movement. Which of these most energize the work of the Church of the Nazarene that you now attend?

3. Read more on Nazarene history. We recommend the following:

Bangs, Carl. *Phineas F. Bresee: His Life in Methodism, the Holiness Movement, and the Church of the Nazarene.* Kansas City: Beacon Hill Press of Kansas City, 1995.

"Historical Statement." In *Manual, Church of the Nazarene, 1997—2001.* Kansas City: Nazarene Publishing House, 1997, 14-24.

Purkiser, W. T. *Called unto Holiness, Vol. 2.* Kansas City: Nazarene Publishing House, 1983.

Smith, Timothy L. *Called unto Holiness, Vol. 1.* Kansas City: Nazarene Publishing House, 1962.

Thumbnail Sketch

WHAT NAZARENES BELIEVE AND PRACTICE

Historical Foundations

The foundation stones on which the Church of the Nazarene is built are as follows:

Classical Christianity—the religion of the New Testament and the Early Church.

Protestant Principles—the theologies of the Protestant Reformation, including the priesthood of believers, the Bible as the Rule of faith and practice, salvation by grace alone through faith alone (not by good works).

Arminian Thought—Jesus made atonement for all. By free grace, each person can choose God and good. Our choice makes a difference; we are not predestined.

Wesleyan Practical Theology—adopting and adapting John Wesley's system of doctrine and pastoral theology, Nazarenes continue to emphasize Wesley's distinctive doctrine of entire sanctification.

Holiness—the revival of Wesleyan teachings on sanctification and Christian perfection that swept across 19th- and early 20th-century America was called the American Holiness Movement. The Church of the Nazarene was at the heart of this movement and is now the largest Wesleyan-Holiness denomination to emerge from it.

Core Beliefs

Nazarene beliefs are rooted first of all in the Bible and shaped by classic Christian doctrine. Ecclesiastically, our Articles of Faith are founded upon the Thirty-nine Articles of Religion of the Church of England as amended and abridged by John Wesley into the Twenty-five Articles of Methodism. From this foundation the Nazarene Articles of Faith and Agreed Statement of Belief are drawn.

The Nazarene General Rules are taken directly from John Wesley's general rules for the Methodist societies. Our Special Rules attempt to relate Wesleyan-Holiness principles to daily life.

The Church of the Nazarene Today

Today 1.2 million Nazarenes worship in 11,857 congregations in 119 countries and world areas. We have 59 schools of higher education with 26,000 students. We have 100 compassionate ministry centers and 700 Good Samaritan churches. The Church of the Nazarene believes it has been raised up to carry on in Christ's name worship, evangelism, nurture, and service.

2 ~ WHAT NAZARENE∫ BELIEVE AND PRACTICE

THE CHURCH OF THE NAZARENE IS A
Christian,
Protestant,
Arminian,
Wesleyan,
Holiness
community of faith. And our creedal statements show it. Our 16 Articles of Faith, Statement on the Church, Agreed Statement of Belief, and General Rules can be found in the appendix of this book and, of course, in fuller form in the *Manual, Church of the Nazarene, 1997—2001.*

The Church

The three paragraphs in our Constitution titled "The Church" once formed an article of faith on the Church. But they were moved to a separate section, and decades later a new article of faith on the Church was adopted. Both statements are theologically rich and revealing.

Our very first line about the Church delivers the Church of the Nazarene from the trap of claiming to be the one true Church. Many of the churches, sects, and cults that you will meet in this book claim that they are the one true Church. But Nazarenes nip such extremism in the bud by declaring, "The Church of God is composed of all spiritually regenerate persons" (*Manual, 1997—2001,* par. 23).[1]

Another statement marks us as a believers' church. The Agreed Statement of Belief bluntly declares that "the right and privilege of persons to church membership rest upon the fact of their being regenerate" (saved, converted, or born again). See paragraph 26 in the *Manual.* Further, the phrase about Nazarene church members as people "who have voluntarily associated themselves together" (par. 25) also marks us a believers' church and not a state church.

The new article of faith (1989) about the Church accents the Church of the Nazarene as a family of faith. Such phrases as "the *community* that confesses Jesus Christ as Lord," "the covenant people," "in the unity and fellowship of the Spirit," and "mutual accountability" (par. 15, italics added) mark us as a believers' church, a biblical faith community.

---

1. *Manual, Church of the Nazarene, 1997—2001* (Kansas City: Nazarene Publishing House, 1997). Any *Manual* paragraphs cited are from this edition; often only paragraph numbers are given.

Classical Christians

Several of our Articles of Faith place us squarely in the orthodox, historic, classical Christian tradition. For example, our first three articles about the triune God, Jesus Christ, and the Holy Spirit show that we accept the classic Christian doctrines about the Holy Trinity. "He, as God, is Triune in essential being, revealed as Father, Son, and Holy Spirit" (par. 1). We also affirm our faith in Jesus Christ as "very God and very man, the God-man" who "died for our sins" and "truly arose from the dead" (par. 2). The Holy Spirit is not just the *energy* or *influence* of God, but the blessed "Third Person of the Triune Godhead" who convicts sinners, "regenerating those who repent and believe [and] sanctifying believers" (par. 3).

Thoroughly Trinitarian, we disagree with those who renounce the doctrine of the Holy Trinity, such as the Mormons, Jehovah's Witnesses, Muslims, and some Pentecostal groups.

Our articles of faith about the second coming of Christ (XV) and resurrection, judgment, and destiny (XVI) also connect us with classic Christianity. We teach that "the finally impenitent shall suffer eternally in hell." But we also affirm "that glorious and everlasting life is assured to all who savingly believe in, and obediently follow, Jesus Christ our Lord" (par. 22). These affirmations point not only to harmony with the Scriptures but also to the ancient Christian creeds. Thus, the Apostles' Creed and the Nicene Creed are often used in Nazarene worship.

Protestant Christians

Other Articles of Faith signal that we are clearly Protestant. Our fourth article shows us to be in tune with the concept of *sola scriptura*. For the first Protestants and for us, *only the Bible* is the divinely inspired Revelation of the "will of God concerning . . . all things necessary to our salvation, so that whatever is not contained therein is not to be enjoined as an article of faith" (par. 4). The early Protestants opposed the notion that the pope and church tradition spoke with as much (or more) authority than the Bible.

Our celebrating only two sacraments (not seven) also marks us as Protestant. We name Christian baptism (for believers or infants) as a sacrament (par. 16). We do not believe that baptism has regenerative powers. Rather, it is "a sacrament signifying acceptance of the benefits of the atonement of Jesus Christ, to be administered to believers. . . . Baptism may be administered [among Nazarenes] by sprinkling, pouring, or immersion" (par. 16). Though Nazarenes usually practice adult "believer's baptism," the baptism of infants is also provided for in both creed and ceremony (pars. 16, 800.2). "Young children may be baptized, upon request of parents or guardians," says the article of faith. Most Nazarenes today practice infant dedication. But infant baptism was a common practice among the earliest Nazarenes. At the annual district assemblies, the general superintendents often baptized babies. The records show that Phineas Bresee, H. F. Reynolds, R. T. Williams, J. B. Chapman, and J. W. Goodwin often performed these services.[2] We really believe in "liberty of conscience" when it comes to baptism.

---

2. Stan Ingersol, "Christian Baptism and the Early Nazarenes: The Sources That Shaped a Pluralistic Baptismal Tradition," *Wesleyan Theological Journal* 25, No. 2 (fall 1990): 34-35.

Our article of faith called "The Lord's Supper" has linguistic and theological roots in Anglican Protestantism. We see Holy Communion as a "memorial" of the "sacrificial death" of "Jesus Christ" (par. 17). Thus, the bread and wine are seen as symbols or "emblems of His broken body and shed blood" (par. 802). This puts us on the Reformed side of Protestantism rather than the Lutheran. Lutherans hold that the literal presence of Christ is in, with, and under the bread and wine.

In the Communion service, Nazarenes examine their hearts before God, meditate on "the death and passion of our Lord," and look forward to His return (pars. 17, 802). Though some denominations permit only members of the local congregation to take Communion, Nazarene churches invite all born-again believers to share in the Lord's Supper regardless of denominational affiliation.

Arminian, Wesleyan, Holiness Christians

James Arminius, a Dutch pastor, had a profound influence on Protestantism, especially the Wesleyan tradition. Arminius became the spokesperson for those who felt that Protestant leaders like Luther, Calvin, and Beza had driven the theological train past the station.

When the Roman Catholics declared the rights of the church and its leaders to determine who would be saved or excommunicated, forgiven or condemned, it drove persons of good faith to take a different position. The Protestant Reformers taught that no pope or church could forgive sins—God alone does that. No pope or church can say who will be saved—God alone decides that. Further, they said, pushing the envelope too far for Arminians, God has predestined who is to be saved and who is to be lost. No pope, church, or person *knows* who will be saved—God alone knows that. Further, nothing that any person can do will change or affect in any way what God has predestined or decreed. In other words, the Protestants said a sovereign God, not the church or its clerics, makes all the decisions.

Soon this hardened into rigid Calvinistic doctrines: Jesus died only for the elect, those predestined to be saved. Everybody else will pay for his or her own sins in hell. "Limited atonement" is this doctrine's official name. "Irresistible grace" was another cast-in-stone doctrine, which meant that those who were predestined to be saved were so overwhelmed by the Spirit and grace of God that they could not resist doing what God wanted them to do. One fruit of this was the eternal security of the believer. Once you have been "elected" to be saved, predestined to receive grace, you cannot resist. There is nothing you can do to change it. You were saved through no effort of your own; nothing you say, think, do, or *choose* can change that, some Calvinists claimed.

James Arminius, though fiercely persecuted for it, preached that Jesus died for all, that all could be saved, that human beings were given free grace. Further, one had to *choose* God and good to be saved.

John Wesley (and others) then built a Protestant theology that expanded Arminian thought. Wesley modified the Thirty-nine Articles of the Church of England, coming up with Methodism's Twenty-five Articles of Faith. The early Nazarenes, part of the American Holiness Movement, adopted much of Wesley's affirmation of faith.

These are reflected throughout our Nazarene creedal statements but particularly in Articles V through X. These deal with sin (original and personal), atonement, free moral agency, repentance, justification, regeneration, adoption, and entire sanctification.

We will not try to unpack all of these faith affirmations here. You will see them interpreted throughout this book as Nazarene doctrines are compared and contrasted with beliefs of Christian and non-Christian religions. Also, you are urged to study these articles in the *Manual* or in the appendix of this book. Nevertheless, a few particular comments will highlight distinctive Wesleyan-Holiness teachings.

If you live in Florida or Louisiana, how many words do you need for snow? Probably only one. Alaskan Inuits, however, have 12 words for snow: one for falling snow, another for snow already on the ground, still another for blowing snow—plus 9 more.

How many words does a Christian need for sin? If you're a Calvinist, one will do—any falling short of God's perfect standard is sin. If you're a Catholic, you need two at least: venial and mortal. If you're a Wesleyan-Holiness Christian, you need a lot of words for sin: inbred sin, sin as act, sin as state, sins of surprise, sins of infirmity, sins of intention, sins of omission, and most of all, sin as a *willful* transgression of a *known* law of God. You could say that Nazarenes are the Inuits of hamartiology (the doctrine of sin).

Our fifth article of faith carefully spells out the difference we see between original sin and personal acts of sin. We stand clearly in the Augustinian camp, believing that we are born in sin. "We believe that original sin, or depravity, is that corruption of the nature of all the offspring of Adam by reason of which everyone is very far gone from original righteousness" (*Manual,* par. 5.1). Our Arminian roots, however, keep us from proclaiming that total depravity has destroyed everything good in the human heart. Arminianism insists on free grace. Wesleyan dogma insists that there are some remains of the image of God in the worst of persons because of prevenient grace. That persuades us to teach that although we are born sinners, we also can find something at the very core of our nature that is positive, godlike, something that can be counted on to seek God and good.

This brings us to Article VII, free agency. When we preach free will, we don't mean uninhibited freedom that New Age thought or certain psychologies teach. We mean that in the moral realm, we have freedom to choose. We have been enabled by prevenient grace (Wesley's term) to choose God and good. Many Christians deny this. But it is part and parcel of the *free grace for all* preached by Arminius, Wesley, and our Nazarene forebears such as Phineas F. Bresee, H. F. Reynolds, A. M. Hills, and R. T. Williams.

Entire sanctification, the principal doctrine that empowered the Wesleyan revival and the American Holiness Movement, is treated in Article X. This doctrine announces the radical optimism of grace taught in the Scriptures and preached by Wesley and his theological offspring. Behaviorism, determinism, Freudian psychology, other social sciences, and some Christian traditions teach that the evil influence of genetics and environment trap a person very early in life and that he or she never overcomes it. The Wesleyan-Holiness people declare a radical optimism for one and all through sanctifying grace. We recognize that people are not impervious to negative environmental forces such as poverty, racism, or parental abuse. Yet we believe and teach that through the riches of the atonement of Christ, there is almost no ceiling on the good things that can happen to anyone—even if his or her current address is a suburb of hell.

Our gift to this dark age is the radical optimism of entire sanctification. Believers can be made holy, sanctified "through and through" (1 Thess. 5:23). Our creed, Article X, calls entire sanctification "that act of God . . . by which believers are made free from original sin, or depravity, and brought into a state of entire devotement to God, and the holy obedience of love made perfect" (par. 13).

This article also cites a doctrine that distinguishes Wesleyan-Holiness people from other groups who use the name "Holiness." Some of them teach holiness as the baptism of the Holy Spirit that empowers the believer for service, but they do not believe that depravity or inbred sin is cleansed. Our article of faith declares that entire sanctification (or the baptism with the Holy Spirit) includes "cleansing of the heart from sin" (par. 13). You see, we take the Bible seriously when it calls believers to be cleansed from "all filthiness of the flesh and spirit" (2 Cor. 7:1, KJV). We believe John was serious when he wrote about the blood of Jesus cleansing us "from all sin" (1 John 1:7, KJV). James calls on double-minded believers to "purify your hearts" (4:8). You see, it wasn't David Letterman who said these things—it was the Holy Bible.

The article of faith on divine healing (XIV) represents the reaction of the Holiness Movement to the "healing revival" that broke out early in the 20th century. Mostly within Pentecostal and Christian Science circles, this "revival" carried healing to such an extreme that medical attention was forbidden. Article XIV simply states our belief that God does, according to His will, intervene and heal people, but we also believe in medical treatment. Anointing the sick and calling the elders to pray is an accepted practice among Nazarenes.

The General Rules

Our General Rules (par. 27) are the same three rules that John Wesley created for the early Methodists. Those who wish to join our fellowship "shall show evidence of salvation from their sins by a godly walk and vital piety" and "shall evidence their commitment to God" (27)

1. "By doing that which is enjoined in the Word of God . . . our rule of both faith and practice" (27.1).

This is explained as loving God with all one's heart, soul, mind, and strength, and one's neighbor as oneself. Being courteous, helpful, and active in compassionate ministry, supporting the ministry, and faithfully attending church are also cited.

2. "By avoiding evil of every kind" (27.2).

Swearing, Sabbath breaking, sexual immorality, quarreling, dishonesty in business or life, pride in dress or behavior, and music, literature, and entertainment that dishonor God are proscribed.

3. "By abiding in hearty fellowship with the church . . . wholly committed to its doctrines . . . and [being] actively involved in its . . . witness and outreach" (27.3).

The Special Rules

The Special Rules (pars. 33-41) represent the church's effort to interpret and apply its Articles of Faith and General Rules to specific needs of a changing culture. Currently, the Special Rules speak against all "entertainments that are subversive of the Christian [life]" (34.1), gambling, membership in oath-bound secret organizations, social dancing, using tobacco or intoxicating drinks, divorce, abortion, and sexual perversions such as homosexual activity or pornographic uses of sex in marriage (34.2-37). The Special Rules speak in favor of Christian marriage, sex as a gift of God, Christian stewardship, storehouse tithing, and support of pastors and other ministers.

What Nazarenes Are Doing in Our World

The Church—our church—has just four things to do: worship, evangelism, nurture, and service. Armed and energized by their Christian, Protestant, Wesleyan-Holiness heritage and theology, Nazarenes everywhere busily carry out their fourfold task.

Worship

Despite any argument to the contrary, nothing more important ever happens on earth than the worship of God. Worship is our church's first privilege and primary duty.

Nazarenes believe that both private and corporate worship are utterly necessary. Popular spirituality today elevates private worship above the corporate worship of God. The guitar-twanging country music artist whose hit song declared, "Me and Jesus got our own thing goin'," spouts a message as phony as plastic parsley on the seafood platter.

Thus, we need to be reminded that whatever else the church is, it is a called-out, worshiping *community*. Maria Harris had a point when she wrote, "One Christian is no Christian; we go to God together or we do not go at all."[3] The Christian life is, after all, a community affair. Both private and public worship are as essential as food and breathing.

Today 1.2 million Nazarenes carry out the mission of worship in 11,857 congregations on 340 districts located in 119 countries and world areas.[4]

Our worship style, like our practice of the sacraments, leaves much to the liberty of conscience. No prescribed Nazarene liturgy exists. A wide range of worship styles may be found among us, from low-church liturgical to very free and spontaneous worship.

The key elements in Nazarene worship include singing, prayer, reading of Scripture, giving tithes and offerings, the Lord's Supper, and preaching.

Music is a great part of Nazarene worship and will often include piano, organ, and other musical instruments. Sometimes choirs or smaller groups will sing, but always there will be congregational singing.

---

3. Maria Harris, *Fashion Me a People* (Louisville, Ky.: John Knox Press, 1989), 77.
4. See the general secretary's report, *Herald of Holiness,* June 1997, special insert, pages not numbered.

What a privilege to join with the fellow pilgrims and, shoulder to shoulder, sing,

> *O Thou in whose presence my soul takes delight,*
> *On whom in affliction I call,*
> *My Comfort by day and my Song in the night,*
> *My Hope, my Salvation, my all!*

—Joseph Swain

Of course, your local Nazarene church may be more into singing praise choruses or maybe psalms.

Prayer by both clergy and laypersons is part of most Nazarene worship services. Invocations, benedictions, pastoral prayers, laypersons leading in extemporaneous prayer, reciting the Lord's Prayer, open altar prayer, sentence prayers, directed prayers, and prayer at the altar at the close of an evangelistic service—all of these are integral parts of Nazarene worship.

The public reading of the Bible is included in most Nazarene services and should be included in all of them. We need more Scripture reading than just the reading of the preacher's text.

Though sometimes neglected by some of our churches, the sacraments of baptism and the Lord's Supper have been honored from our earliest days. Often the revival or camp meeting tent was pitched near a stream or lake so the converts could be baptized. And the final service at nearly every camp meeting and many revivals was a Communion service.

No Nazarene service is complete without the chance to bring our tithes and offerings in support of the church around the world. To us, this is an act of worship.

Preaching is in the anchor position in most Nazarene services—and rightly so. Our churches are pulpits of wood and stone, not shrines or altars of wood and stone. Our pastors are preachers first and priests second. Like the Puritans, we tend to regard the sermon as the "sacrament of the Word."

The critics of preaching, those "carping censures of the world," to use Shakespeare's phrase, seem to be blithely unaware of the high place preaching has in Christian tradition. Dietrich Bonhoeffer declared, "The proclaimed Word is the Incarnate Christ himself. . . . The preached Christ is the historical Christ and the present Christ . . . walking through His congregation as the Word."[5] "So identified is Jesus the Word with the word of preaching," writes Richard Lischer, "that the one proclaimed once again becomes the proclaimer. Insofar as preaching . . . offers the life of God in Christ, it is Jesus himself who is the preacher."[6]

Evangelism

"For God so loved the world that He gave His only begotten Son, that whoever believes in Him should not perish but have everlasting life" (John 3:16, NKJV). This verse expresses the greatest reality known to the human race.

When a person discovers this great reality through the saving grace of God

---

5. Clyde E. Fant, *Preaching for Today* (New York: Harper and Row, 1975), 22.
6. Richard Lischer, *A Theology of Preaching* (Nashville: Abingdon Press, 1981), 74.

in Christ, it is only natural for him or her to want to tell others. And this our Lord commissions us to do: "Go therefore and make disciples of all the nations, baptizing them in the name of the Father and of the Son and of the Holy Spirit, teaching them to observe all things that I have commanded you; and lo, I am with you always, even to the end of the age" (Matt. 28:19-20, NKJV).

Evangelism is not "politically correct" in some religious and cultural settings. It is talking down to people as though you were better than them, the argument goes. But Christians are not acting in arrogance when they share Jesus Christ, the Bread of Life. Rather, as the saying goes, it's a case of one beggar telling another where the bread—or Bread—is. Augustine called the bearer of the gospel a little basket in which the Bread of Life is laid. Could any Christian find a more noble vocation?

Thus, we willingly answer the call to become "ambassadors for Christ, as though God were pleading through us . . . be reconciled to God" (2 Cor. 5:20, NKJV).

Every Nazarene in the world resonates with Paul, who wrote, "I am a debtor both to Greeks and to barbarians, both to wise and to unwise" (Rom. 1:14, NKJV). Nazarenes have taken seriously the Bible promise and imperative "You will receive power when the Holy Spirit has come upon you; and you will be my witnesses in Jerusalem, in all Judea and Samaria, and to the ends of the earth" (Acts 1:8, NRSV).

During the 1992-96 quadrennium about a quarter of a million new Nazarenes were received into membership. The net gain in membership was 146,000. Each of our world regions reported good gains, with Africa and South America showing phenomenal growth.

During the same quadrennium, 24,879 Nazarenes in 1,484 Work and Witness teams paid their own expenses to mission fields, where they donated a cumulative total of 812 years of labor.

Nazarenes give generously for world evangelism, placing $197.6 million in the offering plates for missions during the 1992-96 period. Nazarenes now have 665 missionaries working in 119 countries. Twenty-nine countries have sent their own Nazarenes to mission fields.

But evangelism is not just mission work. Nazarenes evangelize through revival meetings, personal evangelism, lifestyle evangelism, starting new churches, Sunday School outreach, small-group ministries, community and youth programs, and a dozen other methods.

Nurture

This task of Christian nurture is a labor of love and drinks of that same spirit that moved Paul to write to the Thessalonians: "So deeply do we care for you that we are determined to share with you not only the gospel of God but also our own selves, because you have become very dear to us" (1 Thess. 2:8, NRSV).

Our definition of Christian nurture includes everything the church does to teach, to promote spiritual growth, and to make disciples. It includes such things as faith mentoring, Bible study groups, support groups, family worship, spiritual formation, Christian camping, Sunday School, Christian colleges, and just plain Christian fellowship.

The goal is to bring everyone to "the knowledge of the Son of God, to maturity, to the measure of the full stature of Christ" (Eph. 4:13, NRSV). "It is a blessed thing to have fellow travellers to the New Jerusalem," John Wesley wrote. "If you do not find any you must make them, for none can travel this road alone."[7]

Nazarenes conduct many educational enterprises. Strong Sunday Schools have been a Nazarene hallmark around the world. Small-group ministries patterned after John Wesley's classes and bands still flourish. The Nazarene Publishing House is the largest producer of Holiness literature in the world. World Mission Radio and the broadcasting arms of the Communications Division give "Nazarene nurture" an international presence. One nurturing venture that truly characterizes us these days is our colleges, seminaries, universities, and Bible colleges. By 1921 we had 12 institutions of higher learning; now we have 59. These schools educate 26,000 students on their campuses and extension programs. Their annual budget is about $175 million, their assets $307 million.[8] The early Wesleyans started all kinds of schools. We Nazarenes have carried on that tradition with zest.

Nazarenes know what John Greenleaf Whittier was talking about when he wrote,

It need not fear the skeptic's puny hand
While near the school the church shall stand,
Nor fear the blinded bigot's rule
When near the church shall stand the school.[9]

As A. M. Hills, one of the founders of the school that became Olivet Nazarene University, put it, "Spirituality without intellectuality becomes fanaticism, and intellectuality without spirituality becomes infidelity."[10]

Nurture is the very essence of the Wesleyan-Holiness tradition, as this Charles Wesley hymn shows:

Help us to help each other, Lord;
Each other's cross to bear.
Let each his friendly aid afford
And feel his brother's care.

Help us to build each other up,
Our little stock improve;
Increase our faith, confirm our hope,
And perfect us in love.[11]

---

7. Wesley D. Tracy et al., *The Upward Call: Spiritual Formation and the Holy Life* (Kansas City: Beacon Hill Press of Kansas City, 1994), 137.

8. See the education commissioner's report, *Herald of Holiness*, June 1997, special insert, pages not numbered.

9. Donald S. Metz, *MidAmerica Nazarene College: The Pioneer Years, 1966-1991* (Kansas City: Nazarene Publishing House, 1991), 74.

10. Ibid., 46.

11. Charles Wesley, "Help Us to Help Each Other, Lord," in *Wesley Hymns*, comp. Ken Bible (Kansas City: Lillenas Publishing Co., 1982), No. 110.

Service

Christian service is not optional. Maxie Dunnam was right: "A spirituality that does not lead to active ministry becomes an indulgent preoccupation with self, and therefore grieves the Holy Spirit and violates the presence of the indwelling Christ."[12] Mother Teresa put it this way: "There is too much talk. . . . Take a broom and clean someone's house. That says enough."[13]

John Wesley declared, "I do not acknowledge him to have one grain of faith who is not continually . . . willing to spend and be spent in doing all good . . . to all men."[14] Phineas F. Bresee in 1901 wrote in the *Nazarene Messenger,* "The evidence of the presence of Jesus in our midst is that we bear the gospel, primarily, to the poor." Later he added, "I may have faith that moves mountains, and if I lack the great love that stoops to lift men, I am nothing—*no thing.*"

Poverty has reached critical dimensions at a time when many Christians seem co-opted by consumerism and self-interest. But Nazarenes have been energetically reclaiming their biblical and Wesleyan heritage of "spending and being spent" for others. Nazarenes gave nearly $9.5 million for compassionate ministries among the poor and oppressed. The denomination operates 100 compassionate ministry centers and has 700 Good Samaritan churches reaching out to persons in all kinds of emergencies.

There are so many avenues and channels for service among us that to join up with the Nazarenes is a move toward giving your life away in service to Christ and the people for whom He died.

So there you have it—a glimpse of what the Church of the Nazarene believes and practices. If you like what you see, come share the dream.

Review and Reflection

1. Study the Nazarene creedal statements cited in this chapter and included in the appendix. Consult a *Manual* and study the scriptures that are cited in support of the Articles of Faith. Focus on the articles of faith that (*a*) inspire you the most, (*b*) are the hardest for you to understand, and (*c*) trouble you most.

2. Examine the following, and associate each with one of the four tasks of the church.

   a. "Loose the chains of injustice and untie the cords of the yoke . . . set the oppressed free . . . share your food with the hungry . . . provide the poor wanderer with shelter—when you see the naked, . . . clothe him. . . . Then you will call, and the Lord will answer . . . Here am I" (Isa. 58:6-7, 9).

   b. "I now send you, to open their eyes and to turn them from darkness to light, and from the power of Satan to God, that they may receive forgiveness

---

12. Maxie Dunnam, *Alive in Christ* (Nashville: Abingdon Press, 1982), 113.
13. Ibid., 118. Dunnam is quoting from Malcolm Muggeridge's *Something Beautiful for God.*
14. John Telford, ed., *The Letters of the Rev. John Wesley, A.M.,* 8 vols. (London: Epworth Press, 1960), 1:239.

of sins and an inheritance among those who are sanctified by faith in Me" (Acts 26:17-18, NKJV).

c. "The gifts he gave were . . . to equip the saints for the work of ministry, for building up the body of Christ, until all of us come . . . to maturity, to the measure of the full stature of Christ" (Eph. 4:11-13, NRSV).

d. "Oh come, let us worship and bow down; let us kneel before the LORD our Maker. For He is our God, and we are the people of His pasture, and the sheep of His hand. Today, if you will hear His voice: 'Do not harden your hearts'" (Ps. 95:6-8, NKJV).

3. Recently the Board of General Superintendents adopted this statement of mission for the Church of the Nazarene. Examine it in light of our Articles of Faith and what you learned in this chapter.

I. *Mission*

"The mission of the Church of the Nazarene is to respond to the Great Commission of Christ to 'go and make disciples of all nations'" (Matt. 28:19).

II. *Key Objective*

"The key objective of the Church of the Nazarene is to advance God's kingdom by the preservation and propagation of Christian holiness as set forth in the Scriptures."

III. *Critical Objectives*

"The critical objectives of the Church of the Nazarene are 'holy Christian fellowship, the conversion of sinners, the entire sanctification of believers, their upbuilding in holiness, and the simplicity and spiritual power manifest in the primitive New Testament Church, together with the preaching of the gospel to every creature'" (*Manual*, par. 25).

PART II

OUR CLOSEST KIN: METHODIST AND HOLINESS CHURCHES

- Early Wesleyan Foundations

- Methodism in America: Church with the Soul of a Nation

- Our Sister Denominations: The Holiness Churches

Thumbnail Sketch

Early Wesleyan Foundations

Historical Roots

John Wesley (1703-91), preacher's kid and Oxford professor, was the founding father of the Methodist movement. John and his cohorts sought to reform the nation, particularly the church, and to spread scriptural holiness throughout Britain—and beyond. To do this, they created societies, classes, bands, and mentoring pairs to help people in the pursuit of Christian perfection. They also reached out in unprecedented ways to the brutalized masses with food, clothing, health care, education, and the gospel.

Core Beliefs

Early Wesleyanism embraced a theology of grace—prevenient grace, saving grace, sanctifying grace.

The church's aim was the salvation of souls.

Entire sanctification was the engine that drove the movement.

They modeled a conscious choice for the poor and oppressed.

The Wesleyans were committed to the church as a community where Christians helped each other in the pursuit and practice of perfect love.

They embraced orthodox Christianity, including a belief in the *sufficiency* of Scripture to reveal the way of salvation.

Personal religious experience that brings inner assurance of grace marked the early Methodists.

Agreement and Differences

Nazarenes find little to disagree with here. In fact, our own beliefs and practices were modeled after Wesley's by our founding fathers. Though changing times produce adaptations, Nazarenes still believe that it would be difficult to find a more balanced, biblical, and practical starting point from which to carry out the mission to which Christ has called us than the model of those early Wesleyans.

Wesleyanism Today

Though some have taken liberties with the heritage, some 80 denominations worldwide regard Wesley as ecclesiastical ancestor, including the United Methodist Church, The Wesleyan Church, the Free Methodist Church, The Salvation Army, and the Church of the Nazarene.

My heart was strangely warmed. I felt I did trust in Christ, Christ alone for salvation, and an assurance was given me that He had taken away *my* sins, even *mine*.

—John Wesley

3 ~ EARLY WEƒLEYAN FOUNDATIONƒ

WHEN THE BLIZZARD THAT WAS THE INDUSTRIAL REVOLUTION howled through the winter of England's soul in the 18th century, it blew the poor people like maple leaves before a November wind into the cities. And it left them, like leaves, piled in random heaps. Housing conditions were outrageous. Ten persons per unfurnished room was a common arrangement. Horse manure polluted the unpaved streets. It was sometimes piled 14 feet high on both sides of some London thoroughfares. Typhoid, cholera, dysentery, and smallpox ravaged unchecked through the population. Some 90 percent of the population were poor, 40 percent desperately poor. Starvation was a daily reality, as reported in almost every edition of every English newspaper. Graveyard operators maintained gaping "poor holes"—large, common graves left open until the daily flow of corpses of nameless nobodies finally filled them.

Violent crimes were constant. Gambling and gin drinking became the national pastimes. Every sixth building in London was an alehouse. England was easily the most drunken nation in the world. Sports included boxing, bull-baiting, and cockfighting, with hangings occupying the Super Bowl category in the sporting mind. For the children, there were the streets or the sweatshops. School? Only 1 child in 25 attended any school of any kind.

Henry Fielding described the London in which he lived: "The poor are a very great burden and ever a nuisance. . . . There are whole families in want of every necessity of life, oppressed with hunger, cold, nakedness and filth and disease. . . . They starve and freeze and rot among themselves . . . steal and beg and rob among their betters."[1]

A letter from John Wesley that appeared in the *London Chronicle*, *Lloyd's Evening Post*, and the *Leeds Mercury* read in part:

Why are thousands of people starving? . . . I've seen it with my own eyes in every corner of the land. I have known those who could only afford to eat a

---

1. J. B. Whiteley, *Wesley's England* (London: Epworth Press, 1954), 28.

little coarse food every other day. I have known one picking up stinking sprats from a dunghill and carrying them home for herself and her children. I have known another gathering the bones which the dogs have left in the streets and making broth of them to prolong a wretched life. Why are so many thousand people in London, in Bristol, in Norwich, in every county from one end of England to the other, utterly destitute of employment?[2]

Those who did find work labored under the most debilitating working conditions. Twelve- to 15-hour days in the coal mines or the textile mills were the rule. The situation of the miners was desperate. Long hours in the damp bowels of the earth made "rheumatism universal and consumption common."[3] Accidents and poison gas took the lives of miners on a daily basis. One newspaper reported, "The catastrophe from foul air [in the mines] becomes more common than ever; yet as we have been requested to take no particular notice of these things, which, in fact could have little good tendency, we drop the farther mentioning of it."[4]

The coal mines had something for the whole family. Dad worked 15-hour days digging; the kids stood in ankle-deep water for 12-hour shifts operating the pumps. Mom was included too. "Women were employed as beasts of burden and, with chains around their waists, crawled on hands and knees through narrow passages, drawing after them the coal carriages."[5]

Workers as young as 3—and to become old at 20—were recruited by the textile mills, where working conditions rivaled those of the mines.

Thousands of Enclosure Acts drove the people off the common lands. For centuries, the poor had been able to gather firewood, raise cabbages and chickens, parsnips and pigs on the common lands. But now they had no land, no garden, no job. A Leeds journalist declared, "The poor are without relief . . . without fuel, without food, and without the lawful means of securing them."[6]

When lawful means of survival are not available, the unlawful will do. A man being executed for participating in two hunger riots was asked by the *London Chronicle* why he and his pals would do such things. He answered, "We did not desire to hear our children weep for bread and [have] none to give them."[7]

The official government response to such conditions was so fierce that it would make "an eye for an eye" look like a radical mercy movement. It is typified by the report of the Grand Jury of the King's Bench in 1741. This august body was asked to consider the swarms of hungry people who were choking the streets of London. After describing them as a "dreadful nuisance" so "burthen-

---

2. *London Chronicle,* December 17-19, 1772; *Lloyd's Evening Post,* December 21, 1772; *Leeds Mercury,* December 29, 1772.

3. D. D. Thompson, *John Wesley as a Social Reformer* (New York: Eaton and Mains, 1898), 94.

4. *New Castle* (England) *Journal,* March 21, 1767.

5. Thompson, *Wesley a Reformer,* 94.

6. *Leeds Intelligencer,* 1791. Cited in Robert Wearmouth, *Methodism and the Common People of the Eighteenth Century* (London: Epworth Press, 1945), 71-72.

7. *London Chronicle,* September 11, 1762. For more about the social conditions of Wesley's times, see Wesley Tracy, "Economic Policies and Judicial Oppression as Formative Influences on the Theology of John Wesley," *Wesleyan Theological Journal,* spring-fall 1992, 30-56. Also see Wearmouth's book in note 6.

some and disgraceful," the Grand Jury recommended enforcing the laws more vigorously, "that we may not be thus troubled with the Poor."[8]

And enforce the laws they did. No fewer than 250 offenses were punishable by death. Death sentences were dished out for stealing a sheep, a loaf of bread, a piece of cheese, or for trying to pick a pocket. Crimes against the gentry were punished especially harshly. Every Lent and Christmas season, the court system carried out a bloody pageant of death and oppression. The assizes (trials) were the central attraction for many. Balls and business conferences and other social events were held during assize week. Before the trials began, the high-ranking clergyman from the state church would bless, in a sermon to convicts and the crowd, what the court was about to do And what the courts proceeded to do week after week, year after year, was to hand down the same penalty of death to offenders guilty of murder on the one hand or of stealing a piece of bread on the other. Thousands of poor "criminals" were deported as indentured servants to Africa, Australia, and America. Others were whipped, burned, and jailed. Death sentences were passed out to children as young as 10, as England hanged up to 500 of her citizens per year.

Enter John Wesley

Into this scene of judicial oppression, official indifference, and dire poverty walked a little man with a Bible under his arm, John Wesley. Only 5'6" tall and never weighing more than 135 pounds, the Little Giant led England in a revival of religion that has been called the Methodist Revolution. This Christ-centered revolution lifted the social and spiritual life of the brutalized masses, created the British middle class, and gave Christianity a bridge over which it could travel into modern times.

John Wesley was born in 1703 to devout parents. His father, Samuel, was an Anglican priest and scholar. His mother, Susanna, was a remarkable woman of learning and devotion. She gave personal religious instruction to her children besides making a successful school of her home, where she taught other children as well. She was the 25th child sired by her father. She gave birth to 19 children herself. John was her 15th child. He treasured her counsel.

When he was 17, John went to Oxford University. In 1724 he graduated from that school. In 1726 he became a teacher at Oxford's Lincoln College. He received his master's degree from Oxford in 1727, and in 1728 he was ordained as an Anglican (Church of England) priest. Though he would go on to found the Methodist Church, he would remain an Anglican priest all his life.

During his years as a student and teacher at Oxford, John and his younger brother, Charles, became involved with a group of intensely earnest students who wanted more than anything else to do the will of God every hour of every day. They soon attracted pejorative labels—"Bible moths," "Methodists," "the Holy Club." "Methodist" was the one that stuck. While others laughed at them, they gave themselves to devotion, study, and daily work with the sick, poor, and imprisoned.

---

8. *Gentlemen's Magazine,* July 1741.

Next, in 1736, Wesley tried his hand at winning the Indians of Georgia, one of the American colonies, to Christ. His ministry to colonists and Native Americans in Georgia proved more of a failure than a success. He returned to England in less than two years to resume working with his fellow Methodists in London.

Personal Religion

On May 24, 1738, Wesley's long and painful search for a heartfelt personal relationship with Christ came to a fruitful end. "Unwillingly" attending a society meeting where someone was reading aloud Luther's introduction to Romans, wherein the Reformer described salvation by faith alone, Wesley felt his heart "strangely warmed." "I felt I did trust in Christ, Christ alone for salvation, and an assurance was given me that he had taken away *my* sins, even *mine,* and saved me from the law of sin and death."[9]

With this new religion of the heart burning inside, Wesley was ready to take his place alongside such colleagues as George Whitefield in spearheading a revival that changed England and much of the world.

Whitefield and Wesley, among others, took their message to the people by preaching in the fields and streets. Thousands turned out to hear them. Souls who were renewed under his preaching Wesley organized into societies, classes, bands, and mentoring pairs for the nurture of personal religion and the pursuit of Christian perfection.

To date, no one has improved on the pastoral theology and spiritual formation scheme of John Wesley. Besides attending the principal services of the Church of England, the new Methodists met twice weekly in societies for instruction and preaching. Each society member was also required to join a class of 12 persons who met once a week for mutual support and religious instruction. Those who hungered for a still deeper walk with God were, after spiritual examination, invited to join a *band.* This was a group of four to six persons of the same gender who met weekly to share their spiritual journey "without reserve and without disguise." Each meeting began by hearing any spiritual failures that members had encountered that week. Prayer and restoration followed. Next, persons shared the temptations they had encountered along with the strategies and devotions that had delivered them. Wesley felt that Methodism did its best work in the bands.

Wesley also arranged for hundreds of Methodists to be associated in mentoring pairs or twin soul pairs. Spiritual fathers and mothers were directed to mentor specific new Christians. Twin soul pairs were Christians of like faith paired off as spiritual friends and mutual spiritual guides (not spiritual directors). All this—societies, classes, bands, mentoring pairs, and twin souls— Wesley called "Christian conference." It conserved the fruits of revival, produced stronger Christians, provided loving accountability among believers, created an arena for sanctifying grace to be sought and experienced, and pro-

---

9. Richard P. Heitzenrater, *Wesley and the People Called Methodist* (Nashville: Abingdon Press, 1995), 80.

duced deep mutual devotion and lifelong friendships. Wesley's system of family religion was also a form of Christian conference that must be taken seriously.[10]

To William Holland, Wesley wrote, "The Lord has given us to each other . . . that we may strengthen each other's hands in Him."[11] Nothing more astutely sums up the Methodist commitment to Christian conference.

The system of Christian nurture was managed by a cadre of itinerant preachers or helpers, many lay preachers, and an army of class leaders. Wesley's Methodism soon became the most efficient organization or "connexion" in all England. George Whitefield moved from one mass revival meeting to another. Looking back late in his career, he mourned, "Brother Wesley acted wisely. The souls that were awakened under his ministry, he joined in class and thus preserved the fruits of his labor. This I neglected, and my people are a rope of sand."[12]

> *"The Lord has given us to each other . . . that we may strengthen each other's hands in Him."*

Social Responsibility

John Wesley and his Methodists modeled for the world a near-perfect marriage of personal religion and social responsibility. Perhaps no other group has ever lived out the vows of this marriage better. It was not enough for early Wesleyans to attend society, class, band, prayer, and mentoring pair meetings in an all-out pursuit of Christian perfection. No, for them, Christian service was just as much a spiritual discipline as prayer and fasting.

True Christianity brings with it, Wesley believed, "a hunger and thirsting to do good of every possible kind."[13] Wesley called himself God's steward for the poor. "Join hands with God to help a poor man live" was a frequent plea.[14] Every class and band meeting included an offering for the poor. The goal was "to feed the hungry, cover the naked with a garment, and prepare the poor a way of supplying their own wants for the time to come."[15]

Wesley and his people engaged in all sorts of ministries:

1. Schools of many kinds—literacy schools, Sunday Schools, adult education schools, ministerial schools, day schools, residential schools.

2. Sick ministries. London was divided into districts, and Methodists were assigned to visit each sick person at least three times a week, checking on the state of the sick person's soul and health.

3. Medical care. John Wesley established the first free medical clinic in England in 1748.

4. Food and clothing distribution, particularly in London and Bristol.

---

10. See Tracy et al., *Upward Call,* 193-200, for more on Wesley's family religion.

11. John Wesley, letter to William Holland, February 6, 1748, Telford, *Letters,* 2:115.

12. Tracy et al., *Upward Call,* 139. For a fuller treatment of the history and principles of Wesley's Christian conference, see the same source, 133-200.

13. *The Works of John Wesley,* ed. Thomas Jackson, 3rd ed., 14 vols. (reprint, Kansas City: Beacon Hill Press of Kansas City, 1978-79), 8:352.

14. Ibid., 8:267.

15. Ibid., 7:286-87.

5. Ministry to unwed or destitute mothers. The Lying In Hospital in London provided prenatal and postnatal care, religious instruction, and vocational training for about 300 women per year.

6. The Stranger's Friend Society. This was a charity created by Methodists for non-Methodists. It soon spread throughout the land, and even the king and queen contributed to it.

7. The Christian Community ministered to the "paupers and vagabonds" in the London workhouses.

8. A widows' home in London.

9. An orphanage in New Castle.

10. Unemployment relief—jobs for out-of-work Methodists were provided. The project failed, but the attempt was made.

11. Small business loan fund. Methodists who wanted to go into business for themselves could get a loan from a Methodist fund with which to launch it.

12. Prison ministries. In order to join the Bristol Methodist society, one had to pledge to do prison work. Newgate Prison in Bristol was a "region of horror . . . so great was the filth, the stench, the misery, and wickedness which shocked all who had a spark of humanity left."[16] Soon the Wesleyans got a Methodist appointed as warden. The prison was reformed, and the whole kingdom was invited by Wesley to come and see how a prison should be run in a Christian country. Charles Wesley, the hymn writer, was one of the tireless workers who helped make this happen.

There are many people around today who want to purify some aspect of society. But the reform and purification they are urging in public they have long since abandoned in their personal and private life. Not so for those early Wesleyans. They devoted themselves to heart purity, to Christian perfection, to holiness of heart, while at the same time applying sanctifying grace to society. Perfect love means reaching out to one's neighbor. Wesley called sanctifying grace "the medicine of life, the never failing remedy for all the evils of a disordered world, for all the miseries and vices of men."[17]

In 1983 a British statesman was asked to address the International Congress of Socialist Countries. Delegates had gathered—thousands of them—from almost every Communist and socialist country in the world. With the electronic gear in place and the interpreters at the ready, they were set to hear in their own languages the ideas of the speaker of the hour. The British labor secretary was to share the secret of the success of England's social democracy. Why was it succeeding while so many socialist and Communist regimes were seriously crumbling? The speaker told the congress that perhaps the biggest difference was that their countries had learned their lessons from an atheist named Karl Marx, while England had learned its lessons about social responsibility from John Wesley.[18]

---

16. *London Chronicle*, January 1761.
17. John Wesley, *Works*, 7:424.
18. Theodore Runyon, ed., *Wesleyan Theology Today* (Nashville: Kingswood Books, 1985), 9.

The Essence of Methodism

John Wesley created a theology for his times. His every doctrinal innovation can be traced not only to the Scriptures and Christian creeds but also to distinct needs of the times. His teaching against predestination and for free grace, for example, taught his brutalized masses to hope. Their poverty, ignorance, and suffering, far from being what God had planned for them, was to be seen as a contradiction to God's will for them. When Wesley began to teach human freedom and equality, he was attacked by politicians and Anglican clergy for conspiring against divine Providence by changing the estate of the poor.

Wesley's theological method was simple: study the needs of the times, then examine all the resources of the Christian faith, and bring resources and needs together. After Wesley, others would speak of his method in terms of the Wesleyan quadrilateral, a device by which ideas and doctrines are tested by Scripture (first of all), reason (does it make sense?), tradition (what has the Church done and said about this matter in the past?), and experience (is the idea under discussion consistent with the religious experience of God's people?).

The core beliefs of early Methodism include the following:

1. **Salvation is the central aim.** Whatever acts of piety and mercy the Wesleyans gave themselves to, the overarching aim was the salvation of souls. The Methodists took sin seriously. Something has gone wrong with the human enterprise. The human heart, as Albert Outler has said, is a tinderbox of sin. No list of legalisms, no stack of self-help psychology books can cure it.

What is salvation? Wesley said, "By salvation I mean, not barely, according to the vulgar notion, deliverance from hell, or going to heaven; but a present deliverance from sin, a restoration of the soul to its primitive health, its original purity; a recovery of the divine nature; the renewal of our souls after the image of God, in righteousness and true holiness, in justice, mercy and truth."[19]

Shallow activism, the cold rationalism of the deists and latitudinarians, or the empty formalism of Anglo-Catholic ritual would not suffice for the early Wesleyans. They wanted a personal knowledge of Christ as Savior.

2. **Sanctification is both the organizing principle and the most distinctive contribution of Wesleyan spiritual theology.** No doctrine is more characteristic of early Methodism than that of sanctification. Surely the pursuit of Christian perfection, perfect love, or holiness fueled the Wesleyan revival. It is the capstone of all of Wesley's paradigms for spiritual formation. It flies in the face of traditional Protestant thought that declares humankind to be so sinful that they will never get over their depravity in this life. Wesley boldly preached—based on Scripture, reason, tradition, and experience—that the believer's heart can be cleansed from all sin and filled with divine love. To Lawrence Coughlan, Wesley wrote that holiness was "the love of God and our neighbour; the image of God stamped on the heart . . . the mind that was in Christ, enabling us to walk as Christ also walked . . . that deep communion with

19. John Wesley, *Works*, 8:47.

the Father and the Son, whereby they are enabled to give Him their whole heart, to love every man as their own soul."[20]

This was a perfection of heart and intentions, but certainly not of performance. A thousand infirmities that go with being members of a fallen race that bears the brunt of centuries of sin will plague our best efforts. But as Wesley wrote to Dorothy Furly, "I want you to be all love. This is the perfection I believe and teach."[21] To young theologian Joseph Benson, Wesley defined full salvation as "an entire deliverance from [willful] sin, a recovery of the whole image of God, the loving God with all our heart, soul, and strength."[22]

Every Christian generation has produced at least two kinds of Christians. First, there is the ordinary garden-variety believer, who runs hot and cold and who may have just enough religion to feel guilty most of the time. But in every generation, one finds Christians who have somehow discovered a deeper life. They are the exception rather than the rule. John Wesley thought that should be reversed. He personally interviewed 1,000 persons who had found the deeper life. Without exception, they reported that they received sanctifying grace (the deeper life) instantaneously by faith—not by earning it through sacrificial suffering as the mystics taught, and not by gradual growth in grace. There was a gradual process involved, of course. From the moment of conversion, of justification by faith, God had been preparing their hearts for a deeper work of grace. And God continued to cultivate the garden of their heart after they had come into a permanently deeper experience of Christ.

3. **Wesleyanism is anchored in grace.** Salvation by grace alone is so foundational to Wesleyanism that Henry Bett declared, "From the days of Wesley to the present, no Methodist has ever dreamed of grounding the forgiveness of sins on anything but the free grace of God and the redemptive work of Christ."[23] The Wesleyan system is a progression of grace: atoning grace, prevenient grace, justifying (saving) grace, sanctifying grace, perfecting grace, and glorifying grace. Deeds of piety and service are required, but only God's grace saves.

4. **Wesleyanism rests in the sufficiency of Holy Scripture.** "O give me that book! At any price give me the book of God," cried John Wesley. "I have it: here is knowledge enough for me. Let me be *homo unis libri* [a man of one book]."[24] For those early Wesleyans, the Bible was the first and final authority. Yet the Methodist approach to Scripture is wide-scoped, not fundamentalistic. It focuses on biblical principles rather than yanking Bible passages out of context to support some presupposition. The rigid, legalistic debate on inerrancy did not spring from Methodist soil. Methodists believe that Scripture is *sufficient* to reveal to us the way of salvation. To try to prove that no translator made an error—ever—is strangely beside the point to us. Wesleyans take the Bible too seriously to chop it up into proof texts in order to win arguments.

---

20. Telford, *Letters*, 5:101-3.
21. Ibid., 4:188.
22. Ibid., 5:215.
23. Henry Bett, *The Spirit of Methodism* (London: Epworth Press, 1937), 123.
24. John Wesley, *Sermons on Several Occasions* (London: Wesleyan Methodist Book Room, n.d.), 4.

5. Wesleyanism embraces a catholic spirit. The catholic spirit demonstrated by early Methodism did not mean that it was like the Roman Catholic Church. Rather, it means that John Wesley was convinced that what believers had in common in Christ was more important than their denominational differences. That is to say, provincialism and sectarianism are foreign to the Wesleyan spirit. Wesley declared that "God has given no right to any . . . to lord it over the conscience of his brethren."[25] He pled, rather, "Though we cannot think alike, may we not love alike? May we not be of one heart, though we are not of one opinion?"[26] He announced, "If thine heart is as my heart, if thou lovest God and all mankind, I ask no more: give me thine hand."[27]

> *"Though we cannot think alike, may we not love alike? May we not be of one heart, though we are not of one opinion?"*

6. Wesleyanism is Christ-centered. Of Wesley, Albert Outler wrote, "In a hundred different ways, on thousands of different occasions, decade after five decades, his message was Jesus Christ and Him crucified—*Christus crucifixus, Christus redemptor, Christus Victor.*"[28]

7. The genius of early Methodism was creative synthesis. Wesley was committed to the synthetic method. By that is meant that in working out theology, doctrine, polity, or educational philosophy, he consulted a wide variety of sources and resources—some of them religious. Governed by the theological norms of the "quadrilateral" (Revelation, reason, tradition, experience), he braided new ropes to rescue the perishing. He was unafraid to "plunder the Egyptians" of medicine, literature, secular philosophy, or business. For example, where in the Bible would Wesley learn how to establish a credit union/loan fund to help Methodists start their own businesses? He turned to both secular and religious educators to come up with a way to run the Foundery and Kingswood schools.

Governed by the quadrilateral whenever a one-sided traditionalism, rationalism, experimentalism, or biblicism threatened, "there was from the beginning a built-in Wesleyan resistance to each of these approaches pursued in isolation."[29]

8. Early Methodism emphasized vital religious experience. "I want that faith which none can have without knowing that he hath it," prayed the young Wesley.[30] Empty, formal religion does not satisfy the Wesleyan quest for the religion of the heart. Wesley declared, "He wants a religion of a nobler kind, a religion higher and deeper than this. He can no more feed on this poor, shallow, formal thing than he can 'fill his belly with the east wind.'"[31]

---

25. Ibid., 552.
26. Ibid., 549.
27. Ibid., 556.
28. Albert Outler, *Theology in the Wesleyan Spirit* (Nashville: Tidings, 1975), 45.
29. Durwood Foster, "Wesleyan Theology: Heritage and Task," in Runyon, *Wesleyan Theology Today,* 31.
30. Bett, *Spirit of Methodism,* 20.
31. Wesley, *Sermons on Several Occasions,* 297.

Charles Wesley's hymn "For the Anniversary Day of One's Conversion" celebrates the personal religious experience prized by early Methodism:

> Then with my heart I first believed,
> Believed with faith divine;
> Power with the Holy Ghost received
> To call the Saviour mine.

> I felt the Lord's atoning blood
> Close to my soul applied;
> Me, me He loved—the Son of God
> For me, for me, He died![32]

9. **Wesleyanism accents the church as a community of faith.** Early
Methodism is not the religion of the solitary mystic trying to climb the ladder of
illumination or the lone ascetic fighting evil spirits in the desert sun. Wesley
believed that "social holiness" was as genuine as the monastic variety. Therefore,
Methodism prized public preaching, corporate worship, and small-group ministries. The principles of Christian fellowship demonstrated in the societies,
classes, bands, mentoring pairs, and love feast charac-
terize genuine Wesleyanism.

Wesleyanism renounced "private piety that clings to Jesus and ignores the human agonies of this world."

10. Wesleyanism con-
tains a magnetic attraction
to the poor and oppressed.
Wesleyanism renounced
"private piety that clings to Jesus and ignores the human agonies of this
world."[33] Just as Jesus validated His messianic credentials by citing His ministry
to the blind, the lame, the lepers, the deaf, and the poor, Wesleyanism validates
itself by a conscious choice for the poor and oppressed.

The early Methodists set high benchmarks for the 80 churches and denominations that today describe themselves as belonging to the Wesleyan tradition.

Review and Reflection

1. Consider the "near-perfect marriage" of social responsibility and personal religion as described in this chapter. How is this marriage doing in your
local church? in your personal life?

2. Identify the Christian strengths in your life. When it comes to personal
religion, what is your greatest strength? What do you do best? When it comes to
reaching out to those more needy than you, what is your greatest strength?
What do you do best?

---

32. Bett, *Spirit of Methodism*, 26.
33. Outler, *Theology*, 46.

3. List the heart or essence of true Christianity as you see it. Then compare your views with the 10-part essence of early Wesleyanism presented in this chapter. What do you find in Wesleyanism that you want to incorporate into your life?

4. In your quiet time, sing the words to Charles Wesley's hymn "For the Anniversary Day of One's Conversion." It's OK to make up your own tune, right?

Thumbnail Sketch

METHODISM IN AMERICA: CHURCH WITH THE SOUL OF A NATION

Historical Roots

Methodism came to America in the 1760s. Barbara Heck, an Irish immigrant, helped start the first Methodist society in North America in 1768. The Christmas Conference of 1784 in Baltimore created the Methodist Episcopal Church. Francis Asbury, one of Wesley's missionaries, became its strongest leader. African-American Methodism and German Methodism also helped write the story of Wesleyanism in the United States.

Core Beliefs

Orthodox Protestant theology, including the triune God; Christ as Savior; justification by faith; sacraments of baptism and the Lord's Supper; prevenient, saving, and sanctifying grace; and the sufficiency of Scripture. The *Discipline* of the United Methodist Church provides for "exploratory" theologizing, which has engaged the denomination in Black, feminist, liberation, and process theologies.

Agreement and Differences

Nazarenes and United Methodists are in harmony on basic Protestant orthodoxy and Arminian views. Differences come at the scope of theological teaching approved by some Methodists. Nazarenes stick primarily to traditional Wesleyan teachings.

Nazarenes and United Methodists tend to differ on our cardinal doctrine—sanctification. United Methodists commonly promote sanctification as process and Christian nurture. Nazarenes and other churches in the American Holiness Movement prefer Wesley's teaching that entire sanctification has both processive and instantaneous aspects.

American Methodists Today

The United Methodist Church is the second largest Protestant denomination in the United States. Add three African-American Methodist groups, and there are 14 million Methodists in the United States.

Q. What may we reasonably believe to be God's
design in raising up the Methodist preachers?
A. To reform the Continent, and to spread scriptural
Holiness over these lands.
—First *Discipline* of the Methodist Episcopal Church

4 METHODIƧM IN AMERICA: CHURCH WITH THE ƧOUL OF A NATION

THE UNITED METHODIST "CROSS AND FLAME" LOGO is the best-recognized denominational symbol in America. It combines symbols of Christ and the Holy Spirit. Its two tongues of fiery red flame, united at the bottom, also symbolize the 1968 union of the Methodist and Evangelical United Brethren Churches.

United Methodists are a large proportion of worshiping Americans. With over 8.5 million U.S. members, the church is the second largest Protestant denomination in North America and has another 1 million members in other countries. Three predominantly African-American Methodist denominations have another 5.5 million members in the United States.

American Methodism was the product of British Methodism's missionary impulse. Planted in the 1760s, Methodism grew to be the largest American denomination by 1850. This happened because Methodists were not paralyzed by the challenge of competing within a religious environment dominated by Calvinism. At the same time, Methodists became the most American of churches, exposed fully to the stresses of national life. Racism and ethnicity exacted their price, as did democratization. Three traditions developed: a central one embodied by the Methodist Episcopal Church and distinctly African and German forms of Methodism.

Francis Asbury

The first American Methodists were immigrants like Barbara Heck (a native of Limerick, Ireland) who brought their Methodist faith with them. In 1768 Heck helped organize the first Methodist society in America in New York City.[1]

John Wesley sent lay preachers to lead these societies and organize new ones. Earnest but conservative, those preachers returned to England when the

---

1. Arthur B. Moss, "Barbara Ruckle Heck," in *The Encyclopedia of World Methodism*, ed. Nolan B. Harmon (Nashville: United Methodist Publishing House, 1974), 1:1103-4.

American Revolution came. There was one exception: Francis Asbury (1745—1816) alone adapted to the American spirit and remained to supervise the Methodist enterprise. Despite the turmoil of war, Methodism sank deep roots into American culture during the Revolution. The preachers were sufficiently strong as a body to organize the first Methodist denomination in the world in 1784.

Why did the Americans leave Wesley's Church of England and strike out on their own? The factors included

- the sacramental crisis
- an urgency to evangelize the American people
- their acceptance of the daunting challenges of America's physical and social environment

The Church of England's failure to place a bishop in America before or after the Revolution provoked the sacramental crisis. With no bishop, it was impossible under Anglican polity to ordain priests in the New World. The resulting shortage of priests meant infrequent baptisms, Communion, and preaching.

Wesley felt he could not wait for his church to act. In 1784 he authorized Thomas Coke (1747—1814), an Anglican priest like himself, as one of two general superintendents of the American Methodists. Wesley also ordained several lay preachers into the ministry, including Richard Whatcoat and Thomas Vasey. It was entirely irregular by Anglican standards. Only bishops could ordain, but Wesley felt that "emergency ministers" were needed. Coke was authorized to ordain Francis Asbury, whom Wesley appointed as the other general superintendent.

Coke's arrival in America was sensational. Anglicans flocked to his services along the Eastern seaboard, where hundreds were baptized and thousands took Communion. The annual conference of Methodist preachers was announced for late December in Baltimore.

The Christmas Conference established a new church. Wesley had not authorized *that* but could not prevent it. The American preachers were convinced of its necessity. An episcopal government modified by presbyterian elements was approved. Wesley had sent 24 Articles of Religion for the societies. With the addition of one other, they became Articles of Religion for a church. Wesley's published sermons also were adopted as standards of doctrine. The Methodist Episcopal Church was born.

American Methodism retained the Church of England's twofold ordination, first as a deacon and then—after proving oneself—as an elder. Asbury, already a proven minister, was ordained to the ministry on two successive days and inducted into the superintendency on the third. Two Nazarene general superintendents (H. F. Reynolds and J. G. Morrison) were ordained by Bishop John Hurst, whose ordination line goes back to that historic service in which Coke ordained Asbury.

Coke returned to England and traveled frequently between England, Ireland, America, and the West Indies. He was a bishop only when he was on American soil. His death en route to India exemplified early Methodism's restless missionary spirit.

And so Asbury—not Coke or Wesley—was American Methodism's chief founder. What was Asbury like? Albert Outler noted that he was opinionated, authoritarian, and had "no unrecorded ailments." But "his own dedication to poverty, chastity, and obedience was patent." He pushed Methodism forward through zeal, self-abnegation, and Christian fortitude.[2] He was no plaster saint—he was a Methodist saint.

Asbury traveled by horse and carriage the length of the new nation and a full third of its breadth. Sanctified Methodist Richard Whatcoat was elected bishop in 1801 to assist him. Whatcoat was succeeded by William McKendree, the first American-born bishop and a rugged frontier revivalist who commanded the preachers' respect. Under Asbury, Whatcoat, and McKendree, Methodism's strategy for evangelizing North America took shape.

"To Reform the Nation"

Methodists succeeded in the 19th century for several reasons. Among them:
- the circuit rider
- the class meeting and class leader
- the camp meeting revival
- the message
- the appointive system in which ministers were assigned by the bishop

America was largely a frontier society. The Methodist minister traveled a circuit that could have 20 or more preaching points. Bishops deployed the preachers in ways that covered large territories. This also forced the church to rely on strong lay leaders in the interim between pastoral visits. The physical demands were horrendous, and many were worn-out preachers by middle age. Locally, Methodists were organized into classes under spiritual leaders. Preaching and Communion services were held when the ordained minister visited, but some class leaders were also licensed local preachers.

The camp meeting was an effective Methodist tool. Large groups gathered, sometimes by the thousands, with simultaneous preaching in different parts of the camp. Asbury always estimated (by hundreds) the number who were converted, sanctified, and took Communion at these gatherings.

Today it is common to see large Methodist churches in urban areas. But Methodism has always been strongly rural. By following the frontier and ministering to the homesteaders, the Methodists spread more evenly across America than any other denomination.

German Methodism

German Methodism developed from revivalism's influence upon German-American communities. Two primary denominations arose: the United Brethren in Christ and the Evangelical Association (later the Evangelical Church).

The first was formed by Philip William Otterbein (1726—1813), a German Reformed minister, and Martin Boehm (1725—1812), a Mennonite bishop. Both were pietists who stressed a personal relationship with God, an identifiable conversion experience, sanctification, and the witness of the Spirit. After Otterbein first heard Boehm preach in a barn in Pennsylvania, he grabbed Boehm's hand

---

2. Albert C. Outler, "Adventures and Misadventures of Methodism," Second Gray Lecture, Duke University Divinity School, November 8, 1983.

and exclaimed, "We are brothers." Their interest in the warmed heart cut through denominational boundaries, and in 1800 they organized the Church of the United Brethren in Christ.

Both founders had close relations with Methodism. Otterbein laid hands on Asbury at the latter's consecration as bishop, while Boehm belonged to a Methodist class meeting and helped organize a Methodist church on his family's land. His son, Henry, was Asbury's traveling companion and a well-known Methodist minister. The United Brethren had many Methodist features, including a quadrennial general meeting, a strong missionary emphasis, and an episcopacy understood as a general superintendency.

From their ranks came early Nazarene leaders like C. W. Ruth and H. Orton Wiley.

The Evangelical Association was started by Jacob Albright (1759—1808), a son of German immigrants. Educated by Lutherans in Pennsylvania, Albright was influenced by Otterbein's followers. After three of his children died in an epidemic in 1790, Albright sought a deeper experience of grace and joined the Methodist Episcopal Church. He preached in homes and schoolhouses to German folks throughout Pennsylvania, Maryland, and Virginia, organizing Methodist class meetings. In 1807 the classes under his leadership decided to unite as a denomination under Albright's leadership. He was elected bishop but died the next year. In 1816 the group took the name Evangelische Gemeinschaft (or Evangelical Association). Its *Discipline* was patterned after the Methodist Episcopal Church's.

Both denominations aggressively evangelized the Germans pouring into America. Both were committed to Wesleyan revivalism and doctrine throughout the 19th century, and from their ranks came early Nazarene leaders like C. W. Ruth and H. Orton Wiley. In 1946 the two denominations formed the Evangelical United Brethren Church.

"To him [Nast], sanctification was a fact and not a theory; it could be experienced and demonstrated."

The Evangelical United Brethren (EUB) tradition existed partly because Asbury did not want the Methodist Episcopal Church working, in its early years, with another language group. A generation later a new philosophy prevailed. William Nast (1807-89) emerged as a leader in evangelizing German-Americans on behalf of the Methodist Episcopal Church and played a critical role in planting Methodism in Germany itself. Nast belonged to the National Holiness Association. A biographer states that "to him, sanctification was a fact and not a theory; it could be experienced and demonstrated." Eventually, the Methodist Episcopal Church developed several German conferences.

African Methodism

Leon Litwack's *North of Slavery* examined the lives of Black Americans in the North before the Civil War. His findings: that they neither enjoyed equality with Whites nor, in many cases, even enjoyed a humane life. This point is a backdrop for understanding African Methodism, which sprang from discrimination against Black Methodists by White ones.

African Methodism's early history is reflected in the life of Richard Allen (1760—1831), born a slave in Philadelphia and sold to a master in Delaware. Allen was converted through Methodist preaching at age 17. Soon thereafter so was his master, who came to believe that slavery was inherently evil and arranged for Allen to earn his freedom. Allen engaged in secular work and was licensed as a lay preacher in 1784 by Saint George's Methodist Episcopal Church in Philadelphia.

Saint George's White members expected the church's African-Americans to sit in the back and take Communion only after the White members were served. A new gallery built inside the church was designated as seating for Black worshipers. In 1787 two trustees pulled Absalom Jones and one other up from their knees during prayer for being outside the designated area. Allen led a walkout of the Black members, and a new congregation was organized. But the people voted to affiliate it with the Episcopal Church. Allen disagreed with that decision and remained in the Methodist Episcopal Church.

Allen's dream of a Black Methodist church in Philadelphia finally was realized in 1794. Bethel Church was dedicated by Francis Asbury, who ordained Allen a deacon in 1799. Friction between the races persisted, however. A dispute over whether Bethel's property would be controlled by its members or the White-dominated conference led to Bethel's break with the Methodist Episcopal Church.

A similar pattern of segregated seating and offensive Communion procedures had strained relations between White and Black Methodists in other cities. Allen joined representatives of similar congregations to organize the African Methodist Episcopal Church in 1816 and was its first bishop. Its *Discipline,* Articles of Religion, and General Rules were nearly identical to the Methodist Episcopal Church's.[3]

A similar denomination took shape in New York City in 1820. The Zion Methodist congregation voted to be independent after the New York Conference refused to support a plan for an African Conference within the Methodist Episcopal Church. James Varick, ordained in 1822, was the first general superintendent. The name of African

The A.M.E. Zion Church actively opposed slavery; its members included Frederick Douglass and Harriet Tubman.

Methodist Episcopal Zion Church was adopted.[4] Like the African Methodist Episcopal (A.M.E.) Church, the A.M.E. Zion Church actively opposed slavery; its members included Frederick Douglass and Harriet Tubman.

A third expression of Black Methodism originated in the South after the Civil War. The Methodist Episcopal (M.E.) Church, South (its formation is described in the next section of this chapter), had over 200,000 slave members

---

3. Frederick E. Maser and George A. Singleton, "Further Branches of Methodism Are Founded," in *History of American Methodism,* ed. Emory S. Bucke, 3 vols. (New York and Nashville: Abingdon Press, 1964), 1:601-9.
4. Ibid., 609-14.

in 1860, but only 20,000 Black members remained a decade later as the A.M.E., A.M.E. Zion, and M.E. Churches successfully recruited Black members during Reconstruction. Southern Blacks had demonstrated a desire to control their own churches, so the M.E. Church, South, provided for its remaining African-American members to organize a self-governing body. The Colored Methodist Episcopal Church was created in 1870. Its membership originally was restricted to those of African descent. In 1954 its name changed to the Christian Methodist Episcopal (C.M.E.) Church.[5]

Today the A.M.E. Church's members total 3.5 million, while the A.M.E. Zion Church has over 1.2 million members. The C.M.E. Church's membership is 718,000.[6] The doctrines of these churches are nearly identical. Mary Love, editor of A.M.E. Zion literature, writes that the major beliefs of her church include
- the Apostles' Creed
- The Articles of Religion of the M.E. Church
- the sacraments of baptism and Holy Communion
- conversion
- sanctification
- the witness of the Spirit
- emphasis on the means of grace[7]

Two early women preachers in this tradition—Jarena Lee (A.M.E.) and Julia Foote (A.M.E. Zion)—left vivid testimonies to the grace of entire sanctification and were instrumental in leading others into it. "How to Obtain Sanctification" was the last chapter of Foote's autobiography.[8]

Democracy and Slavery

The issue of equal lay representation at Annual and General Conferences reflected the new nation's social impulses upon religion. Resistance to these trends by religious conservatives led to the Methodist Protestant schism in 1830. The Methodist Protestant Church had a church president instead of bishops and gave the laity representation at all levels of church governance. Methodist Protestants also were more liberal on the issue of women in the ministry. Anna Howard Shaw, denied ordination by the Methodist Episcopal Church, joined the Methodist Protestant Church, which ordained her in 1880.

No issue afflicted the Methodist Episcopal Church more than slavery, the driving issue in the Wesleyan Methodist schism (1843) and a significant factor in the Free Methodist schism (1861). Both new churches were staunchly abolitionist. Slavery was so divisive that the 1844 General Conference decided to split the Methodist Episcopal Church into two: a church for the North and another

---

5. Frederick A. Norwood, *The Story of American Methodism* (New York and Nashville: Abingdon Press, 1974), 274-76.

6. Kenneth B. Bedell, ed., *Yearbook of American and Canadian Churches, 1996* (Nashville: Abingdon Press, 1996), 250-51.

7. Mary A. Love, "African Methodist Episcopal Zion Church," in *An Encyclopedia of Religions in the United States: One Hundred Religious Groups Speak for Themselves*, ed. William B. Williamson (New York: Crossroad Publishing Co., 1992), 219.

8. Julia A. Foote, *A Brand Plucked from the Fire: An Autobiographical Sketch* (Cleveland: Printed for the Author, 1886), 122-24. The book has numerous references to entire sanctification.

for the South. The Northern church retained the original name. The other became the Methodist Episcopal Church, South. Few events so dramatically demonstrate the temporary triumph of the world over the gospel.

Why didn't the doctrine of Christian perfection redeem this situation? It is a compelling question. Advocates of Christian holiness could be found on all sides of the slavery issue. Phoebe Palmer and many close associates would not condemn slavery publicly in order to keep

Bonds of national unity significantly weakened after Baptists, Methodists, and Presbyterians split over slavery.

peace within the church, but the New England Conference's abolition-minded editor, Gilbert Haven (later bishop), had no such reservations, and his aggressive Holiness crusade had personal and social dimensions. By contrast, Lovick Pierce, a patriarch in the Methodist Episcopal Church, South, was a consistent preacher of entire sanctification but also a defender of the South's "liberty" to keep and hold slaves. C. C. Goen argues in *Broken Churches, Broken Nation* that the bonds of national unity significantly weakened after Baptists, Methodists, and Presbyterians split over slavery. A nation, after all, is more than its government, and many different social bonds knit it together. The failure of the churches preceded and prepared the way for a baptism in blood. The advocates of Christian perfection were not unified any better or worse than others on this vital issue.

Reunion

The lingering bitterness of regionalism and the Civil War affected American Methodism for generations. When Northern and Southern branches of the Methodist Episcopal Church finally held reunion discussions, the Methodist Protestants were also invited to the table. In 1939 a three-way reunion occurred in Kansas City, and the newly reunited denomination became simply The Methodist Church.

Connecting the branches of the Methodist tree was not over. Methodists and German Methodists had interacted for generations. In 1968 the Methodist Church and the Evangelical United Brethren also merged, creating the United Methodist Church.

In the 1980s and 1990s United Methodists and the African Methodist churches also have discussed union. The Black churches have serious concerns to weigh. As critical agents in African-American history, they must decide whether to surrender their distinctive identities in order to create a new Methodism. On the other hand, a 14-million-member church in which 40 percent of the members are African-American would be a witness to Christian unity unparalleled in American Christianity's history. How will this story end?

All four Methodist churches participate in the Church of Christ Uniting movement. Ten denominations have moved toward a covenant relationship in which each retains its distinctive identity but participates at certain levels in one another's ministries. The four Methodist churches contain well over half the membership of the denominations involved in the Church of Christ Uniting.

United Methodist Theology

What does the United Methodist Church teach today? The *Discipline* (1996) gives the church's basic theological affirmations:

- faith in the mystery of salvation in and through Jesus Christ
- belief that God's redemptive love is realized in human life by the activity of the Holy Spirit in personal experience and in the community of believers
- the essential oneness of Christ's Church
- that the United Methodist Church is part of Christ's universal Church "when by adoration, proclamation, and service we become conformed to Christ"
- scriptural authority in matters of faith
- justification by grace through faith
- "the sober realization that the church is in need of continual reformation and renewal"
- understanding God's reign as both present and future[9]

Each aspect ties the United Methodist witness to the Church Universal. But a further summary notes "distinctive Wesleyan emphases":

- prevenient grace
- justification by grace
- assurance of present salvation
- sanctification and perfection, described primarily as a process of growth in grace
- faith as "the only response essential to salvation" yet dead without works of mercy
- Christian fellowship as essential both for the nurture and mission of the Body of Christ[10]

The *Discipline* contains two creeds: the Twenty-five Articles of the Methodist Episcopal Church (1784) and the Confession of Faith of the Evangelical United Brethren Church. Both reflect basic Protestant orthodoxy, including the doctrines of the Triune God; the sufficiency of Scripture; original sin; justification by faith alone; and the sacraments of baptism and the Lord's Supper. Methodism's Twenty-five Articles are also followed by one on "Sanctification" carried over from the *Discipline* of the Methodist Protestant Church. This article stresses sanctification as process. Of greater interest, however, is the article on "Sanctification and Christian Perfection" from the Evangelical United Brethren Confession, which affirms,

- "We believe that sanctification is the work of God's grace . . . by which those who have been born again are cleansed from sin in their thoughts, words and acts, and are enabled to live in accordance with God's will, and to strive for holiness without which no one will see the Lord."
- "Entire sanctification is a state of perfect love, righteousness and true holiness which every regenerate believer may obtain."

---

9. *The Book of Discipline of the United Methodist Church, 1996* (Nashville: United Methodist Publishing House, 1996), 41-42.

10. Ibid., 43-46.

- "Through faith in Jesus Christ this gracious gift may be received in this life both gradually and instantaneously, and should be sought by every child of God."[11]

While official doctrine is expressed in these articles of faith, a section of the *Discipline* titled "Our Theological Task" emphasizes that the church has a continuing theological vocation. It states that the church "encourages serious reflection across the theological spectrum. . . . We are called to identify the needs both of individuals and of society and to address those needs out of the resources of Christian faith. . . . Theology serves the Church by interpreting the world's needs and challenges to the Church and by interpreting the gospel to the world."[12] Thus, Methodists believe that "exploratory theologies"—feminist theology, liberation theology, Black theology, process theology, and other schools of thought—assist them in reaching out to the contemporary world.

A set of United Methodist social principles are included in the *Discipline*. They establish a theological framework for Christian moral thinking in four broad areas: the natural world, the compassionate community, society, and economics.

A final section titled "The Ministry of All Christians" calls the church "the people of God" and teaches that all Christians are ministers, that baptism marks one's entry into the ministry of the church, and that "the impulse to minister always moves one beyond the congregation toward the whole human community." Thus a belief in lay ministry permeates United Methodist thought as it did earlier on the frontier.

Within this framework of the ministry of all Christians, "ordained ministers are called by God to a lifetime of servant leadership in specialized ministries among the people of God." United Methodists ordain two types of specialized ministers: deacons and elders.[13]

The 1996 General Conference reversed two centuries of American Methodist practice on two major issues. Double ordination—first as a deacon, later as an elder—was changed to single ordination, either as a permanent deacon or as an elder. United Methodist ordination practice now lines up with that of most denominations, including the Church of the Nazarene.

Second, United Methodists decided to become an international church. For two centuries their missionaries helped raise independent Methodist churches in other countries. Now mature mission conferences can remain in the United Methodist Church if they choose. The impetus for rethinking global strategy came from bishops outside North America who questioned whether national boundaries should shape denominational ones. As the United Methodist Church repositions itself as an international body, how will its experience with this issue compare with ours?

11. Ibid., 62.
12. Ibid., 71.
13. Ibid., 107-17.

United Methodists also practice *inclusiveness*. Women and racial/ethnic minorities are always well represented at public gatherings of the church. This intentional commitment to include all groups may reflect a strong desire to overcome the divisions in Methodism's earlier history, but it also represents a sense of what Pentecost is about.

Nazarene and Methodists

What do we owe the United Methodist Church? More, frankly, than we owe to any other denomination:

- our quadrennial General Assembly
- our *Manual*, patterned originally after the *Discipline*
- our system of districts and district superintendents
- our general superintendency
- our basic theology
- our General Rules
- our ordination practices
- the majority of our major founders
- district ownership of local church property

Early Nazarene theologian A. M. Hills claimed that "the Church of the Nazarene is the fairest flower that has ever bloomed in the Methodist garden, the most promising ecclesiastical daughter the prolific Mother Methodism has ever given to the world."[14] General Superintendent E. F. Walker insisted, "Scratch a real Nazarene, and you will touch an original Methodist; skin a genuine Methodist, and behold a Nazarene."[15] Both Hills and Walker were former ministers in Presbyterian and Congregational churches. Despite that fact (or perhaps because of it), they understood the underlying Methodist identity of their new church.

Hills's essay, published for the Church of the Nazarene's 25th anniversary, cited Nazarene continuity with Methodism in six primary areas: pioneer leadership, soul winning, missionary endeavor, theological scholarship, spiritual inheritance, and education for a Christian culture.

Methodist influence permeated the early course of study for ministerial preparation. Young Nazarene preachers were required to read John Telford's *Life of John Wesley* and Wesley's sermons. The systematic theologies of Methodists John Miley and Thomas Ralston were used to teach basic Wesleyan theology until H. Orton Wiley's *Christian Theology* appeared in 1940. Even A. M. Hills's systematic theology, listed on the course of study from 1932 to 1940, was an alternate to Ralston's text, not the choice text itself.

What differences, then, separate the two denominations? What makes the Church of the Nazarene distinctive and different?

First, Nazarenes are distinctly Evangelical and embrace a traditional Wesleyanism. Official United Methodist doctrine expresses orthodox theology, but the range of beliefs among the church's theologians, pastors, and members is much more diverse than the *Discipline* indicates. United Methodists have been

---

14. A. M. Hills, "The Silver Jubilee Anniversary," *Herald of Holiness,* November 22, 1933, 10.
15. E. F. Walker, "New Denominations," *Nazarene Messenger,* April 1, 1909, 7.

so ecumenical and broad-minded that in some times and places they have embraced the radically ultraliberal, and in other times and places the reactionary conservative. These tendencies reflect a truth: a church that identifies too fully with its culture will be subject to the fault-line fractures of that culture. Does it then lose its prophetic voice or ability to speak a word from beyond culture?

This tolerance for other theologies has discouraged many traditional Wesleyans within the United Methodist Church. Nevertheless, a Wesleyan-Holiness component in United Methodism maintains a vigorous camp meeting tradition and supports Asbury College, Asbury Theological Seminary, and Taylor University. Their influence is felt in the Christian Holiness Partnership and the Wesleyan Theological Society. Their contribution to the Wesleyan-Holiness tradition's vitality is considerable when one considers that Asbury Theological Seminary trains more ministers than the next three largest Wesleyan-Holiness seminaries combined. United Methodists who reflect the Wesleyan-Holiness tradition exist, then, within a theologically pluralistic church. By contrast, the Church of the Nazarene maintains a traditional Wesleyan focus.

This leads to another major difference: the Church of the Nazarene's founders created a believers' church. This concept was not stated as clearly as our doctrine of holiness. But it was vocalized and underlay the founders' thinking about the church's purpose. The believers' church required a clear testimony to a converted life from its members. It was set against a mainstream Methodism that the founders believed had been seduced by American culture. For instance, Nazarene rejection of secret oath-bound societies reflected their belief that the Methodists who belonged to such groups were allowing other loyalties to compete with their loyalty to fellow believers in Christ. The early Nazarene passion to take the gospel to the poor reflected a similar disenchantment with a mother church they believed was too seduced by rising middle-class prosperity.

The Nazarene founders also were revolutionaries who made all clergy and lay offices in the church open to women. Methodist women still struggled for laity rights, and full clergy rights lay another half century down the road. But Nazarenes simply went ahead and did it. That issue no longer divides us today, and United Methodists have a significantly higher percentage of women pastors. In addition, they have female district superintendents and bishops.

Another difference lies in the basic understanding of how a person typically becomes a Christian. Nazarenes emphasize Christian conversion, both among their own youth and in their outreach to unchurched people. United Methodists, on the other hand, largely emphasize Christian nurture as the primary way of coming to Christ. Altar calls are largely unknown in United Methodist churches around large urban areas, whereas Nazarene pastors periodically sense a need to preach in a fashion that calls people to a decision.

Additionally, a corresponding difference exists in the basic stance on sanctification. Many United Methodists take sanctification very seriously but regard John Wesley's particular theology of holiness, and its possibility of entire sanctification, as an oddity just as the Calvinists of Wesley's day did. Wesley emphasized three phases of sanctification: initial sanctification (regeneration, the new birth), progressive sanctification (before and after entire sanctification), and entire sanctification (the moment perfect love expels the tendency toward sin). Most United Methodists affirm progressive sanctification only, although we noted the Wesleyan-Holiness minority within United Methodism.[16]

Methodism is a worldwide family of churches connected to us by historical ties. The World Methodist Council's member churches include the United Methodist, African Methodist Episcopal, African Methodist Episcopal Zion, and Christian Methodist Episcopal Churches. The Free Methodist and Wesleyan Churches, the denominations most nearly like our own, also belong to this council. The World Methodist Council's official handbook includes information about the Church of the Nazarene and other nonmember churches that "have a distinctive Methodist tradition and emphasis." It also includes our worldwide statistics in its studies showing Methodist penetration country by country.

Methodism does not account fully for our identity, but it accounts for much of it. The history of American Methodism through the 1890s, with its moments of tragedy and grace, is also our history. And the pages of history we and our children write will be further chronicles in the story of Wesley's heirs.

Review and Reflection

1. Identify the following persons:
   Francis Asbury

   Harriet Tubman

   Richard Allen

   A. M. Hills

   Mary Love

   Barbara Heck

   H. F. Reynolds

   Julia Foote

   H. Orton Wiley

   Martin Boehm

Which of the above persons would you most like to meet and talk with?

---

16. Other differences between Nazarenes and United Methodists include the following:
- United Methodist pastors are appointed to churches by the bishop rather than called by the congregation.
- The United Methodist General Conference is composed of equal numbers of elected lay and clergy delegates; bishops and heads of church agencies are not allowed to vote at General Conference and can speak only under special rules.
- United Methodism is organized at five levels: General Conference; Jurisdictional Conference (regional), where bishops are elected and assigned; Annual Conference; district; and local church. The Church of the Nazarene only exists at three levels: general, district, and local. The Nazarene district assumes the functions of both the United Methodist district and the United Methodist Annual Conference.

2. Identify the following ideas as treated in this chapter:
Abolition

Sanctification

Conversion

Sacraments

Ordination

Prevenient Grace

Which of these is most important in your life right now?

3. The Wesleyan tradition has an amazing vitality. Write a prayer or a poem in which you express your positive feelings about your own Wesleyan heritage.

4. Suppose you were working with a group of junior high kids, and you were to teach them about their Wesleyan heritage as presented in the preceding two chapters of this book. A bumper sticker exercise is part of the lesson plans. What "starter" bumper sticker ideas would you introduce to your students?

Thumbnail Sketch

OUR SISTER DENOMINATIONS: THE HOLINESS CHURCHES

Historical Background

The 19th-century Holiness Movement brought forth new churches that took as their mission the heralding of the gospel of entire sanctification. Most sprang directly from Wesleyan roots, including The Wesleyan Church, the Pilgrim Holiness Church, the Free Methodist Church, the Church of Christ (Holiness), The Salvation Army, and, of course, the Church of the Nazarene. The Church of God (Anderson, Indiana) and the Church of God (Holiness) shared a similar dream and message. The Evangelical Friends married Wesleyan doctrine with their Quaker heritage.

Core Beliefs and Family Differences

The core beliefs of the churches treated in this chapter include the traditional doctrines of the Trinity, inspiration of Scripture, and salvation by grace through faith in Jesus Christ. All but one are Arminian in theology and Wesleyan in doctrine.

Some "family differences" include the rejection of sacraments by The Salvation Army, opposition to denominational organization and to creeds by the Church of God (Anderson), and the Keswickian sanctification teachings and mild Calvinism of the Christian and Missionary Alliance.

Wesleyan-Holiness Churches Today

The churches treated in this chapter report a constituency of about 4 million. Add to that 1.2 million Nazarenes and the membership of a dozen more smaller denominations not discussed in this chapter, and you have a formidable army of like-minded Christians.

5 ~ Our Sister Denominations: The Holiness Churches

THE SEVERAL DOZEN HOLINESS CHURCHES in North America fall into four groups. Those most closely related to the Church of the Nazarene share our Methodist roots and our Evangelical Wesleyan-Holiness theology. The major ones are The Wesleyan Church, the Free Methodist Church, The Salvation Army, and the Church of God (Anderson, Indiana). The Church of God (Holiness), Church of Christ (Holiness), and Bible Missionary Church are smaller churches that also merit our attention.

Another group of churches have non-Methodist origins. Influenced by the 19th-century Holiness revival, they incorporated Wesleyan holiness into their doctrine and Methodist revivalism into their practice, yet they retain key aspects of their original tradition. Major churches in this tier are the Brethren in Christ and the Evangelical Friends International.

A third tier is composed of churches that teach entire sanctification as a second work of grace and also embrace 20th-century Pentecostalism. These are discussed in a later chapter.

The fourth tier has one representative, the Christian and Missionary Alliance, which teaches a second work of grace but not the Wesleyan-Holiness view. It represents the Keswick-Holiness tradition. Nevertheless, it is similar to the Wesleyan-Holiness churches.

Wesleyan-Holiness Relationships

Wesleyan-Holiness churches interact through two primary fellowships. The Christian Holiness Partnership began in 1867 as the National Camp Meeting Association for the Promotion of Holiness, better known as the National (and later Christian) Holiness Association. The oldest Holiness association in the world, it once inspired scores of state, county, and local organizations. Methodists tightly controlled it at first, but today its members include the larger Wesleyan-Holiness bodies in North America, several smaller ones, and many evangelical United Methodists. Early Nazarene leaders Phineas F. Bresee and C. W. Ruth served the association in key positions. B. Edgar Johnson and Jack W. Stone are among the Nazarenes who have done so more recently. One of its key auxiliaries is the Wesleyan Theological Society, founded in 1965. The International Wesleyan-Holiness Women Clergy Conference, which meets every two years, is also related to the Christian Holiness Partnership.

The Interchurch Holiness Convention (IHC) was created in the 1950s to serve the more conservative Holiness Movement in North America. IHC-related groups are committed to the patterns of revivalism that flourished in the early 20th-century Holiness Movement and are culturally conservative, sometimes tending toward legalism. Many deplore evils that they perceive taking root in the larger Holiness denominations. The IHC's annual meeting draws several thousand people and functions as a large meeting for the smaller Holiness churches in the same way that General Conference and General Assembly activities function in the larger ones.

The Wesleyan Church

The Wesleyan Church enshrines a paradox. It is the oldest and yet the youngest of the major Wesleyan-Holiness churches. It was produced by the merger of the Wesleyan Methodist and Pilgrim Holiness denominations in 1968, but each parent body had an older history.

The Wesleyan Methodist Connection began in 1843 when Orange Scott, Luther Lee, and other foes of slavery withdrew from the Methodist Episcopal Church, whose bishops had stifled internal debate over the abolition issue. The Wesleyan Methodists stood for two principles: the abolition of slavery and a church without bishops.

Wesleyan Methodism's radical tendencies were shown in other ways. The Seneca Falls Convention, launching the women's rights movement, was held in a Wesleyan Methodist sanctuary, while Luther Lee preached the sermon at the ordination of Congregational minister Antoinette Brown, the first woman ordained in America.

Orange Scott soon died. After the Civil War, Lee and other surviving founders returned to the Methodist Episcopal Church, since slavery was no longer an issue, and the Methodist Episcopal Church was mounting a major program to educate and assist newly freed slaves. Adam Crooks, however, opposed the reunion movement. In the 1870s he helped the remaining Wesleyan Methodists find a new sense of purpose by leading them to identify more closely with the national Holiness revival.

The Pilgrim Holiness Church was one of the bodies that emerged from that revival. It began as the International Holiness Union and Prayer League, a fellowship founded in 1897 by Martin Wells Knapp (Methodist), Seth Rees (Quaker), and C. W. Ruth (Holiness Christian Church). Knapp also founded God's Bible School in Cincinnati and edited *God's Revivalist,* a popular Holiness paper. In 1901 Knapp died, and Ruth joined the Nazarenes. Rees withdrew over a dispute with Mrs. Knapp in 1905. George Culp, a man of Fundamentalist bent, became the key leader as the group evolved slowly into a denomination known by 1913 as the International Apostolic Holiness Church.

Like the Church of the Nazarene, the International Apostolic Holiness Church gathered many small independent works. Some had Nazarene links, like the Holiness Christian Church, whose Pennsylvania Conference united with Nazarenes in 1908 while other conferences united with the International Apostolic Holiness Church in 1919. William Lee's People's Mission Church in Colorado was another. It affiliated with the Nazarenes in 1911 but withdrew one year later. It joined the Pilgrim Holiness Church in 1925.

The most memorable link was Seth Rees. His brief ministry among Southern California Nazarenes involved a stormy relationship with several men from Bresee's inner circle. In 1917 Rees's large congregation in Pasadena was disorganized by the district superintendent in a drastic attempt to "save" the district. Rees had many Nazarene supporters but did not appeal this decision to the General Assembly. Instead, he formed the Pilgrim Church with about 400 former Nazarenes. In 1922 the Pilgrim Church united with the International Apostolic Holiness Church, adding Rees's 457 members to a total church membership of around 13,000.[1] This brought Rees back into fellowship with a group he had cofounded a quarter century before. The Pilgrim Holiness Church name was adopted at this time, and Rees later was its general superintendent.

> *The Wesleyan Church and the Church of the Nazarene have been the primary groups to gather up the fragmented Wesleyan-Holiness world in the 20th century.*

The Wesleyan Methodist/Pilgrim Holiness merger into The Wesleyan Church in 1968 was a further consolidation. The Wesleyan Church and the Church of the Nazarene have been the primary groups to gather up the fragmented Wesleyan-Holiness world in the 20th century. The Wesleyan Church's educational institutions include Houghton College (New York) and Indiana Wesleyan University (Marion, Indiana). The church has approximately 171,000 members in North America and a total worldwide constituency of over 300,000.[2]

The Free Methodist Church of North America

Benjamin Titus Roberts was the primary founder of the Free Methodist Church in 1860. As a Methodist pastor in western New York, Roberts was committed to the doctrine of Christian perfection. He voiced active opposition to growing doctrinal laxity, slavery, and Freemasonry's growth among laity and clergy. But his chief concern was to include the poor in the church's life. He spoke against pew rent, a common method (in those days) of raising money for local churches that gave preference to the rich and discriminated against the poor. Roberts tried to persuade one of his congregations to become a "free church." When that failed, he tried enlisting their help to plant a free church elsewhere in the city.

Roberts wrote a strong article against the tendencies he deplored, coining the term "New School Methodists" for those who had "compromised" with the world. He was put on church trial for unbrotherly conduct, found guilty, and censured. The next year he was tried for ignoring his censure by reprinting the

---

1. Paul Westphal Thomas and Paul William Thomas, *Days of Our Pilgrimage: History of the Pilgrim Holiness Church* (Marion, Ind.: Wesley Press, 1976), 95; Lee M. Haines and Paul William Thomas, *An Outline History of the Wesleyan Church*, 3rd ed. (Marion, Ind.: Wesley Press, 1985), 126-27.

2. Kenneth B. Bedell, ed., *Yearbook of American and Canadian Churches, 1997* (Nashville: Abingdon Press, 1997), 251, 258; Frank S. Mead and Samuel S. Hill, *Handbook of Denominations in the United States*, 10th ed. (Nashville: Abingdon Press, 1995), 303.

article and distributing it more broadly. It had indeed been reprinted, but Roberts denied doing it. However, another minister testified that Roberts had handed him the pamphlets and urged him to distribute them. Roberts was found guilty and expelled from the Methodist ministry. The chief witness against him later demonstrated a poor memory in other matters.

Roberts established two "free churches" in Buffalo while appealing his case to the General Conference. Other Methodists had established independent "free churches" in the Midwest. When Roberts's appeals were denied by the 1860 General Conference, he joined with others to form the Free Methodist Church and was elected as its first general superintendent. (In 1910 the Methodist Episcopal Church admitted making errors and posthumously restored Roberts's credentials and good standing.)

Roberts strongly advocated the ordination of women and aligned himself with the laboring class in their conflict with industrialists. His strong witness to entire sanctification was not incidental to his social views. He believed that perfect love had personal and social dimensions and that the gospel should be preached especially to the poor.

After Roberts's death, the term "general superintendent" was replaced by "bishop." Like the Wesleyan Methodist Church, Free Methodism has been centered largely in the Northeastern and upper Midwestern United States. Free Methodists operate several liberal arts institutions, including Seattle Pacific University. The Free Methodist Church has an inclusive membership of over 80,000 in the United States and Canada.[3]

The Salvation Army

The Salvation Army began in the slums of London in 1865. Originally named the Christian Mission, its focus was the conversion of sinners and the entire sanctification of believers. Many features considered unnecessary to this end—including the sacraments—were discarded. Its founders, William and Catherine Booth, reorganized it in 1878 as The Salvation Army and gave it a military structure. Ministers were "commissioned" as "officers" and given military type rank instead of being ordained. Lay members were called "soldiers." Their commitment to ministry among the poor resulted in an increasingly strong social ministry to complement its evangelistic one. In 1890 William Booth's *In Darkest England and the Way Out* spelled out a program of social and moral reform. By that date The Salvation Army was operating in North America, Australia, and Europe.[4]

George Railton brought the movement to America in 1890. Corps (churches) were established in New York City, St. Louis, and other urban areas. Three of the Booths' children led the American work, including Evangeline Booth. She headed the work in Canada (1896—1904) and the United States (1904-34) before becoming The Salvation Army's fourth "general" and leading the worldwide movement (1934-39). Samuel Logan Brengle, an outstanding

3. Bedell, *Yearbook of Churches, 1997*, 249, 255.
4. E. H. McKinley, "William Booth," in *Dictionary of Christianity in America*, ed. Daniel G. Reid et al. (Downers Grove, Ill.: InterVarsity Press, 1990), 175-76.

preacher and teacher, was a popular revivalist and holiness exponent within the larger Wesleyan-Holiness Movement. The Salvation Army has nearly 171,000 full members in the United States and Canada. Its inclusive North American membership (including children and associate members) is nearly 550,000.[5]

Church of God (Anderson, Indiana)

Another early Holiness church was related less closely to Methodism. The Church of God Reformation movement originated through Daniel Sidney Warner's ministry. Warner opposed all denominations as evil. He regarded entire sanctification as a source of spiritual power and unity that would make nonsectarian Christianity a triumphant reality. In 1881 he founded the *Gospel Trumpet* to promote his views regarding the restoration of "true Christianity." The Church of God Reformation movement was promoted by bands of itinerant gospel workers who preached on street corners, ministered in slums, and held church revivals.

After Warner's death, Church of God leaders backed away from his claim that the movement was "the true Church" and began cooperating with other Holiness bodies. Today it is active in the Christian Holiness Partnership and the National Association of Evangelicals. It remains congregational in government and has no formal creed. An annual camp meeting in Anderson, Indiana, draws around 20,000 people and serves as the church's convention.

The national offices are also located in Anderson, together with a college (Anderson University) and seminary (Anderson School of Theology). Its *Christian Brotherhood Hour* radio broadcast has blessed millions around the world. Renowned preacher and homiletics teacher James Earl Massey is a minister in the church. Its North American adherents number over 228,000, and its worldwide constituency is nearly a half million.[6]

Church of God (Holiness)

Others followed the Anderson folks down a sectarian path, including the Church of God (Holiness), which stemmed from the Southwestern Holiness Association, centered in Missouri and Kansas. The association was gripped by strong antidenomination fervor in 1882. Under A. M. Kiergan's influence, an independent congregation was organized in Centralia, Missouri, in 1883. Kiergan's message of restoring the "true gospel" (holiness) and "true church order" (radical congregationalism) inspired other Churches of God to spring up in the area. John P. Brooks of Illinois joined the Church of God (Holiness) in 1886 and six years later set forth a detailed and systematic argument for the union of "true holiness" and congregationalism in his book *The Divine Church.*[7] Today the Church of God (Holiness) perpetuates the emphases of its founders

---

5. Bedell, *Yearbook of Churches, 1997*, 250, 257.

6. John W. V. Smith, *The Quest for Holiness and Unity: A Centennial History of the Church of God (Anderson, Ind.)* (Anderson, Ind.: Warner Press, 1980), 37-40, 44-80; *The First Century*, ed. Barry L. Callen, 2 vols. (Anderson, Ind.: Warner Press, 1979), 1:25-29, 43-54; Williamson, *Encyclopedia of Religions*, 80.

7. A. M. Kiergan, *Historical Sketches of the Revival of True Holiness and Local Church Polity from 1865-1916* (Fort Scott, Kans.: Church Advocate and Good Way, n.d.; reprint, 1972), 34-42; Clarence Eugene Cowen, *A History of the Church of God (Holiness)* (Overland Park, Kans.: Herald and Banner Press, 1949), 17-32.

and regards its congregational government as scripturally prescribed. Its head-quarters are in Overland Park, Kansas. Its estimated membership is under 4,000.

Church of Christ (Holiness) U.S.A.

Charles Price Jones and C. H. Mason were among the black Southerners expelled from Baptist circles in the late 1890s for preaching Wesleyan doctrine. Jones led in organizing the Churches of God in Christ, but dissension fell upon the group after Mason accepted tongues-speaking Pentecostalism in 1907. Mason and his Pentecostal followers were expelled. Jones reorganized the work under the name Church of Christ (Holiness). Jones was a gifted gospel song-writer whose contributions include "Deeper, Deeper" and "I Would Not Be Denied." He was a friend of early Nazarene leader J. O. McClurkan. Fraternal delegates from the Church of Christ (Holiness) addressed the 1923 and 1940 General Assemblies of the Church of the Nazarene. Nazarenes responded to the first occasion by sending a delegation to the Church of Christ (Holiness) national convention in 1924, but no union resulted from these contacts. Jackson, Mississippi, is the headquarters of the denomination, which supports a college there. It reported over 9,000 members in 1965.[8]

Bible Missionary Church

The Bible Missionary Church was organized by conservatives who left the Church of the Nazarene in the mid-1950s in the belief that Nazarenes had grown worldly. The realization that the 1956 General Assembly would not ban television viewing by Nazarenes was one of the precipitating factors. The Bible Missionary Church's early membership was not drawn solely from Nazarene circles but also attracted people from other larger Holiness denominations. Glenn Griffith, a for-mer Nazarene district superintendent, was an early leader but left the Bible Missionary Church because it allowed divorced Christians into membership, a stance he opposed. The church operates Bible Missionary Institute at Rock Island, Illinois, and publishes the *Missionary Revivalist*. It rejects most 20th-century Bible translations and champions the use of the King James Version.

Brethren in Christ

The River Brethren emerged from successive waves of revivalism flowing through Pennsylvania's German-American communities in the late 1700s. Like Mennonites and German Baptist Brethren, the River Brethren cleaved to a strong believers' church ideology and embraced Christian pacifism. But they disagreed with Mennonites on the mode of baptism and with German Baptist Brethren on baptism's significance in the Christian life. Thus they chose an independent path. The Brethren in Christ name was adopted in the mid-19th century.

By 1890 some had migrated to Kansas and were exposed to Holiness revivalists, such as George Weavers, founder of the Hephzibah Faith Missionary Association in Iowa. After Kansas Brethren accepted the Wesleyan view of entire sanctification, the doctrine gradually worked its way back east. In 1910 the

---

8. Charles Edwin Jones, *Black Holiness: A Guide to the Study of Black Participation in Wesleyan Perfectionist and Glossolalic Pentecostal Movements* (Metuchen, N.J.: American Theological Library Association and the Scarecrow Press, 1987), 45-46.

church adopted a statement on sanctification that aligned it with the Wesleyan-Holiness Movement. The Roxbury Camp Meeting in Pennsylvania has long been a center of Wesleyan-Holiness influence in the church's life.

The Brethren in Christ Church cultivates ties to both Anabaptist and Wesleyan traditions. It participates in Mennonite World Fellowship and the compassionate ministries of Mennonite Central Committee, yet it also belongs to the Christian Holiness Partnership. Messiah College in Grantham, Pennsylvania, is its primary educational institution.

Evangelical Friends

The Evangelical Friends International is a fellowship of Quaker yearly meetings (state organizations) that embrace the Wesleyan view of entire sanctification. The Evangelical Friends constitute one of the four basic divisions within the American Quaker community that are discussed in another chapter. The Ohio, Kansas, and Northwest Yearly Meetings are among the bodies composing the Evangelical Friends International.

David Updegraff, Dougan Clark, and Walter and Emma Malone played important roles in promoting the Wesleyan doctrine of holiness among 19th-century Quakers. The Malones established a Holiness evangelistic institute in Cleveland that today is Malone College. George Fox University in Oregon, Friends University in Kansas, and Malone College in Ohio are among the Quaker schools related in varying degrees to the Holiness Movement.

Christian and Missionary Alliance

Several noted American Holiness revivalists preached in England in the mid-19th century. As a result, an annual convention was founded in Keswick, England, to perpetuate the message of a second and deeper work of God's grace subsequent to conversion.

But the Keswick view of holiness differs in ways from the Wesleyan-Holiness preaching that gave rise to it. The Keswick Convention emphasizes the baptism of the Holy Spirit as an experience of power for Christian living and service but rejects Wesleyan theology's insistence that entire sanctification represents a cleansing from original sin. Keswickians teach that the baptism of the Holy Spirit suppresses sin rather than cleansing it from the heart. It became a type of holiness for mild Calvinists. Revivalists associated with D. L. Moody brought Keswick theology from England to America in the late 19th century.

The Christian and Missionary Alliance (CMA) is the sole denomination that exists to perpetuate Keswick teaching. It was founded by A. B. Simpson, a Presbyterian, in 1897. Simpson preached a fourfold gospel of Jesus as "Savior, Sanctifier, Healer, and Coming King." The formula represents a doctrinal core centered in conversion, sanctification, divine healing, and the premillennial second coming of Christ. The CMA has nearly 187,000 full members in North America, with an inclusive membership (children and associate members) of nearly 390,000. Its worldwide membership has been estimated at over 2 million.[9]

---

9. Bedell, *Yearbook of Churches, 1997,* 248, 253; D. P. Hollinger, "Christian and Missionary Alliance," in Reid et al., *Dictionary of Christianity in America,* 251-52.

A Relevant Tradition for the Modern World

What role does the Wesleyan-Holiness tradition play in the modern world? Does it have resources for meeting human needs, or are we just another circle of heart-happy pietists sitting over in the corner, holding hands, and singing "Heavenly Sunshine"?

Holiness people are, indeed, heart-happy pietists, but not irrelevant ones. The late Harvard-trained historian (and Nazarene minister) Timothy L. Smith drew attention to the socially positive aspects of revivalistic perfectionism in his 1955 classic study of mid-19th-century religion, *Revivalism and Social Reform.* Smith showed that Christians of perfectionist persuasion played important roles in the campaign against slavery. They also identified with the concerns of the poor and helped raise the status of women to one of equality with men. His pioneering historical study was coupled with the pleas for compassion in Carl F. H. Henry's *Uneasy Conscience of Modern Fundamentalism* (1947) and David O. Moberg's *Great Reversal* (1972). Together these three writings played a key role in the revival of Evangelical social responsibility after World War II. The rebirth of Nazarene Compassionate Ministries in the 1980s was one of the happy consequences as Nazarenes and other Wesleyans renewed their covenant with their own founding principles.

Other writers also draw freely from this tradition, including Howard Snyder, author of *The Problem of Wine Skins, The Radical Wesley, Community of the King, Liberating the Church,* and additional titles published by InterVarsity Press and other publishers. Snyder's works deal with contemporary issues in the Church and always address a wide audience. But he also writes from a perspective shaped by the spiritual and ethical resources of his own Free Methodist Church and the broader Wesleyan-Holiness tradition.

Similar commitments shape the writings of Donald W. Dayton, author of *Discovering an Evangelical Heritage* (1976), a member of The Wesleyan Church, and Nazarene pastor Michael J. Christensen, author of *City Streets, City People* (1988) and *The Samaritan's Imperative* (1991). Ronald J. Sider, a Brethren in Christ theologian, is the founder of Evangelicals for Social Action and the author of *Rich Christians in an Age of Hunger* (1977). Sider is more self-consciously shaped by the Anabaptist side of his denomination, but John Wesley would have little trouble endorsing Sider's book on Christian responsibility in an era of great spiritual and human need.

A pietist tradition? Yes. And one, we trust, that's fit for citizenship in both heaven and earth.

Review and Reflection

1. The number of like-minded Christians in the 10 churches treated in this chapter and the 22 member denominations of the Christian Holiness Partnership is significant. What if these millions of Holiness Christians worked together more closely? If you were a denominational leader or an officer in the Christian Holiness Partnership, in what arenas would you seek united action?

    a. Becoming one huge denomination

    b. United voice on key social issues

    c. Joint Sunday School curriculum

    d. Book publishing

    e. Television and radio broadcasting

    f. Ministerial education

    g. Missionary program

    h. _____

    i. _____

2. Are some of the churches discussed in this chapter located in your town or neighborhood? What is the quality of the relationships and cooperative ministries between them and your own church? What could you do to make things even better?

3. Review all the chapters in Parts 1 and 2 of this book, and get your Wesleyan-Holiness heritage well in mind. It is your home base, the standard with which other churches and movements will be compared throughout the rest of this book.

PART III
THE LITURGICAL CHURCHES

- The Eastern Orthodox Churches
- The Roman Catholic Church

Thumbnail Sketch

THE EASTERN ORTHODOX CHURCHES

Historical Roots

All Christians trace their faith back to Jesus and the apostles. But the Eastern Orthodox believers do so directly. Some Orthodox congregations can trace their origins back to the presence in their own city of the apostles themselves. Christianity was conceived in the East, born in the East, and spent its childhood there before venturing westward.

Most Christians in the Middle East, Turkey, Greece, the Balkan countries, Ukraine, and Russia belong to the Orthodox tradition.

Core Beliefs

Orthodoxy is the church of the crucial councils of the early Christian centuries. The Orthodox believe in the Trinity, the person and divinity of Jesus Christ, and the full divinity of the Holy Spirit as described by the councils of Nicaea and Chalcedon. They believe the seven church councils are the unchangeable, infallible authority for the church, outranking even the Bible.

Orthodoxy teaches that Christ was the Second Adam, and that the "All-Holy, immaculate, most blessed and glorified Lady, Mother of God, and Ever-Virgin Mary" was the Second Eve.

The goal of redemption is sanctification, or Christian perfection.

Agreement and Differences

Nazarenes agree with Orthodox believers on the nature of the Trinity, the Holy Spirit, and Jesus Christ. We have built on their views of Christian perfection as interpreted by John Wesley. We agree with them about heaven and hell and about personal responsibility and free will. We differ on the Bible. Nazarenes affirm it to be the highest authority. Orthodoxy sees the Bible as subordinate to tradition. We differ in the mode of worship and on the manner in which redeeming grace is received. In the Orthodox way, an infant may receive baptism for remission of sin, chrismation for receiving the Holy Spirit, and then receive first Communion—all in the same service. They trust not in a personal experience or encounter with God for salvation, but upon the eternal power of the church to declare one redeemed.

Orthodoxy Today

More martyrs have died for their faith in the 20th century than in all preceding ones. Most Christians dying for their faith in this century have been Orthodox victims of Communism. There are about 160 million Orthodox believers today, 5 million in North America.

God became man so that man could become god.
—Athanasius

THE EAJTERN ORTHODOX CHURCHEJ

WHAT DO YOU THINK OF WHEN SOMEONE SPEAKS of a "fast-growing church"? A megachurch in a megalopolis with a charismatic pastor and a program tuned into the consumerized "full-service church" frenetically giving the customer whatever he or she wants? How about an ancient church, as old as Christianity itself, with an ancient liturgy given in an ancient language?

Surprisingly enough, the Eastern Orthodox churches form one of the fastest-growing religious bodies in North America. Their church signs will read Greek Orthodox, Russian Orthodox, Albanian Orthodox, American Carpatho—Russian Orthodox, Bulgarian Orthodox, Romanian Orthodox, Serbian Orthodox, Syrian Orthodox, or the Orthodox Church in America. Though precise statistics are hard to come by, there are some 160 million Orthodox believers. When you add their "cousins" in the five non-Chalcedon churches, the Oriental Orthodox, and the Church of the East, the total comes to about 187 million Christians.[1]

The growing Orthodox presence in America now approaches 5 million, with the Greek Orthodox believers accounting for half that total. That worship is carried on in an ethnic language doesn't keep Americans away. "It is incredible but nonetheless true that a couple of million Americans now regularly worship in ancient Greek, Arabic, or church Slavonic, of which they do not understand one word in a hundred."[2]

What is the appeal of this obscure cluster of faith communities? For one thing, the Orthodox provide the stability of a tradition nearly 2,000 years old. They are changeless if anything, basing their creeds on the earliest Christian councils. Their goal is "to preserve the Doctrine of the Lord uncorrupted, and firmly adhere to the Faith He delivered to us, and keep it free from blemish and diminution . . . neither adding any thing, nor taking any thing from it."[3] Talk about stability—"There are congregations today that trace their origins to the

---

1. Ted A. Campbell, *Christian Confessions* (Louisville, Ky.: Westminster/John Knox Press, 1995), 19.
2. Patrick Henry Reardon, "The Other East," *Books and Cultures*, March-April 1996, 7.
3. Letter in G. Williams, *The Orthodox Church of the East in the Eighteenth Century,* 17, quoted in Timothy Kallistos Ware, *The Orthodox Church* (New York: Penguin Books, 1993), 196.

very presence, in their own cities, of Jesus' apostles."[4] Given the fact that Christianity started in the East and moved west, the Eastern Church is "the mother of us all." Going back to our Christian roots is what many people want, and some are finding those roots in Orthodoxy.

Further, the Orthodox treasure "a deep sense of divine mystery in worship."[5] For contemporary children of the Enlightenment, overdosed on rationality, analysis, and technology, the holy mysteries have a lot of appeal.

Some are attracted to the hierarchical authority of the Orthodox Church. Sick of each person being a law unto himself or herself, some people find security in the way the Orthodox obey church authorities. Neither theology nor church polity is put to popular vote. Democratizing the church would be a sin of the rankest sort to the Orthodox mind. Bishop Timothy Kallistos Ware calls the bishop a "monarch."

Another attraction to Orthodoxy is the love for the arts. The holy icons, statuary, paintings, and architecture fill a void in hearts starved for aesthetics. How different from the Evangelical and Fundamentalist approaches that often make war on the arts!

The holy icons, statuary, paintings, and architecture fill a void in hearts starved for aesthetics.

The order of the Orthodox Church appeals to many in our fragmented world. No guessing about what will happen at church for them. They won't be wondering whether it will be a chancel drama, a Christian rap group, a sports celebrity, or a Sandi Patty concert at church this Sunday. Every Sunday has its special place in the Christian year with its own liturgy.

Another thing that appeals to this generation of Americans is the Orthodox teaching that the aim of the Christian life is to become so like God that you yourself become divine or deified. The longing after divinization of human nature, or holiness, finds Christian foundations in Orthodox teachings.

The Orthodox Heritage

The Beginnings

Christianity was conceived in the East, born in the East, and spent its childhood there before it hiked westward. Persecution and martyrdom marked the first three centuries. White martyrdom (a believer abandoning everything he or she loves for Christ's sake) and red martyrdom (dying for Christ's sake) formed the foundation stones of the universal Church.[6]

Christians were forced to think hard and seriously about what they were living and dying for. Challenges from gnosticism, modalism, and other ideologies called the Church to come to consensus about what they believed about the nature and being of God, Christ, and the Holy Spirit. By the end of the second

4. Campbell, *Christian Confessions,* 19.
5. Reardon, "The Other East," 6.
6. Ware, *Orthodox Church,* 15.

century, a doctrine or practice, to be authoritative, had to pass the test of continuity with Hebrew scripture, the apostolic writings, an accepted creed, and apostolic succession.[7]

The Church of the Seven Councils

From A.D. 325 to 787, the search for Christian consensus on matters relating to the nature and being of the Trinity, particularly Christ, continued. The first of the ecumenical councils was called in 325. It met at Nicaea and ruled that Arianism was heresy. Arius held that Christ was a creature, that is, a creation of God. Though the emperor sympathized with Arius, the council declared that Jesus Christ is "God from God, light from light, true God from true God, of one substance with the Father, begotten and not created."[8]

In 381 the Council of Constantinople upheld the action of 325 and created what is today recited as the Nicene Creed. The Council of Ephesus in 431 rejected the Nestorian teaching that Christ was really two persons with two different natures, one human and the other divine. The Chalcedon Council (451) ruled against Nestorianism and also against the preachers of Monophysitism, who held that Christ was one person with one nature. The council of bishops at Chalcedon declared that Christ was indeed one person with two natures. Some Christians could not accept this decision and to this day continue as "non-Chalcedon Christians." Today we know them as the Syrian Church of Antioch, the Armenian Church, the Coptic Church (Egypt), the Syrian Church in India, and the Ethiopian Church.[9]

The Trinitarian and Christological teachings of Chalcedon were upheld in the next two ecumenical councils (553 and 680), though serious attempts were made to reconcile the Monophysite churches.

The seventh and last of the ecumenical councils of the undivided church was held in 787 at Nicaea. It dealt with the use of images in worship. Is the use of icons idolatry? Some felt that the use of images, paintings, or statues was clearly idolatrous, and they went about smashing icons in order to purify the church. The bishops at Nicaea II ruled that image breaking (iconoclasm) was wrong, that images may be used in worship. Images could be honored or venerated, but not worshiped. Worship (*latreia*) is for God alone.[10]

The Orthodox believers to this day, in all countries and with one accord, declare that the decisions of the ecumenical councils (and not the pope) are infallible and authoritative. They seek to preserve their teachings.

Separation from Rome

The south wind softly stirs the leaves on the eucalyptus trees in the courtyard of the Church of the Holy Wisdom in "second Rome" (Constantinople), the seat of the Byzantine Church. In a few minutes a service will begin in the church. It's the summer of 1054. Cardinal Humbert, flanked by two other repre-

7. Campbell, *Christian Confessions*, 22.
8. Ibid., 24.
9. Ware, *Orthodox Church*, 4.
10. Campbell, *Christian Confessions*, 26.

sentatives of Pope Leo IX, enters the sanctuary and approaches the altar. But he does not pray. He does not prepare to administer the blessed sacrament. He pulls from his robe a legal document. He places it on the altar. He and his silent companions then head for the western door of the Church of the Holy Wisdom. A deacon steps forward and stares at the document. It is a declaration of excommunication! It announces that the Eastern patriarch, Michael Cerularius, and the other leaders in Constantinople are excommunicate and anathema—outside the communion of Christian faith and cursed. The deacon picks up the document and runs to catch up with Cardinal Humbert. He begs him to take his document back. But Humbert shakes the dust from his feet and says, "Let God look and judge." Cerularius responds by excommunicating the three delegates from Rome. The mutual anathemas stood until about 30 years ago, when Pope Paul VI and the patriarch of Constantinople agreed to remove them.[11]

This incident in the summer of 1054 climaxed a growing schism between East and West within the Church. The separation followed the lines of cultural differences. The Greek-speaking East and the Latin-speaking West had gone their separate ways in politics, in culture, and now in religion.

One of the sharpest points of dispute came up when the pope ruled Roman Christians could incorporate a change in the way the Nicene Creed was recited in worship. Nothing could have inflamed the East more—the ecumenical councils were infallible and authoritative. They must be obeyed by all. Only an ecumenical council could change a doctrine! Certainly no single bishop, acting on his own, could change the creed—not even the bishop of Rome!

The change had to do with the famous *filioque* phrase, which you once memorized to pass a church history test. To you it was only a word. To the Eastern Christians it was a doctrinal and a political transgression that could not be overlooked. The Roman Church, the Eastern believers thought, had diminished the role of the Holy Spirit. The historic creed had always said that the Spirit "proceeds from the Father." The pope had, without support of an ecumenical council, approved the addition of *filioque*—which means "and the Son." Thus the Spirit was seen to be inferior to the Son. The East traditionally put more emphasis on the work of the Spirit than did the West, who seemed bound and determined to have a Christ-centered theology, even if it meant tinkering with an "infallible" creed. Though two Western councils (Toledo, 589, and Frankfort, 794) had approved this change, the Orthodox could not bear it.

Expansion Northward

Shut off from the south by the Monophysite Coptic and Ethiopian Churches, pressed on the east and south by militant Muslims, and excommunicated by the West, the Orthodox Church moved north. Strong Orthodox communities were established in Ukraine, Serbia, Bulgaria, Albania, Romania, Poland, Czechoslovakia, Georgia, and Russia.

Before the end of the seventh century, the Muslims had captured Palestine, Syria, and Egypt. Thus, three of the ancient patriarchates of the Orthodox

---

11. See Ware, *Orthodox Church*, 43-44, and Campbell, *Christian Confessions*, 27-28.

Church—Jerusalem, Antioch, and Alexandria—once again fell under persecution. After hundreds of years of threat and war, Constantinople, the throne city of the Orthodox Church, fell to the Muslim armies of the Ottoman Turks. The Church of the Holy Wisdom became an Islamic mosque.[12]

With so much of its domain under Muslim rule, the Orthodox mantle shifted to Russia. Moscow became the "third Rome." For the next several hundred years, the Russian Orthodox Church produced many miracles of grace. A missionary monasticism conquered the outer regions, while the churches and priests worked in the cities. Through the centuries, the Russian church developed a cadre of distinguished saints, including Basil the Blessed, Maximus, Nilus, Joseph, Nikon, Avvakum, Tihkon, Seraphim, Alexis Khomiakov, and Innocent.

The Church Under Communist Rule

The first three centuries are regarded by historians as the age of martyrdom. But according to one source, "more Christians have died for their faith since 1900 than in all previous centuries put together, and the majority of these have been Eastern Orthodox."[13] Perhaps no regime in history has killed more Christians than the Communist Party in Russia. Ted Campbell reports that 12,000 Russian priests were martyred.[14] Timothy Ware says, "The sum total of priest-martyrs must extend to tens of thousands." He also cites the execution of 130 bishops, noting that this list is incomplete.[15] As Stalin declared, "The Party cannot be neutral towards religion. It conducts an anti-religious struggle against all and any religious prejudices."[16]

Rooting out the Christian religion was not left to the secret police alone. The education system was to make this its aim.

"A Soviet teacher . . . is obliged not only to be an unbeliever himself but also to be an active propagandist of godlessness among others, to be the bearer of . . . militant . . . atheism. Skillfully . . . and persistently, the Soviet teacher must expose . . . religious prejudices . . . in school and out of school, day in and day out."[17]

Such persecution revealed who the spiritual heroes were—they suffered and died for the faith. But the bootheel of persecution also exposed the weak and those who were willing to collaborate with the enemy in order to save themselves.

Some of the top leaders in the Russian Orthodox

Some bishops actually had KGB code names—including the present patriarch of Moscow, Aleksii II (Ridiger).

---

12. Campbell, *Christian Confessions*, 30.
13. Reardon, "The Other East," 7.
14. Campbell, *Christian Confessions*, 31.
15. Ware, *Orthodox Church*, 149.
16. Ibid., 145.
17. F. N. Oleschuk (formerly secretary of the League of Militant Atheists), in *Uchitelskaya Guzeta*, November 26, 1949. Cited in Ware, *Orthodox Church*, 147.

Church seem to have worked hand in glove with the Communist oppressors. Some bishops actually had KGB code names—including the present patriarch of Moscow, Aleksii II (Ridiger).[18] In 1930 Metropolitan Sergius, head of the Russian Orthodox Church, attended the World Council of Churches meeting and declared that there had never been any persecution of Christians under the Communist Party. This was a clear betrayal of the new Russian martyrs who had made Russia red with their blood. Those who sought to defend Sergius called it a "necessary sin"—one of many that Sergius resorted to in an alleged effort to save the church from extinction.[19] Throughout the 70-year rule of the militant atheists, one church leader after another remained either quietly submissive to or overtly supportive of the Communist wolves who were devouring their flock. Opposition would have meant certain destruction. Collaboration, some said, while not heroic, might be a prudent way to preserve the church.

Not everyone agreed. Aleksandr Solzhenitsyn, in a 1972 "Lenten Letter" to the head of the Russian Orthodox Church, wrote, "By what reasoning is it possible to convince oneself that the planned *destruction* of the spirit and body of the Church under the guidance of the atheists is the best way of *preserving* it? Rescuing it *for whom?* Certainly not for Christ. Preserving it *by what means?* By falsehood? But after falsehood by whose hands are the holy sacraments to be celebrated?"[20]

The Orthodox history under Communism is at once a sad and glorious affair. The sins of the collaborating hierarchy and the blood of the faithful martyrs makes it so.[21]

The collapse of Communism has brought a new religious freedom to Russia. Orthodoxy has seen a significant revival, though there is a shortage of priests, seminaries, and theological literature. The new religious freedom has also brought another challenge to Orthodoxy—Evangelical Protestants on every corner. At a dedication of a Nazarene ministry center building in Kyiv, Ukraine, on September 29, 1996, for example, the local secretary of religion made a speech and said that in Kyiv alone there are 70 denominations at work.

The Orthodox resent this as an intrusion. They have never felt any significant connection with Protestantism, considering it "hatched from the egg which Rome had laid."[22] They feel more affinity to their non-Chalcedon cousins and even to Anglicanism than they do to Roman Catholics and Protestants. They particularly resist the Protestant domination of the World Council of Churches. Thus, the Orthodox regard missionaries as proselytizers who deny the integrity of Orthodoxy in its own social context. Leaders of the Russian Orthodox Church in 1997 pressured the Yeltsin government into passing a law limiting Christian mission activity and prohibiting the sending of new missionaries by churches who were not already in Russia 15 years ago.

---

18. Cited by Reardon in reviewing Alexander F. C. Webster, *The Price of Prophecy: Orthodox Churches on Peace, Freedom, and Security* (Grand Rapids: Wm. B. Eerdmans Publishing Co., 1996).

19. Ware, *Orthodox Church,* 154.

20. Ibid., 159.

21. For more on this intriguing subject, see Webster's book cited in note 18 as well as Daniel B. Clendenin, *Eastern Orthodox Christianity: A Western Perspective* (Grand Rapids: Baker Book House, 1996), and Nathaniel Davis, *A Long Walk to Church: A Contemporary History of Russian Orthodoxy* (San Francisco: Westview Press, 1996).

22. Ware, *Orthodox Church,* 2.

Orthodoxy in the United States Today

Given the fact that all the historic Orthodox centers have suffered under governments more or less hostile, their international effectiveness has suffered. When the patriarchate in Moscow or Constantinople was unable to service the needs of the Orthodox "in diaspora," new regional and ethnic hierarchies were developed. Thus, the Orthodox communities in America today are fragmented and disorganized.

Most Orthodox groups in the United States are under the supervision of an "old country" patriarch. Membership tends to run along ethnic and national lines. For example, many Orthodox churches will have the flag of Greece, Ukraine, Lebanon, or Syria posted among the holy icons. Further, in some cases, the governments of the nations involved regard the United States congregations as political outposts that can be used to promote their interests.

Such realities make unification of the United States Orthodox difficult. For example, in 1994 American bishops from several Orthodox groups gathered and drew up a plan to create a unified American Orthodox Church. The plan failed because of the opposition of Patriarch Bartholomew I of Constantinople. He objected to the plan "with a vehemence boding on irrationality."[23] Why? Perhaps it is because he operates under the eye of a Muslim government and needs the political leverage of being in ecclesiastical jurisdiction over 2.5 million U.S. Greeks.[24]

Even with the hindrances of ethnicity, nationalism, and language barriers, dynamic forms of Orthodoxy are breaking forth in the United States. For example, the Evangelical Orthodox Church was formed in the 1980s by a group of baby boomers. They combine folk songs, guitar music, and the Byzantine liturgy, incense, and icons. They were received by the Antiochian Orthodox Diocese of America, and the ordination of their priests was recognized unilaterally.[25]

Orthodox and Nazarene Beliefs Compared

At some points Nazarenes will say "Yea and amen" to the doctrines of Orthodoxy. At other points we will differ with conviction and respect.

Tradition

As much as Nazarenes may treasure their traditions, the Orthodox prize theirs far more. Their tradition includes the creeds of the ecumenical councils, the teachings of the church fathers, the canon laws, the liturgy service books, the holy icons, and the Bible. "Orthodox Christians of today see themselves as heirs and guardians to a rich inheritance . . . and they believe it is their duty to transmit this inheritance unimpaired to the future."[26]

Note that the Bible is just one part of an authoritative tradition for the Orthodox. It stands on par with the creeds, laws, the fathers, and the liturgy, but

---

23. Reardon, "The Other East," 7.
24. Ibid.
25. Campbell, *Christian Confessions,* 32.
26. Ware, *Orthodox Church,* 196.

it does not stand above them. This is distinctly different from the Protestant doctrine of *sola scriptura,* that is, Scripture alone as the rule of faith. Nazarenes are thoroughly Protestant in their view of the Bible as the final Arbiter on matters of doctrine and practice.

The Doctrine of God

Nazarenes believe that "God is Triune in essential being, revealed as Father, Son, and Holy Spirit."[27] Though the term "revealed" could be at risk in the hands of a modalist, it is our understanding that there is one divine essence, three distinct Persons, with the totality of the essence dwelling concurrently in each Person. We are not as concerned about the nuances of Trinitarian faith as the Orthodox. For example, we can readily use the Nicene Creed (East) and in the very next service recite the Apostles' Creed (West) and never know the difference.

The Orthodox believe that the Western Christians emphasize the unity of God to the detriment of the distinct Persons.

Ted Campbell, using creedal statements from Orthodox literature, summarizes the Orthodox statement on the Trinity: "God is three 'Persons' in one 'substance.' . . . The three Persons differ in the 'modes of origin' (the Father is unbegotten, the Son is begotten, and the Spirit proceeds), and . . . the three Persons 'interpenetrate' each other in all acts of God."[28]

Nazarenes would agree with the Orthodox that wherever God is at work, it is the work of the Holy Trinity and not the work of an "errand boy" sort of deity. We would also agree with them that God is transcendent (different from us and beyond our ability to comprehend Him) but also personal and incarnate.

Jesus Christ

Both Nazarenes and Orthodox accept the Chalcedon definition of the nature of Christ. Orthodox Christians would like the Nazarene affirmation that Christ is "the Second Person of the Triune Godhead; that He was eternally one with the Father; that He became incarnate by the Holy Spirit and was born of the Virgin Mary, so that *two whole and perfect natures,* that is to say the Godhead and manhood, are thus united in one Person very God and very man, the God-man."[29]

The Nazarenes would also agree with the Orthodox on the mission of Jesus, the Son of God. He came to save us from our sins. Sin had obscured the path to God, but "Jesus Christ, by uniting humankind and God in His own person, reopened for us the path to union with God."[30] Jesus showed us what likeness to God looked like and "set that likeness once again within our reach. Christ, the Second Adam . . . reversed the effects of the first Adam's disobedience."[31]

27. *Manual, Church of the Nazarene, 1997—2001,* 26.
28. Campbell, *Christian Confessions,* 39.
29. *Manual, Church of the Nazarene, 1997—2001,* 26-27, italics added.
30. Ware, *Orthodox Church,* 225.
31. Ibid.

But the Orthodox would also want to add a few words to us about the way we worship Christ. Why do you in the West, they would inquire, grieve so much over Christ the Victim, rather than celebrating Christ the Victor? In Orthodox worship, the glory of the conquering Christ is celebrated with joy—every Sunday. Thus, the Transfiguration and the Resurrection are the highest holy days on the calendar. In the West, Christmas (the Incarnation) and Good Friday (Crucifixion) far exceed the Transfiguration. Both traditions make the Resurrection central to the faith.

There is more than aesthetics at stake here in the Orthodox mind. They believe that the Catholic and Protestant worshipers spend too much time trying to sympathize and agonize with the suffering Savior. The Western Christians also see the Crucifixion too much in legal terms, with Jesus trying to satisfy an angry Father God and to "pay the penalty" for us in some Anselmic or Calvinist justice system. When the Orthodox meditate on the Crucifixion, they are more likely to concentrate on Christ's conquering of sin, death, and hell in our behalf. Their hearts turn to praise rather than agonizing before the Cross. Do they have something to teach us?

> *"From one point of view, the whole 'aim' of the Incarnation is the sending of the Spirit at Pentecost."*

The Holy Spirit

"Christ's work of redemption cannot be considered apart from the Holy Spirit's work of sanctification," writes Orthodox Bishop Timothy Kallistos Ware.[32] He goes on to say, "From one point of view, the whole 'aim' of the Incarnation is the sending of the Spirit at Pentecost."[33] Russian saint Seraphim of Sarov declared, "The true aim of the Christian life is the acquisition of the Holy Spirit of God."[34] Surely Nazarene believers everywhere will resonate with such proclamations.

At the beginning of each day, the devout Orthodox Christian recites the morning prayer that includes these words:

O heavenly King, O Comforter, the Spirit of Truth . . . come and abide in us. Cleanse us from all impurity, and of [by] Your goodness save our souls.[35]

Though Nazarenes and Orthodox differ on how to receive the fullness of the Spirit, they are on the same page when it comes to articulating the doctrine of the Spirit. The Nazarene Articles of Faith include these affirmations: "We believe in the Holy Spirit . . . He is ever present and efficiently active in and with the Church of Christ, convincing the world of sin, regenerating those who repent and believe, sanctifying believers, and guiding into all truth as it is in Jesus."[36]

---

32. Ibid., 229-30.
33. Ibid., 230.
34. Ibid.
35. Ibid., 230-31.
36. *Manual, Church of the Nazarene, 1997—2001*, 27.

Mary, the Mother of Jesus

The Orthodox honor Mary as the most exalted human creature. She is, they believe, more glorious than the angels in heaven. Each time she is mentioned in the weekly liturgy, her full title is given: "Our All-Holy, immaculate, most blessed and glorified Lady, Mother of God, and Ever-Virgin Mary."[37]

"If Christ is the New Adam," writes Bishop Kallistos Ware, "Mary is the New Eve." He quotes Jerome: "Death by Eve, life by Mary."[38] While officially rejecting the Roman Catholic view of the Immaculate Conception, the Orthodox practice comes very close to it.

Nazarenes, of course, must part company with our Orthodox friends here. In line with traditional Protestantism, believing in the priesthood of all believers, we honor the saints, the "faithful departed," but we don't pray to or through them in worship or venerate them with holy icons.

Humanity: Creation and Fall

Both Nazarene and Orthodox Christians believe that human beings are created in the likeness of God, as the Scriptures teach. Thus, we are "His kin," which means that "between us and Him there is a point of contact and similarity."[39] The Orthodox teach that the *likeness* of God in which Adam and Eve were created included *holiness, immortality, reason,* and *freedom* (the power and ability to do God's will). These terms define four attributes of God and describe what godliness is. The *likeness* of God, the Orthodox teach, was lost in the fall of Adam, and only the *image* remains. The *image* retained in all human beings consists of *reason* and *freedom*.[40]

Holiness and immortality were lost in the Fall. Therefore, the purpose of salvation and the quest of the Christian life is to regain what was lost: holiness and immortality.

Reason and freedom are retained, and with them comes the grace of God that makes it possible for persons to choose God and good. The Orthodox believe in free will and free grace. They find the Calvinist doctrines of predestination, moral inability, and limited atonement abhorrent. John Wesley's statements about free and prevenient grace and limited human freedom are very close to the Orthodox teachings.

The Orthodox and the Wesleyan-Arminian traditions share a strong belief in original sin. "In losing holiness they [our first parents] fell into sin; in losing immortality they became susceptible to disease, corruption and death."[41] These positions have been echoed by many theologians in our own Wesleyan-Holiness tradition.

Orthodoxy makes little or no attempt to describe the mystery of how original sin passes from generation to generation. No scientific study of genetics is suggested. They are content to teach that "cut off from God, Adam and his

---

37. Ware, *Orthodox Church*, 257.
38. Ibid., 259.
39. Ibid., 219.
40. Campbell, *Christian Confessions*, 48.
41. Ibid.

descendants passed under the domination of sin and of the devil. Each new human being is born into a world where sin prevails . . . a world in which it is easy to do evil and hard to go good."[42]

John Wesley taught, in harmony with Orthodoxy, that individuals are not personally guilty for Adam's sin. They bear the marks of that sin but do not carry the guilt.

The Wesleyan-Holiness tradition holds another doctrine about original sin in common with Orthodoxy. Some Holiness theologians have called it the doctrine of "extensive original sin," as opposed to the "intensive original sin," taught by classic Protestantism. Wesleyanism and Orthodoxy teach that the results of the Fall "extend" to every part of the person, affecting all areas of life (the mind is darkened, the will enfeebled, and so on). The likeness or image of God is impaired but not crushed or destroyed. Bishop Ware writes, "Orthodox do not say, as Calvin said, that human beings after the fall are utterly depraved and incapable of good desires. They cannot agree with Augustine . . . that human beings are under a 'harsh necessity' of committing sin . . . and . . . lack freedom."[43]

The Aim of Salvation

The aim of salvation for the Orthodox is "godlikeness" or, to use their own language, *theosis,* meaning "deification" or "divinization." To the Catholic Christian and the Reformed believer, this sounds incredibly arrogant. To the New Age devotee, it sounds like a pleasing self-fulfillment dictum.

But Orthodox thinkers past and present have taken seriously the words of Scripture that say, for example, "Jesus answered, 'Is it not written in your law, "I said, you are gods"?'" (John 10:34, NRSV). He was quoting Ps. 82:6: "You are gods, children of the Most High, all of you" (NRSV). And what of these words from Christ's high-priestly prayer?—"that they may all be one. As you, Father, are in me and I am in you, may they also be in us" (John 17:21, NRSV).

In addition to scriptural authority, the Eastern fathers (held to be equals or near equals with Scripture in the infallible tradition) taught that "God became man so that man could become god." These words of Athanasius were restated by several others, including Irenaeus.[44] Basil defined a Christian as one who had received the command to become a god. The Orthodox liturgy for Holy Thursday includes these words attributed to Christ: "In my kingdom . . . I shall be God with you as gods."[45]

Therefore, for the Orthodox, salvation means to becomes so godlike that divinization or Christian perfection is not a misnomer. They do not believe that this happens all at once, but that it takes a lifetime of devotion to attain as the believer works in cooperation with the Holy Spirit.

There is a unique connection between the Orthodox teaching of *theosis* and the Wesleyan doctrine of entire sanctification. John Wesley found in the teach-

---

42. Ware, *Orthodox Church,* 223.
43. Ibid.
44. See Michael J. Christensen, "Theosis and Sanctification: John Wesley's Reformulation of a Patristic Doctrine," *Wesleyan Theological Journal* 31, No. 2 (fall 1996): 72.
45. Ware, *Orthodox Church,* 231.

ings of the Eastern fathers sure foundations for his teaching of Christian perfection, holiness, or entire sanctification.[46] Wesley was so impressed by the teachings of perfect love that he studied in the Eastern fathers that he reprinted several of their works and made them required reading for his preachers. Wesley's *Christian Library,* first published in 50 volumes as textbooks for Kingswood School, carried the six epistles of Ignatius of Antioch, Polycarp's "Epistle to the Ephesians," and 23 sermons by Macarius the Egyptian. In such works Wesley found much of his vocabulary about Christian perfection and entire sanctification.

Here are a few representative passages from Wesley's edited version of Macarius:

1. Believers have a natural desire for purity and perfection.

A person may see a bird flying and wish that he, too, could fly. "Just so a man may be willing to be pure, and without blame . . . but he has not the wherewithal to compass it . . . unless he receive wings. . . . Beseech God that He would give us the wings of a dove."

2. Perfection is available in this life.

"Unless the soul shall in this world receive the sanctification of the Spirit through much faith and prayer . . . it is unfit for the kingdom of heaven."

3. Perfection is preceded by self-denial, though it is wrought by grace.

Spiritual riches are "purchased only with labour, and pains, and trials, and many conflicts." But the obtainment of them "is owing to the grace of God." The seeker must then "by habitual violence esteem himself as nothing . . . [and do] righteous works without number." Still such a soul "demeans itself . . . as if it had wrought nothing at all."

4. Perfection usually includes a fiery encounter with the Holy Spirit, who purifies the soul.

"The soul that has renounced the world . . . and received the heavenly fire . . . is . . . set free from all the corruptions and the affections. . . . Things of the world appear . . . as impertinent superfluities." Sin is rooted out and man receives "the original formation of Adam in his purity." The sincere seeker may then expect "an entire redemption from sin, and the darkness of the affections: that being purified by the Spirit, sanctified in soul and body, it may be made a vessel clean prepared for the . . . residence of Christ . . . the pure habitation of the Spirit."

5. The purifying encounter with the Spirit leads to a Spirit-filled life of holiness.

"As a stone in the bottom of the sea is every way surrounded with water; so

46. The connection between Wesley's doctrine of perfection and that of the Eastern fathers has been explored by a number of scholars. The following sources are among those recommended for further reading: Paul M. Bassett and William M. Greathouse, *Exploring Christian Holiness,* vol. 2, *The Historical Development* (Kansas City: Beacon Hill Press of Kansas City, 1985); Ted Campbell, *John Wesley and Christian Antiquity* (Nashville: Kingswood Books, 1991); Randy L. Maddox, *Responsible Grace: John Wesley's Practical Theology* (Abingdon Press, 1994). Among several useful articles on the subject in the *Wesleyan Theological Journal* are Luke L. Keefer Jr., "John Wesley: Disciple of Early Christianity," vol. 19, No. 1 (spring 1984); John G. Merritt, "Dialogue Within a Tradition: John Wesley and Gregory of Nyssa Discuss Christian Perfection," vol. 22, No. 2 (fall 1987): 92-116; and Christensen, see note 44 above.

are those cleansed by the Spirit every way drenched by the Holy Spirit and made like Christ." The sanctified ones are "blameless, spotless and pure."[47]

Wesley stopped well short of endorsing *theosis,* the deification of the believer. Without the foundations of the Orthodox fathers, however, Wesley would have had to search for a new vocabulary for his pastoral theology. What Wesley did find in them was a radical optimism of grace that declares that there is almost no ceiling on the good things that can happen in, to, and through the sanctified believer.

Wesley saw in the Eastern fathers a high degree of Christian perfection or holiness that he believed could be lived by ordinary Christians in the workaday world. Whether it is a Wesleyan speaking of entire sanctification or an Orthodox Christian speaking of deification, one question needs to be asked: How do good works, acts of piety, and acts of mercy relate to the obtaining or attaining of the aim of salvation?

When Wesleyans speak of the restoration of the image of God (entire sanctification), they are thoroughly Protestant. Both justifying and sanctifying grace come *sola gratia,* that is, by grace alone. Wesley taught that works of piety and mercy are necessary in a secondary way but certainly not meritorious. No number of deeds of piety or service can sanctify a believer. Only God does that as a gift of grace through faith.

Orthodoxy, while maintaining a high view of grace, makes good works essential to achieving deification or holiness. The performance of them is somewhat meritorious in *attaining* holiness. Protestants are troubled by the role that the Orthodox give to *attaining* or *achieving* Christian perfection. Wesleyans speak of *obtaining* holiness as a gift of grace through faith but stop short of teaching that holiness can be *attained.*

Receiving Salvation

Strong similarities exist between the Orthodox and Wesleyan traditions when it comes to the doctrine of salvation. They are not nearly so compatible when it comes to how to receive saving and sanctifying grace.

To begin with, the Wesleyans (and all other churches in the Augustinian tradition) have a lot to say about justification by faith alone. The Orthodox are not nearly so concerned about such forensic matters. They speak often of forgiveness of sins but sparingly of justification.

The entry into the Christian life is also quite different in the two traditions. Evangelical Wesleyans insist that entry into the true Christian life comes through a conversion experience, a personal encounter with the living Christ involving confession, repentance, and saving faith. For the Orthodox (as well as for Roman Catholics and classical Protestants), the entry into the Christian life

---

47. The Macarius quotations are from John Wesley's *Christian Library Consisting of Extracts from and Abridgements of the Choicest Pieces of Practical Divinity which have been Published in the English Tongue.* Originally published 1749-55, these quotations are from the 1819 edition, vol. 1, pp. 81-178. This particular treatment is taken from Wesley D. Tracy, "The Wesleyan Way to Spiritual Formation: Christian Spirituality in the Letters of John Wesley" (S.T.D. diss., San Francisco Theological Seminary, 1987), 14-15.

occurs at baptism—as an adult or an infant. Bishop Kallistos Ware declares, "Through Baptism we receive full forgiveness of sin, whether original or actual; we 'put on Christ,' becoming members of His Body, the Church."[48]

Throughout the whole order of salvation, the Wesleyans and the Orthodox represent widely differing views. The Orthodox depend on the "infallible" tradition, apostolic authority, and the sacred liturgy of the church. Salvation has nothing to do with how they feel or what they may individually experience. Rather, they know they are saved because of the infallible word of the true Church. Since God has given the church the authority to dispense saving and sanctifying grace, why not do it as soon as possible? Thus, the infant is baptized for remission of sin, he or she receives chrismation (a ceremony in which it is believed the infant receives sanctifying grace and the gift of the Spirit), and then the baby receives his or her first Communion—all in the same service.

Most Wesleyans would feel that to do this is to put far too much emphasis on the authority of the church to declare who is and who isn't in a state of grace. One wonders why in preserving the tradition of the elders, the Orthodox did not preserve the early practice of baptism being preceded by some three years of study, devotion, testing, and probation by each candidate. That was the typical practice before Emperor Constantine made Christianity the law of the empire. Most Wesleyans would question the prudence and the right of any church to declare all the works of grace accomplished through a ceremony.

Though some Wesleyans have always permitted infant baptism, it has never been meant to take the place of a personal conversion experience when the individual reaches the age of accountability. Further, the gift of the sanctifying Spirit cannot be bestowed by any church ceremony, Wesleyans believe. The Wesleyan tradition is, for better or worse, a system that values saving and sanctifying encounters with the living God, that is, certain types of religious experiences, far more than it values creedal or ecclesiastical authority.

Heaven and Hell

Both Wesleyan and Orthodox Christians believe in eternal rewards and punishments—heaven and hell. The Orthodox counter objections that the existence of hell would slur the reputation of a loving God, saying, "Hell is nothing else than the rejection of God.'. . . Hell is not so much a place where God imprisons humans, as a place where humans, by misusing their free will, choose to imprison themselves."[49]

Worship and the Sacraments

Baptism is by immersion in Orthodoxy. The person is immersed three times, once for each Person of the Trinity. Seldom is baptism by another Christian church recognized as valid by Orthodoxy. And baptism "by sprinkling or smearing is quite simply not real Baptism at all."[50] Wesleyans usually permit

48. Ware, *Orthodox Church*, 278.
49. Ibid., 262.
50. Ibid., 278.

the baptismal candidate to select the method of baptism preferred. Further, if a person has been baptized by another Christian church, Wesleyans recognize it as valid and do not rebaptize.

Holy Communion, or the Eucharist, is a rich tradition in the Orthodox Church. Only those who are Orthodox can receive it, and only those Orthodox who have prepared by fasting are expected to participate. The bread is leavened, not unleavened. The bread and wine are understood to be the true body and blood of Christ. The Communion elements become, for the Orthodox worshiper, a sacrifice. And since Christ is present in the elements, the sacrifice offered is once again Christ himself. And this sacrifice is offered to the Holy Trinity in behalf of the living and the dead.

In the Wesleyan tradition, Holy Communion is offered to all believers, regardless of church membership. The bread and the wine are understood to be *symbols* of the body and the blood of our Lord.

Wesleyans celebrate two sacraments, baptism and Holy Communion. The Orthodox add five more: chrismation, confession, holy orders, marriage, and the anointing of the sick.

Worship among the Wesleyans usually follows the free church style, with a wide variety of practices acceptable. Orthodox worship is highly liturgical. Every day of the Christian year has specific significance, whether it is St. James Day on October 23 or Mary the Mother of God Day on August 15 or Circumcision of Christ Day on January 1. The service books prescribing Orthodox liturgies throughout the year take up 20 volumes.

There are 12 great festivals (feasts) during the year. Seven of them are feasts celebrating Jesus; five honor Mary. A number of minor festivals are also celebrated, such as the one in honor of St. Nicholas the Wonderworker on December 6 and the Nativity of St. John the Baptist on June 24.

Since the Orthodox also believe that "fasting and self-control are the first virtue, the mother, root, source and foundation of all good," the calendar is punctuated with five great fasts.[51]

Orthodox worship is conducted without benefit of pews. The congregation stands during the entire service. In the United States the typical service runs for one to two hours. But in earlier times, people usually stood through a seven- or eight-hour service. No musical instruments are used, but the service is sung or chanted.

The Church

The Orthodox Church believes that it is the one true Church. Some say this with Christian humility. They are quick to say that this does not make them better than other people. That they belong to the one true Church is but a gift of grace. They may cite the words of Metropolitan Eulogy: "Have not the saints passed beyond the walls that separate us, walls which . . . do not mount up as high as heaven?"[52] They are also likely very active in national and international

---

51. Ibid., 300.
52. Ibid., 307.

ecumenical meetings. On the other hand, some Orthodox simply tell you that there is no salvation outside their "one true Church."

While some Wesleyan-Holiness groups may have acted as if they were the one true Church, it has never been their creed. It is hard to find a tradition that has been more ecumenical than the Wesleyan. From John Wesley's sermons "Against Bigotry" and "The Catholic Spirit" on to the present day, Wesleyans have extended the right hand of fellowship to almost all who believe in the Bible and in Christ as Savior.

Review and Reflection

1. Suppose you are going to teach this chapter to a Sunday School class of college-age students. The session is limited to 45 minutes. You must prioritize.

   a. What three concepts or chunks of content rank high on your "must cover" list?

   b. What feelings and appreciations would you try to foster? Why?

   c. What actions (deeds, behaviors) do you hope result from your class session? What do you want your students to *do?*

   d. How would your teaching change if you were to teach junior highs? Or senior citizens?

2. Were you surprised that the Wesleyan and Orthodox traditions have so much in common? Read again the section on "Orthodox and Nazarene Beliefs Compared." Put a plus (+) by every idea that is new. Mark an upward arrow (↑) by each point that inspires or comforts you. Put a question mark (?) by ideas that you don't understand, thus marking them for further study.

3. Meditate on the idea in this chapter that seems most pleasingly remarkable to you. Make notes, and then telephone, fax, or E-mail a friend about this idea that has become a "serendipitous epiphany" (happy revelation) to you.

THE ROMAN CATHOLIC CHURCH

Historical Roots

The legion of Christians who conquered the Roman Empire called themselves the "catholic" (universal) church. As the bishop of Rome rose in significance and power over the other bishops of the Mediterranean world, the "catholic" church began to take on a Romanesque identity. With the official split between Eastern and Western Christians, the Roman Catholic Church became the church of western Europe and other points west. Headquartered in Vatican City and Rome, and claiming that Peter was the first pope, the Roman Catholic Church directs the largest Christian body in the world.

Core Beliefs

The Roman Catholics believe in the triune God. They believe in Jesus Christ, the Son of God, born of a virgin, and Savior of the world. They believe in the person and work of the Holy Spirit. They venerate Mary as "the Mother of God" and the only human being (except Jesus) to be born without original sin. Catholics believe theirs is the one true Church but that God will be merciful to some Protestants. They honor the Bible as inspired, but it does not outrank Catholic authorities. Catholics oppose premarital sex, homosexual activity, birth control, and abortion.

Agreement and Differences

Nazarenes are in harmony with the Roman Catholics on the doctrines of the Trinity, the Son of God, the Holy Spirit, sin, and redemption. Differences arise over the place of the Bible, which is the final Authority for us but one of several authorities for them. We do not venerate Mary or proscribe birth control, but we do oppose abortion, homosexual activity, and adultery. We as Protestants affirm salvation by grace alone through faith. Catholics see grace as the primary means of salvation, but one must partially pay for salvation through various disciplines, service, and suffering. Nazarenes also disagree with the Catholic dogma of confession to a priest.

Roman Catholics Today

One person out of every 6 in our world is a Roman Catholic. That adds up to 1 billion persons. Twenty-three percent of the United States population identified themselves as Catholics in 1993.

Our past embraces the good, the bad, and the ordinary, and we who are Catholic accept it all as ours. We trace ourselves back to the Church of the Apostles. . . . There have been Judases in the Church in every age, but there have been far more saints.

—Father Oscar Lukefahr

THE ROMAN CATHOLIC CHURCH

THOUGH OUTCAST AND OUTLAWED, the early Christians conquered the Roman Empire. The Holy Spirit descended on the 120 believers on the Day of Pentecost and set that little community of faith ablaze with evangelical fire. When the hammer of persecution struck the Jerusalem church like an anvil, the sparks of divine fire showered the Mediterranean world as those heroes of faith went everywhere preaching the gospel. That church, like Jesus, belongs to all of us who take the name Christian.

That church called itself the "catholic" or "universal" Church of Jesus Christ at least as early as A.D. 110. Ignatius of Antioch in his *Epistle to the Smyrmaeans* wrote, "Wherever Jesus Christ is present, we have the catholic Church."[1] Polycarp, the martyred bishop of Smyrna, wrote in A.D. 156 of "the holy catholic church."[2] And Saint Cyprian of Carthage about A.D. 250 wrote a treatise titled *The Unity of the Catholic Church.*[3]

The Roman Catholics

In this chapter we will speak of the Roman Catholic Church as the community of faith that existed after the Edict of Milan in the year 312. At that time Emperor Constantine saw a vision of the Cross and was told, "By this sign conquer." Though he himself was not baptized until the day of his death, his edict made Christianity a legal religion in the empire. By 381 Emperor Theodosius made it illegal to practice any other faith in the empire.

---

1. Richard P. McBrien, *Catholicism* (San Francisco: Harper, 1989), 3. McBrien cites Ignatius as dying around A.D. 107. Others date his *Epistle to the Smyrmaeans* at A.D. 110 or 120.

2. Richard S. Taylor, ed., *Beacon Dictionary of Theology* (Kansas City: Beacon Hill Press of Kansas City, 1983), 96.

3. Paul L. Williams, *Everything You Always Wanted to Know About the Catholic Church but Were Afraid to Ask for Fear of Excommunication* (New York: Doubleday, 1989), 8.

The growth of Christianity accelerated. Powerful centers of Christian influence developed in Alexandria, Antioch, Jerusalem, Byzantium, Carthage, Ephesus, and Rome. More and more, the bishop of Rome came to be recognized as the "first among equals" in the fellowship of bishops. Rome was located at the heart of the empire, was home to the fastest-growing part of the Church, and was building a reputation as the champion of orthodox teachings.

As noted in the previous chapter, the years between 325 and 787 formed the era of the seven councils at which the Christian Church hammered out its orthodoxy. Councils at Nicaea, Constantinople, Ephesus, and Chalcedon clarified the standard Christian doctrines of the Trinity and the nature of Christ. These dogmas were confirmed by ecumenical councils in 553 and 680 and still form orthodox Christian beliefs.

Political and Religious Power: Use and Abuse

When Attila the Hun threatened Rome in the fifth century, it was Pope Leo I who saved the city, not the civil emperor. A few years later when the Vandals sacked Rome, it was Leo who limited the destruction to 14 days and more or less saved the city. About the same time, Leo found time to write and deliver the defining doctrine of the Trinity that carried the day at the Council of Chalcedon. He also established the doctrine of the papacy as Peter's own office and the pope as the very voice of Peter and Christ. Thus, secular and sacred leadership were combined in the church's highest office. The pope assumed authority of king and emperor of the empire and the church. And it trickled down. "Bishops replaced the Roman prefects, becoming the central source of order in the cities. Archbishops supplanted the provincial governors. The Synod of Bishops succeeded the provincial assembly."[4]

With the church in charge (more or less) of both the secular and religious seats of power, we should expect a veritable millennial reign of peace and paradise. But it didn't happen. In fact, the millennium between 500 and 1500 would provoke no one to think of peace or paradise.

The Roman Catholic Church did a lot of good. It was the fountain of learning, the force for civilization that parried the blows of the invading barbarians. It established rule by law and became the most stable organization in western Europe. Monasteries served as mission frontiers, and the gospel was carried to every nook and cranny of Europe. Popes like Gregory I (590—604), Gregory VII (1073-85), and Innocent III (1198—1216), mystics like Bernard of Clairvaux (1090—1153), preachers like Dominic (1170—1221), and theologians like Thomas Aquinas (1224-74) made great contributions for God and good that still affect us today. "It took centuries, but the popes, aided by Christian princes, pacified and baptized a continent and called it Christendom, Christian Europe."[5]

The lures of worldly power proved too strong for some, however. The papacy and other high offices became political plums for which no sacrifice in terms of honor and character was too great to pay. Some popes sold ecclesiastical positions to

4. Ibid., 11.
5. Bruce L. Shelley, *Church History in Plain Language* (Waco, Tex.: Word Books, 1982), 493.

the highest bidder and then created new positions so they could ring up still more sales. Family members and friends of the popes were made cardinals and bishops. By the end of the eighth century, the popes ruled not only the papal states in Italy but also most of Portugal, much of Spain, and all of England, Ireland, Bulgaria, Corsica, Sardinia, and Sicily, from which revenues were energetically extracted. Taxes were levied on Christians, extortion was practiced, indulgences peddled. Some of the worst popes tortured competitors, poisoned opponents, openly took mistresses and sired children, and presided over the grossest sexual orgies imaginable.

Rodrigo Borgia was one of the worst. He bought the votes of 13 cardinals for 5,000 ducats and became Pope Alexander VI. At the time of his election, he had already fathered four illegitimate children by his main mistress and boasted of many more by his legion of lovers. Upon his election, he took a new mistress and named 19 political cohorts to the office of cardinal. He created several openings for his friends by poisoning cardinals who were already in office. He extorted money from the clergy and was known as a ruthless erotomaniac. One party recorded in the diary of Burchard, a papal employee, notes that on October 30, 1501, "50 naked Roman harlots" had been retained for the amusement of Pope Alexander and his daughter, Lucrezia Borgia.

When Alexander finally died in 1503, the city wildly rejoiced. The citizens burned the houses of the fake cardinals that he had appointed. "The whole city . . . crowded about the corpse in St. Peter's Church, and were not able to satisfy their eyes with the sight of the dead serpent."[6]

Such abuses provoked the Protestant Reformation and eventually the Catholic Counter-Reformation as people of good conscience could no longer ignore the fact that something had gone terribly wrong with the "Christian" enterprise. Purging, renewal, and reformation were necessary.

Reformation and Counter-Reformation

At first the Roman Church did nothing when Luther and his German believers bolted from the Catholic flock. Many supposed that, like other hotheaded reformers, Luther would be excommunicated, and upon his death, his following would fade away. Slowly the realization came that the rent in the church fellowship was permanent.

Many Catholics had already been searching for ways to reform the church. The Protestant Reformation helped them put their cause on the table. Pope Paul III, himself repentant over his four illegitimate children, appointed a commission of cardinals to study church reform. Its 1537 report declared that the papal office was too secular, that both cardinals and popes needed to turn their attention to spiritual matters. Bribes, prostitution in the Holy See, abuses of indulgences, and evasion of church law by high-ranking officials had to cease.[7]

The attention of Catholic Christians turned back to basic reasons for the church's existence. A revival occurred through the influence of Spanish aristocratic mystics John of the Cross, Saint Teresa of Avila, and Ignatius of Loyola,

6. Williams, *Everything You Always Wanted to Know*, 19-20.
7. Shelley, *Church History*, 292.

the founder of the Jesuits. Reforms also happened in other countries headed by leaders like English lawyer Sir Thomas More; the archbishop of Milan, Charles Borromeo; and the missionary to the Calvinists, Francis of Sales.[8] Francis Xavier carried the gospel of the Jesuits to India, Ceylon, Malaya, and Japan.

In a less exemplary mode, Popes Paul III, Paul IV, and the "saintly zealot Pius V" vigorously conducted the Roman Inquisition that extirpated Protestants from Italy, securing that country as a base from which to fight Protestants in the North.[9]

The Council of Trent (1545-63) was called to deal with concerns that the clamor for reform had raised. After affirming that there would not have been a Protestant Reformation had it not been for the "ambition, avarice, and cupidity" of high-ranking clergy, the council proceeded to condemn the principles and written works of Luther, Zwingli, Carlstadt, and Calvin.[10] Traditional Roman Catholic positions were reinforced against such Protestant principles as *sola scriptura*. Scripture was not enough, they reasoned—after all, the church existed before the Bible, created the Bible, and had jurisdiction over its interpretation.

The Trent conferees also struck down *sola fide*. Faith alone was not enough to bring salvation. Even the popes "have to earn their way to salvation like any other Catholic."[11] *Sola gratia* was also denounced. Salvation was indeed by grace, but salvation could not be achieved without penitential works and the sacraments administered in the one true Catholic Church.

Theologically, the Council of Trent was an angry denunciation of Protestants. Traditional Catholic theology remained about the same. Preserved were the pope as monarch, the seven sacraments, the Latin sacrificial mass, indulgences, icons, veneration of saints, confession to priests, and the primacy of church tradition over Scripture. "The council's work was essentially medieval; only the anger was new."[12] That anger would be expressed in inquisitions, civil wars, and persecutions as both sides declared themselves the true Church.

Administratively, the Council of Trent made some productive decisions. Bishops were to live holy lives. Seminaries were to be established. Unfortunately, since the Protestants were making a veritable "paper pope" of the Bible, the curriculum was to be scholastic rather than biblical. Further, the council abolished the position of "indulgence seller."

The Modern Roman Catholic Councils

Two general councils of the Roman Catholic Church have transpired since the Council of Trent. Vatican I came to pass in 1869-70 in Rome under the direction of Pope Pius IX. Vatican I was again a defensive council. It moved to reinforce the power of the prince of the church. It picked up the general doctrine of papal infallibility and made it specific dogma. More than 80 bishops voted against the legislation in its original form, and 55 bishops formally absented themselves when

8. Ibid., 290.
9. Walter A. Elwell, ed., *Evangelical Dictionary of Theology* (Grand Rapids: Baker Book House, 1984), 276.
10. Ibid., 1109.
11. Williams, *Everything You Always Wanted to Know,* 20.
12. Shelley, *Church History,* 296.

the final vote on the edited proposal came up.[13] The vote carried, however, and from that day forward, Catholics have been required to believe that when the pope makes official announcements (speaks ex cathedra) about faith and practice, it is the very voice of Peter and Christ and is, therefore, infallible and not subject to challenge or change.

Vatican II, held in the 1960s, was different. For the first time in history, a general Catholic conference was held *for* something, not *against* something. The purpose was, according to Pope John XXIII, to bring the church up-to-date and make it relevant to the everyday life of Christians. Most of the compromises and adjustments were, in fact, steps toward the principles of Protestantism. It seemed that the Catholic Church was finally saying that those who had left her had good reason to do.

1. It was affirmed that the laity had a priestly service to fulfill. They were to take over many of the local church functions that had always before been left up to the priests. This was a step toward the Protestant doctrine of the priesthood of all believers.

2. The liturgy was simplified. The mass was to be given in the language of the people—not in Latin.

3. While still affirming the Catholic Church as the true Church, Vatican II declared that this did not mean that people in other churches would go to hell. Luther and Calvin were still heretics, but those who were raised in their traditions—raised in invincible ignorance of the true Church—would not be held guilty by God or the Catholic Church. They were termed not heretics but "separated brethren." This was a radical change from Trent. Protestant churches could be a way to salvation. But then, non-Christian religions could be a way to God as well. Vatican II regarded religions, as Yves Congar put it, "as an ordinary way of salvation and Christianity as an extraordinary way."[14]

4. The Bible was given more prominence in Catholic life by Vatican II. It still did not rise above tradition, councils, and ex cathedra pronouncements by the pope. But lay study of the Bible was strongly encouraged for the first time.

5. The infallibility of the pope was muted by an equal emphasis on the importance and authority of the council of bishops.

These and other measures were moves toward Protestant ideals and toward a democratized church where the will of the laity and the bishops are taken seriously by cardinals and popes. Though the Roman Catholic Church remains an absolute monarchy—only the position of pope is attained by election—democratic principles have been let in.[15]

The changes were so dramatic that many rank-and-file Catholics were not prepared for them. Conservatives thought the changes added up to compromise with the Protestants' heretic and secular popular opinion. Many thought that the moves, while elevating the laity, diminished the priesthood. Some 8,000

---

13. Elwell, *Evangelical Dictionary*, 1134.

14. Bernard Lauret, ed., *Fifty Years of Catholic Theology: Conversations with Yves Congar* (London: SCM Press, 1988), 15.

15. Williams, *Everything You Always Wanted to Know*, 31.

American priests left the ministry between 1966 and 1972. Enrollments in Catholic seminaries in America decreased by 31 percent during those years.[16] Roman Catholicism has had a sort of identity crisis after Vatican II.

Since Vatican II, Catholics and Protestants have worked together in interesting ways. Does this foreshadow a time when Christianity will once again be united?

A Survey of Roman Catholic Beliefs

1. Do Catholics believe in the triune God?

Yes. The orthodox beliefs about the Holy Trinity were worked out in the early ecumenical councils and are affirmed by Roman Catholics and by most Protestant churches, including the Church of the Nazarene.

2. Do Catholics believe that Jesus was fully human and yet fully God? That is, do they believe in the Incarnation?

Yes. They clearly teach the orthodox doctrines about the Incarnation and the nature of Jesus Christ, as does the Church of the Nazarene.

3. Do Catholics believe that the Holy Spirit is fully God and not just a messenger for God the Father and the Son?

Yes. Though the Eastern Orthodox challenge the *filioque* usage in the Catholic versions of the creeds, Roman Catholics repeatedly affirm the divinity of the Third Person of the Trinity, the Holy Spirit.

4. Do Catholics believe in the virgin birth and resurrection of Jesus?

Yes. They refer to the Gospel of Luke and the Gospel of Matthew in support of the Incarnation, as do we. Catholics also teach the real, bodily resurrection of Jesus Christ.

5. Do Catholics view Mary the mother of Jesus the same way that Nazarenes do?

No. They call her *theotokos*, the "Mother of God," rather than the mother of Christ. This label has intended to protect the divinity of Jesus against certain early heresies. Catholics teach the Immaculate Conception. On December 8, 1854, Pope Pius IX, speaking ex cathedra, that is "infallibly," made it mandatory for Catholics to believe that Mary was the only human being other than Jesus ever born without original sin. Catholic theology taught that original or Adamic sin is passed down genetically from generation to generation, thus the necessity for the Immaculate Conception of Mary in order to make the birth of the divine Son of God possible. Mary, they say, was without sin and "full of grace" from her conception. "Therefore, Mary in holiness surpassed the beautitude of Adam and Eve and the angels who were capable of sin, while Mary was not."[17]

6. Do Catholics pray to Mary?

Yes, but not in the same way that they pray to God. They claim to *worship* God but only *venerate* Mary. They believe that given Mary's special status as the mother of God, she can help them by interceding with her Son in their behalf. Thus, they often pray for her to pray for them. She has a special place above all

16. Shelley, *Church History,* 479.
17. Williams, *Everything You Always Wanted to Know,* 67.

saints. She is viewed as the "New Eve"—just as Jesus is seen as the "New Adam"—without sin and the spiritual mother of us all. "Vatican II taught explicitly . . . that Mary is one of us, a member of the Church, and one of those redeemed by Christ."[18]

7. What else do Catholics teach about Mary that is different from what most Protestants teach?

Catholics teach that Mary remained a virgin throughout her life. They regard the brothers of Jesus mentioned in the Bible as spiritual brothers or children of Joseph by a former marriage. They also are required to believe in the Assumption of Mary. The only ex cathedra pronouncement of a pope in the last 100 years included the teaching that at the end of Mary's life Christ gave her victory over death, and that since she had never sinned, she was "assumed" or "translated" directly to heaven into complete union with her Son.[19]

8. Do Catholics pray to other saints?

Again, they prefer the term "veneration" over prayer or worship, but prayer to deceased persons is a common practice. "We pray to God—Father, Son, and Holy Spirit—as the source of all blessings. We pray to the saints in the sense," writes Oscar Lukefahr, "that we ask them to pray with us and for us, to be near us in love and friendship and to lead us closer to Jesus."[20] To the Catholic mind, the line between the living and the dead is very faint. Persons alive or dead are considered church members whom they might ask to pray for them in much the same manner that you might ask your pastor to remember you in prayer as you face a tough decision. Among Protestants the doctrine of the "priesthood of all believers" has replaced praying to the saints.

9. What do Catholics teach about the sacrament of the Lord's Supper?

The Lord's Supper (Holy Communion, Eucharist) is one of the areas over which Catholics and Protestants have always disagreed. Both practice this holy sacrament but disagree about what goes on during the service. Catholics insist that the bread and wine actually become the real body and blood of Jesus. Most Protestants regard the bread and wine or juice as *symbols* of Jesus' broken body and shed blood.

Both traditions encourage spiritual examination before receiving the sacrament. Fasting and confession to the priest of any mortal sin must precede Communion for Catholics. The sacrament also nourishes spiritual life, draws us closer to God and to each other, and foreshadows the return of our Lord. For Catholics, it is also a sacrifice that occurs during the mass. Drawing on the idea of the Passover lamb whose blood saved the Israelites, Catholics see the Eucharist as a sacrifice for their own sins. The real Christ is present in the bread and wine, they believe, and the body and blood of Jesus are offered to God as a holy sacrifice in payment for their sins.

In Catholic worship, the Eucharist is the central focus of the service. In Evangelical churches, the focus of the typical service is the sermon. Catholics

---

18. Oscar Lukefahr, *We Believe . . . A Survey of Catholic Faith* (Liguori, Mo.: Liguori Publications, 1995), 68.
19. Ibid., 69.
20. Oscar Lukefahr, *The Privilege of Being Catholic* (Liguori, Mo.: Liguori Publications, 1993), 125.

believe that the real Christ is present in the sacrament offered again as a sacrifice for sin. Many Protestants and Evangelicals agree with Lutheran Dietrich Bonhoeffer that if the preacher faithfully preaches the saving words of Christ, the historical Christ is present, walking among the congregation, offering redemption. The aim of both kinds of worship is to bring the worshiper to Christ in saving, reconciling relationship. The Catholic service does this through the *sacramental sacrifice,* the Evangelical through the sacrament of the *preached Word* and the invitation.

10. What does the Catholic Church teach about baptism?

Catholics teach that baptism brings four blessings: the forgiveness of sin (personal and original), regeneration (new life in Christ), union with God, and membership in the church. The rather elaborate ceremony includes baptism by immersion or pouring.

Though Catholics believe baptism is the occasion of forgiveness of sin, they do not say that baptism saves them. Baptism (of desire or actual) is necessary to salvation, they say, but it alone does not save. Catholics are careful not to say they are "saved." That is Calvinistic Protestantism, they believe. Some Protestants say that once they have accepted Jesus as Lord and Savior, they are eternally saved. Catholics do not believe that salvation is a one-time-only affair.

Instead of salvation as a singular experience, they see it as a journey. It is a journey begun in baptism, the first of three initiation sacraments. Baptism is followed by first Communion and then by confirmation. Oscar Lukefahr compares the journey of salvation to traveling by ship through the waters of this life to the safe haven of eternity. "The ship has been built. Christ has done everything necessary by his life, death, and resurrection to bring us to heaven. . . . But we must book passage on the ship and become an active part of the crew. We must 'work out' our salvation."[21] Lukefahr goes on to say, "The Bible shows that it is possible to 'jump ship' and choose the wrong destination."[22] Thus, Catholics will not say they are *saved* until they make it safely to heaven.

The Nazarene doctrine of baptism is not as complicated or as central to our Christian living. We regard baptism as an outward sign of an inward grace. That grace is saving or justifying grace that comes in an encounter with Christ in which we confess and repent of our sins and put our trust in Jesus as Savior and Lord. After such a conversion experience, one may be baptized, thus testifying to all that he or she is a believer and wants to be known always as a disciple of Christ. Thus, baptism is not necessary, we believe, to salvation. What counts is a saving personal relationship with Jesus Christ. Baptism is, however, important, a blessing not to be missed. Our *Manual* states, "While we do not hold that baptism imparts the regenerating grace of God, we do believe that Christ gave this holy sacrament as a sign and seal of the new covenant."[23]

A fairly new program among Catholics is called Rite of Christian Initiation of Adults. In this ministry, the Catholics are returning to the ancient plan of

---

21. Lukefahr, *We Believe,* 94-95.

22. Ibid., 95.

23. *Manual, Church of the Nazarene, 1997—2001,* par. 800.2, 246.

preparing adult converts for baptism. It has several steps and may take years to complete. Step one is the *Period of Inquiry,* in which the prospect learns the basic truths about the faith. Step two is the *Catechumenate,* a period of more intensive instruction. Step three is *Enlightenment and Purification.* During Lent the candidate is led in study and prayer that climaxes at Easter with baptism, confirmation, and the holy Eucharist.[24] Often led by laymen as part of the new (1992) catechism, this program has been quite productive.

11. What is confirmation?

Confirmation is the third initiation rite that gets one started on the path to heaven. Baptism brings forgiveness and regeneration. Holy Communion is, among other things, a sacrament of sanctifying grace. Confirmation is also a sacrament of sanctification. More precisely, it is viewed as giving the gift of the Holy Spirit to the believer. "Confirmation is our Pentecost," one Catholic priest declares.[25] It brings the fruit of the Spirit and gives power for service. Nazarenes also believe in regeneration (saving grace) and sanctifying grace, but as we have seen earlier, these are regarded as matters of personal experience that a mere ceremony cannot usually deliver.

For Catholics, entry into the Christian life is something that happens over time. One catechist writes, "Conversion to Jesus Christ . . . is a fairly arduous event that takes time and the nurture of candidates by faith-filled members of the community."[26] Does it seem to you that Nazarenes can teach their Catholic brethren something about personal relationships with God, while they could teach us something about thoroughly preparing prospects for discipleship?

12. Do Catholics practice sacraments besides baptism and Holy Communion?

The Roman Catholic catechism lists seven sacraments. There are three sacraments of initiation—baptism, Eucharist, and confirmation; two of healing—penance (or reconciliation) and healing of the sick; two of service and mission—holy orders and marriage. Most Protestant groups, including the Church of the Nazarene, recognize only baptism and Holy Communion as sacraments.

13. Do Catholics teach that salvation is by grace alone?

No. They do teach that grace is the primary source of salvation. Without the gracious love of God and the atonement of Christ, no one would have any hope of salvation. But given that, they teach that one must by his or her own works, piety, suffering, and service earn, or partially pay for, his or her salvation. Catholics are sure to say this around Calvinistic and Lutheran Christians who have historically declared that salvation is a matter of predestination. Salvation depends on God and God alone, they say—there is not one thing you can do to make yourself worthy of salvation. Thus, classic Protestants speak of *obtaining* or *receiving* salvation. They never speak of *attaining* it or *achieving* it, as Catholics often do.

---

24. Lukefahr, *We Believe,* 93.

25. Ibid., 97.

26. Raymond A. Lucker, Patrick J. Brennan, and Michael Leach, eds., *The People's Catechism* (New York: Crossroad Publishing Co., 1995), 149.

John Wesley, our spiritual ancestor, tried to find a middle road between the classic Protestant view of grace and Catholic view of works. He said that good works (acts of piety and acts of mercy) were necessary in a secondary sort of way, but that they were never to be regarded as earning or meriting salvation or even a little part of it. Good works were simply what any Christian should and would do. Wesley declared that he did not regard a person as having one grain of faith if he (or she) was not willing "to spend and be spent" for others.

14. What is the Catholic doctrine about penance?

Penance is one step in the Catholic practice of confession or reconciliation. First is *contrition*, or sorrow for one's sins. Second comes *confession* to a priest. Third, the priest assigns a proper *satisfaction* or *penance*. This is an effort to make up for the damage that one's sins caused. The closest thing to this in Evangelical teaching is the practice of restitution. The convert is expected to pay back money that was stolen, apologize for falsehoods whispered, and so on.

In the early centuries, Catholic penances were often severe. If a person, after baptism, committed adultery or engaged in homosexual acts, he or she was excommunicated for 15 years and commanded to abstain totally from sexual activity for the rest of his or her life. Homicide, sorcery, and incest could be forgiven only after 20 years of repentant excommunication. Denying Christ under persecution was the gravest sin. The penance was segregation to the "weepers'" part of the church for the rest of their lives, where they would in a loud voice mourn their sins every Sunday as the devout gathered for worship. They were not allowed to take Communion again—until the hour of their death.[27]

Things are much more lenient today, but the Catholic Church has a long history of accountability and penance. After contrition, confession, and the assignment of penance, the priest grants *absolution,* or forgiveness of sins. The Catholic tradition of purgatory is connected with the idea of penance. If one dies before getting all due penances performed, purgatorial fires will purify the soul, making the person ready for heaven eventually.

15. Why do most Protestants disagree with the idea of confessing sins to a priest?

Both experience and wisdom indicate that there are times when one needs to add to his confession to God confession to a Christian pastor or friend. But the Protestant principle of the priesthood of all believers includes the conviction that confession to God is what brings forgiveness and reconciliation. It is not up to a priest to tell us whether or not we are forgiven. The Bible promise is enough: "If we confess our sins, he is faithful and just to forgive us our sins" (1 John 1:9, KJV).

Part of the Protestant revolt against the Catholic confessional was that it gave priests far too much control over one's life. When a mere human can give or withhold forgiveness and assign any punishment or penance that he pleases, dreadful abuses are all but guaranteed. Very few Bible passages can be recruited to support the idea of confessing to a priest, but Roman Catholic tradition upholds it.

---

27. Williams, *Everything You Always Wanted to Know,* 284, 288.

16. Do Catholics believe that the Bible is inspired?

Yes, but it does not have the authority for them as it does for most Protestant believers. We believe that the Bible is the final Word on matters of faith and salvation. Catholics hold that the church created the Bible for its own use and therefore has power to add books to the canon and interpret the Bible officially. The Bible is the church's book. Though they view the Bible as the Word of God, they hold that church tradition, infallible papal decrees, and theological councils have authority equal to that of the Scriptures.

17. Do Catholics believe that theirs is the one true Church?

Yes. Though they are seeking now to reach out to Protestants, Jews, and certain other religions, Vatican II says, "They could not be saved who, knowing that the Catholic Church was founded as necessary by God through Christ, would refuse to enter it. . . . It is through Christ's Church alone, which is the all-embracing means of salvation, that all fullness of the means of salvation can be obtained."[28]

> *The Catholic Church does not bless divorce. It also warns members that sex within marriage must be restrained and not lustful.*

This does not mean that Catholics believe that other Christians are going to be lost eternally. Vatican II also said, "One cannot charge with the sin of separation those who at present are born into these communities [Protestant churches] and in them were brought up in the faith of Christ, and the Catholic Church accepts them with respect and affection as brothers."[29]

18. Does the Catholic Church teach a biblical standard of sexual morality?

Yes. The Roman Catholic Church vigorously teaches against premarital sex, adultery, and homosexual activity. Catholics oppose abortion. The Roman Catholic Church does not bless divorce. It also warns members that sex within marriage must be restrained and not lustful. On these matters the Church of the Nazarene and the Roman Catholic Church have quite similar ideals.

The Roman Catholic Church officially regards masturbation as a mortal sin and prohibits artificial birth control. These two matters Nazarenes have left to individual conscience and pastoral guidance.

Recent polls show that most American Catholics do not share their church's position on divorce, premarital sex, and birth control.[30]

Today there are over 1 billion Catholics in our world. That adds up to one-sixth of the world's population. The Roman Catholic Church is by far the largest body of Christians in the world. About 23 percent of the population of the United States in 1993 identified themselves as Catholics. United States Catholics number almost 60 million and worship in about 20,000 churches.[31]

---

28. Ibid., 117.
29. Ibid.
30. See ibid., 247.
31. Mead and Hill, *Handbook of Denominations,* 270.

Review and Reflection

1. In 2 Pet. 1:5-7, we are given four pairs of qualities that should mark the mature Christian.

faith and *virtue* (KJV) (goodness)
knowledge and *self-control*
perseverance and *godliness* (piety)
kindness and *love*

2. Think about this chapter in terms of knowledge and self-control.

a. Knowledge

List several facts you did not know before you read this chapter. Be sure to include both positive and negative facts.

List one topic in this chapter about which you would like to know more. (Check the author's footnotes for a first step in further study.)

Think of a friend who is or has been a Roman Catholic. In what ways has this chapter equipped you to converse with your friend more intelligently? How has it helped you with understanding him or her? What do you admire in that friend? in his or her faith?

b. Self-control

What facts, ideas, or statements in this chapter provoke the idea of self-control?

3. Suppose that you just moved to a new town. Your neighbor brings over a cherry pie to welcome you. Religion comes up. You tell your new neighbor that you are Nazarene. She replies, "We're Catholic. How is your belief different form ours?" What would you say?

Don't worry if you can't spit out a perfect answer without reading this chapter again. One way to answer would be to graciously cite the Protestant principles:

Sola gratia (grace alone),
Sola fide (faith alone),
Sola scriptura (Scripture alone), and the
Priesthood of all believers.

4. Ponder the other three pairs of qualities for mature Christians from 2 Pet. 1:5-7.

PART IV

CLASSICAL PROTESTANT CHURCHES

- The First Protestants: Lutherans Rearrange the Christian World

- Calvin and His Kin: Presbyterian and Reformed Churches

- Catholic and Reformed: The Anglican Paradox

THE FIRST PROTESTANTS: LUTHERANS REARRANGE THE CHRISTIAN WORLD

Principal Leader

Martin Luther, Augustinian monk turned Reformer, was the most important leader of the Lutheran Reformation. He presided over the Reformation in Germany and influenced it in other countries. Luther and his disciples dramatically changed Christianity.

Core Beliefs

Justification by grace through faith in Christ.

The Bible as the Church's final Authority.

The priesthood of all believers—not just the ordained few.

The conviction that doctrine and spiritual experience must merge in the spiritual life.

The belief that Christ is literally present in the Communion elements.

Agreement and Differences

Nazarenes eagerly embrace these Protestant principles taught by Luther: justification by faith, salvation by grace (not works), the authority of Scripture, and the priesthood of all believers.

We differ, however, on the nature of the Church, the Lord's Supper, baptism, worship styles, and the doctrine of sanctification.

Today's Lutheran Christians

Today there are 68 million Lutherans in 100 denominations worldwide. The largest North American Lutheran body is the Evangelical Lutheran Church in America, with 5.2 million members.

**Each man must do his own believing,
just as each must do his own dying.**

8 ~ THE FIRJT PROTEJTANTJ: LUTHERANJ REARRANGE THE CHRIJTIAN WORLD

PROTESTANTISM EMERGED IN THE EARLY 16TH CENTURY as a new force in Christianity. It assumed four basic forms by 1600: Lutheranism, the Reformed (or Calvinist) tradition, Anabaptism, and Anglicanism. Each had its own genius, purpose, and spirit. And each contributed to the streams that have blended to create the Church of the Nazarene.

On the Road to Reformation

Lutheranism, like a wedge, cracked open Catholic Europe. It did not emerge in a vacuum. Sixteenth-century Europe was in ferment. Lutheranism was preceded by a renewed emphasis on preaching fostered in the monastic orders founded by Francis of Assisi and Dominic, in England by the followers of John Wycliffe, and in Czech Bohemia by the disciples of Jan Hus. The Reformation, a product of this renewal, created Protestant churches that sustained and perpetuated the preaching revival.

Renaissance humanism also prepared the way for the Reformation. Catholic humanists preferred their theology with both feet on the ground. Some disdained abstract theology and studied Greek, Roman, and biblical literature instead of philosophy. Their research in ancient texts led to new methods of translation and study. The Dutch humanist Erasmus (ca. 1466—1536), a New Testament scholar, prepared a new text of the Greek New Testament, while Johannes Reuchlin (1455—1522) spearheaded renewed interest in the study of Old Testament Hebrew. Their work on the Greek and Hebrew texts enabled Martin Luther and other Reformers to translate the Bible into the common languages of their day.[1]

Luther and the Reformation in Germany

Martin Luther was born in Saxony, a German state in the Holy Roman Empire. After taking a degree at the University of Erfurt, he became an

---

1. Williston Walker, *A History of the Christian Church*, 2nd ed. (New York: Charles Scribner's Sons, 1959), 291-97.

Augustinian monk and priest. The Augustinians sent him to Wittenberg's new university for further study. There Luther completed an advanced degree and succeeded his mentor, Johann Staupitz, as professor of biblical theology.

But Luther was plagued by a terror of God. When he read Paul's words on the "justice of God," Luther felt himself judged and found guilty by the Great Judge. His anxiety did not abate until he realized that the "justice of God" was not a doctrine of terror but of liberation. God's justice is a judgment that frees, not condemns, the sinner. Luther came to understand that God's justice is at one with His justification (or acceptance) of the sinner through grace.

Luther reworked his personal theology from this standpoint, relying especially on Paul's Epistles to the Romans and Galatians. He called the theology of medieval Catholicism, with its rarefied philosophical structures, a "theology of glory" and set his simple "theology of the Cross" over against it.

Luther's theology of the Cross emphasized humanity's radical sinfulness, the heart "turned in on itself" that makes one unable to be saved apart from God's grace. But Luther also emphasized God's radical decision to forgive sins. Christians *are* just because they are justified by God's grace through faith. This doctrine is called "justification by faith." But grace—God's initiative—is its main point. Faith, for Luther, is the way God chooses to bestow saving grace. Faith is understood primarily as "trust" rather than "belief." Even devils believe in God; but they do *not* place their *trust* in God!

The distinction between "law" and "gospel," derived from Paul, was important in Luther's theology. He had experienced the Catholic system of salvation as legalistic. Not all Catholics experienced it so, but Luther and many others did. The doctrine of justification by grace cut through the legalism. Lutherans ever since have emphasized the distinction between law and gospel.

Ministry and Worship

Luther's theological breakthrough had implications for the Church and ministry. Roman Catholicism drew a hard-and-fast line between clergy and laity. Catholics held that men may choose either marriage or ordination (never both) as their service to God. But Luther argued that every Christian is a minister called by God through baptism to participate in the Church's ministry to

The priesthood of believers makes us responsible ministers to one another and to the world.

the world. This idea was called "the priesthood of believers." Ordained clergy—set aside to preach, administer the sacraments, and lead the flock of Christ—symbolize the whole Church's calling. The priesthood of believers makes us responsible ministers to one another and to the world. This doctrine also implied that laity should have some role in governing the church.[2]

Luther believed that worship should be conducted in the people's own languages, so he heavily edited Catholicism's Latin mass and then translated it into

---

2. Paul Althaus, *The Theology of Martin Luther* (Philadelphia: Fortress Press, 1966), 323-32.

German. He translated the Bible for the same reason—a critical step for the German language and culture. Germany was many states under many princes, but Luther's translation helped standardize the language. As Germans worshiped and read the Scriptures in their native tongue, a sense of nationhood slowly developed. A similar dynamic worked in other countries as Protestantism reinforced the emerging European nationalism and hastened the disintegration of the Holy Roman Empire, which had existed since Charlemagne in the ninth century.

> ***Without doubt, the Protestant parsonage was one of the greatest gifts to emerge from the Lutheran Reformation.***

Luther initiated many other changes that shape our lives as Protestants. Early Christians had accepted writings into the Old Testament that Jewish rabbis had not accepted into their canon. Luther excluded these writings, which Protestants call the Apocrypha, in his German translation of the Bible. Other Protestant Reformers followed his lead, so that Protestantism's Old Testament conforms to the Jewish canon but differs slightly from the Roman Catholic and Eastern Orthodox canon.

Luther advocated a married clergy, for he was no longer bound to Roman Catholicism's belief regarding the mutually exclusive nature of marriage and ordination. As the Lutheran Reformation progressed, Saxony's monasteries and convents closed, and Luther helped the nuns find husbands. To set a good example, he married one himself—Katherine von Bora. They had three sons and three daughters. Theirs was a rich family life. Without doubt, the Protestant parsonage was one of the greatest gifts to emerge from the Lutheran Reformation.[3]

Another of Luther's changes was in the number of sacraments. Catholicism and Orthodoxy had seven, but Luther finally accepted only baptism and Holy Communion. He defined a sacrament as an act commanded by Christ to which the promise of His Word is bound. This "Word" is the living Christ who comes to Christians, according to His promise, through the sacraments. Sacraments are basic elements of life—water, bread, and wine—to which the Word is *conjoined*. In Luther's view, one does not appropriate the grace offered in the sacrament simply by partaking of it. It must be apprehended by faith (or trust) in God's promise. Luther wrote that the sacraments "must be called efficacious in the sense that, when faith is indubitably present, they most assuredly and effectively impart grace."[4]

Roman Catholicism offers only the Communion bread to the laity, while both cup and bread are offered to the priests. Luther changed this practice and offered the laity the cup as well. His lead was followed by later Protestant churches.[5]

---

3. Heiko A. Oberman, *Luther: Man Between God and the Devil* (New York: Image Books, 1992), 277-83.

4. Martin Luther, "The Pagan Servitude of the Church," in *Martin Luther: Selections from His Writings*, ed. John Dillenberger (Garden City, N.Y.: Anchor Books, 1961), 249-359, esp. 293-303. Quote on 300.

5. Ibid., 256-59.

Luther developed a unique view of Communion, for he did not break completely with Catholicism's idea that Christ's body and blood are really in the Eucharistic elements. In 1529 his associate, Philip Melanchthon, tried to create a united front with Swiss Reformers; but Luther argued with Zurich Reformer Ulrich Zwingli on this point: what did Jesus mean at the Last Supper when He said, "This is my body"? Zwingli said that Jesus used figurative language and meant that the bread signifies His body. Luther understood the "is" to be literal. They could not agree, so Melanchthon's united front did not materialize.

Catholics used Aristotle's philosophy to explain their literal interpretation of Jesus' words, but Luther had no interest in using philosophy to explain the Scriptures. He grounded his version of Christ's "real presence" in a simple, plain reading of Scripture, arguing that Christ's body and blood are "in, over, and under" the Communion elements in a real and literal sense. Lutheranism's unique view is called *consubstantiation*.[6]

Brave Heart

Luther's life alternated between the tedium of his study and moments of high drama. He excelled in debates and used this forum to advance ideas and win followers to his cause. When the early Reformation forced a crisis upon Germany, Luther was forced to defend his ideas before Charles V, the Holy Roman Emperor, and the German Diet (Parliament). Told finally to recant, Luther refused, crying, "Here I stand. I can do no other, so help me God." The emperor issued a warrant for Luther's arrest, and Luther lived under its threat throughout his life. But Luther had the confidence of many German princes, including his own, Frederick of Saxony, who protected him.

The emperor issued a warrant for Luther's arrest, and Luther lived under its threat throughout his life. Fortunately for Luther, the Turks invaded Austria at this time, and Charles V devoted the next 10 years to defending Europe from their threat. By the time the Turks were pushed out, the Lutheran Reformation was firmly established in many parts of Germany. Luther remarked to associates that while he and his friend sat in the garden drinking German beer, the Word of God went forth reforming the church. The point was clear: Luther worked diligently for the Reformation cause, but its success was God's work, not Luther's.

Philip Melanchthon

Philip Melanchthon (1497—1560) was "the only humanist for whom Luther had an enduring, almost unexplainable respect."[7] Melanchthon emerged as the other important early Lutheran theologian after Luther—a considerable accomplishment for a classics scholar and philosopher who was never ordained. Luther disdained philosophy; Melanchthon specialized in Aristotle. Luther's many writings were produced in response to developing situations; Melanch-

---

6. David C. Steinmetz, *Luther in Context* (Bloomington, Ind.: Indiana University Press, 1986), 73-75.
7. David C. Steinmetz, *Reformers in the Wings* (Philadelphia: Fortress Press, 1971), 69.

thon produced the first Lutheran systematic theology, *Loci Communes* (1521), which examined the doctrines of the Christian faith within a system in which justification by faith was the controlling idea.

Later editions of *Loci Communes* show Melanchthon's growing independence from Luther on certain points. He rejected predestination, which Luther (under Augustine's influence) held. He asserted that humans have a degree of free will and can cooperate with God by assenting to their own salvation. He also veered from Luther's doctrine of consubstantiation and embraced a view of Christ's spiritual, but not bodily, presence in Communion.[8]

There were other points of disagreement. Melanchthon understood law and works in a more positive light than Luther. On these points, and in his view of the sacrament of Communion, Melanchthon was closer to John Calvin and the Reformed tradition than to Luther. After Luther's death, Melanchthon was severely attacked by conservative Lutherans who regarded any deviation from Luther as heresy.[9]

The relationship between Melanchthon and Luther is not unlike that between John Wesley and John Fletcher. Just as Melanchthon's theology bore Luther's strong imprint but differed from his mentor's, so Fletcher's doctrine of holiness was rooted in Wesley's but differed in certain respects. Wesley's holiness theology was rooted in the doctrine of Christ, Fletcher's in the doctrine of the Holy Spirit. Yet Fletcher was Wesley's designated successor to lead the Methodists of England. These two examples teach us that theological traditions do not originate as "pure" but usually contain diversity at the outset.

The most important doctrinal statement in early Lutheranism, the Augsburg Confession (1530), was written principally by Melanchthon. It was presented to Emperor Charles V with the endorsement of various Lutheran princes and free cities. Though rejected by Charles and the Roman Catholic Church, the Augsburg Confession became a rallying point for the Lutheran cause.[10]

The Spread of Lutheranism

Lutheranism spread through much of Germany, though some areas remained Catholic and others became Calvinist. Lutheranism's triumph was more complete in Scandinavia, where the state churches in Sweden, Denmark, Norway, and Finland became Lutheran. The same occurred in Iceland. Luther's theology also made inroads in Holland and the Baltic nations. Its ideas, debated throughout Europe, spurred other vigorous Protestant movements.

Lutheran Pietism

The Reformation battle largely was fought at the level of doctrine. Logical arguments presented in public debates and in apologetic and polemical writings promoted Protestant ideas. Intellectual vitality was emphasized in this era of religious disputes. Luther's era was followed by a period called Protestant

---

8. Ibid., 69-81.

9. John Dillenberger and Claude Welch, *Protestant Christianity: Interpreted Through Its Development* (New York: Charles Scribner's Sons, 1954), 78-85.

10. Walker, *History of the Christian Church*, 334-35.

scholasticism, noted for the vigilance of Lutheran pastors and theologians to protect their new orthodoxy against Catholic and Protestant foes. Was it possible in this atmosphere to be a champion of the new Protestant orthodoxy but know little from personal experience about what these doctrines were about? A century after Luther, some pastors argued that orthodoxy was not enough and that Lutheranism's potential had not been realized fully. They believed that a further reform of Protestant spirituality was needed. The movement to connect church doctrine more fully with spiritual life is called Pietism.

The early leaders of German Pietism were Philip Jacob Spener and Auguste H. Francke. A pastor, Spener formed circles of earnest disciples who met for Bible study and prayer. The members spoke of justification by faith in personal terms and were accountable to one another as disciples. This experiment revived Spener's churches, and others adopted his methods. Under the influence of his disciple Francke, the University of Halle became a leading disseminator of pietist methods and spirituality. Nicholas von Zinzendorf, educated at Halle, founded the Moravians, a pietist sect that influenced John Wesley. Pietism affected other Protestant denominations too.[11] Historian Ernest Stoeffler identified Pietism's main themes: a new dynamic in preaching, a renewal of pastoral care, devotional life and literature, an interest in mission and social outreach, and an emphasis on discipleship.[12]

Lutherans in America

Henry Muhlenburg was sent from Halle to America in the 1700s to pastor three Lutheran churches formed by German and Dutch immigrants. In 1748 he organized these and other Lutheran congregations into the first Lutheran synod in America. His crucial work as a pastor and organizer have earned him recognition as the principal leader of Lutheranism in colonial America.

European immigration reached flood stage in the 19th century, and Lutheran immigrants set up denominations in America that reflected their national origins. New Lutheran denominations were also set up according to whether the members preferred a pietist form of Lutheran church or a more confessional (or doctrine oriented) form. Pietism was the dominant expression of Lutheranism in America during most of that century.

A once-bewildering mosaic of Lutheran denominations has slowly coalesced together into fewer and fewer separate groups. By 1995 the overwhelming majority of American Lutherans were embraced within the Evangelical Lutheran Church in America, with 5.2 million members, and the Lutheran Church—Missouri Synod, with 2.6 million. The Wisconsin Evangelical Lutheran Synod has 415,000 adherents, and several smaller Lutheran bodies exist.[13]

Missouri Synod Lutherans and Wisconsin Lutherans derive their names from their headquarters location, not because their membership is principally located in these states. Both are Fundamentalist churches with strict views of bib-

---

11. Theodore G. Tappert, "Introduction," in Philip Jacob Spener, *Pia Desideria* (Philadelphia: Fortress Press, 1964), 1-28.

12. F. Ernest Stoeffler, *The Rise of Evangelical Pietism* (Leiden: E. J. Brill, 1965), 1:965.

13. Bedell, *Yearbook of Churches, 1996*, 2.

lical inerrancy. They strongly oppose women's ordination or pastoral leadership. Wisconsin Lutherans serve Communion only to their own members, and both churches appear doctrinaire to most people of Wesleyan-Holiness persuasion.

The Evangelical Lutheran Church in America (ELCA) is much more diverse. It was created in 1988 through the merger of the Lutheran Church in America and the American Lutheran Church. Both merging bodies had large Scandinavian-American components. There was also a third merger partner: the Association of Evangelical Lutheran Churches, former Missouri Synod Lutherans who left that denomination in 1976 over policies of its Fundamentalist leadership. Many of the ELCA's parent groups were pietist bodies and emphasized Christian living more than doctrinal precision. The ELCA is one of America's mainline denominations, but it is located on the conservative end of that spectrum.[14]

Lutheran churches are liturgical. Their order of worship resembles that of the Roman Catholic mass. Luther insisted on weekly celebration of the Eucharist, but American Lutherans are more likely to do so monthly.

Because of their adherence to the Augsburg Confession and other confessions of faith, Lutheranism is a body of "confessional churches" that emphasize doctrinal continuity with the Reformers.

European Lutherans retained the office of bishop. In the United States, a bishop heads each synod of the ELCA. The Lutheran Church—Missouri Synod, on the other hand, calls its synod leaders "presidents."[15]

There are about 68 million Lutherans worldwide. Nearly 100 denominations from 50 countries participate in the Lutheran World Federation, which meets every six years to witness to Lutheran unity. The federation also sponsors theological study and the translation and publication of Lutheran literature. Lutheran World Service, a department of the federation, provides emergency and relief services to tens of thousands of refugees and poor annually.[16]

Lutherans and Nazarenes Agree . . .

Nazarenes and other Wesleyans are deeply indebted to Martin Luther and his followers. Luther's new understanding of the gospel added important new dimensions to Christianity.

Luther's doctrine of *justification by grace* through faith was appropriated, via Philip Melanchthon, by the Church of England. John Wesley, a member of that church, made this doctrine one of the theological "landmarks of the Wesleyan revival."[17] This vital doctrine is a baseline in all Protestant churches. It is reflected in the Church of the Nazarene's Articles of Faith (Article IX) and in typical Nazarene preaching. New members affirm their personal experience of God's saving grace appropriated through faith when they join a Nazarene church and enter into covenant with other believing members of the congregation.

---

14. Martin E. Marty, "Lutheran Churches in America," in Reid et al., *Dictionary of Christianity in America,* 670-74.

15. Williamson, *Encyclopedia of Religions,* 198, 204.

16. J. D. Sutherland, "Lutheran World Federation," in Reid et al., *Dictionary of Christianity in America,* 678.

17. See Robert E. Cushman's essay "The Landmarks of the Wesleyan Revival" in his anthology, *Faith Seeking Understanding* (Durham, N.C.: Duke University Press, 1981), 51-52.

The *priesthood of believers* has also powerfully influenced Nazarene life. The American Holiness Movement never accepted the idea that the clergy were to direct everything. Indeed, the American Holiness Movement arose through the initial work of Methodist laywomen led by Phoebe Palmer and her sister. Many local and even state Holiness associations were led by laypersons, and lay preachers played an important role in Nazarene origins. We continue to see the laity as ministers in their own right and include laypersons at every level of church governance, from the local church through the General Assembly.

Lutheran *Pietism* has also shaped Nazarenes, though its influence was refracted through John Wesley's Anglican lens and modified by the North American environment. Pietist modes of spirituality are traditionally the primary spiritual vehicles in Nazarene life. Prayer meetings, revivals, strong missionary interests, extemporaneous prayer (rather than printed prayer), and much of the religious vocabulary of Nazarenes is rooted in historic Protestant Pietism.

A host of other innovations that date to Luther shape Nazarene life, including married clergy, the Old Testament canon, and our acceptance of two sacraments.

. . . and Differ

Where do Nazarenes and Lutherans differ? First, Wesley's distinctive theology took shape 200 years after the Reformation, when some of the inherent weaknesses in Luther's theology had become more apparent. Like the Church of England itself, Wesley's theology reflects themes drawn from Protestant Reformers but also from Catholic and Eastern Orthodox writers. So the Wesleyan theological reservoir is wider than Luther's was.

This is true especially in Wesley's understanding of grace as prevenient, justifying, and sanctifying. The doctrine of prevenient grace was from Catholicism, his concept of justifying grace from Luther, and his view of sanctifying grace draws principally from Catholic and Eastern Orthodox sources. For Luther, *faith* is what God requires of us. For Wesley, *love* wrought by faith is what God requires. The points are similar but not identical.

This difference appears in Luther's understanding of the justified Christian as one who is *simul justus et peccator* ("at once justified and a sinner"). Luther believed that through faith we appropriate God's forgiveness of sins and are justified by grace, but he saw the Christian life as a continual battle against original sin that is not won in this lifetime but only through death. So Christians, in his view, are still sinners, but they are sinners whom God counts as righteous through Christ. Sanctification is a continual process that is incomplete at death. His view is called *imputed righteousness*. Wesley, however, argued that sanctifying grace is *imparted* to the believer and that it actually changes the believer's inward disposition. The gift of salvation brings a real change, not only in our standing before God but also *in us*.

Another difference between Nazarenes and Lutherans is over the doctrine of *the Lord's Supper*. The Lutheran doctrine of consubstantiation is not held by any other Christian church. It is a distinctive Eucharistic doctrine that marks Lutherans out from other Christians.

Worship style is another area of difference. In Lutheranism, Pietism did not displace liturgical worship but was a supplement to it. Nazarenes, on the other hand, brought Pietism into the sanctuary and made it their dominant mode of worship. Nazarene pietism, however, has been shaped by the camp meeting and revival tradition.

Finally, the Nazarene concept of *the general church* is quite different. When Lutherans think of their denomination, they always think in national terms. Nazarenes, on the other hand, think in international terms. Our church is a global church, and we strive to be world Christians.

Our debt to Lutheranism is great. But our denominational emphasis and doctrines have been shaped by other Christian traditions as well, particularly Anglicanism and its Methodist offshoot. Our debt to Lutheranism is only one of many debts.

Review and Reflection

1. What role did Renaissance humanism play in the Reformation? How did this humanism differ from secular humanism?

2. How have you personally experienced the doctrine of justification by faith? What part does it play in your own theological thinking?

3. How does Luther's doctrine of consubstantiation differ from the Nazarene concept of Holy Communion?

4. What are some areas you see in which Lutheran Pietism influences Nazarene beliefs and practices?

CALVIN AND HIS KIN:
PRESBYTERIAN AND REFORMED CHURCHES

Principal Founder and Leader

John Calvin (1509-64) is considered the primary father of Reformed theology. He led the Protestant Reformation in Switzerland and France. His *Institutes of the Christian Religion* form the foundations for Reformed churches today.

Core Beliefs

Total depravity
Unconditional election
Limited atonement
Irresistible grace
Perseverance of the saints

The soil in which this TULIP grows is the doctrines of God's absolute sovereignty and predestination.

Agreement and Differences

We share with Reformed Christians beliefs in the Holy Trinity, the authority of Scripture, the priesthood of all believers, and salvation by grace.

Nazarenes, however, beg to differ with every petal of the Reformed TULIP.

Today's Reformed Christians

The main American denominations springing from Reformed roots, with their approximate membership totals, are as follows:

- Presbyterian Church (U.S.A.), 3.7 million
- United Church of Christ, 1.5 million
- Reformed Church in America, 309,000
- Presbyterian Church in America, 268,000

Reformed churches in other countries include the Church of Scotland, the Dutch Reformed Church, and the Swiss Reformed Church.

end is to glorify God, and to enjoy him forever.
—Westminster Shorter Catechism

CALVIN AND HIS KIN: PRESBYTERIAN AND REFORMED CHURCHES

JOHN WESLEY NAMED THE PAPER for his Methodist followers the *Arminian Magazine*. The title distinguished the *Wesleyan* Methodists from the *Calvinistic* Methodists led by George Whitefield, a colleague to whom Wesley was indebted for many things—but not his theology.

We often use the terms "Calvinism" and "Arminianism," but what do they mean? Calvinism is a system of theology that developed in Switzerland. It became one of the great Reformation traditions. It is often referred to as "Reformed theology," for John Calvin was not the first (nor the only important) theologian to shape this perspective.

Zwingli

Ulrich Zwingli (1484—1531) was Zurich's outstanding preacher when Luther's writing stirred the Reformation tempest. A proficient Greek scholar and humanist, he quickly grasped the implications of Luther's new theology but developed his own theology of the Word. The issue of Scripture's authority spurred Zurich's Reformation onward, not the issue of personal salvation, as it had for Luther. Zwingli arranged public debates to promote Protestant teachings and led Zurich to purge Catholic elements from its religious practices.[1]

Zwingli emphasized the Holy Spirit as the Author of Scripture and indispensable Guide to its interpretation. He affirmed *sola scriptura*—the principal of Scripture as the final authority in deciding matters of faith. His *Commentary on True and False Religion* (1525) showed how important the Holy Spirit was in his baptismal theology. Zwingli insisted that water baptism and Spirit baptism are both necessary to make a Christian. One may experience water baptism first and Spirit baptism later, or the order may be reversed, or they may coincide, but inner and outer baptism are both necessary, in Zwingli's opinion, for salvation.[2]

---

1. A useful survey of Zwingli's career is found in John T. McNeill's *History and Character of Calvinism* (London: Oxford University Press, 1954), 18-52. The book also contains a minibiography of John Calvin's life and thought.
2. Ulrich Zwingli, *Commentary on True and False Religion* (Durham, N.C.: Labyrinth Press, 1981), 185-97.

Zwingli's theology of Communion provoked his greatest public disagreement with Luther. Zwingli rejected Catholic and Lutheran versions of Christ's bodily presence in the consecrated bread and wine. When Jesus said, "This is my body," Zwingli understood Him to say that the bread signifies His body. The words are symbolic, Zwingli said, and doctrines of Christ's bodily presence merely confuse the symbols with the things they signify. Zwingli was adamant: the Catholic mass, which reenacts the Eucharist, does not have power to forgive sins. The forgiveness of sins comes only through the unrepeatable act of Jesus' death and resurrection. The Eucharist always points back to the Cross.[3]

When a Swiss Catholic army attacked Zurich, Zwingli defended his city. He perished in the Battle of Kappel in 1531. His dying words, reportedly, were from Socrates: "They may kill the body but not the soul."[4] His body was dismembered and burned, but Zurich's Reformation endured and spread to other Swiss cities.

John Calvin

John Calvin (1509-64) was the Reformer of Geneva. Born in France, he trained in biblical studies, as Luther and Zwingli had done, earning degrees at Paris and at other French universities. A religious conversion in about 1533 changed his life and outlook.

Calvin moved to Switzerland in 1535. His *Institutes of the Christian Religion* (1536) first appeared in Basel. A small book at first, it reappeared in ever larger editions throughout his lifetime. The final edition, with over 80 chapters, set forth Reformed theology's central themes.

Calvin was passing through Geneva, stopped to visit, stayed to lecture, and was appointed as one of its preachers. He drew up plans for a model Christian state but was banished due to conflict with city officials. He moved to Strassburg and ministered to exiled French Protestants for three years. There he married a widow. He was invited back to Geneva in 1541 and remained there until his death. He wrote many biblical commentaries. He introduced a new Protestant liturgy to Geneva's churches that emphasized congregational singing.

The Presbyterian System

One of Calvin's innovations was to restructure Geneva's churches. He identified four church offices that he believed Christ instituted: pastor, teacher, deacon, and elder. In the Geneva system, the pastors preached, met weekly to discuss the Scriptures, and instructed ministerial candidates. They also met quarterly to discipline those in their ranks who had offended. The pastors were all equal, without a bishop or superior officer over them. Deacons cared for the poor. Teachers educated the young. The elders—12 laymen—met weekly with pastors to apply church discipline against lay offenders.[5]

Democratic elements—the laity's participation in governance, the lack of a

---

3. Ibid., 233-34.
4. McNeill, *History and Character of Calvinism,* 52.
5. Lefferts A. Loetscher, *A Brief History of the Presbyterians,* 4th ed. (Philadelphia: Westminster Press, 1983), 25-26; McNeill, *History and Character of Calvinism,* 161-68.

bishop or superintendent—marked the Genevan way. This model became the heart of the presbyterian form of church government.

The Theater of God's Glory

John Calvin adopted Luther's doctrine of justification by grace through faith and saw its truth confirmed in Scripture and his own experience. But he placed this doctrine in a larger context, namely his view of predestination. He believed that God mercifully chooses to save certain individuals but not others, in spite of their sins. How did he gain this understanding?

Calvin began with the majesty of Almighty God, who creates the world as the theater of His glory. God's divine glory is reflected in two arenas: nature, where God creates and sustains; and the redemptive drama, where God shows divine purity and love through the mercies of His Son, Jesus Christ.

God gives "common grace" to all, causing the sun to shine and the rain to fall on good and wicked alike. While some may feel that the natural laws governing the universe with machinelike efficiency indicate God's remoteness, Calvin saw it differently. He regarded nature's laws as signs of God's continuing presence and action.

Common grace is given to all, but redemptive grace, Calvin thought, is offered only to some. "Predestined" is a scriptural term that Calvin understood in a distinctive way—as "predetermined" for saving grace. God chooses—out of the mass of sinful and alienated humanity—individuals to enjoy the benefits of Christ's atonement. They are not chosen due to any inward or outward merit, but simply to participate in God's redemptive drama. Calvin's view of predestination is linked, then, to the idea of "limited atonement"—the notion that Christ's death does not offer the possibility of salvation to all, but only to those God has preselected to save.

> *Paul Tillich, a 20th-century theologian, noted, "It is remarkable how little Calvin had to say about the love of God."*

The drama of redemption unfolds in human history. At the final Judgment, God shows His glory and power by saving those who were elected to receive divine mercy and justly punishing those who were not.[6]

Paul Tillich, a 20th-century theologian, noted, "It is remarkable how little Calvin had to say about the love of God. The divine glory replaces the divine love. When he speaks of the divine love, it is love toward those who are elected. The universality of the divine love is denied."[7]

And yet Calvin's doctrine of predestination actually assured his flock! It affirmed that there is a merciful God who redeems some, even though no one *deserves* divine grace. In an age riddled with superstitious belief in witchcraft and astrology, Reformed theology taught Christians that their fate did not lie in

---

6. McNeill, *History and Character of Calvinism*, 208-14.
7. Paul Tillich, *A History of Christian Thought* (New York: Simon and Schuster, 1968), 270.

the stars nor is subject to an evil spell. Individual destiny was in the hands of God, who demonstrates justice and mercy.

Calvin pointed to specific signs of election—a love for the church, spiritual things, and right living. These indicate (but not prove) that God's grace is effective for salvation in one's life. Those whom God elects are drawn to grace. They do not choose it; it chooses them. But it does become real. Therefore, God has appointed certain ways of making divine grace effective in the lives of the elect.

The sacraments, the Scriptures, preaching, and the living community of faith are among God's methods to bring His elect to salvation. These means prepare the chosen ones for grace and strengthen those who are given saving faith. Calvin joined other Protestant Reformers to affirm *sola fide,* by "faith alone," as salvation's basic principle. By faith alone the elect receive saving grace. By faith alone they continue in its promises. But this faith is a gift, given only to a few.

Can "the elect" backslide in Reformed thinking? Only in a limited sense. They can fall away from the church, but they do not lose God's saving grace. Just as a beloved child can destroy his or her life with alcohol or drugs but still be loved, so the elect can slip into sinful ways without losing God's promise of salvation. Indeed, sin is understood in Reformed theology essentially as straying from God's perfection. So Calvinists often say that we sin daily in thought, word, and deed.

Calvin agreed with Luther and Zwingli that infants should be baptized. He argued that infant baptism was the sign of covenant relationship among Christians just as circumcision testified to covenant relationship among the Jews. One need not despair, however, if an unbaptized infant dies. If God has predestined that child for salvation, then the child is truly saved, regardless.

Calvin readily responded to those who objected that the New Testament does not mention infant baptism. The Scriptures, he said, never mention that women partook of the Lord's Supper, but who would bar them from this sacrament on an argument based on silence? No one. Then why bar infants from baptism when the argument for doing so is also based on silence? Calvin, Luther, and Zwingli all agreed that baptism relates more to the faithful covenant community than to one's individual salvation.[8]

The Third Use of the Law

Luther and Calvin disagreed over the law's relationship to the gospel. Luther contrasted law and gospel, depicting the "two uses of the law" in a negative light. The law's first use, Paul made clear, is to reveal our sin before God, convict us, and prepare us to receive the gospel as the sole basis of salvation. The second use of the law is to restrain evildoers. As free people in Christ, Christians live by faith, not law. But the whole world is not made up of Christians. So the law restrains those who do not live by faith in Christ. For Luther, law and gospel stand in tension.

Calvin went beyond Luther, writing about "the third use of the law"—its ability to shape our lives as disciples by giving moral guidance. In this respect, the

---

8. John Calvin, *Institutes of the Christian Religion,* ed. John T. McNeill, trans. Ford Lewis Battle (Philadelphia: Westminster Press, 1960), 2:1324-33.

law teaches and has a positive function in Christian life. It shapes and gives content to Christian character.[9] The Ten Commandments, for instance, help inform the godly conscience. New England Puritans—spiritual descendants of Calvin— typically had these "Two Tables of the Law" mounted in their sanctuaries. John Wesley was closer to Calvin, not Luther, on this important Reformation debate.

Calvin's embrace of the "third use of the law" gave Reformed theology a different attitude toward the world than Luther's theology did. It made Calvinists more optimistic about the gospel's ability to transform societies and promote social justice. Many Calvinists saw religious and secular law as agents in Christ's work of renewing nations and communities.

Reformed Churches Proliferate

Calvin's theology and the presbyterian system of church government provided a strong alternative to Roman Catholicism. The doctrine of predestination made the Catholic system of penance unnecessary, while Presbyterianism— rooted in collegiality and lay participation—was antithetical to Catholicism's hierarchical structures. While Lutheranism retained features of the Catholic mass, Reformed worship did not. It put the sermon, not the Eucharist, at the center of worship. So Catholicism's fiercest foes tended to gravitate toward the Geneva model. "Geneva and Rome" came to represent opposite poles. Denominations descended from this tradition are usually distinguishable by the "Reformed" and "Presbyterian" label in their names.

The Geneva model spread. Some German states became Reformed, and in the 19th century secular rulers forced most of Germany's Lutheran and Reformed churches to cooperate in one state church. Today Germany's Protestant state church views both the Lutheran and Reformed traditions as its own.

The Reformed tradition had greater impact on three other state churches— the Swiss Reformed Church, the Dutch Reformed Church, and the Church of Scotland. All embraced the Geneva way, restructuring church government and theology along similar lines. The French Huguenots, bitterly driven from their native lands in the 17th century, also followed the Reformed tradition. Calvinist sympathizers also have composed a significant body of ministers within the Church of England from the Reformation to today, including the Puritans. Most English and American Baptists also accept many key tenets of Reformed theology but disagree with its concepts of church government and infant baptism.

The Dutch and Scots were influential in disseminating the Reformed tradition worldwide. Dutch colonists took the Reformed church to South Africa, Asia, and America. Scots took it to North Ireland, where antagonism between Scotch-Irish Presbyterians and Catholics have disturbed that island's peace ever since. Scottish immigrants also established Presbyterianism in America, joining the Puritan founders of New England's Congregational Church and the continental immigrants who brought the Swiss, German, and Dutch Reformed Churches with them.

---

9. Ibid., 1:348-66, esp. 360-62.

Arminius Takes Aim

Calvin's successors took Reformed theology to new extremes. Theodore Beza embraced a view called "double predestination." Beza reasoned that if God predestines some to salvation, then He just as surely predestines the others to damnation. Some Reformed thinkers asserted that God's decision to save and damn was the first decree, and the decision to create the world was made in order to carry out that intention.

Another group of Reformed churchmen moved in a different direction and embraced a very different understanding of salvation. It was called Arminianism, after Dutch theologian James Arminius (ca. 1559—1609). Holland, England, and later America became the chief centers of Arminian thought.

Arminius studied with Beza in Geneva before he was installed as a preacher in Amsterdam in 1587. He played an important role in establishing the Reformed Church in Holland. In 1603 he became professor of theology at Leiden University. Arminius saw himself as a faithful son of the Dutch Reformed Church in spite of the different understanding he developed on predestination and issues linked to it.

Arminius agreed with Calvin's doctrine of total depravity, the idea that there is no merit in us that can lay a claim on God for our salvation. But he held that Christ's atonement offers salvation to every person. Scripture, he believed, teaches that Christ intended the benefits of His atonement to be *universal,* not *limited* as Calvin taught. They also are *conditional*—based on faith and repentance—not *unconditional* and *irresistible* as Calvin understood them to be for "God's elect."

Arminius's logic led to another conclusion: since faith is conditional, one who has accepted God's saving grace can lose it by backsliding through severe or persistent sin. This contrasted starkly to Calvin's doctrine of the perseverance of the saints, which was grounded in his view of predestination.

Arminius had powerful Dutch supporters, but his doctrines were condemned 10 years after his death by an international council of Reformed theologians meeting in Dort, Holland. The Arminians were forced from the Dutch Reformed Church and established a separate denomination, the Remonstrant Church, which still exists in Holland.[10] But the struggle between Calvinism and Arminianism was far from over. Its critical arenas shifted to England and America, among other places.

Controversy in Britain and America

Calvinism and Arminianism have a long and complicated history in England and America, and only a few milestones can be enumerated.
- Under John Knox's resourceful leadership, the Church of Scotland embraced Reformed theology and presbyterian government.
- Reformed theology influenced the English Reformation and its Thirty-nine Articles of Religion drawn up under Archbishop Thomas Cranmer's guidance.

---

10. McNeill, *History and Character of Calvinism,* 263-66. The definitive biography of Arminius in English is Carl Bangs, *Arminius: A Study in the Dutch Reformation* (Nashville: Abingdon Press, 1971).

- The Church of England eventually positioned itself as a via media —a middle way—between Rome and Geneva. It came to see itself as Catholic *and* Reformed.
- The Puritans were originally members of the Church of England who disagreed with the principle of the via media and wanted to exclude all Catholic elements and abolish the office of bishop from the church.
- When James I came to England's throne in 1603, the Puritans presented him with a list of demands. He ignored all but one: their request for a state-authorized translation of the Bible in English.
- The leaders of the via media party were known by the early 1600s as Arminians, since many of them had come to reject predestination and related doctrines of Reformed theology.
- The Puritan-Arminian conflict began as religious, became political, and finally was a cause of the English Civil War in the 1640s, which the Puritans won.
- The Puritans controlled England for a decade and a half but could not agree on a government for the Church of England. Some advocated Presbyterianism, like the Church of Scotland, but others insisted on strict congregationalism.
- The Westminster Assembly was English Puritanism's high-water mark. A convocation of Puritan preachers and theologians, it produced the Westminster Confession of Faith (1647) and the Westminster Catechism —landmark documents in Presbyterian history.
- Once the Puritans were overthrown and the via media reestablished (1661), the presbyterian and congregational parties left the state church and formed separate denominations.
- America's New England Puritans had their greatest affinity with old England's congregational party but were part of the Church of England in theory (not practice) until the American Revolution. They became the Congregational Church and merged with the Evangelical and Reformed Church in 1957 to create the United Church of Christ.
- Immigrant Scots brought Presbyterianism to the American frontier, where they competed with Baptists (who shared their Calvinism but not their church government) and Methodists (who opposed their government *and* theology).
- Early English Methodism had a Calvinistic wing led by George Whitefield and a Wesleyan-Arminian wing led by John Wesley.
- A quarrel over predestination estranged Wesley from Whitefield, and for several years they did not speak to each other. Wesleyan Methodism became the leading proponent of Arminian theology in England and America.
- Some of Whitefield's followers remained in the Church of England and were the base for its Evangelical party. Wesley's followers in England and America eventually separated from the mother church. After Whitefield's death, the term "Methodist" increasingly came to mean "Wesleyan."
- When Methodism came to America in the 1760s, it entered a religious

culture dominated by Reformed churches and modes of thought. But by 1850 the Methodist Episcopal Church was America's largest denomination, and its Arminian principles were affecting the beliefs and behavior of people in Presbyterian and Reformed Churches. Methodists did not simply accept the dominant religious culture but started changing it.

- Methodist clergy often debated Calvinist preachers. Predestination was a favorite topic.
- Nazarene theologian H. Orton Wiley represented the Arminian viewpoint in a 1959 discussion of grace and election with Reformed theologians Carl Henry and Roger Nicole and Anglican theologian Geoffrey Bromiley. It was printed in *Christianity Today*.[11]
- Most nondenominational Bible studies teach Scripture from a Reformed perspective even when their leaders claim that they "want to teach only God's Word, not man's." This is true of most parachurch groups, including Bill Gothard's Institute in Basic Life Principles seminars and Campus Crusade for Christ, which teaches a mild Calvinism.

Reformed Denominations in America

The largest Reformed church in America is the *Presbyterian Church (U.S.A.)* with almost 3.7 million members. It is the accumulation of at least 10 church mergers in the past 250 years.[12] Its roots lie in the first American presbytery (local association of churches), formed in 1706 and in the first American synod (regional body), which formed 10 years later.

Presbyterians divided in the 1830s into New School and Old School parties. New School Presbyterians were open to revivalism, while the Old School was more consistently Calvinistic. Other divisions soon appeared. The New School divided into separate Northern and Southern churches over the slavery issue, while the Old School did the

The Reformed people nearest to America's heart are the New England Puritans, who shaped the idea of America as a haven for religious refugees.

same once the Civil War began. New and Old School Presbyterians in the North eventually reunited. Old School Presbyterians in the South evolved into the dominant Presbyterian church in that region. In 1983 the Northern and Southern Presbyterians reunited, creating the Presbyterian Church (U.S.A.).

The Reformed people nearest to America's heart are the New England Puritans, who shaped the idea of America as a haven for religious refugees. By 1800 the Puritan churches had evolved into the Congregational Church. In the 19th century Congregationalists worked closely with Presbyterians under the Plan of Union, an agreement by which the two denominations agreed not to compete in planting churches on the frontier. This insured that the resources of

11. "The Debate over Divine Election," *Christianity Today* 4, No. 1 (October 12, 1959): 3-18.
12. Bedell, *Yearbook of Churches, 1996,* 94.

both groups were used more effectively to establish the Reformed tradition in the West. An example of this cooperation is found in the ministry of Presbyterian revivalist Charles Finney, who pastored several Congregational churches. Outstanding Congregationalist preachers include pastor-theologians Jonathan Edwards and Horace Bushnell, abolitionist Lyman Beecher and his son, the noted pulpiteer Henry Ward Beecher.[13]

In 1961 the Congregational Church merged with the Evangelical and Reformed Church, creating the *United Church of Christ*. David Stowe, brother of retired Nazarene general superintendent Eugene Stowe, was a United Church of Christ missionary and headed his denomination's world mission agency. Today this denomination has 1.5 million members in the United States.[14]

Neither the Presbyterian Church (U.S.A.) nor the United Church of Christ require strict fidelity to traditional Reformed theology today. Both have allowed members to accept 20th-century theologies. At the same time, there are still congregations, pastors, and laity in these denominations who adhere to traditional versions of Reformed theology.

> *At least two generations of Phineas F. Bresee's ancestors were married in the Dutch Reformed Church in Albany, New York.*

Two other Reformed denominations are noteworthy. The *Reformed Church in America* dates to the founding of a Dutch Reformed congregation in 1628 in New Amsterdam (now New York City). The denomination grew through continuing Dutch and German immigration and was greatly augmented in the 19th century. At least two generations of Phineas F. Bresee's ancestors were married in the Dutch Reformed Church in Albany, New York. The denomination's present name, adopted in 1867, represented its growing German membership and the Americanization of its Dutch base. The Reformed Church in America is an Evangelical body with an inclusive membership of over 309,000. Television preacher Robert Schuller is a member of this denomination, as was Norman Vincent Peale. It is a charter member of the National Council of Churches and the World Council of Churches and projects a conservative influence within these ecumenical bodies.[15]

The *Presbyterian Church in America (PCA)*, a relative newcomer, was organized in 1973 by congregations opposed to the merger talks that created the Presbyterian Church (U.S.A.) a decade later. The PCA has an inclusive membership of 268,000. It holds a strict view of biblical inerrancy and strongly opposes women's ordination, which it views as compromise with biblical guidance. Reaction to women's ordination in the Presbyterian Church (U.S.A.) fueled the defection of conservatives from that body into the PCA during the 1980s. The

---

13. L. W. Wilshire, "Congregationalism," in Reid et al., *Dictionary of Christianity in America*, 309-11.

14. Bedell, *Yearbook of Churches, 1997*, 257.

15. E. J. Bruins, "Reformed Church in America," in Reid et al., *Dictionary of Christianity in America,* 985-86.

PCA adheres strictly to the Westminster Confession and Westminster Catechism.[16]

Korea

Presbyterian missionaries were the first Protestants to arrive in Korea in the 19th century. Today over 20 percent of South Korea's 44 million citizens are Presbyterians. They account for over half of that country's Christians and for 60 percent of its Protestants. Yim Sung Bihn, a seminary professor in Seoul, believes that the "democratic church structure coupled with a respect for elders" that is fundamental in Presbyterianism fits well with Korean culture. He notes that Korean Baptists and Methodists have adopted Presbyterian features.[17]

Similarities . . . and Differences

John Wesley, stout foe of Calvinism, presided at a Methodist conference (1745), which affirmed that "the truth of the gospel lie[s] very near . . . to Calvinism . . . within a hair's breadth." What on earth did they mean?

Wesley and his associates listed three fundamental points where Calvinists were right: (1) in "ascribing all good to the free grace of God," (2) in denying that people have a *natural* free will to choose the gospel, and (3) in denying that humans have any natural merit that saves us; rather, the good we do is a response to God's grace, not a claim upon it."[18]

What about this matter of denying that we have "a natural free will"? Do we not *choose* to be Christians? Indeed. But Wesleyan theology asserts that our ability to choose God is a *gracious* ability—given by God through prevenient grace—not a natural ability. Our natural free will was marred by sin, but God graciously restores our ability to respond to the gospel. Wesley's (and our) argument with Calvinism turns not on whether free will is natural or gracious, but on whether God's gift of gracious ability extends to all or only a preselected few. Traditional Calvinists say only to a few. We say to everyone.

There are other fundamental points where Wesley—and Nazarenes—agree with the Reformed tradition: on Scripture as the primary authority for deciding doctrine (*sola scriptura*); on the reality of original sin, which strips us of any claim upon God for salvation based upon merit; and faith in Christ as God's design for communicating saving grace. We, like Wesley, also tend to agree with Calvin's "third use of the law"—its ability to shape and inform Christian discipleship.

Our critical differences emerge around a cluster of doctrines linked to grace and election. Like Arminius, we believe that

- Christ's atonement was for all (not just a few).
- Salvation is conditional on faith and repentance (not unconditional for those who are elect).
- God's gracious offer of salvation can be resisted (not irresistible for the elect).
- Saving grace can be lost by severe or persistent sin.

16. A. H. Freundt, "Presbyterian Church in America," ibid., 929-30.
17. "Presbyterian Groups Grow Rapidly in Korea," *Christian Century*, September 25—October 2, 1996, 888.
18. John Wesley, *Works*, 8:284-85.

Other critical differences with Calvinism are related to what Wesley brought to our theology over a century after Arminius. Among them:

- Prevenient grace drawing us toward salvation
- Sanctification as God's inward work that begins in the new birth (regeneration) and leads, through His grace, to entire sanctification of our heart
- Faith as the method by which God sanctifies the heart (not good works and not separation from the body)

Another basic difference: Reformed churches view their presbyterian government as scriptural. It has theological, not just organizational, meaning to them. We understand church government quite differently and deny that a particular pattern of church organization is taught in Scripture. In theory, our polity combines principles and pragmatism in ways central to carrying out our mission. In practice, Nazarene government combines episcopal, presbyterian, and congregational elements. Our assemblies, based on the Methodist system of conferences, show elements of presbyterian influence on Methodism and on us. So, too, does the practice of electing ministerial candidates to elder's orders at district assembly and inviting ordained elders to participate in the laying on of hands for new ministers.

The Reformed tradition has played a critical role in Protestant development and contributed elements to Nazarene practice and belief. But fundamental differences over the way of salvation and Christian holiness place us altogether in another category.

Review and Reflection

1. Recruit a study partner (maybe your pastor) to help you put in your own words the concepts behind TULIP as well as the Nazarene and Wesleyan-Holiness challenges to this system. Start by defining terms. Then come up with affirmations of faith that state the position from both sides. Enter these in your journal or notebook.

Reformed Belief

Total depravity
Unconditional election
Limited atonement
Irresistible grace
Perseverance of the saints

Wesleyan Affirmation

_____

_____

_____

_____

_____

2. What in the Reformed tradition do you most respect or admire? At what point do you most vigorously disagree with Reformed thinking?

3. In what kind of ventures could your church join with Reformed churches in your community?

- Joint Easter and Christmas services
- Food and clothing distribution
- Citywide revival campaign
- The ministerial alliance
- Advocacy programs for better housing for the poor
- Youth ministry—camps, recreation programs
- Ministry to the disabled or ill, such as hospice service
- Dialogues on race relations
- Other _____
- Other _____

What do you think of the slogan "Doctrine divides; service unites"?

4. If you have a friend who attends a Reformed church, see if he or she is comfortable with talking about the things that both churches can do (separately or together) to minister in Christ's name today.

CATHOLIC AND REFORMED: THE ANGLICAN PARADOX

Historical Roots

Church of England (Anglican) roots reach deep into Christian history. Its spirituality is rooted in the Celtic saints. Anglicanism began in the desire of Henry VIII to have a male heir. When Rome refused his request to divorce his wife, he took English Christians out of the Catholic church. Anglicanism's Protestant spirit is rooted in John Wycliffe and the thirst for church reform. Its theology and worship roots are in the thought and liturgy of Thomas Cranmer.

Core Beliefs

A Protestant view of the authority of Scripture. Belief in the Apostles' and Nicene Creeds. The practice of liturgical worship. The Thirty-nine Articles of Religion. The *Book of Common Prayer* shows that worship is the central concern of this church.

Agreement and Differences

The Nazarene tradition is more directly influenced by the Anglican Reformation than by Luther or Calvin. Our spiritual ancestors, John and Charles Wesley, were Anglican priests all their lives. Our Articles of Faith, originally formulated by Phineas F. Bresee, bear the influence of the Twenty-five Articles of Religion of the Methodist Episcopal Church, which John Wesley extracted from Anglicanism's Thirty-nine Articles of Religion. Our Articles of Faith on original sin, the Trinity, Christ, justification by faith, the sacraments, and the Bible sound like the Anglican creed.

We worship differently. Though Wesley found the seeds for his doctrine of holiness in Anglicanism, the way we think about the holy life is different from that of conventional Anglicanism. The range of Anglican beliefs is broader than Nazarene beliefs, which stay closely to Wesleyan-Arminian teachings.

Anglicans Today

Anglicans number approximately 70 million in 35 denominations worldwide. The Church of England—mother church of the Anglican communion—is the largest. The Episcopal Church is the principal Anglican denomination in the United States, with 2.5 million members. The Anglican Church in Canada has 850,000 members.

The "nearest of any . . . to the primitive Church."
—Archbishop William Laud

10 CATHOLIC AND REFORMED: THE ANGLICAN PARADOX

ANGLICANISM IS A WORLDWIDE COMMUNION of churches that trace their origin to the Church of England. The English Reformation began in Henry VIII's decision to separate the English church from the Roman Catholic Church and accelerated under his son Edward. Catholic and Protestant martyrs alike were created before Anglicans found their niche. The Church of England became the church of the via media (middle way)—Catholic *and* Reformed.

Celts and Catholics

When the Roman army withdrew from England, it left behind a small Christian population among the native Celts, who developed an indigenous church. A Celtic monk, Patrick, evangelized Ireland. Irish monks in turn planted monasteries along the coasts of Scotland and northern Europe.

England lacked the big cities that encircled the Mediterranean Sea, so Celtic Christianity developed very different patterns. Abbots (heads of monasteries) were the highest administrators in the Celtic church and outranked bishops. The office of bishop in the Celtic church was purely *spiritual*. Chosen as models of sanctity, bishops were charged with ordaining priests and raising the people's spiritual life.[1]

Angle and Saxon invaders brought pagan deities to England with them. But Christian reinforcements appeared when Pope Gregory the Great sent missionaries in 596 from Rome. Led by a monk named Augustine, they evangelized Kent and established a center at Canterbury. Augustine became a Roman Catholic bishop the next year. He laid plans to evangelize Britain and divide it into 12 episcopal areas. But his plan did not acknowledge the jurisdiction of the Celtic bishops already there.

The Celts evangelized England from the north, the Catholics from the south. Their missions eventually overlapped, and in 663 the Synod of Whitby determined England's religious future. The Northumbrian king chose the Catholic way, and English Christianity joined the mainstream of European

---

1. John R. H. Moorman, *A History of the Church in England,* 3rd ed. (London: Adam and Charles Black, 1973), 3-11; Stephen Neill, *Anglicanism* (London: Penguin Books, 1958), 8-11.

Christianity. Celtic patterns gave way to Catholic ones, and the pope became England's spiritual head. But Britons remembered their Celtic past. Bede (ca. 672—735), scholarly monk of Jarrow, saw to that in his *Ecclesiastical History of the English People.* Celtic rigor fused with Catholic vigor, especially among the Irish, who kept the lamp of Christian knowledge burning brightly when it dimmed later in most of Europe.[2]

John Wycliffe

A renaissance under the Saxon king Alfred the Great came and went, and then the Saxon kings vanished in the Norman Conquest of 1066. William the Conqueror replaced Saxon bishops and abbots with French clerics, and the Church of England was more tied to the Continent than ever.

Three hundred years later, an Oxford scholar named John Wycliffe (ca. 1320-84) emerged as a champion of church reform. His followers, called Lollards, were university men who popularized Wycliffe's ideas among ordinary folk. Wycliffe's principles included

- translating the Bible into the language of the people;
- affirming Scripture as the highest authority in matters of doctrine;
- the predestination of the elect to grace, meaning that God (not the Catholic sacramental system) determines who is saved and damned;
- restricting the papacy;
- emphasizing preaching as a greater means of grace than the Eucharist;
- simplicity as a key characteristic of apostolic character.

His disciples paid dearly for their devotion to reforming principles. Nearly all lost academic positions, and some were burned as heretics. But they made an impact on England. Wycliffe's ideas soon spread through Europe, inspiring a vigorous reform movement in Czech Bohemia under Jan Hus.[3]

When the English church separated from Rome in the 16th century, echoes of two traditions in its past ran counter to the Roman Catholic ethos: a Celtic past that preceded Romanism, and a heritage of Wycliffian dissent.

The Reformation

Lutheranism grew from Luther's quest for a new understanding of the gospel, and the Reformed tradition from Zwingli's logical outworking of the idea of scriptural authority. Anglicanism, on the other hand, originated in Henry VIII's desire to divorce his first wife after secretly marrying a second in the hope of producing a male heir. The pope refused to grant a divorce, and Parliament at Henry's instigation severed the church in England from the Roman Catholic Church. The pope's authority over the English church was then divided between the monarch and the archbishop of Canterbury.

At first the English Reformation was limited to reforming church government, abolishing monasteries and convents, and confiscating monastic lands and other assets for the crown. Henry harbored many Catholic sympathies but had his son educated by Protestants. Moreover, Thomas Cranmer, archbishop of

---

2. Moorman, *History of the Church in England,* 18-36.
3. Ibid., 118-22.

Canterbury, was much farther down the Protestant road in his personal thinking.

Cranmer made secret plans to reform Anglican worship and theology after Henry's death. Henry opposed clergy marriage; Cranmer secretly had a Lutheran wife he had married in Germany. Cranmer's theology leaned toward Calvinism. His opportunity to advance the Reformation came when young Edward ascended to the throne.

Cranmer produced articles of religion that Parliament adopted for the Church of England. He also helped produce the *Book of Homilies*—sermons that set forth Anglican doctrine on essential matters such as justification by faith. His greatest achievement was the *Book of Common Prayer,* introduced in 1549 and revised three years later. Cranmer wrote it in such a way that English citizens of different persuasions could find it meaningful. It contained prayer services for morning and evening worship, Sunday services, and services for holy days.

Edward died after six years, and his half sister, Queen Mary, tried vigorously to reestablish the Roman Catholic faith. Cranmer was burned at the stake in Oxford, as were Bishops Hugh Latimer and Nicholas Ridley. Over 250 others were also executed for heresy. But Mary's reign was also short, and she was succeeded by her half sister Elizabeth.

Anglicanism's via media was established under Elizabeth. Like Henry, she was Catholic at heart but a political realist. The daughter of Henry's second wife, she was a bastard child in Roman Catholic eyes and an illegitimate monarch. She allowed the religious refugees who had fled to Europe in Mary's reign back into England, and these "Marian exiles" brought a deeper understanding of Protestantism's logic and inner workings. Matthew Parker, once a Lutheran, became archbishop of Canterbury. Cranmer's articles of religion were the basis for the Thirty-nine Articles of Religion adopted by Parliament, and Cranmer's revised prayer book was restored.

Logic of the Via Media

What does it mean when a church is both Catholic and Reformed? How did Cranmer, Parker, and others see their church?

- They saw the Church of England as a church with roots in primitive Christianity.
- The Scriptures were worked thoroughly into Anglican worship—more so than in any other branch of Christianity.
- They embraced the Early Church fathers, the first commentators on Scripture, who shaped the doctrines of the Trinity and Christ's nature and defined the New Testament canon of Scripture.
- The Catholicism of the church fathers was regarded as more basic and universal than that of Roman Catholicism, with its claim of papal supremacy. Anglicans saw themselves as full participants in a Catholic tradition much broader than that of Rome.
- The episcopacy (or church with bishops) was an important bulwark against heresy in early Christianity. Bishops were retained as another point of identity with primitive Christianity.

The Anglican Reformers did not fully repudiate their medieval heritage. They rejected Roman Catholic additions to the broad Catholic tradition, such as papal authority. But they didn't throw out everything that was medieval. Both Celtic and Catholic saints remained models of holiness. At the same time, the Anglican Reformers

- embraced the Reformation doctrine of justification by faith;
- rejected Roman Catholic views of the sacraments, especially transubstantiation;
- affirmed scriptural authority in matters of church doctrine.

They were Protestant in another sense. Monasteries and convents remained closed, so the English church after Henry had a very different spiritual feeling to it than that of the Middle Ages.

Catholic in some respects, Anglicanism was shorn of Roman trappings. Protestant in doctrine, it was not doctrinaire. A leading 17th-century archbishop, William Laud, wrote that the Church of England was the "nearest of any church now in [existence] to the primitive church."[4]

Puritans

Some of Elizabeth's subjects rejected the ideal of the state church as a via media and sought change. Marian exiles, especially, wanted to dispose of the *Book of Common Prayer* and purge all that they considered a Roman Catholic remnant. They opposed episcopacy (governance by bishops), since John Calvin had taught that presbyterianism was the "true scriptural method." Members of this party were called "Puritans."

The via media party, on the other hand, could show that episcopacy existed in the first century—reflected, for instance, in the writings of Ignatius of Antioch (ca. 100)—and that bishops had played major roles in protecting the faith from heresy and in evangelizing the unsaved. The argument over the episcopacy revolved around issues of biblical and historical interpretation that neither side would concede. The protracted struggle continued for three generations before erupting in the reign of Charles I into the English Civil War.

The Civil War was a temporary Puritan triumph. Charles I and Archbishop Laud were beheaded, the *Book of Common Prayer* was thrown out, and Geneva's Calvinistic worship was brought in. But Puritanism was losing its focus. By 1660 it was divided into factions—presbyterian and congregationalist factions within the state church, Baptists and Quakers outside it. Some smaller Puritan groups expected Christ's imminent second coming. With little common purpose except to oppose the High Anglicans, the Puritans were unable to govern after their general, Oliver Cromwell, died. As Albert Outler stated, they proved that "prophets cannot rule" and "radicals cannot sustain consensus."[5] Anglicanism and the monarchy were soon restored.

During this conflict, Calvinism began withering away among High Church Anglicans. Archbishop Laud and others in his circle were Arminian in theology before the Civil War. With Anglicanism reestablished, the presbyterian and independent parties left the Church of England to set up new denominations, taking the leadership of English Calvinism with them.

---

4. Paul Avis, *Anglicanism and the Christian Church* (Minneapolis: Fortress Press, 1989), 139.
5. Albert C. Outler, "The Methodist Reformation," First Gray Lecture, Duke University, November 1983.

In the centuries that followed, three other religious movements also shaped Anglicanism: Evangelicalism, Anglo-Catholicism, and liberal theology.

Religion of the Heart

The Church of England's Evangelical party grew out of the 18th-century Evangelical Revival. That revival involved two sets of leaders and two theologies. The Arminian Methodists, led by the Wesleys, eventually became a separate denomination. Some of the Calvinistic Methodists, led by George Whitefield and supported by Selena, Countess of Huntingdon, also left the state church, but some stayed in. Whitefield was an important figure in the Evangelical Revival and America's Great Awakening. He traveled to America several times and established an orphanage in Georgia. Sometimes on good terms with the Wesleys and sometimes estranged (usually over theology), Whitefield combined social compassion with fervent revivalism. Lady Huntingdon's college, Trevecka, inspired the name of Trevecca Nazarene University in Nashville. Cambridge University was hospitable to the Evangelicals for a time and became a center of Evangelical influence.

A generation later, an Evangelical politician, William Wilberforce (1759—1833), played a central role in abolishing the slave trade in the British Empire (1807) and laying the

> *Lady Huntingdon's college, Trevecka, inspired the name of Trevecca Nazarene University in Nashville.*

groundwork for slavery's total abolition in 1833. A network of Evangelicals around Wilberforce, known as the Clapham Sect, worked diligently to outlaw cruel sports that victimized animals and people. They supported education reform, labor laws, helped form the Church Missionary Society, and secured a law that opened India to Christian missions. They met in banker Henry Thornton's drawing room to design legislative and public relations strategies and had evening prayer together before returning home.

They were convinced that England faced a moral crisis, so their Evangelical ethics were broad and social, not narrow and individualistic. They stood against the economic interests of their own class when that seemed necessary to being good disciples.[6] This blend of Evangelical religion and social conscience was reflected in the career of the liberal prime minister William Gladstone, and it is reflected today in the ministry of Evangelical writer and preacher John R. W. Stott.

Anglo-Catholics

The Evangelical Movement's passion eventually gave way to that of the 19th-century Oxford Movement. Its leaders were John Henry Newman, John Keble, and Edward Pusey. One of their objectives was to assert the church's spiritual independence from the state. In a nation where Parliament elected the Church of England's bishops, the Oxford reformers wanted to demonstrate that the church's existence depended on the gospel, not on acts of Parliament.

---

6. David L. Edwards, *Christian England* (Grand Rapids: Wm. B. Eerdmans Publishing Co., 1984), 3:83-94.

An objective was to uncover the roots of early Christian liturgy and to renew Anglican worship practices. Pusey, an Old Testament scholar, studied the Hebraic roots of early Christian worship. Newman explored patterns of Christian worship reflected in the writings of the Early Church fathers. They insisted that liturgical renewal was vital. But they also romanticized the church of the Middle Ages, drew close to Roman Catholicism, and criticized the Protestant Reformers. They spread their views through inexpensive tracts. Newman eventually converted to Roman Catholicism, but Keble and Pusey remained steadfast Anglicans. The Anglo-Catholics who followed them experimented with many new liturgical forms.

Liberal Theology

Another tendency emerged in 19th-century Anglican theology: a liberal Anglicanism with roots in the *broad church* movement. It minimized denominational distinctives and advocated a broad platform where those of many persuasions (and little persuasion) could stand together. Liberal theology had other roots, too, including new social theories, Darwinism and the new sciences, and higher criticism of the Bible.

J. Frederick Denison Maurice (1805-72) helped shape theology's new mood. Raised a Unitarian, Maurice converted to a Trinitarian view of God and became an Anglican priest and theologian. He saw Christ as the true Head of the human race who reconstitutes humanity through His atonement. Sin, for Maurice, is a failure to understand *who* and *what* we are in relation to Christ. It is confusion about our true identities. Conversion may be dramatic or not, but it always involves a new and penetrating clarity about our relation to Christ and others.

Maurice advocated Christian socialism. His view of history was thoroughly Christian and contradicted Karl Marx's dialectical materialism. The impetus for Christian social responsibility, Maurice asserted, arises out of Christ's self-giving to us. Maurice helped found a workingman's college in London so ordinary workers could gain some education. He was also the first Anglican theologian to deny in his writings the doctrine of the everlasting punishment of the wicked. He argued that "eternal punishment" was a quality of punishment, not a length of time.[7]

England is largely secular today. With low church attendance, its great cathedrals are national treasures more than houses of worship.

England is largely secular today. With low church attendance, its great cathedrals are national treasures more than houses of worship. In 1963 Bishop John Robinson addressed the skeptical soul of secular people in his book *Honest to God.* The Evangelical and Anglo-Catholic parties—at odds a century ago—are more charitable toward each other today as they face threats to Christian orthodoxy arising from secularism and liberal theology.

7. Moorman, *History of the Church in England,* 355-56.

Episcopalians

American Anglicanism dates to the early British settlement at Jamestown, Virginia (1607). By 1775 the Church of England was established by law in a majority of American colonies, including all those of the South.

The colonists were under the Bishop of London. With no bishop on American soil to ordain clergy, ministerial candidates traveled to England for ordination. English priests were also sent to the colonies to assist them, but there was still a chronic shortage of priests in the colonies—made worse when the English priests fled during the American Revolution. Those remaining, like Methodist-minded Devereaux Jarratt of Virginia, were stretched to the limit preaching and providing the sacraments to corners far removed from their regular parish.

American independence wrought change. Thomas Jefferson's statute on religious liberty became part of Virginia's constitution and disestablished Anglicanism there. Other states adopted a similar measure, as did the federal government.

Further change came when the Methodists withdrew in 1784 to organize the Methodist Episcopal Church. Five more years passed before the remaining Anglicans organized the Protestant Episcopal Church, commonly known as The Episcopal Church. Who can gauge for the Episcopalians the loss of the Methodists? In 1775 Anglicanism was the third largest denomination in America, and the Methodist societies were quite small; by 1850 the Methodists were the largest denomination in America, and the Episcopalians were fifth.

The Episcopal Church, Anglicanism's primary expression in the United States, has an inclusive membership of 2.5 million members. Its General Convention is divided into a House of Bishops and House of Deputies. The latter is composed of equal numbers of elected lay and clergy delegates. Legislation must pass both houses, though on some issues separate votes by clergy and laity are required. The Anglican Church in Canada is that country's principal Anglican denomination and has a membership of about 850,000.[8]

The Episcopal Church was strongly evangelical until the Anglo-Catholic movement was felt in America. In reaction, a group withdrew in 1783 to form the Reformed Episcopal Church, a Calvinistic denomination of under 7,000 members in the United States.[9]

Although Episcopalians have a reputation for liberal tolerance, the first women priests were not ordained in the United States until the 1970s, and the same did not occur in the Church of England until the mid-1990s. The strongest opposition to women's ordination came from Anglo-Catholics, some of whom have united with the Roman Catholic Church as a result. In the United States several small Anglo-Catholic denominations splintered off from the Episcopal Church over the women's issue and changes in the 1928 Prayer Book.

Anglican Writers

The English spiritual tradition is not limited to the *Book of Common Prayer.* It is also evident in several writers who have influenced contemporary Chris-

---

8. Bedell, *Yearbook of Churches, 1996,* 129, 246, 253.
9. Ibid., 255.

tianity, including C. S. Lewis, Evelyn Underhill, and Dorothy Sayers. Underhill specialized in devotional literature, and her study of Christian mysticism reflected deep personal interests. Lewis's fiction and nonfiction works have been popular since the 1960s, including *The Chronicles of Narnia* series for children. Sayers, a novelist, used fiction (including detective stories) to explore spiritual matters.

The Anglican Communion

The growth of the worldwide Anglican Communion was connected with the British Empire. Today over 35 self-governing Anglican churches have over 70 million members in 164 countries.[10] About once a decade, bishops of the Anglican churches gather in England for the Lambeth Conference. Over 500 bishops attended the 1988 conference, and over 700 were expected in 1998. In 1888 the Lambeth Quadrilateral was adopted as a set of theological landmarks. They affirm

- the Holy Scriptures of the Old and New Testaments as the only rule and ultimate standard of faith;
- the Apostles' Creed as a baptismal creed and the Nicene Creed as a statement of faith;
- the two sacraments of baptism and Lord's Supper ministered with Christ's words of institution;
- the historic episcopate, adapted locally to the needs of various nations and people.[11]

Anglican Distinctives

What distinguishes Anglicans? The Thirty-nine Articles of Religion have been interpreted widely by Calvinists and Arminians, Evangelicals and Anglo-Catholics. Anglicanism's focus, therefore, lies elsewhere, and that is in the *Book of Common Prayer.* Anglicans do not unite around a creed so much as around the reality of the Church as the worshiping people of God. The *Book of Common Prayer* contains a format for different worship services—Sunday worship, holy days, and morning and evening prayer. It also contains devotional material. Scripture is liberally sprinkled throughout these services, and the book is suitable for family and private worship.

Bishop Stephen Neill identifies other characteristics of Anglicanism:

- *Biblical quality.* This is expressed in creeds and liturgy, and Neill insists that "the Anglican Churches read more of the Bible to the faithful [during worship] than any other group of churches," and Anglican laity are urged to read the Scriptures in their home.[12]
- *Liturgical.* Members are expected to attend worship regularly and partake of the Eucharist. The aim of liturgical worship "is not that of producing immediate emotional results, but of gradually building up a settled res-

---

10. The Worldwide Anglican Communion home page <http://www.aco.org/index.htlm#index>, March 25, 1997.

11. F. L. Cross and E. A. Livingstone, eds., *The Oxford Dictionary of the Christian Church,* 2nd ed. (Oxford: Oxford University Press, 1974, rev. 1983), 795.

12. Neill, *Anglicanism,* 418.

olute will to holiness, based more on the direction of the will than on the stirring of the emotions."[13]

- *Continuity.* Anglicans embrace their Celtic, Catholic, and Protestant roots. They have a keen sense of belonging to the Church Universal.
- *Episcopacy.* The episcopacy is viewed as an apostolic link to early Christianity and as a tie to the Church in all ages.
- *Saintliness.* A life of holiness is affirmed, although Anglicans understand its moral dimensions and obligations differently than Nazarenes do. The strong spiritual core at the base of Anglican life is reflected in the *Book of Common Prayer.*[14]
- *Comprehensiveness,* or inclusiveness. In the Church of England, this takes the form of gathering all the different segments of the English people into one church. "Is it not desirable," Neill asks, "that, among those who are agreed on the fundamentals of the Christian faith, there should be a measure of latitude in interpretation?"[15]

Anglican Influences

The doctrinal statements in the Nazarene *Manual* are closer to the Thirty-nine Articles than to any other Reformation creed. The reason is simple: Phineas F. Bresee prepared Articles of Faith for our church that were adapted from the Twenty-five Articles of Religion of the Methodist Episcopal Church. John Wesley, in turn, had adapted those from the Thirty-nine Articles.

> *The doctrinal statements in the Nazarene Manual are closer to the Thirty-nine Articles than to any other Reformation creed.*

A line of descent marks our doctrinal lineage. It can even be traced in specific phrases in our *Manual,* such as these on original sin:[16]

Thirty-nine Articles (Church of England)

Original sin . . . is the fault and corruption of the nature of every man, that naturally is engendered of the offspring of Adam, whereby man is very far gone from original righteousness, and is of his own nature inclined to evil, so that the flesh lusteth always contrary to the Spirit.

Twenty-five Articles (Methodist)

Original sin . . . is the corruption of the nature of every man, that naturally is engendered of the offspring of Adam, whereby man is very far gone from original righteousness, and of his own nature inclined to evil, and that continually.

Nazarene Manual (1908)

Original Sin is that corruption of the nature of all who are engendered as the offspring of Adam, whereby everyone is very far gone from original righteousness, and is inclined to evil, and that continually.

---

13. Ibid.
14. Ibid., 424.
15. Ibid., 426.
16. Harmon, *Encyclopedia of World Methodism,* 1:149; *Manual, Pentecostal Church of the Nazarene* (Los Angeles: Nazarene Publishing Co., 1908), 26-27; *Manual, Church of the Nazarene, 1997—2001,* 27-28.

Nazarene Manual (1997)

We believe that original sin, or depravity, is that corruption of the nature of all the offspring of Adam by reason of which everyone is very far gone from original righteousness . . . and inclined to evil, and that continually.

Anglican roots of Nazarene belief are evident in other doctrines, sometimes in identical phrases, sometimes in their general thrust, including those on

- the triune nature of God
- the work of Christ
- justification by faith alone
- the Scriptures
- baptism and the Lord's Supper (including the precise term "Lord's Supper")
- free will as God's gracious gift, not our natural ability

There are other linkages as well.

Our Wesleyan theology of salvation. The Wesleyan theology of salvation parallels the principle of the via media. Wesley married the Protestant emphasis on justification by faith with the Catholic (and Eastern Orthodox) emphasis on saintliness, or holiness. He understood more thoroughly than Catholic and Protestant predecessors that the faith that justifies the Christian generates evangelical love, or holiness, and that faith and love form an indivisible unity.

Paul Bassett has clarified the importance of the quest for holiness in pre-Reformation writers by showing how the *idea* of entire sanctification was expressed in the Early Church and in the Middle Ages as "entire devotement" to God. This was especially the goal of monastic life. But Wesley saw the pursuit of Christian perfection as the calling of all Christians and linked its attainment to the Protestant concept of grace through faith.

The doctrine of Scripture. The Church of England's Article VI, titled "Of the Sufficiency of the Holy Scriptures for Salvation," dates to the Protestant Reformation. "Sufficiency of Scripture" means that the Bible is the definite Guide to salvation, and that anything not found in the Bible cannot be imposed as an article of faith or considered necessary for salvation. John Wesley carried this doctrine over into Methodism's Articles of Religion, and it was taught through the Methodist course of study to our Nazarene founders of Methodist background. This has preserved the concept of Scripture in Anglicanism and Methodism from the static biblicism found in some Reformed thinkers.

The word "inerrantly" was added to the Nazarene article on Scripture in 1928, but it was done so strategically. Our statement reads that the Bible "inerrantly reveal[s] the will of God concerning us in all things necessary to our salvation." Thus the principle of sufficiency was preserved. H. Orton Wiley, who was writing his three-volume *Christian Theology* at the time, influenced the strategic positioning of this word.[17]

What essential differences separate Anglicanism and the Church of the Nazarene? They fall in three broad areas: doctrine, worship, and latitude.

---

17. Paul Merritt Bassett, "The Theological Identity of the North American Holiness Movement: Its Understanding of the Nature and Role of the Bible," in *The Variety of American Evangelicalism,* ed. Donald W. Dayton and Robert K. Johnson (Knoxville, Tenn.: University of Tennessee Press, 1991), 72-108.

Doctrine. The Nazarene *Manual* contains specific articles of faith that represent the heart of Wesleyan theology. These include statements on

- repentance,
- new birth (regeneration) and adoption by God,
- entire sanctification.

These are doctrines of spiritual life that were influenced by Pietism and took definite shape in John Wesley's theology. They are not necessarily inconsistent with Anglicanism, but neither are they specified there. But we specify them, and they distinguish us and our kin in the Wesleyan-Holiness tradition from other churches that came before us.

Worship. The *Book of Common Prayer* specifies an order of worship for a variety of occasions, but very little is specified in Nazarene worship. Our worship traditions have been shaped by the camp meeting, prayer meeting, revival, and evangelistic crusade. The public testimony, extemporaneous prayer, and kneeling at the altar rail in response to an invitation to receive Christ or to press on to Christian perfection are aspects of a very different worship tradition. The typical Sunday morning service of worship in the Church of the Nazarene reflects the personality and instincts of a particular pastor and people, not the cadences of the *Book of Common Prayer.*

Degree and type of doctrinal latitude. The doctrines of Anglicanism have been affirmed by radically diverse Christian groups, and that high degree of diversity seems unlikely in the Church of the Nazarene. Our Articles of Faith provide less "elbow room" and are oriented in a definite Protestant, Arminian, and Wesleyan direction. Nevertheless, the extent of this difference is less than it was a generation ago as Nazarene participation in parachurch movements with Calvinistic and Pentecostal biases are reshaping popular thinking in the church.

The Anglican tradition is important in Christian history and to Nazarenes. Our lineage splits off with the decision of American Methodists to form their own separate church. Nevertheless, it is through our Anglican roots that we are oriented most strongly toward the Protestant Reformation and to the Christian Church before the Reformation.

Review and Reflection

1. Sentence Stems

Finish these sentence stems in your own words:

If I had a lunch date with an Anglican pastor or friend tomorrow, one thing I would be sure to bring up is . . .

Two new things I learned from this chapter are . . .

If I could ask one question about the connection between the Wesleyan-Holiness way of doing religion and the Anglican heritage, it would be . . .

If I had to make a presentation on this chapter to a small group or to a class of adult students, the three most important ideas or facts that I would emphasize are . . .

2. *Book of Common Prayer*

John Wesley, Anglican priest and founder of Methodism, taught his people to use printed prayers as well as praying in their own words in both personal and corporate worship.

Here is one of Wesley's favorite prayers from the *Book of Common Prayer.* An Americanized version of this prayer appears in the Nazarene hymnal, *Sing to the Lord,* No. 58. Try it out in your devotions. Repeat this prayer until it becomes your own. Ponder its words. Wesley said it was the very outline of the holiness he taught and preached. Church of England worshipers to this day pray this prayer before taking Communion.

Following Wesley's advice to combine written and extemporaneous praying, pray this prayer from your heart. Then follow the leadings of the Spirit and your own spirit, and proceed to pray in your own words about whatever seems appropriate.

> *Almighty God,*
> *To whom all hearts be open,*
> *All desires known,*
> *And from whom no secrets are hid,*
> *Cleanse the thoughts of our hearts,*
> *By the inspiration of Thy Holy Spirit,*
> *That we may perfectly love Thee,*
> *And worthily magnify Thy holy name.*
> *Through Jesus Christ, our Lord.*
> *Amen.*

Part V
THE BELIEVERS' CHURCH TRADITION

- The Peace Churches: Anabaptists, Brethren, and Quakers

- The Baptists: A Priesthood of Believers

- Unity and Simplicity: The Christian Church (Disciples of Christ)

The Peace Churches:
Anabaptists, Brethren, and Quakers

Historical Roots

Anabaptists are rooted in the radical religious ferment of early 16th-century Europe. The complex movement sought a believers' church free from state interference. Many early Anabaptists were burned, hanged, or drowned. Menno Simons, from whom Mennonites take their name, was the best-known leader.

The Church of the Brethren was founded in 1708 by Alexander Mack in Schwarzenau, Germany. It blended the Anabaptist view of the church with German Pietism.

The Quakers, founded by George Fox and taught by Robert Barclay, came into existence in England a century before the Wesleyan revival sprang up. The teaching of the "inner light" distinguishes the Quakers.

Core Beliefs

1. Christian pacifism—refusal to participate in war—characterizes the peace churches today.

2. Separation of church and state.

3. Adult believers' baptism rather than infant baptism. (Quakers, however, believe in the baptism of the Spirit only.)

4. Discipleship, shunning worldliness, and a personal relationship with God characterize the peace churches.

5. Church discipline of backsliders.

Agreement and Differences

The Nazarenes share a believers' church perspective, redemptive social action, and the emphasis on discipleship and church discipline.

We disagree with all three peace churches on their respective theologies of the sacraments. While we respect the peace witness of the pacifist churches, we do not require our members to refuse military service.

Peace Churches Today

Contemporary Anabaptist churches include the Mennonite Church, General Conference Mennonite Church, Mennonite Brethren, Old Order Amish Church, and the Hutterite Brethren. Altogether, these groups have some 335,000 adherents in North America.

The Brethren began in Europe and reorganized in America on Christmas 1723. Now seven Brethren denominations have 256,000 members.

North American Quakers have several denominations, totaling about 124,000. Several early Nazarene leaders had Quaker backgrounds.

11 ~ THE PEACE CHURCHES: ANABAPTISTS, BRETHREN, AND QUAKERS

ITS HARD TO THINK OF A QUAINT AMISH COUPLE, riding in their horse-drawn buggy, as martyrs. What connection could they have to a pious German woman of another century, strapped to a ladder laid across a fire? Or what connection could there be between a congregation of 18th-century London Quakers —their hour-long worship punctuated by few words—and a relief worker feeding the starving in Bangladesh?

Quite a lot, as it turns out.

The Sermon on the Mount holds a special place in the theology and ethics of three families of churches: Anabaptists, Brethren, and Quakers. Generally, these groups reject the idea that Christians should participate in warfare. In the 20th century, their "peace witness" has led them into ministries of reconciliation, social justice, and worldwide networks of voluntary social service.

These groups are linked to another big idea that has exercised a powerful influence on modern Protestantism: the concept of the believers' church. The 16th-century Anabaptists were the modern pioneers of this theory. They rejected the legitimacy of official state churches, arguing that God's visible Church on earth should be composed only of those who testify to being regenerated and who voluntarily associate together. Quakers, Baptists, and Brethren emerged in subsequent centuries as faith traditions that also strongly embraced the believers' church concept.

While believers' churches are small in Europe, where state churches predominate, and in South America, where Roman Catholicism is strong, they are the dominant pattern of Christianity in North America, Africa, and Asia. The influence of Quakers in Pennsylvania, Delaware, and New Jersey, and Baptists in Rhode Island, made these places laboratories of religious freedom that influenced the ideals of the new American nation. Thus, the believers' church emphasis of these "peace churches" has given them greater influence on other religious groups than many realize.

The Radical Reformation

The Anabaptist movement was part of the "radical Reformation." The radical Reformation was not a cohesive wing like the Lutheran and Reformed wings. The radical wing included Socinians, precursors of modern Unitarianism, and

Spiritualists, who believed that all church organizations were fallen and sinful. To Spiritualists, the only church that counted was the "invisible Church" of true believers known only in God's heart and mind.

By contrast, Anabaptists joyfully embraced the idea of the visible Church in the world. But they sought to rescue the Church from those who linked it to the state's power. They believed that the Roman emperor Constantine's embrace of Christianity in the early fourth century was fatal for Christianity's spiritual health. From that point on, they believed, secular rulers had corrupted the religion of "the Powerless One" sent by God to save the world. Anabaptists saw this as a major flaw in Eastern Orthodoxy, Roman Catholicism, and the major branches of the Reformation.

"Anabaptist" means "rebaptized one." All those baptized as infants had to be rebaptized the first time they joined an Anabaptist congregation. Why? Because Anabaptists placed the highest importance on the holiness and integrity of the visible Church. Since baptism signifies incorporation into Christ's Church, they reasoned that it should be administered to those who show adult repentance and give evidence of regeneration. When their own children were born, they did not baptize them, as the Lutherans and Presbyterians did. They waited for their children to make their own public profession of faith.

These ideas of the Church and sacraments set Anabaptists apart from other churches of their day.

Anabaptist Origins

Anabaptism developed simultaneously in several parts of Europe. Its stronger centers were in Switzerland, southern Germany, Moravia, and Holland. The movement had a complex early history.

- Zurich was an early center. Conrad Grebel and Felix Manz led a group who concluded that Zwingli's reforms did not go far enough and that infant baptism was not supported by Scripture. They rebaptized one another on January 21, 1525. City officials viewed them as disturbers of the peace and persecuted them. Manz and his wife were put to death in 1527. As an ironic gesture, drowning was the mode of execution.
- Michael Sattler, once a Catholic monk, led a strong Anabaptist congregation in Strassburg, Germany. In February 1527, he presided over an Anabaptist assembly that convened in Schleitheim. It adopted seven articles of belief Sattler largely had written. He was burned to death three months later by Austrian officials.
- Other Anabaptist leaders perished between 1527 and 1529. These included Balthasar Hubmaier, burned to death in Vienna; George Blaurock, burned in the Tyrol; and Hans Hut, who died of disease and starvation in an Augsburg prison.
- Apocalypticism—the view that the world will soon end violently—captured the imagination of some Anabaptists in the 1530s. Jan Matthys, a Dutch baker, preached that he was a prophet sent to help bring in God's kingdom. Followers from Germany and Holland streamed to Münster, their New Jerusalem, and seized the city. Polygamy and a communistic

social order prevailed until the German princes recaptured the city and executed the leaders.

- Anabaptism made notable inroads into German Lutheranism until the Münster debacle. Afterward, its influence subsided.
- Menno Simons (1492—1559), a former Catholic priest, joined the Anabaptist movement shortly after the Münster episode. He was deeply moved by it, for he saw the Anabaptists of northern Europe as sheep without a shepherd. His pastoral style was crucial in preserving Anabaptism in Holland and northern Germany. Menno taught that Christ's gospel is one of peace, love, and service. Mennonites take their name from him.
- By 1540, two major Anabaptist denominations were coming into existence: Mennonites and Hutterites.
- Jan van Braght, Dutch Mennonite pastor, published *The Martyr's Mirror* in 1660. It dealt with the broader history of Christian martyrdom but emphasized Anabaptist martyrdom. The book has shaped Anabaptist self-understanding ever since. It reminds modern Mennonites that the way of Christian pacifism is not always an easy one.

Persecution

Why were Anabaptists persecuted by Catholics and Protestants alike? One reason is that Anabaptism developed in a time of social turmoil. The Peasants' Revolt in Germany (1524-25) was a climactic moment of class struggle, followed a decade later by the Münster episode. Anabaptism appealed to the poor and socially disenfranchised, and any movement that did so was regarded with suspicion by authorities.

Moreover, if the poor opted out of the state church while the wealthy did not, this would undercut the religious unity that princes usually enforced to help maintain social stability. The teaching that Christians should not participate in combat was also viewed with alarm. Rulers need soldiers to advance their aims. Roman Catholics tended to execute Anabaptist leaders for heresy. Protestants executed them for sedition.

Anabaptist Distinctives

The seven articles of religion that Michael Sattler presented to the Anabaptist conference in Schleitheim form the key document of early Anabaptist belief. The Schleitheim Confession states that:

- Baptism can be administered only to those who have repented and truly believe that Christ has taken away their sins, and accordingly have amended their lives.
- Church discipline is to be applied to those who backslide. They are to be dealt with privately, and if that does not lead to correction, they should be banned publicly before the congregation partakes of the Lord's Supper.
- The Lord's Supper is reserved only for those in the covenant community.
- Believers are to be separated from sin and evil. Worldliness is to be shunned.
- The "shepherd in the church" (pastor) must be a person of good character, chosen by the congregation.

- Members of "the flock" are to refrain from holding government office or from helping government officials wield "the sword" of secular power. God has instituted secular power to control evildoers. But Christians live by a higher law of love.
- Christians are not to swear oaths. Instead, their character is to be so high that swearing an oath would not add one whit to their credibility, for their yes always means yes, and their no always means no.[1]

The distinctive themes are clear: separation from the world, including the exercise of secular power; repentance; amendment of one's life; baptism as a sign of repentance and affiliation with the community of faith; and the church as a righteous, or holy, community.

While not every early Anabaptist was a pacifist, the Schleitheim principles were adopted by the movement's third generation, and they came to characterize all the Anabaptist groups that endured.

American Anabaptists

Dutch Mennonites eventually experienced toleration. But those in German states were constantly subject to military service. In the 1700s many moved to Pennsylvania. Still others emigrated to Russia at Catherine the Great's invitation, living there prosperously for several generations and blending German and Russian cultures. After 1880 many of the Russian Mennonites went to North America.

In North America the *Mennonite Church* was organized in colonial Pennsylvania. One of the earliest appeals against slavery by a religious group was issued by its Germantown, Pennsylvania, congregation. The Russian immigrants who later settled on farms on the Great Plains and western Canada tended to join a Mennonite Church offshoot, the *General Conference Mennonite Church*. Nearly half of its members live in Canada. The two denominations have committed themselves to a merger that should unite over 160,000 believers by 2000. The doctrinal basis for their merger is a new confession of faith titled "A Confession of Faith in a Mennonite Perspective."

Other Russian immigrants formed the *Mennonite Brethren* Church. Unlike traditional Anabaptists, Mennonite Brethren practice revivalism and reflect the impact of the pietist movement on Mennonite communities in Russia. There are 50,000 Mennonite Brethren in North America, the majority living in Canada.

The *Old Order Amish Church* is the most conservative branch of Mennonites. Followers of Bishop Jacob Ammann, they separated from other Mennonite bodies in 1693, migrating to America in the 1700s. Theirs is a network of house churches, each with a bishop and two other clergy chosen by lot to serve for life. To preserve themselves from cultural influences that they deem harmful, the Amish have built a cultural wall between themselves and the outside world, rejecting certain modern technologies and practices but not others. Nearly 81,000 Amish live in the United States, and an indeterminate number are in Canada.[2]

---

1. "The Schleitheim Text," *Gospel Herald,* February 27, 1977, 153-56.
2. Bedell, *Yearbook of Churches, 1997,* 257.

The *Hutterian Brethren* form another Anabaptist group. Their inclusive membership is over 41,000. They live in 375 colonies across North America and publish religious materials in English and German. Their children are taught to be bilingual. Their name derives from Jacob Hutter, who during the Reformation taught a doctrine of community of goods, using the Jerusalem church in Acts 2 as his model.[3]

Other Mennonites of German descent live in Mexico, Central America, and South America. In the 20th century, Mennonite missionaries have also taken their faith to Africa, Asia, and other world areas. The Meserete Kristos Church in Ethiopia, planted by Mennonite missionaries, has had indigenous leadership for a quarter century and currently has over 50,000 members.[4] The Mennonite World Conference, held every decade, brings together Mennonites from different nations, cultures, and races. It is held on a different continent each time.

Church of the Brethren

Nearly 200 years after the Reformation, the German Baptist Brethren emerged in Schwarzenau, Germany. They borrowed the Anabaptist view of the church and united it with the spiritual style of another movement called Pietism.

The Brethren founder was Alexander Mack, who in 1708 was rebaptized with seven others in the Eder River. Like all pietists, they taught the need of "awakening" to one's sinful condition and experiencing "the new birth." They conducted prayer meetings. Pietists such as John Wesley created discipleship groups within the state churches. But the Brethren insisted on a church free of state connections, marked by believers' baptism, a confession of personal faith in Christ as a condition for church membership, and the application of church discipline to backsliders. The Brethren also embraced Christian pacifism.

The Brethren insisted that the New Testament teaches baptism by immersion only. And they held that immersion must be administered three times (for Father, Son, and Holy Spirit) by leaning forward, not backward, into the water. Because they "dunked" baptismal candidates, the Brethren were also known as "Dunkards" and "Tunkers."

The Brethren were persecuted for their pacifism and for their attitude toward the state church, which they insisted was fallen. Most Brethren migrated to America beginning in 1719, and they organized an American church on Christmas Day, 1723.

Colonial Brethren were related closely to the Ephrata Cloister in Ephrata, Pennsylvania, a group of pietists who lived communally, and whose founder— Conrad Beisell—belonged to the Brethren for several years. They were also linked to Christopher Saur, a Germantown printer and pietist who published the first German-language Bible in America and played a critical role within the German-American community of the 1700s. In the 19th century, the Brethren followed the frontier and carved out farms in the wilderness.

---

3. Ibid., 88, 256.
4. Mennonite Central Committee, 1996 Workbook: Ethiopia, at:
<http://www.mbnet.mb.ca/mcc/workbook/1996/ethiopia.html>.

The emphasis on Evangelical spirit and faith, coupled with Anabaptist views of discipleship and church, provided a solid basis for Brethren unity for a century and a half. But the movement suffered a three-way split in the 1880s in the face of cultural pressures.

Ultraconservatives broke off and took the name *Old German Baptist Brethren.* They emphasize plain dress (their women wear bonnets) and maintain strong ethnic German traditions. Their 5,600 members registered a growth rate of only 20 percent in over 100 years.

The Progressive Brethren were on the other end of the spectrum. They sought to bring the Brethren up to date by adopting methods used by larger Evangelical churches. The Progressive Brethren today exist in two denominations: *The Brethren Church (Ashland, Ohio),* with fewer than 14,000 members, and the *Fellowship of Grace Brethren Churches,* with about 40,000 adherents.

The great majority of Brethren were in the middle. They modernized but did so more slowly than the Progressive Brethren. Some identified with liberal Protestantism. They took the name *Church of the Brethren* in 1908 and currently have about 143,000 members in the United States.[5] The Church of the Brethren maintains a strong "peace witness," which has not been the case with the Progressive Brethren denominations.

Quakers: The Inner Light

Every theology has controlling insights—powerful ideas at the center that shape the larger point of view. The controlling insight in Quaker theology is based on John 1:9, which speaks of Christ as "the true light, which enlightens everyone" (NRSV). To George Fox, the founder of the Quakers, this verse meant that Christ's light shining in each person means that God has already established a relationship with each one, making him or her a person of the utmost worth.

Fox preached the doctrine of the inner light throughout England in the middle part of the 17th century. His followers were called Friends, though others called them Quakers, as they were thought to "quake" in the Spirit. Robert Barclay, a Scot, was their prominent early theologian, and William Penn was an early convert.

What is the inner light? It cannot be identified simply with the conscience, for the conscience is culturally conditioned to some extent. Only to the extent that conscience is God-shaped can it be identified with the Quaker doctrine. But the inner light is greater even than this aspect of conscience; it is a path, and if it is followed, it can lead one to a personal knowledge of God.

The inner light is a source of personal revelation of God that exists apart from the Bible. But it does not conflict with the Bible, Quakers insist, for what God reveals to you or to another will not conflict with what God revealed in other times and places. The Bible is a record of revelation and thus a guide to all who follow the inner light today.

The doctrine of the inner light was viewed as heresy by the Puritans, who emphasized God's revelation in Scripture. Friends who preached in 17th-century

---

5. Membership statistics for Church of the Brethren and sister churches are from Bedell, *Yearbook of Churches,* 1997, 253-57.

Massachusetts were flogged and sometimes hanged. But the Friends did not back down. They were saying that doctrine must be experienced, not simply received by the mind.

The inner light idea transformed everything about Quaker life and ethics. It completely altered the Quaker theology of the sacraments. The Friends reinterpreted baptism and the Lord's Supper in completely spiritual terms. To them the true baptism is baptism in the Spirit; true communion is the communion of Christians through the Holy Spirit.

The inner light also stood at the center of Quaker worship. The Anglican *Book of Common Prayer* was thrown out, along with every other kind of structured service. The Quaker meeting had no agenda and no priests to lead it. Once the meeting began, all was steeped in silent prayer and meditation except when someone spoke out in song, prayer, or exhortation at the prompting of the Spirit. Even today in those Quaker churches where silent worship still prevails, it is not uncommon for there to be two or three brief "testimonies" of 5 to 10 minutes each, with the rest of the service made up of silent meditation.

The inner light affected Quaker ethics. It is a reason why Friends took the Sermon on the Mount with such literal application. If the inner light is within each person, how can I bear arms against others and kill them when God has already staked a claim on those lives? Pacifism did not free Friends from military language, however. They talked of "the Lamb's war" that Christ wages against iniquity. They preached that weapons of forgiveness and compassion used by soldiers in the Lamb's war exceed in power the carnal weapons of destruction used by kings and emperors.

Quakers were also early and fervent foes of American slavery. How can one hold in bondage a fellow human being in whom Christ's inner light is present? They were generally fair in their dealing with Native Americans and paid them for the land they used despite the fact the British monarch had "granted" that land for their use.

Quakers and Religious Liberty

Quakers were important in shaping American religious liberty. Persecuted in England, many sought a more humane life in the New World. In Delaware, Rhode Island, and New Jersey, they constituted an important social and political block that fostered toleration of religious minorities. Their influence was greatest in Pennsylvania, however, which was transferred by the English king to William Penn to settle a debt. There they established what they hoped would be a model government for the world. They dominated the colonial legislature for several generations.

This illustrates a point: unlike Mennonites and Brethren, Quakers were involved in government affairs. Ironically, their attempts at a model government ended in the mid-1700s when the governor of Pennsylvania, appointed by the king, issued a bounty for the scalp of any Native American, regardless of gender or age. The Friends resigned from the legislature in horror and protest and were succeeded by men whose principles were quite different.

The way in which the Quaker experiment in Pennsylvania ended discouraged many Friends. But the *Journal of John Woolman,* a classic in American religious autobiography, begins soon after this period, as Friends found their social purpose renewed in their witness against slavery.

Quaker Denominations

The Quaker service of worship is called the meeting, and the house of worship is "the meetinghouse." But local meetings are part of larger bodies called Yearly Meetings. The various Yearly Meetings were linked for several generations, but this changed in the 1830s.

A liberal group led by Elias Hicks moved toward a Unitarian view of God. Hicks argued that "Christ was the Son of God in the same sense that all people were." He denied traditional doctrines of Christ's atonement, original sin, and the devil. He regarded the Bible as inferior to one's immediate experience of God.[6] The Hicksites were not some small minority, and these teachings created strong dissension. The Baltimore Yearly Meeting was in Hicks's camp. Other Yearly Meetings suffered schism. By 1830 American Friends were divided. Bitterness continued between *Orthodox Friends* and Hicksites for many years. In 1900 the Yearly Meetings in the Hicksite tradition organized the *Friends General Conference,* which has 31,400 members today.

Other disruptions occurred over innovations in Quaker worship and fellowship with non-Quakers. Many Friends reacted to Hicksite liberalism by moving into an Evangelical mainstream dominated by Methodists, Baptists, and Presbyterians. Joseph John Gurney, who led Quaker Evangelicals in England and America, nearly repudiated the whole idea of the inner light because his views had conformed so thoroughly to those held by other Evangelicals. The Gurneyites eventually became a majority of America's Orthodox Friends, according to Quaker historian Thomas Hamm.[7]

Not all Orthodox Quakers wanted to join the Evangelical mainstream, however, and regarded the Gurneyites as compromisers. John Wilbur led traditionalists who held fast to the old ways, rejecting Hicksite and Gurneyite innovations alike. Wilbur's followers are known as Conservative Friends. They were clearly a minority and pulled out of existing Yearly Meetings to establish new ones. Their connection, which has dwindled to about 1,800 members, is known as the *Religious Society of Friends (Conservative).*[8]

One further division affected the movement: through the influence of the American Holiness Revival, there were Gurneyites who adopted the Wesleyan view of the new birth and entire sanctification. Some joined other Holiness churches. Edgar P. Ellyson, an early Nazarene general superintendent, and his wife, Mary Emily Ellyson, came into the Church of the Nazarene from the Holiness Quakers. So, too, did Susan Fitkin, founding president of the Nazarene World Missionary Society. Seth Rees, who had a brief but eventful ministry in the Church of the Nazarene, did the same. But most "revival Quakers" remained

---

6. Thomas Hamm, *The Transformation of American Quakerism* (Bloomington and Indianapolis: Indiana University Press, 1988), 16.

7. Ibid., 27.

8. Bedell, *Yearbook of Churches, 1997,* 257; J. Gordon Melton, *The Encyclopedia of American Religions,* 2nd ed. (Detroit: Gale Research Co., 1987), 489.

in the Society of Friends and created their own fellowship. Currently those in the United States and Canada are known as the *Evangelical Friends International —North America.* They have just under 9,000 members.[9]

The remaining Gurneyites created their own denominational structure in 1902, known today as the *Friends United Meeting.* Their United States membership is about 44,000.[10] They were influenced by modern liberal theology in the early 20th century. Rufus Jones, perhaps the leading 20th-century Friend, emphasized the mystical aspects of Quaker theology in light of conclusions he believed that modern biblical criticism had demonstrated.

The pattern of worship in Friends United Meeting and Evangelical Friends churches is now programmed, with offering, song, and sermon. A period for silent meditation usually remains, however, as an influence from earlier days. Conservative Friends and Friends General Conference services typically perpetuate traditional Quaker worship.

Peace Church Social Witness

Jesus said that if someone strikes you on the cheek, you should turn the other cheek (Matt. 5:39). He also said, "Blessed are the peacemakers" (v. 9). "Being a peacemaker" implies being active, not passive, in the face of evil. Twentieth-century peace churches have taken seriously the mandate to be peacemakers.

The Brethren in Christ participated in founding Church World Service, an interchurch agency providing disaster relief and social services in Christ's name around the world. Quakers and Mennonites have their own networks: the American Friends Service Committee and Mennonite Central Committee. Mennonite Disaster Service is another agency that is well known for quickly getting work teams to sites where disasters have occurred. Another area where members of peace churches excel is in medicine. This is largely a by-product of serving in noncombatant roles—often in health-related fields—during times of war.

Nazarenes and the Peace Churches

Nazarenes share several vital points of interest with the peace churches. First, the Church of the Nazarene is a believers' church and makes profession of faith a condition of church membership. This characteristic is inherited from the Anabaptist heritage. Nazarenes in America are indebted further for the way the peace churches fostered an atmosphere in which all believers' churches could thrive during an early and critical time in American history.

Nazarenes share with the peace churches an emphasis on discipleship. This common thread is expressed both in the individual's personal journey with God and socially. The strong support Nazarenes give to Nazarene Compassionate Ministries indicates that we share the peace churches' desire to make a positive social witness in the name of Jesus Christ.

Beyond these general areas of agreement, we also share things with individual peace churches:

• The pietist heritage with the Brethren.

---

9. Bedell, *Yearbook of Churches, 1997,* 255.
10. Ibid.

- Similarities between our Wesleyan doctrine of prevenient grace, where we see God at work to some degree in every person, and the Quaker doctrine of the inner light.
- We agree with Mennonites and Brethren on the importance of the sacraments but disagree with the way Quakers spiritualize these tangible ways in which God is presented to us.

However, the Church of the Nazarene is not a peace church in the classical sense that Friends, Mennonites, and Brethren are. We do, however, take steps to protect those Nazarenes who are conscientious objectors to military service, and we have always worked to ensure that they are accorded the same status given to conscientious objectors in other denominations.

Another difference is that the peace churches do not share our Anglican-Methodist heritage, which shapes us distinctly. Although Quakers arose in England, they repudiated Anglicanism thoroughly. Some of our doctrinal statements descend from Anglicanism and tie us into that Reformation tradition. Similarly, the Wesleyan aspects of our heritage are foreign to the three peace churches, except among the Evangelical Friends.

Review and Reflection

1. Your new neighbor tells you that he and his family are Mennonites. You want to talk about the teachings and practices that you as a Nazarene and your new neighbor hold in common. What points will you bring up?

Infant baptism

Military service

A believers' church

Holding government office

Holiness

Church rules

Compassionate ministries

Open Communion

Pledge of allegiance

Ethiopian missions

Mennonite home page on the World Wide Web

2. Review the section on the Church of the Brethren. What do you believe is the main contribution that this group has made to American religious and social life?

3. Compare and contrast the Church of the Nazarene with Quakers on

Pacifism

Baptism

Lord's Supper

Prevenient grace

Worship styles

Personal holiness

Inner light

Authority of Scripture as *the* Revelation of God

THE BAPTISTS:
A PRIESTHOOD OF BELIEVERS

Historical Background

The first Baptist congregation appeared near London in 1612. Roger
Williams helped establish the first Baptist church in America in 1639. The first
Baptist college was the College of Rhode Island, now Brown University.
Landmark Baptists, however, deny these origins, tracing their ecclesiastical
existence back to Jesus himself.

Core Beliefs

Specific beliefs vary among the many Baptist congregations, but generally
held Baptist doctrines include
1. The autonomy of the local church
2. Ordinances rather than sacraments
3. The priesthood of all believers
4. Religious freedom
5. Soul liberty—freedom to make personal choices on matters of faith and
morals
6. Baptism of adult believers by immersion only
7. A believers' church of the regenerate only
8. Simple, vernacular worship style

Agreement and Differences

Nazarenes share common ground with many Baptists on such points as the
believers' church, the priesthood of all believers, and worship style. Nazarenes
disagree with immersion-only baptism, the Baptist view of the sacraments, and
most vigorously with the Calvinist views of salvation that characterize the
majority of Baptist denominations. (See chapter 9.)

Nevertheless, Nazarenes have been influenced by the Baptist dominance of
20th-century Evangelicalism. They have influenced us in the way we worship,
baptize, regard women (in ministry and life), and organize and operate Sunday
Schools.

Baptists Today

The Baptist World Congress represents 191 Baptist organizations with 41.6
million members; 32.7 million are in North America. These totals do not
include several Baptist denominations who do not participate in the Baptist
World Congress.

Baptists you know—William Carey, Martin Luther King Jr., Walter Rauschenbusch, Charles H. Spurgeon, Billy Graham, Jimmy Carter, and Bill Clinton.

12 ~ THE BAPTISTS: A PRIESTHOOD OF BELIEVERS

THE NAME "BAPTIST" CONJURES MANY DIFFERENT IMAGES. What does it conjure for you? Are Baptists Calvinists or Arminians? Fundamentalists, moderate Evangelicals, or theological liberals? Are they mission-minded or antimissionary? Would they rather hold a revival or march for social justice? Do Baptists ordain women, or do they not?

If you're White and have lived in the American South, you probably answered that Baptists are Calvinists, that some are moderate Evangelicals while many are rigid Fundamentalists, that they are revivalistic and mission-minded, and that they oppose the ordination of women.

But if you are one of more than 10 million African-Americans who belong to a Black Baptist denomination, your view of who Baptists are and how they think would be different. You would view the Baptist Church as an activist and socially responsible church. You would remember the critical role of Baptist leaders, including Martin Luther King Jr., in the civil rights struggle of the 1960s.

If you lived near the University of Chicago, founded under Baptist auspices a century ago, you might have still another image of Baptists. You would know of some who are theological and social liberals. You might even be aware of the influence of Baptist theologian Walter Rauschenbusch on the development of the social gospel's theology in the early 20th century.

Each description in the first paragraph fits one Baptist group or another. That some Baptist churches are Calvinistic while others are not reflects a basic point. There is a theological core that unites all Baptists, but that core is not a particular understanding of the way of salvation. Rather, it is a specific set of beliefs regarding the essential nature of the church and its relation to discipleship.

Here's one other question to ponder: are Baptists largely an American phenomenon, or are they a worldwide movement?

Baptist Origins

The Baptist tradition originated in England early in the reign of King James I. The Anglican Reformation was nearly 50 years old. The Church of England required its priests to use Thomas Cranmer's *Book of Common Prayer* in all public worship. And this was a problem for Puritans, a faction within the church. The *Prayer Book* was an abridgment of older Roman Catholic worship manuals, edited to reflect Protestant theology. But Puritans wanted to "purify" the Church of England of *all* Roman Catholic influences and alter the liturgy so that it conformed to the style of worship developed by John Calvin in Geneva.

Several small groups left the Church of England in the midst of the Puritan agitation. The Brownists and the Barrowists, two of the earliest, set up independent congregations.

The first Baptist congregation was started in Spitalfields, near London, in about 1612. Its founder was Thomas Helwys, and his church differed from other Separatist churches in that it rejected infant baptism. Instead, it taught believers' baptism. This doctrine of the Church was similar to that of the Anabaptists. Like them, Helwys insisted on a regenerate church membership, believers' baptism, the discipline of backsliders, and the separation of church and state. But he rejected Mennonite pacifism and other ethical commitments flowing from the pacifist stance. He believed that Christians could serve in government without violating their consciences, something Mennonites did not accept. Helwys penned a booklet calling for freedom of worship and dedicated it to King James. As a result, he was imprisoned and never freed.[1]

But that first Baptist congregation endured, and by 1644 there were 47 Baptist congregations in England. They were known as General Baptists, for they held to Arminian views of God's grace, believing that Christ's atonement for sin was for everyone who would believe in Him, and that any person could be saved by grace through faith.

There was another type of Baptist church emerging by this time, however, known as Particular Baptists. The first Particular Baptist congregation was founded in about 1640. They were Calvinistic. "Particular" referred to their Calvinistic belief that Christ had not died for everyone but only for the special (particular) few God had predestined for salvation before the world began.[2]

Which group would control the Baptist future?

Early Baptists in America

Roger Williams, founder of the Rhode Island colony, helped establish the first Baptist church in America at Providence in 1639. He withdrew from it a few months later. Over a century later the College of Rhode Island (now Brown University) was established in Providence as the first Baptist college in America.

The Great Awakening of the mid-1700s stimulated Baptist growth in the Northeast. During the Awakening, some of the revived Congregationalists accepted Baptist views on believers' baptism and the strict independence of the local church. Meanwhile, Shubal Stearnes and Daniel Marshall promoted Baptist life in the South and had great success in the Carolinas.

A growing Baptist witness in Virginia was also vital. After American independence, Virginia's Baptists joined Presbyterians to lobby for Thomas Jefferson's

---

1. Durnbaugh, *Believers' Church*, 97-99.
2. Ibid., 99.

clause on religious liberty, which was designed to separate the Anglican church from the government of the new Commonwealth of Virginia. Baptist voices helped the clause become part of the Virginia Constitution, which in turn influenced the First Amendment to the Constitution of the United States.

By 1800 Baptists were poised for significant growth. As America's frontier moved ever westward, Methodists and Baptists excelled in reaching the new settlements. In 1776 Baptists claimed nearly 17 percent of all church members in America, while Methodists claimed only 2.5 percent. By 1850 Methodists had increased their share to over 34 percent and were the largest church group in America, while Baptists cornered nearly 21 percent. How well were these churches doing? The third-largest Protestant church—Presbyterians—had less than 12 percent of America's church members.

So the 19th century was the Methodist century in some respects. But the 20th century became the significant century for Baptist growth. By 1900 Baptists and Methodists were nearly equal in numbers. Roman Catholics had overtaken both churches to become the largest denomination in America, its numbers swelled by steady immigration from Europe, especially Ireland, Italy, and Germany. Baptists began outpacing Methodists and in the early 20th century surpassed them to become the largest Protestant block in America. Baptists historically have been strongly anti-Roman Catholic. Could Baptist and Roman Catholic growth in America be linked in some way?

Baptist Associations

Baptist churches are fiercely local and independent. So how do they relate to one another? The primary way is through local, state, and national "associations" of churches, sometimes called "conventions."

The first association of denomination-wide scope was spurred into existence by missionary interests. Adoniram and Anne Judson and Luther Rice were sent as Congregational missionaries to India. But by the time they reached their destination, they had become persuaded that infant baptism was unscriptural. They embraced believers' baptism, a position contrary to Congregationalist beliefs. Baptists in America rallied to support these missionaries, whom they had not sent but who now represented their views. Rice eventually returned to America and became an advocate of missions.

According to Baptist historian William Brackney, Rice "conceived of a system of regional and local societies which would unite in one *general society* to carry forth the one great task of missionary endeavor. The original expectation was that local or regional organizations would meet annually and the *general* or national body would meet triennially. From 1814 to 1826, this was practically the case."[3] Christian education, home missions, and publishing interests also became concerns of the Triennial Convention.[4]

---

3. William H. Brackney, "The General Missionary Convention of the Baptist Denomination, 1814-1845: An American Metaphor," *Baptist History*, July 1989, 14.

4. B[ruce] L. Shelley, "Baptist Churches in the U.S.A.," in Reid et al., *Dictionary of Christianity in America*, 111.

Not every Baptist, however, supported these innovations. Daniel Parker led anti-mission Baptists opposed to cooperative work, Sunday Schools, and missionaries. They were staunch Calvinists who believed that God would save those He willed to save without human agency. And they argued that there was no scriptural support for founding missionary societies. Many of the anti-mission churches became Primitive Baptist churches.

The bulk of America's Baptists supported the Triennial Convention, however. It was a uniting force in Baptist life until 1845, when the issues of slavery and regionalism overwhelmed the Convention, just as they had done to the Methodist General Conference the year before. The slavery issue moved to the fore after Northern Baptists learned that Triennial Convention funds supported home missionaries in Texas who were slaveholders. In the uproar, the Triennial Convention divided along regional lines into two bodies, a Southern Baptist Convention and a Northern Baptist Convention.

Doctrinal Core

W. H. Porter and Philip Jenks identify several foundational principles for Baptist thought and life:

- *Autonomy,* or the belief that each local church is independent.
- The *associational principle,* in which Baptist churches participate together in areas of common witness, especially missions, Sunday Schools, home missions, and higher education.
- *Ordinances,* a term preferred in place of the word "sacraments," since most Baptists view baptism and the Lord's Supper as practices required of Christians, rather than as grace-bearing events for the Church.
- *Priesthood of all believers,* an important Anabaptist concept, is also central in Baptist life. This principle means that all Christians are ministers to one another and to the world.
- *Religious freedom* is an important idea in Baptist life, beginning with Thomas Helwys's desire to have freedom to worship in a way different from that required by English law. There is not always unanimity among Baptists on the exact place to draw the line of religious liberty, however. While many Baptists in the South support prayer in public schools, other Baptists are staunch opponents of the practice.
- *Soul liberty,* or the idea that individuals are competent to decide for themselves matters of Christian faith and morals as they study the Scriptures and are led by the Holy Spirit.[5]

> *"Soul liberty" is the idea that believers are competent to decide for themselves matters of Christian faith and morals as they study the Scriptures and are led by the Holy Spirit.*

---

5. Willis Hubert Porter and Philip E. Jenks, "Baptists," in Williamson, *Encyclopedia of Religions,* 30.

Calvinist or Arminian?

The core convictions identified by Porter and Jenks lie at the heart of all Baptist life. But these convictions by themselves do not answer other important questions: *Who* will be saved? And *how* will that be accomplished?

Baptists do answer these questions as well, but not with one voice. They unite either Calvinism or Arminianism with their ecclesiology (doctrine of the church). General Baptists, who were Arminians, were strong during much of America's colonial period. By 1800 that was changing rapidly. Particular, or Calvinistic, Baptists began to outpace General Baptists to such an extent that most Baptist churches today are Calvinistic. Some are mildly so; others are strongly so. One smaller group of Baptists who forthrightly embrace Arminianism are known today as Freewill Baptists.

Landmarkism

A new theology arose within the Baptist movement of the mid-19th century that produced great change among Baptists in the South. It was the "Old Landmark" movement, and it asserted that Baptist churches did not originate in England but were, in fact, "true churches" that exist in a thread of unbroken continuity that goes clear back to the New Testament. Indeed, Jesus himself, it was asserted, was the true Founder of the Baptist lineage.

James A. Graves of Tennessee and James Pendleton of Kentucky popularized Landmark beliefs through books and periodicals. Graves, editor of the *Tennessee Baptist,* enjoyed regional prominence and had an effective platform for propagating his views. Landmark Baptist beliefs include the following:

- Only Baptist churches are true churches.
- Only baptism by immersion administered in a Baptist ("true") church is true baptism; immersions that took place in a non-Baptist church were called "alien immersions," while baptisms by other modes (sprinkling or pouring) were disregarded completely.
- Closed Communion, or the idea that the Lord's Supper is restricted to members of the local church.
- Rejection of cooperative ventures with non-Landmark churches, including those with other (non-Landmark) Baptists.[6]

Graves and Pendleton did not deny that there were Christians in other denominations. But those denominations, and their congregations, were mere "religious societies," not churches in any biblical sense.

Graves was especially antagonistic toward Methodism. He rejected its doctrines of grace, its baptism of infants, and its episcopal form of church government. Perhaps Methodists were his special targets because they were the Baptists' major competitors for the allegiance of the American people. Graves's major anti-Methodist publication, *The Great Iron Wheel,* portrayed Methodist structures as unscriptural and oppressive. Methodists who responded argued that the New Testament does not establish one particular form of church govern-

---

6. M. G. Bell, "Landmark Movement," in Reid et al., *Dictionary of Christianity in America,* 629-30.

ment, and that there was as much New Testament validity for episcopacy as there was for the most rabid congregationalism.

Landmarkism made considerable headway in the Southern Baptist Convention. Historian James Tull states that by Graves's death (1893) it was the "prevailing Baptist ideology in Tennessee, southwest Kentucky, northern Alabama, Arkansas, Mississippi, Texas, and Louisiana." It never captured the *whole* Southern Baptist Convention, and in the 20th century it receded within the denomination, the victim of new scholarly interest in Baptist origins. But Tull notes that the Landmark movement's influence still taints the Southern Baptist mind. Its lingering influence is seen in "the virtual disappearance of the doctrine of the universal church" from Southern Baptist thought today. It is also reflected in the antagonism of Baptists in the South toward the ecumenical movement and their disregard for baptisms performed in other churches. Landmarkism also became the underlying theology of two 20th-century denominations that remained separate from the Southern Baptist Convention.[7]

The Central Tradition in North and South

The Triennial Convention's division over slavery in 1845 created two major Baptist denominations in America, one for the North and one for the South. Around these two major bodies smaller ones also existed: Freewill Baptists, several African-American denominations, Swedish Baptists, and Landmark-oriented denominations. A surprisingly large number of Baptist congregations remained completely unaffiliated with any denominational body.

The American Baptist Churches in the U.S.A. After the division of 1845, Northern Baptists perpetuated the mission legacy of the Triennial Convention through the American Baptist Missionary Union. By 1904 they were supporting 520 missionaries around the world. A stronger denominational organization was created in 1907, and the name Northern Baptist Convention was adopted. This later changed to American Baptist Convention, for the word "Northern" seemed increasingly inappropriate and limiting as the denomination spread into the West and even into the South. Since 1972 the denomination has been known as the American Baptist Churches in the U.S.A.

American Baptists have formed a very diverse church. Thirty-seven percent of their present membership is African-American. Other racial minorities comprise another 3 percent. Thus, it is one of the most racially heterogeneous denominations in America.

Unlike most Baptist churches, American Baptists ordain women to the ministry and are affiliated with the National Council of Churches and the World Council of Churches. In 1997 they reported slightly over 1.5 million members in the United States.[8]

---

7. James E. Tull, "Landmark Movement," in *Encyclopedia of Religion in the South,* ed. Samuel S. Hill (Macon, Ga.: Mercer University Press, 1984), 399-401.

8. B. Gray Allison, "Notable Achievements in Missions and Evangelism Since 1845," *Baptist History,* July 1989, 33; Claude L. Howe Jr., "A Portrait of Baptists in America Today," ibid., 50-51; Bedell, *Yearbook of Churches, 1997,* 252.

The Fundamentalist Fellowship, a group originally from within the Northern Baptist Convention, withdrew from the denomination in 1947 over the perceived liberalism of some Northern Baptist missionaries. They reorganized as a denomination, the *Conservative Baptist Association of America*. In 1997 it reported 200,000 members.[9]

The Southern Baptist Convention reported nearly 15.7 million members in 1997, making it the largest Protestant denomination in the United States today. Its reach extends into all 50 states, but the great bulk of SBC membership remains solidly in the South. In North Carolina, for instance, one in every two churchgoers attends a church aligned with the Southern Baptist Convention. In a way that is characteristic of few other churches, regionalism still defines much that is typical of the Southern Baptist character.

How was that "Southern" identity shaped? Largely through identification with the slave economy and the political values and structures sustaining it. The Southern preachers who developed "biblical rationales" to morally justify Black slavery were primarily Baptists who asserted that the Bible teaches that people are inherently unequal—a premise diametrically opposed to a principle upon which American freedoms were founded.

Further, Southern Baptists stood for secession from the Union and supported the Confederate cause without reservation. Their fortunes and identity were intertwined so strongly with a region whose religious life they dominated that its social and economic vices were also theirs.

Northern and Southern Methodists reunited in the fourth generation after the Civil War, demonstrating the moderating influences that time and perspective

> *In the South, Baptist fortunes and identity were so intertwined with the region's culture that its social and economic vices became their own.*

eventually brought to Methodist life. Most Southern Baptists, by contrast, take pride in their regional identity and would never dream of reuniting with their Northern counterparts. Extreme tendencies toward regionalism were reinforced further by Landmarkism, which deepened Southern Baptist isolation and provincialism.[10]

Southern Baptists have made great strides in home and foreign missions through denominational programs. Indeed, from 1845 to 1907 the denominational program of the Southern Baptist Convention was more centralized than that of Northern Baptists. Since 1925 the Cooperative Program has linked state Baptist conventions with the Southern Baptist Convention, sustaining national programs through reliable and systematic funding directly from state conventions, rather than local churches. The basic independence of the local church, however, is still protected. Congregations can withdraw from state conventions, and no decisions made by state or national conventions are binding on a local church.

---

9. Melton, *Encyclopedia of Religions*, 388; Bedell, *Yearbook of Churches, 1997*, 254.
10. Walter Shurden, "Southern Baptist Convention," in Hill, *Encyclopedia of Religion in the South*, 722.

Southern Baptists have been featured prominently in the news of recent years. Two recent presidents of the United States, Jimmy Carter and Bill Clinton, are lifelong Southern Baptists. Charles Stanley and other notable Southern Baptist preachers are also visible, as televised series from their local churches are aired across North America.

Southern Baptists have also been newsworthy for their public contentiousness in the 1980s and 1990s. A determined effort by Fundamentalists with political and theological agendas began moving through the South in 1979. There is an ironic feature of the Southern Baptist organization: the members of all denominational boards and seminary boards are appointed by the president of the denomination. By holding on to the office of president year after year, Fundamentalists have successfully reshaped those boards to reflect their will.

Ostensibly, the Fundamentalist drive arose to protect the doctrine of "scriptural inerrancy" from perceived liberalism. But the Fundamentalists have been notable opponents of the ordination of women—an issue that turns on the *interpretation* of Scripture, not on the *doctrine* of Scripture. Clearly, hidden agendas were also at work. The hierarchicalism of the Old South, dressed in other garb, still persists.[11]

Dissenters from the Central Tradition

Black Baptists. While Southern Baptists were joining their hearts and minds more tightly to the economics and politics of slavery, Black Baptist churches were slowly forming in America. In their own churches, African-Americans experienced freedom. They chose their own worship style and leaders, and they supported their own religious institutions. The Black church was virtually the only sector of public life in which African-Americans had complete self-determination. By 1821 Black Baptists had sent their first missionaries overseas.

The first Baptist associations that African-Americans formed were in the North. They were not permitted to do the same in the South until after the Civil War. In 1895 the Baptist Convention of America was formed through the mergers of several associations. A split in 1915, and a further split in one of those, has resulted in three dominant Black Baptist denominations today.

The National Baptist Convention, U.S.A., is the primary body to emerge from the original Baptist Convention of America. With 8.2 million members, it is the largest African-American denomination today. Its missionary work is limited to Africa and the Bahamas. *The National Baptist Convention of America* broke off from the National Baptist Convention, U.S.A., in 1915 over a church property dispute and today has 3.5 million members.

The *Progressive National Baptist Convention* resulted from a split in the National Baptist Convention, U.S.A., in 1961 over democratic structures. The public issue was whether denominational leaders should serve for life or for limited terms of service. Those who insisted on limited terms formed the Progressive National Baptist Convention after their attempts to reform the mother church failed. Underneath the surface there were other differences. The

11. Eldon G. Ernst, "The Baptists," in *Encyclopedia of the American Religious Experience*, ed. Charles H. Lippy and Peter Williams (New York: Charles Scribner's Sons, 1988), 1:564-65.

two bodies approached the looming civil rights struggle in different ways, with the National Baptist Convention, U.S.A., taking a more conservative approach and the Progressive National Baptist Convention taking a more activist one. Civil rights leaders Martin Luther King Jr. and Jesse Jackson were among the denomination's noted clergy. By 1997 it had 2.5 million members. Peggy Shriver's study in 1989 showed that the denomination's structure was more systematically developed than that of its sister churches. The Progressive National Baptist Convention tradition of noted preachers includes Howard Thurman and Gardner C. Taylor.[12]

All three of these Black Baptist denominations participate in the National Council of Churches and the World Council of Churches.

Freewill Baptists. Among the groups that remained aloof from the Triennial Convention were Freewill Baptists, who dissented from the Calvinism characteristic of most Baptist churches in America. Thorough Arminians, Freewill Baptists affirm Christ's universal atonement. Today's *National Association of Freewill Baptists* traces its roots to the ministry of Paul Palmer, who organized an Arminian Baptist church in North Carolina in 1727. As Freewill Baptists spread through the South, they organized local conferences and in 1921 created a national structure.

The Great Awakening of the 18th century spurred the formation of other Freewill Baptist churches in New England. This group stayed aloof from the Southern body, however, and in 1911 most of its churches united with the Northern Baptist Convention. Some churches rejected this option, however, and in 1935 they merged with the Freewill Baptists of the South to form the National Association of Freewill Baptists. Its headquarters in Tennessee serves a constituency just under a quarter million members.[13]

Landmark Denominations. Because of their Landmark views, some Southern groups objected strongly to the cooperative program of the Southern Baptist Convention, viewing it as unscriptural. The loosely constructed *American Baptist Association* was created when two smaller Landmark bodies united in 1924. Ben Bogard, fiery Fundamentalist from Arkansas, was a leading figure in this church. The American Baptist Association reported a quarter million members in 1986. Another Landmark body, the *Baptist Missionary Association of America,* was organized in 1950 and has slightly over 230,000 members.[14]

Primitive Baptists. Primitive Baptist churches stem from the anti-mission movement of the early 1800s. They are strict, hard-core Calvinists and radical congregationalists. There are over a dozen Primitive Baptist conventions, but none is very large. Most Primitive Baptist groups do not have publishing houses, though a few do.

Other Groups. The North American Baptist world has many other groups. The *Baptist General Conference* was known originally as the Swedish Baptist Church. Gustaf Palmquist migrated to America in 1852 and organized the

12. Williamson, *Encyclopedia of Religions,* 39-44; Melton, *Encyclopedia of Religions,* 64, 400-401; Bedell, *Yearbook of Churches, 1997,* 256-57.
13. Bedell, *Yearbook of Churches, 1997,* 94-95, 256.
14. Ibid., 44, 52, 252-53.

denomination soon afterward to evangelize Swedish immigrants. Though small—it has just over 135,000 members—it sustains extensive missionary work around the world.[15]

The *General Association of Regular Baptist Churches* is more Fundamentalist in nature. It originated when conservatives withdrew from the North Baptist Convention in 1932. Its members must affirm premillennialism. Its membership is slightly over 135,000 members.[16]

Various Baptists in Canada united in the 1940s and 1950s to form the two largest Baptist denominations there. *Canadian Baptist Ministries* (known earlier as the Baptist Federation of Canada) is a federated body that unites four smaller conventions scattered in different regions of Canada. Its membership in 1997 was 130,000 members. The federation exists primarily as a missionary arm to support work on other continents. The *Fellowship of Evangelical Baptist Churches* is a more conservative body. Its founders objected to liberalism among the groups who created Canadian Baptist Ministries. The Fellowship of Evangelical Baptist Churches has slightly over 72,000 members.[17]

One Missionary

One of the most famous Baptists is William Carey (1761—1834). He is often called the Father of Modern Missions, a title that is not accurate. But he *was* the father of Baptist missions. Over the objections of hard-shell Calvinists, Carey and others founded the Baptist Missionary Society in London in 1792. It sent him and his family to India the next year. In various cities, including Calcutta, he labored for over 40 years without a furlough, preaching, teaching, and translating the Scriptures into native languages. Carey was an able publicist for the missionary cause and did much to inspire young missionaries.

Two Preachers

Every tradition is proud of its great preachers, and Baptists are no exception. No 19th-century preacher was better known than Charles H. Spurgeon. During his 38-year pastorate at London's New Park Street Church, membership increased from 232 to 5,311 members. The congregation built the famous Metropolitan Tabernacle to hold the thousands who thronged to his preaching. Spurgeon was a rigid, uncompromising Calvinist and in some respects was one of the last of the Puritans.

No 20th-century Baptist is better known or loved than Billy Graham, whose evangelistic crusades have penetrated every inhabited continent. Graham's personal journey from fiery young Fundamentalist to elder statesman of Evangelical Christianity mirrors many basic changes in modern society. In the early 1950s Graham blended an anticommunistic message with his gospel of redemption. By the mid-1980s he was preaching behind the iron curtain and understood more clearly than most that great spiritual and social unrest would produce fundamental changes in Communist countries.

---

15. Melton, *Encyclopedia of Religions*, 401; Bedell, *Yearbook of Churches, 1997*, 251.

16. Bedell, *Yearbook of Churches, 1997*, 86, 255.

17. Ibid., 141, 149, 248-49; and Shelley, "Baptist Churches in the U.S.A.," 113.

Three Social Prophets

People often forget that the Baptist tradition also has produced great social prophets. Walter Rauschenbusch, a Northern Baptist, was the most thorough exponent of an early 20th-century theology known as the Social Gospel. In *Christianity and the Social Order,* he argued that Christians had substituted a "gospel of the church" for Jesus' more radical "gospel of the Kingdom."

Clarence Jordan, a Southern Baptist, founded Koinonia Farms near Americus, Georgia, in 1942. It was a racially integrated Christian community that endured the violent reactions of local racists. Jordan believed that Christians should live daily according to the Sermon on the Mount. His four-volume *Cotton Patch Version of the New Testament* used Southern idiom and culture as the setting for his paraphrases. Millard Fuller, a lawyer who came to live at Koinonia Farms, founded Habitat for Humanity as an extension of Koinonia Ministries.

Martin Luther King Jr., the best-known Baptist social leader, embraced a theology of nonviolent activism at Boston University. This undergirded his leadership in the civil rights cause in the 1950s and 1960s. Like Jordan, King was called a communist by detractors who feared the social changes he sought. His foes reveled in tales of moral failure in his private life, yet King took a stand against the sin of racism that few of his critics had the courage or moral discernment to do.

Baptists Worldwide

All of the major Baptist denominations in North America participate in the Baptist World Alliance, which has 191 constituent member organizations in 200 nations. The alliance sponsors the Baptist World Congress, which meets every five years. The membership in Baptist World Alliance-affiliated churches totals 41.6 million worldwide. Of these, 32.7 million members are in North America, and nearly half of those are in the Southern Baptist Convention. The total number of Baptists worldwide and in North America is somewhat higher, since Primitive Baptists, other Landmark groups, and many unaffiliated congregations are not represented in the Baptist World Alliance.[18]

Nazarenes and the Baptist Tradition

Baptists and Nazarenes share a number of common characteristics:
- Baptists are among the other groups (including Mennonites and Disciples of Christ) with whom Nazarenes share a common believers' church perspective and emphasize a regenerate church membership.
- The simple, Evangelical style that characterizes Nazarene worship is typical of nearly every Baptist denomination.
- The musical tradition of Baptists and Nazarenes is close, and—except for songs that are doctrinally distinctive—a large number of songs and gospel music are interchangeable.

---

18. Baptist World Alliance web site, <http://www.baptistnet.org/fellowship/memberbodies/index.htm>, October 1, 1997.

While we agree with Baptists on some important matters, there are fundamental points of disagreement concerning doctrine and practice:

- The great majority of Baptists hold views of salvation rooted in Reformed (Calvinist) theology, which Nazarenes—anchored firmly in the Wesleyan-Arminian tradition—find contrary to sound biblical interpretation.
- Differences include our doctrines of prevenient grace, empowered free will, entire sanctification, and the assurance of the Spirit—doctrines that define *who we are* and *how we see the world.*
- The Nazarene doctrine of the ministry differs from that held by most Baptist churches. We embrace the ordination of women and celebrate their gifts of leadership in the Body of Christ. A few Baptist groups agree with our position on this, but most do not.
- The Church of the Nazarene disagrees with the Baptist insistence on the necessity of believers' baptism. Instead, we permit infants to be baptized upon the request of their parents.
- Further, Baptists generally hold that immersion is the only scriptural mode of baptism. The Church of the Nazarene denies this and provides full liberty of conscience to candidates for baptism, who may choose the mode that is in accord with their personal beliefs.
- Nazarenes teach freedom from sin through entire sanctification. Most Baptist groups teach that we sin daily in word, thought, and deed.
- Nazarenes and other Wesleyans teach that one must maintain an ongoing relationship with God in order to be finally saved. Most Baptists believe that once one is born again, his or her sins are forgiven—past, present, and future. The person can never again be "unsaved" and is "eternally secure" regardless of present sin in daily life.

The Baptist Challenge

The Southern Baptist Convention's rise to dominance in American religion poses a challenge to Nazarenes. We have edged ever closer to the Evangelical mainstream during our 20th-century journey, but that mainstream is increasingly influenced by Baptist modes of thought and action. Some Nazarene scholars speak of the "Baptistification" of the Holiness Movement. Our situation differs sharply from that of the 19th century, when Methodists were the dominant Evangelical church, and

The Baptist influence on Holiness churches has been so strong that some Nazarene scholars speak of the "Baptistification" of the Holiness Movement.

Wesleyan ideas shaped a large segment of Evangelicalism. Today the sheer numbers of Baptists in America force us to take notice of their influence.

In *Southern Cross: The Beginnings of the Bible Belt,* historian Christine Heyrman provides the basic grist for understanding the challenge. Evangelical religion, she correctly notes, was not indigenous to the South and had to adapt itself to modes of social organization and philosophy already in place in order to penetrate that region. It had to accept slavery and the hierarchical view of human relationships necessary to sustain the worldview of a slaveholding people. That hierarchical universe did not die with the Confederacy. It continued to live on in certain forms of Southern Evangelicalism that were idealized. Heyrman argues that if we wish to understand some of the basic tensions in American Evangelicalism today, we must know something about this history.[19]

The Southern Baptist Convention is the largest Protestant body in the United States. It is also the largest (but by no means only) organization promoting a style of Evangelical Christianity that views hierarchical relationships in church and world as scriptural and other styles as unscriptural. This influence threads its way through discussions of the role of women in church and society, and it affects modes of governance.

Our distinctive Wesleyan-Holiness heritage has a worthwhile contribution to make to a religious world whose uncritical assumptions are popular Baptistic ones. How well will we maintain our distinctive identity in the years ahead?

Review and Reflection

1. Some member of your family or at least a close friend has surely been a staunch Baptist. List the important elements in this person's personal religious views. Then relate them to the core Baptist beliefs you read in this chapter. Is this family member or close friend in tune with:

- Freewill Baptists?

- American Baptists?

- Southern Baptists?

- Landmark Baptists?

2. Consider the social reform leaders among the Baptists: Walter Rauschenbusch, Clarence Jordan, Martin Luther King Jr. Compare them with John Wesley's work with the poor and oppressed.

3. Evaluate the theological difference between Nazarenes and the majority of Baptists in these areas:
- prevenient grace

- empowered free will

- entire sanctification

- eternal security

---

19. Christine Leigh Heyrman, *Southern Cross: The Beginnings of the Bible Belt* (New York: Knopf, 1997).

Unity and Simplicity: The Christian Church (Disciples of Christ)

Founding Fathers

Barton W. Stone, a Presbyterian pastor in Cane Ridge, Kentucky, fostered a revival in 1801 that became one of the cornerstones of the Christian Church (Disciples of Christ). Thomas and Alexander Campbell, Scottish Presbyterians transplanted to Pennsylvania, founded the other branch of the movement that united in 1832 to form the Christian Church (Disciples of Christ).

Core Beliefs

The founding fathers, tired of Presbyterian and Baptist structures and strictures, wanted to restore the New Testament Church with no denominational hierarchy and no creed but the Bible. "Where the Bible speaks, we speak. Where the Bible is silent, we are silent." They sought to unify the fragmented Christianity of the American frontier under the banner of simple biblical religion. "In essentials, unity" was another of their slogans. The "essentials" included the New Testament as the final church Authority, adult believers' baptism by immersion only, Holy Communion for the immersed only, local church autonomy, and the right to interpret the Bible for oneself.

Agreement and Differences

Nazarenes agree with the Disciples on a high view of biblical authority, Jesus Christ as the one Savior, human free will and responsibility, commitment to missions, and the idea that all Christians are ministers. Differences come at the failure of the Disciples to clearly declare belief in the triune God, in their insistence that baptism is necessary for salvation and must be by immersion, the nature of sanctification, and the provision of rules for church members.

The Restoration Movement Today

The movement to restore pure New Testament religion and unify all Christians has split into four churches. The Christian Church (Disciples of Christ), more or less liberal, has about 1 million members. The Christian Church (Independent), more or less moderate, has 1.2 million. The Churches of Christ, conservative, have 1.7 million in the United States, 3.3 million worldwide. The International Church of Christ, radically conservative, has 85,000.

The Bible, the whole Bible, and nothing but the Bible.

13

Unity and Simplicity: The Christian Church (Disciples of Christ)

W<small>HERE</small> THE BIBLE SPEAKS, WE SPEAK. Where the Bible is silent, we are silent."

"In essentials, unity. In nonessentials, liberty. In all things, charity."

Such noble visions launched one of the largest churches native to American soil. The Christian Church (Disciples of Christ) was born to march under twin banners: restoration of the modern church to the pure standards of the New Testament Church, and the unification of all believers in one "Christian" church.

The restoration vision was to be achieved by simple attention to the Bible. The Bible, in reality the New Testament, was to be the only authoritative source for the doctrine, practice, and governance of the church. What could be more ideal?

One principle helped make that vision only a hope. The movement firmly believed that one of the *essentials* was the right for all Christians to interpret the Bible for themselves. They were finished with the strictures of European churches, they wanted nothing to do with loyalty-oath vows of denominations, and they wanted no state church to hand down official interpretations of the Scriptures. But this principle made the agreements required for unity even harder to come by.

Another sticking point was that the Disciples of Christ wanted to elevate the New Testament far above the Old Testament. Their neighbors on the frontier, the Presbyterians, Methodists, and Baptists, regarded the whole Bible as Christian Scripture. They did not take kindly to the demotion of the Ten Commandments, the 23rd psalm, and the creation stories.

Yet the dream of Christian unity was powerful. The early Disciples really thought that Christians, sick of the dizzying array of denominations hawking their wares on the American frontier, would rally behind their call to unity under simple Bible religion. Many did.

The religious denomination was an American innovation. In Europe, "confessional" churches were organized around a creedal statement such as the Heidelberg Confession or the Westminster Confession. Further, most European countries blessed and supported a state church. American democracy had separated church and state. Every religious outfit was on its own. The multiplicity of new churches was baffling. Bizarre doctrinal creations cluttered the idea market. The competition was fierce. Surely the people were tired of religious huckstering and would now turn to the Disciples' call to unity under plain biblical religion.

A Look at Origins

The very name Christian Church (Disciples of Christ) illustrates how hard it is to unify Christians. This church gets its name from two merging entities. At the dawn of the 19th century, the followers of Barton Stone in Kentucky and southern Indiana called themselves simply "Christians" or the "Christian Church." The followers of Thomas and Alexander Campbell called themselves "Disciples of Christ."

Barton Warren Stone

One of the four men usually regarded as principal founders of the Disciples of Christ church was Barton Warren Stone. Stone was born in 1772 in Port Tobacco, Maryland, the only founder of this religious tradition to actually be born in America. His parents were Anglican, but he became a Presbyterian minister. He became a pastor in Kentucky in 1796.

By 1800 the camp meeting part of the Second Great Awakening was in full swing in Kentucky. Stone attended a camp meeting in Logan County, Kentucky, in 1801 and went home to start a similar meeting in his pastorate at Cane Ridge. Preachers of every brand arrived on the scene, as did somewhere between 10,000 and 25,000 other persons. For a week, the camp meeting went on and would have lasted longer except food and shelter could not be provided for so many.

Cane Ridge was reported far and wide as the "greatest outpouring of the Spirit since Pentecost."[1] Ahlstrom calls it "a watershed in American church history, and the little log meetinghouse around which multitudes thronged and writhed has become a shrine for all who invoke the 'frontier spirit' in American Christianity."[2]

Most of the people in attendance at Cane Ridge were unlettered and crude; their worship was the same. The meetings were marked by "unrestrained zeal in seeking salvation through wrestling bouts with the devil."[3] These were punctuated by such bodily agitations as jerking, barking, laughing, dancing, falling, and the singing exercise.

What Barton Stone saw rising from the Cane Ridge revival was a vision of what Christians could accomplish when they got their hearts off sectarian doctrines and vested denominational interests. Methodist, Baptist, and Presbyterian

---

1. Ahlstrom, *Religious History,* 433.
2. Ibid.
3. Louis Cochran and Bess White Cochran, *Captives of the Word* (Garden City, N.Y.: Doubleday, 1969), 30.

preachers had all worked together with watershed results. Stone's vision came to possess his soul.

What his Presbyterian peers saw in the Cane Ridge phenomenon was one of their number cavorting with uneducated preachers in outrageous emotional excess. Stone, however, was as impatient with them as they were with him. Calvinistic predestination did not fit well on the frontier, where men and women daily carved their own future out of the wilderness with their own hands. In a land of freedom where free choices, free land, and free enterprise dominated, the Presbyterian structure and stricture seemed strangely out of place. Thus, the times gave an Arminian flavor to the developing movement's theology.

Along with several other preachers, Stone declared their independence from the Presbyterian Synod of Kentucky. Stone's followers were known simply as "Christians." They declared their intention to "sink into union with the Body of Christ at large."[4] Their preachers would not learn from books of theology but from the Bible. "It is better," they declared, "to enter life having only that one Book, than having many, to be cast into hell."[5]

Thomas and Alexander Campbell

Thomas Campbell belonged to the Seceder branch of Presbyterians in Scotland. After a troubled ministry in Northern Ireland, Thomas came to America in 1807. His early ministry in America was also troubling. Running afoul of two Presbyterian denominations, he was soon without a church.

In Washington, Pennsylvania, Thomas created the Christian Association. He announced that he was open to communing with all Christians, and in opposition to his Calvinist background began to declare (to the delight of the Arminians in the region) that Christ died for all persons and not just the "elect." With the "ideal of the union of all Christians flam[ing] up in his heart more brightly than ever,"[6] Campbell drew up his famous *Declaration and Address* to which the movement still looks for guidance. In it he declared that

- The true Church of Christ is "essentially, intentionally, and constitutionally one."
- The supreme authority for the Church is the New Testament. The Church can give no new commandment on any topic on which the Bible is silent. The road to salvation is clearly spelled out in the New Testament, and its instructions should be followed precisely.
- Creeds, confessions, and articles of faith have value for instruction, but since they are mere *interpretations* of Scripture, they are not binding or necessary to salvation and cannot be used as a test of faith.
- Since the New Testament Church had no denominational hierarchy or structure, each local church is to be self-governing. Denominations are evidence of our sinfulness, and such division among Christians is a horrid evil; all Christians should love each other.[7]

---

4. Mark G. Toulouse, *Joined in Discipleship* (St. Louis: Chalice Press, 1992), 27.
5. "The Last Will and Testament of the Springfield Presbytery" in Cochran and Cochran, *Captives of the Word*, 31.
6. Stephen J. England, *We Disciples* (St. Louis: Christian Board of Publication, 1946), 12.
7. For other summaries of this document, see ibid., 14-16; Cochran and Cochran, *Captives of the Word*, 6-7.

Campbell believed that, for the most part, 1,800 years of church history had been a doleful mistake. It was time to start over, restore the ancient order of things. His goal was to "take up the work of Christ where the apostles had laid it down."[8]

By 1809, when Campbell's son, Alexander, joined him from Scotland, the Christian Association was ready to become a church. One of the first official acts of the Brush Run Church, as it was now called, was to ordain Alexander Campbell. The Campbells applied to have Brush Run admitted as a Presbyterian church. The proposal was curtly denied. Soon the church joined the Redstone Baptist Association.

During this process, the Campbells became convinced that the only biblical baptism was immersion. Thus, on June 12, 1812, the Campbells were rebaptized by immersion in Buffalo Creek by a Baptist preacher, Matthius Luce. From that moment on, adult believer immersion became the one true baptism for the movement.

Alexander Campbell, educated at Glasgow, nurtured in Restorationism by John Glas and Robert Sandeman (men with whom John Wesley jousted more than once) as well as being named after wealthy Restorationist James Alexander Haldane, soon proved to be a strong leader. As a preacher and debater, he was almost without peer on the frontier. He also established himself as a journalist, editing his own paper, the *Christian Baptist*. In the pulpit and on the printed page, Alexander thundered out arguments about the errors of the creed makers Luther and Calvin, the evils of denominationalism, the sins of educated clergy, the need to restore the "ancient order of things," and the absolute necessity of baptism by immersion for the remission of sins.

> From that moment on, adult believer immersion became the one true baptism for the movement.

The Campbells were soon in trouble with the clergy of the Redstone Baptist Association and promptly joined the Mahoning Baptist Association in Ohio.

In 1821 Alexander met a young preacher, Walter Scott. They had both studied Glas and Sandeman as well as James Alexander Haldane and Robert Haldane. Both were products of their times, Enlightenment rationalists. "Both were as one in agreeing with [John] Locke . . . that the New Testament is the only court of appeal; and that Reason is its only arbiter."[9]

Campbell soon brought about the appointment of Walter Scott as the evangelist for the Mahoning Baptist Association. At first, the goal was to reform the Baptist association from within along the lines of the Restorationist vision. But before long, many of the preachers "confused their task of restoring the One Great Church with the more immediate and joyful job of destroying the present ones."[10] Scott himself seems to have been swept up in this mission to dismantle

8. England, *We Disciples*, 18.
9. Cochran and Cochran, *Captives of the Word*, 23.
10. Ibid., 42.

both Baptist and Methodist churches. After a Baptist-bashing revival in Salem, Ohio, he is reported to have said while riding away in triumph, "Who will now say there is a Baptist church in Salem?"[11]

Alexander Campbell and Walter Scott revisited the emotionalism that characterized frontier religion. Seekers at the revivals and camp meetings often went through extreme emotional agony. "Dying out" to sin might take an hour, or it might take months. The rational Presbyterian in his or her blood could not handle this emotional evangelism. They came up with a "shorter way" to salvation, one that was based on reason and the authority of the New Testament. It had a great appeal to those who were not about to fall at a mourners' bench and bawl out their search for God.

Scott's five-finger sermon, preached thousands of times, epitomizes the evangelistic appeal. Scott would raise his hands and lead the congregation in a drill of the way of salvation. The thumb stood for faith—believing that Jesus was the Son of God and the Savior. The first finger stood for repentance—turning away from sin to God in Christ. The second finger stood for baptism—immersion as an act of obedience to the command of Jesus himself, an act without which no one's sin will be remitted, though he believe and repent with all his heart. The third finger stood for forgiveness of sin, which occurred automatically (whether you felt a spiritual frenzy coming on or not). The little finger stood for the gift of the Holy Spirit, which all converts received at this point in the process.

This formula, observes Stephen J. England in *We Disciples*, provided a "rational and dignified . . . emphasis on what man could do toward his own salvation."[12] Forgiveness was not based on an emotional overthrow but "on the basis of God's own promise."[13]

This "elimination of emotion as the evidence of the forgiveness of sins . . . sounded the death knell of the mourner's bench as an instrument of evangelism in some circles."[14]

To Model Unity and Restoration

With each group about 10,000 strong, the followers of Barton Stone and Alexander Campbell united in 1832. It was a noble effort to unify Christians around simple biblical faith. Both groups preserved their own names: Christian Church (Disciples of Christ). Debates over denomination-like structure, missionary societies, calling ministers "Reverend," open or closed Communion, and serving Communion to unimmersed persons threatened schism. But by 1870 they had grown to 350,000.

The "in opinion, liberty" doctrine posed certain risks. Many of the more liberal came to take the unity plank in the platform as the primary reason for their existence. Some seemed ready to make almost any concession or compromise in order to keep the family together. "In opinion, liberty" served as their banner of rally.

---

11. Ibid., 47.
12. England, *We Disciples*, 43.
13. Ibid.
14. Ibid., 46.

On the right wing, some conservatives took the restoration of the primitive Church as the primary reason for existence. No musical instruments or choirs, no Communion for the unimmersed, no church auxiliaries that are not prescribed in the New Testament, no use of Sunday School literature—why would anyone want to study anything but the Bible? "In essentials, unity" seemed to be their banner of rally. Soon, however, the "right-wing tendency [was] displayed largely in the direction of multiplying the essentials."[15]

Some of the sermons in *The Living Pulpit of the Christian Church* (1868), a 589-page collection of homilies by leading Disciple pulpiteers, show just how strong a rigidity peculiar for a unification movement had grown. Let this glance at a sermon by Winthrop Hartly Hopson be representative. In "Baptism Essential to Salvation," he declares that those who go about in a revival or camp meeting telling folks that they can be saved merely by praying, repenting, and believing are spouting "an infidel sentiment" that is "absurd . . . false, [and] wicked." To so teach is "unmitigated wickedness." He goes on to proclaim, "The baptized penitent believer . . . will receive remission of sins. No other man will." To the question, "But will I be damned if I am not baptized?" Hopson answers, "Certainly. Why not?"[16]

Trouble in Paradise

The experiment to unify Christians survived the Civil War, while many other denominations split North and South. But "it is a tragic fact that the union, so happily brought about in 1832 and so successfully tested by the fires of civil warfare, should have proceeded to defeat itself in the half century after the . . . war."[17] By 1906 a group of conservative congregations deserted the "brotherhood" over the music question. They called themselves the Churches of Christ and sought more than ever to restore their worship to the very New Testament pattern.

Those in the liberal wing found fewer and fewer "essentials" around which to build unity.

During the 1920s, another group broke off from the Disciples because of the latter's embracing of theological liberalism, or modernism. Key in this situation was the acceptance of higher criticism of the Bible by many Disciples. The authority of the Bible was seriously undermined. And for a movement born and sustained by "the Bible, the whole Bible, and nothing but the Bible," this was a shuddering earthquake that could not be ignored.

Biblical criticism even weakened the one thing that distinguished the early movement—baptism by immersion. Within six years after Alexander Campbell died, scholars discovered the *Didache*, an Early Church document older than

---

15. Ibid., 64.

16. *The Living Pulpit of the Christian Church: A Series of Discourses, Doctrinal and Practical, from Representative Men Among the Disciples of Christ,* ed. W. T. Moore (Cincinnati: R. W. Carroll and Co., 1868), 291, 300-301.

17. England, *We Disciples,* 29.

some of the New Testament books themselves. The problem: this ancient document described baptism by pouring. Water was to be poured on the convert three times "in the name of the Father, Son, and Holy Spirit."

Those in the liberal wing found fewer and fewer "essentials" around which to build unity. Even the assumption that the Early Church was worthy of being restored had been questioned for decades. Was the Early Church really free of strife and sin? Is Corinth a model for us? Herbert L. Willett, dean of the Disciples Divinity House in Chicago, declared, "Restoration of the conditions prevailing in the apostolic churches is both impossible and undesirable."[18]

Mark Toulouse points out another hazard that befell the Restorationist vision: "Nostalgia sees history as a simpler time, a safer time, a more certain time. . . . It gives the impression that the present's only hope is in recreating the past. . . . Nostalgia is really one of the great enemies of history, because it distorts the picture."[19]

With the movement's faith in the Bible undermined, its distinguishing practice (immersion) being second-guessed, the Restoration principle being called a faulty assumption, and the brotherhood fractured into three churches, tough days lay ahead.

By 1932 the 100th anniversary of the Stone-Campbell movement to unite all Christians was itself tragically fractured. The Disciples of Christ went on to become a mainline denomination, liberal in theology, with a highly educated clergy, active in ecumenical organizations and movements, and with lectionary sermons in most pulpits.

Today the Disciples of Christ is the smallest of the principal entities springing from the Stone-Campbell movement. Like other mainline denominations, their membership has shrunk in recent decades. Today barely 1 million followers in 4,031 churches are to be found in the United States. At one time the movement had 5 million adherents. Now the Disciples have a typical denominational structure (though local congregations enjoy much autonomy). They are represented in the National Council of Churches, the World Council of Churches, and the Consultation on Church Union.

The Churches of Christ, the group that departed in 1906, is now the largest Restoration group. They have 1.7 million adherents in 13,000 congregations in the Southern and Southwestern United States and another 1.6 million in the 75 countries in which their missionaries work. They operate 21 colleges, several of them in Europe. They publish 117 periodicals. In the Churches of Christ the original teachings of the Campbells are most rigidly endorsed. Fundamentalism is embraced and liturgical forms shunned, though worship is expected to be conducted in a dignified manner.

The Christian Church (Independent) is the name used by the second group that broke away from the Disciples. Reports show them to have a membership of

18. Cochran and Cochran, *Captives of the Word*, 235.
19. Toulouse, *Joined in Discipleship*, 65.

1.2 million in the United States. They support 30 colleges. Standard Publishing in Cincinnati is associated with this group.[20] Generally the Christian Church (Independent) folks represent the moderate voice among the Stone-Campbell ecclesiastical descendants.

An energetic, fast-growing, and ultraradical group has recently sprung up from Church of Christ roots. Kip McKean's International Church of Christ (formerly the Boston Church of Christ) has declared that its parent body is a backslidden, worldly, dead church. McKean invites those who really want to be saved to join the International Church of Christ. He says it's God's only true Church in these times and that no one is likely to be saved who has not been baptized in this church. Now numbering some 85,000 in 60 congregations, this group seems to have picked up the weaknesses of both the Restorationist and Shepherding Movements rather than their strengths. The International Church of Christ has been frequently charged with very abusive practices.

Thus the conservatives, the moderates, and the liberals in the Restorationist Movement have gone their own ways. How strange that these categories should, in the end, be stronger that the Restorationist vision itself! But let there be no doubt—each group sees itself as living out the dominant values of its rich heritage.

Common Ground Between Nazarenes and the Restoration Churches

Given the diversity among the religious bodies that emerged from the Restoration Movement, it's hard to say exactly what they believe and practice. Therefore, in this discussion we will cite only a few core beliefs that tend to represent the whole movement.

1. **Jesus Christ, Savior and Lord.** Nazarenes heartily endorse this statement from the Disciples of Christ *Design:* "We confess that Jesus is the Christ, the Son of the Living God, and proclaim him Lord and Savior of the world."[21]

2. **A high view of the authority of the Bible.** Both Nazarenes and the Restorationists endorse the Protestant doctrine of *sola scriptura*. Both claim that the Bible is the final rule for faith and practice. The Restorationists tend to be more literal in invoking the Bible as the rule for churches. While recognizing that there is a promise and fulfillment factor between the Testaments, Nazarenes view both Old and New Testaments as Christian Scripture. The Restoration tradition, however, elevates the New Testament to the real place of authority.

3. **Human beings are free and responsible.** The Holiness Movement and the Restoration Movement were born in America, where individual freedom and democracy are prized. These factors elbowed their way into the religion of both groups. This put them in opposition to the determinism of both the religious (predestination) and secular (behaviorism) varieties.

4. **Missionary minded.** Both Nazarenes and the Restoration churches make missions a priority.

---

20. For a comparative chart of the beliefs and practices of the churches in this tradition, see Cochran and Cochran, *Captives of the Word,* 254. See Mead and Hill, *Handbook of Denominations,* 94-101, for more statistical and structural detail of the churches in the Restoration Movement.

21. D. Duane Cummins, *A Handbook for Today's Disciples* (St. Louis: Bethany Press, 1981), 23.

5. Every Christian is a minister. The Christian Church's *Design* declares, "The fundamental ministry within the church is that of Jesus Christ. . . . By virtue of membership in the church, every Christian enters into the corporate ministry of God's people."[22] Nazarenes also believe that lay ministry is very important. The Nazarenes, however, from the start had a higher view of the ordained clergy than did the early Stonites and Campbellites. The Restoration churches, however, have now come to appreciate the value of an educated and ordained ministry.

Points of Difference

While we share much in common, there are differences between the Nazarenes and the Restoration churches.

1. Emphasis on sanctification. Building on a Wesleyan foundation, Nazarenes make entire sanctification their distinctive doctrine. We believe that it has both gradual and instantaneous dimensions, but at some point after conversion, the Christian's heart may be brought into "complete devotement" to God, and in a second definite work of grace, the believer is cleansed from inward sin and filled with the love and power of the Holy Spirit. The Christian is not to live as a slave to sin or as a pilgrim who constantly and repeatedly is victimized by sin. The Restoration churches don't have anything against pure hearts or being filled with the Spirit. But they believe that all this happens at baptism, the gift of the Spirit being the fifth step in the formula for salvation. I raised the question of sanctification with a friend of mine who is a pastor in the Christian Church. He said, "In my circles, the question almost never comes up. It's not something that we naturally emphasize."

2. The nature of Christian baptism and conversion. Nazarenes believe that baptism is an outward sign of an inward grace already received. It is a public testimony of one's experience of salvation by grace through faith and of one's intention to live as a dedicated Christian. The Restorationist generally believes that baptism is an integral part of the salvation formula. Without baptism no one can be saved, many of them believe. Nazarenes believe the Scriptures teach that repentance of one's sins and confession of faith in Christ as gracious Savior brings forgiveness and adoption into the family of God. Typically, Restorationists have taught that the salvation formula is (1) affirmation of belief that Jesus is both Son of God and Savior, (2) repentance of sin, (3) baptism, (4) forgiveness granted and received, and (5) the gift of the Spirit bestowed.

For most in the Restoration tradition, salvation is simply not possible without step three—baptism. Some churches will not serve Communion to an unbaptized person. It is "baptism [that] purges all things that have diminished the life of our spirit. The old life is buried, new life is born, sins are forgiven. Baptism represents a . . . moral cleansing, a transformation of the soul, a receiving of grace."[23]

---

22. Ibid., 50-51.
23. Ibid., 28.

Disciples of Christ educator Ronald E. Osborn wrote, "Instead of offering salvation to those who longed for it . . . too many Disciples spent their time trying to prove that no one could be saved who had not followed this [baptismal] formula."[24] In proposing a rational, objective formula rather than an experiential, subjective, "know so" salvation, the Disciples were trying to overcome the emotionalism that plagued both the times and their own Cane Ridge origins. The Campbell side of the heritage in particular resisted the "frenzied or mystical or compulsive . . . violent . . . conversion of the camp meetings, where frightened sinners agonized for . . . an assurance . . . and found release in those strange states of bodily agitation which we associate with 'Holy Rollers' or rock musicians."[25]

In some places, the objective baptismal ritual for salvation was soon reduced to a legalism that Wesleyan-Holiness people found quite incompatible with their own doctrine of inner assurance of salvation.

We differ with the American Restoration churches on their claim that true Christian baptism is by immersion and immersion only. The Nazarene article of faith that says that "baptism may be administered by sprinkling, pouring, or immersion, according to the choice of the applicant"[26] is baffling to our Restoration friends.

3. The doctrine of God. "We believe . . . that . . . God is Triune in essential being, revealed as Father, Son, and Holy Spirit."[27] With this statement, the first Nazarene article of faith begins. The churches of the Restoration Movement have never officially affirmed a belief in the Trinity.

The churches of the Restoration Movement have never officially affirmed a belief in the Trinity.

They believe in God the Father. They insist, generally, on the divinity and humanity of Jesus Christ. But no doctrine of the Holy Spirit has gained dominance among these people who fervently believe that all Christians may interpret the Bible for themselves. Clearly, founder Barton Stone was anti-Trinitarian, calling the Holy Spirit simply "the energy of God."[28] Alexander Campbell taught that the Holy Spirit was a product of the Scriptures and only worked through the Scriptures and had an existence separate from the Father and the Son. This could lead to tritheism, but some say that it at least makes Trinitarian faith a possibility in the Restoration tradition.

4. Rules for church members. Nazarenes have produced a set of General Rules and a list of Special Rules that prescribe the way the holy life should be lived. Apparently we have believed that Christians need specific guidance about such matters as divorce, abortion, lotteries, the cinema, tobacco, liquor, dancing, secret orders, and the use of sleeping pills and stimulants.

24. Ronald E. Osborn, "A Future for Disciples of Christ," in *Classic Themes in Disciples Theology,* ed. Kenneth Lawrence (Fort Worth: Texas Christian University Press, 1986), 147.
25. Ibid., 146.
26. Article XII, *Manual, Church of the Nazarene, 1997—2001,* 32.
27. Article I, ibid., 26.
28. Cummins, *Handbook for Today's Disciples,* 25.

The Restorationists, on the other hand, seek to have no rule book but the Bible. D. Duane Cummins, a Disciples of Christ leader, says, "On matters of personal morality Disciples hold a deep confidence in the ability of individuals to form judgments for themselves."[29]

Working Together

We do not cite the similarities and differences between the Nazarenes and the American Restoration churches in an effort to score more points than they. This book is not about declaring our brothers and sisters in Christ as heretical or inferior.

Rather, the comparisons and contrasts cited in this chapter should be viewed as an effort to inform. As we and Christians of all traditions join forces against the common challenges of our non-Christian, postmodern culture, we need to know each other. We need to know our strengths, our vulnerabilities, our prized heritages, and yes, our baggage that we bring to these grand and awful times.

The words of John Wesley seem to fit: "Think not the bigotry of another is any excuse for your own. . . . Beware of retorting. . . . Let him have all the bigotry to himself."[30]

Review and Reflection

1. Getting Things Straight

   a. Which branch of the early Restoration Movements has the most in common with Nazarene origins: the Barton Stone/Cane Ridge folks or the Campbellites?

   b. Compare the Disciples' view of Scripture with that of the Nazarenes, the Lutherans, and Eastern Orthodoxy.

   c. Contrast the Disciples' and Nazarene views of baptism, the Trinity, sanctification, and Holy Communion.

2. Putting Ideas to Work

   a. In what ways does this chapter equip you to counsel helpfully with a friend or neighbor raised in the Restorationist tradition?

   b. If you are visiting a Disciples or Churches of Christ church with a relative, how will you instruct your children regarding the Communion service?

   c. In what ministries could your church join with a Christian Church (Disciples of Christ) congregation? What types of cooperative ventures would be best to avoid?

3. Devotion Time

Meditate on the quote from John Wesley with which this chapter closes: "Think not the bigotry of another is any excuse for your own. . . . Beware of retorting. . . . Let him have all the bigotry to himself."

---

29. Ibid., 46.
30. John Wesley, "A Caution Against Bigotry," in *Sermons on Several Occasions*, 547.

Part VI

PENTECOSTAL AND CHARISMATIC CHURCHES

- Pentecostals and Charismatics

- Nazarenes in Dialogue with Pentecostals and Charismatics

Thumbnail Sketch

PENTECOSTALS AND CHARISMATICS

Historical Overview

The Pentecostal/Charismatic landscape is divided into six major sectors:

- *Wesleyan-Holiness Pentecostals* emerged from the American Holiness Movement.
- *"Finished Work" Pentecostals* rejected entire sanctification and broke off from Wesleyan-Holiness Pentecostals.
- *"Jesus Only," "Unitarian," or "Oneness" Pentecostals* deny the doctrine of the Trinity and teach that Jesus is the name of God and that believers should be baptized only in Jesus' name.
- *Charismatic fellowships* exist within most mainline denominations (including the Roman Catholic Church) or are nondenominational or interdenominational (such as the Full Gospel Business Men's Association).
- *New Charismatic denominations*, such as Calvary Chapel and the Vineyard Fellowship, are emerging from the Charismatic Movement of the late 1960s and 1970s.
- The fringe of independent radical churches and ministries.

Core Beliefs

All six sectors embrace the gifts of the Holy Spirit mentioned by Paul, including speaking in unknown tongues, interpretation of tongues, prophecy, and healing.

Most also embrace such traditional beliefs as the inspiration of the Bible, the deity of Christ, the Virgin Birth, and Christian conversion. Beliefs about baptism, baptism with the Holy Spirit, and entire sanctification vary among Pentecostal/Charismatic groups.

Agreement and Differences

Nazarenes share orthodox views with the majority of Pentecostals/Charismatics: Scriptural authority, the deity of Christ, the Virgin Birth, and Christian conversion. But Nazarenes question and challenge the heterodox views of the Trinity held by Oneness Pentecostals, and we challenge the idea that tongues-speaking is the evidence of Spirit baptism, an idea held by all Pentecostals. We also question what C. B. Jernigan called the "unbridled emotionalism . . . that led its weaker members astray." Nazarenes also reject the belief in three works of grace taught by one branch of the movement.

Pentecostals and Charismatics Today

Principal bodies in North America include

- Church of God in Christ: 5.5 million members.
- Pentecostal Holiness Church: 150,000 in the United States; 2.3 million worldwide.
- Church of God (Cleveland, Tennessee): 730,000 in North America; 4 million worldwide.
- Assemblies of God: 2.3 million in the United States; 22 million worldwide.
- International Church of the Foursquare Gospel: 224,000 in the United States; 2 million worldwide.
- Pentecostal Assemblies of the World: 1 million in the United States.
- United Pentecostal Church International: 600,000 in North America; 2.3 million worldwide.
- New Charismatic denominations such as Calvary Chapel and Vineyard Christian Fellowship have a combined 1,230 congregations in North America.

Q. Are tongues-speaking Pentecostals our brothers in Christ?
A. Some of them are; others are our sisters in Christ.

—William McCumber, *Herald of Holiness*, September 1, 1984

14 ~ PENTECOSTALS AND CHARISMATICS

YOU ARE SEATED AT AN OLD-FASHIONED REVIVAL MEETING in an open-air tabernacle. The sawdust trail separates you from the Pentecostal evangelist. But wait! The revivalist ridicules the doctrine of the Trinity as a crude belief in three Gods and insists that only those baptized in the name of "Jesus only" are true Christians. Now he asks if some present previously baptized "in the name of the Father, Son, and Holy Spirit" need to be rebaptized!

The scene is much different in a South Bend, Indiana, house near Notre Dame University. An eclectic group of Roman Catholics meet for informal worship: students, townspeople, and several university staff and faculty members. During prayer, the soft but unmistakable murmur of "speaking in tongues" is heard from several participants.

Or imagine a large African-American church in Memphis. Loud, vibrant music draws the congregation to its feet more than once. Near the end of the sermon, the preacher states passionately that some present have been saved and sanctified but need to press on and receive the baptism of the Holy Spirit "with tongues."

Last, enter an Assemblies of God church in Springfield, Missouri, for a Sunday morning service. The worship differs little in style or content from that in the nearby Church of the Nazarene. Similar mix of hymns and praise choruses. Similar pastoral prayer. Similar sermon. Slight nuances of terminology, but never a sermon on—or even a mention of—entire sanctification.

Each setting represents a different aspect of Pentecostal/Charismatic religion, a world of immense diversity.

The relationship between Wesleyan-Holiness and Pentecostal/Charismatic churches often seems equally as complicated. Wesleyans have viewed Pentecostals as good folks who have "gone off the deep end," while Pentecostals (returning the favor) have viewed us as good folks who have stopped short of the authentic baptism of the Holy Spirit.

Our tradition and theirs both originated as revival movements that teach a work of divine grace in Christian life after conversion. Indeed, 20th-century Pentecostalism originated *in* the American Holiness Movement. The oldest Pentecostal denominations—including America's largest—are *both* Wesleyan-Holiness *and* Pentecostal in theology.

Sorting It Out

A distinction is sometimes made between Pentecostals and Charismatics, the latter also referred to as "neo-Pentecostals," though the distinction is less and less relevant. Pentecostalism emerged early in the 20th century. The Charismatic Movement sprang from a similar revival movement that began in the 1960s.

The Pentecostal/Charismatic landscape is divided into six major sectors:

- *Wesleyan-Holiness Pentecostals* emerged from the American Holiness Movement.
- *"Finished Work" Pentecostals* rejected entire sanctification and broke off from Wesleyan-Holiness Pentecostals.
- *"Jesus Only" or "Unitarian" Pentecostals* deny the doctrine of the Trinity and teach that Jesus is the name of God and that believers should be baptized only in Jesus' name; they broke off from the Finished Work people.
- *Charismatic fellowships* exist within most mainline denominations (including the Roman Catholic Church) or are nondenominational or interdenominational (such as the Full Gospel Business Men's Association).
- *New Charismatic denominations,* such as Calvary Chapel and the Vineyard Fellowship, are emerging from the Charismatic Movement of the late 1960s and 1970s.
- The fringe of independent radical churches and ministries.

All six sectors embrace "the gifts of the Holy Spirit" mentioned by Paul: speaking in unknown tongues, interpretation of tongues, prophecy, and healing. Indeed, a significant difference between our classical Wesleyan-Holiness tradition and the Pentecostal/Charismatic traditions is this: the Wesleyan way of salvation and discipleship is wrapped up in the "fruit of the Spirit," while Pentecostals and Charismatics focus their worship and community around the "gifts of the Spirit."

The Fire

Modern Pentecostalism has some significant origins in the Midwest, a region crisscrossed by Holiness revivalists. One was Benjamin Irwin, whose "third blessing heresy" foreshadowed Pentecostalism. Irwin preached, based on his interpretation of Matt. 3:11, that a "baptism of fire" followed the baptism of the Holy Spirit. In 1898 the Fire Baptized Holiness Church was founded around this doctrine. Irwin soon taught other baptisms—of dynamite, lyddite, selenite, and "oxidite"—alienating (in one historian's words) "all but the most entranced of his followers."[1] After he was reportedly seen drunk in Omaha, a leading Holiness paper dubbed him "whiskey baptized," and Irwin withdrew from the ministry. His church declined rapidly and nearly disappeared.

---

1. Charles Edwin Jones, "Benjamin Hardin Irwin," in Reid et al., *Dictionary of Christianity in America,* 582-83.

C. B. Jernigan, an early Nazarene leader, witnessed "the fire" in Texas Holiness camp meetings. Jernigan judged it to be unbridled emotionalism that discredited the Holiness Movement and led its weaker members astray. Some of "the fire teachers imbibed still more fanatical doctrines," he noted, and "among them was 'demon possession.' . . . They had demons of sickness: and various other kinds of demons that tormented the sanctified. The doctrine of demon possession was not very widespread, but played havoc wherever it took root."[2]

The Apostolic Faith Movement

Another Holiness revivalist, Charles F. Parham, articulated a different and more coherent theology of three works of grace. Parham briefly pastored a Methodist church in Eudora, Kansas, but did not pursue ordination, claiming a dislike for bishops and Methodist church order. He became a freelance evangelist, conducting revivals in eastern Kansas. He emphasized faith healing and Christ's premillennial second coming, and he established a faith home and school of evangelism in Topeka.

In 1900 Parham asked the students to study Acts and identify any outward signs that could be interpreted as "the initial evidence" of the baptism of the Holy Spirit. The students concluded that speaking in tongues could qualify as that sign. Parham agreed and urged the students to seek it. On January 1, 1901, Agnes Ozman spoke in tongues after a New Year's Eve watchnight service. Parham and others also did so in coming days.

Parham and his disciples believed that they were speaking in known but unlearned languages, not tongues of angels. They were confident this gift of languages would enable them to play an important role in world evangelization. The movement came to be called the Apostolic Faith. Its theology emphasized

- conversion,
- entire sanctification as a second work of grace,
- baptism in the Holy Spirit with tongues as the initial evidence.

Unlike Irwin's theology, there was no "fire." Instead, the baptism of the Holy Spirit was separated from entire sanctification and defined as a separate and third work of grace, with tongues verifying its reception.

The Apostolic Faith spread in southeast Kansas and adjacent areas of Missouri, Arkansas, and Oklahoma, taking root in small mining communities. By 1905 Houston and surrounding towns were also a center of the Apostolic Faith as Parham's revivals there met with success. The Bible school was moved to Houston, where Parham led a growing revival movement until 1907, when he was arrested on a morals charge in San Antonio. He was never brought to trial but left Texas amid rumors that he had signed a confession and agreed to leave the state. Whatever the facts were, his Texas followers rejected his leadership thereafter. An earlier effort to take control of the Azusa Street revival in Los Angeles had failed, and Parham returned to Kansas, where he led a small denomination from his headquarters in Baxter Springs, Kansas, until his death in 1929.[3]

---

2. Jernigan, *Pioneer Days of Holiness Movement*, 152-54.
3. For an excellent biography of Parham, see James R. Goff Jr., *Fields White unto Harvest: Charles F. Parham and the Missionary Origins of Pentecostalism* (Fayetteville, Ark., and London: University of Arkansas Press, 1988).

Azusa Street

A Black Holiness evangelist named William J. Seymour (1870—1922) was one of Parham's students in Houston. Since Parham had no inclination to challenge the mores of the segregated South, Seymour listened to lectures from the hallway while white students sat in the classroom. Yet the segregated Seymour—the "least of these"—became a significant figure in Pentecostal history.

Seymour went to Los Angeles to preach in 1906. When his Apostolic Faith theology was rejected by the Holiness group that had brought him, he opened an independent mission on Azusa Street and started a revival meeting. The secular and religious press gave it considerable attention, and evangelists and visitors from around the nation knelt at Seymour's altar and spoke in tongues, receiving the "baptism of the Holy Spirit." The meetings continued for three years, and the Azusa Street revival's influence radiated to virtually every part of North America and even to Europe, Asia, and Africa. The mission evolved into a church that Seymour pastored until his death.

The Azusa Street revival's influence radiated to virtually every part of North America and even to Europe, Asia, and Africa.

Charles Parham's basic theology was disseminated widely through the Azusa Street revival. Florence Crawford, a white associate of Seymour's, launched a separate branch of the Apostolic Faith in the Pacific Northwest.

Principal Branches of Pentecostalism Today

Pentecostal Holiness Churches (Three Works of Grace)

Proselytes took the Apostolic Faith's theology to the South and Midwest, where the first Pentecostal denominations were formed. Three major denominations emerged that embraced the three-works-of-grace theology.

The Church of God in Christ. The Church of God in Christ reports a membership of 5.5 million members. A predominantly African-American church, it originated in 1895 as a Wesleyan-Holiness denomination through the ministries of Charles H. Mason and Charles Price Jones, former Baptists. After Mason accepted Pentecostal-Holiness teachings at Azusa Street Mission, however, the leaders went separate ways, Jones to establish the Church of Christ (Holiness). The Church of God in Christ has grown rapidly in the past three decades. The largest Pentecostal denomination in America, it is also the largest church that teaches entire sanctification as a second work of grace. It is governed by local bishops.

Pentecostal Holiness Church. The Pentecostal Holiness Church was organized when the remnants of Irwin's Fire Baptized Holiness Church merged with the Holiness Church of North Carolina, which A. B. Crumpler founded in 1900. After a majority of his people accepted Pentecostal views in 1908, Crumpler abandoned the ministry and returned to the Methodist Church as a layperson. The significant early leader of the Pentecostal Holiness Church was Joseph H. King. It is now known as the International Pentecostal Holiness Church, with headquarters a short distance from Southern Nazarene University in Bethany, Oklahoma. Oral Roberts, raised in a Pentecostal Holiness parsonage, was its best-known preacher in the 1950s.[4] The church currently has just over 150,000 members in the United States but nearly 2.3 million members worldwide.[5]

The Church of God (Cleveland, Tennessee). Another Pentecostal-Holiness church emerged in Tennessee. The Christian Union, founded in 1886, became the nucleus of a small connection of Holiness churches in which tongues-speaking was a characteristic by late 1896. At the second General Assembly in 1907, the name Church of God was adopted. A. J. Tomlinson was the first general overseer until his autocratic ways led to his dismissal in 1923. Church headquarters are located in Cleveland, Tennessee. By 1995 the denomination had over 722,500 members in the United States, nearly 8,000 in Canada, and almost 4 million worldwide. The church does not ordain women but permits them to serve as preachers and evangelists. It observes the ordinances of baptism by immersion, the Lord's Supper, and foot washing.[6]

The Finished Work Controversy

Pentecostalism grew theologically diverse as it proliferated. William H. Durham (1873—1912), a former Baptist, was one of the first to publicly challenge the underlying Holiness teachings in early Pentecostalism. Durham's North Avenue Mission in Chicago was an important link in spreading Pentecostalism to Brazil, Italy, and South America. By 1910 Durham was preaching against entire sanctification. Historian William Menzies states that Durham was convinced that the doctrine was vague and could not be verified in a tangible way.

Durham articulated a view known in Pentecostal circles as "the finished work of Calvary" theory of sanctification. He taught that the problem of sin in the Christian life is dealt with at conversion and that the unfolding of this work in the Christian life is a gradual process of sanctification.[7]

Durham's arguments persuaded former Baptists, Presbyterians, those from the Christian and Missionary Alliance, and others with a background of mild Calvinism. A second round of denominational formation began. Those uncomfortable with the doctrine of entire sanctification withdrew from the earlier Pentecostal churches and linked with independent missions and congregations to form church bodies more compatible with their beliefs.

The Assemblies of God. The most prominent denomination to spring from the Finished Work controversy was the Assemblies of God, organized in 1914 at Hot Springs, Arkansas. Under the chairmanship of Eudorus N. Bell, it adopted a congregational form of church government. It spread rapidly in the South and in

---

4. An excellent history of the church is Vinson Synan's *Old-Time Power: A History of the Pentecostal Holiness Church* (Franklin Springs, Ga.: Advocate Press, 1973).

5. Bedell, ed., *Yearbook of Churches, 1996*, 254; International Pentecostal Holiness Church web site, at <http://www.iphc.org/docs/hisherit.html>, March 26, 1997.

6. Bedell, *Yearbook of American Churches, 1996*, 251. Also Susie C. Stanley, "Churches of God," in Reid et al., *Dictionary of Christianity in America,* 279. Also the Church of God (Cleveland, Tenn.) home page, at <http://www.mindspring.com/~cog/cog3.htm>, March 31, 1997.

7. William W. Menzies, "The Non-Wesleyan Origins of the Pentecostal Movement," in *Aspects of Pentecostal-Charismatic Origins,* ed. Vinson Synan (Plainfield, N.J.: Logos International, 1975), 90-92.

major cities across the United States. By the 1950s it was penetrating smaller Midwestern towns like Eudora, Kansas, where Charles F. Parham had pastored the Methodist church. In 1995 the Assemblies of God reported just under 1.4 million full members and an inclusive membership of 2.3 million for the United States. Its worldwide membership was much higher: over 22 million.[8] Nationally known ministers of the Assemblies of God have included former television evangelists Jim and Tammy Faye Bakker of the PTL Club and Jimmy Swaggart.

International Church of the Foursquare Gospel. Aimee Semple McPherson, a flamboyant evangelist briefly associated with the Assemblies of God, was a former Salvation Army worker. She and her first husband were ordained by William Durham before going to China as missionaries. Robert Semple died in Hong Kong, and Aimee returned to America with their child. She developed a popular evangelistic career, known simply as "Sister Aimee." In 1923 she dedicated the 5,300-seat Angelus Temple in Los Angeles, the mother church of what developed into the International Church of the Foursquare Gospel. Its four primary theological principles emphasize Jesus as Savior, Baptizer (with the Holy Spirit), Healer, and Coming King. Today the International Church of the Foursquare Gospel has just over 2 million members worldwide, of whom approximately 224,000 live in the United States.[9]

Oneness Pentecostalism

The Assemblies of God church was only months old when a controversy shattered its peace. Evangelist Frank Ewart began preaching that baptism was to be administered in the name of Jesus only, not in the name of "the Father, the Son, and the Holy Spirit." This was based on several places in Acts in which groups were said to "believe in the name of Jesus" and were baptized in His name. Ewart and other

Evangelist Frank Ewart began preaching that baptism was to be administered in the name of Jesus only, not in the name of "the Father, the Son, and the Holy Spirit."

supporters were forced to defend their interpretation in light of Jesus' own words in Matthew: "Go and make disciples of all nations, baptizing them in the name of the Father and of the Son and of the Holy Spirit" (28:19).

As the "Jesus only" folk marshaled evidence for their baptismal formula, their basic concept of God shifted until they denied the doctrine of the Trinity altogether. Oneness Pentecostals came to hold that Trinitarianism is really tritheism—belief in three Gods, not one. They asserted that "Jesus" is the true name of the one God and that "Father," "Son," and "Holy Spirit" are merely *titles*. Thus, when Jesus says to baptize "in the name of the Father and of the Son and of the Holy Spirit," the reference is to the *name* (Jesus), which these *titles* signify.

---

8. Assemblies of God Pentecostal Fellowship home page, <http://www.cyberramp.net/~gdm/index.html>, March 17, 1997.

9. International Church of the Foursquare Gospel home page, <http://www.foursquare.org/detail.html>, March 7, 1997.

Oneness Pentecostals, then and now, hold that those who have not been baptized by the correct formula are not true Christians, since they have not fulfilled Jesus' command. Moreover, within the Oneness camp two different understandings of the way of salvation emerged:

- The group closest to traditional Protestantism sees the new birth as a conversion experience, typically followed by baptism in the name of Jesus and by the "baptism of the Holy Spirit" with tongues as the initial evidence.
- A different group of Oneness Pentecostals, however, holds that the new birth is not equated with a conversion experience per se but with a process that begins in repentance, continues in water baptism by immersion in the name of Jesus only, and is completed through Holy Spirit baptism, which is accompanied with tongues. Only those who complete this whole process experience the new birth. As one Oneness body states, "The various aspects of faith and obedience work together in God's grace to reconcile us to God."[10] The new birth becomes a legalistic formula.

The Oneness controversy divided the Assemblies of God for two years. Even E. N. Bell, a principal founder, was rebaptized by the "Jesus only" formula before J. Roswell Flowers and others brought him back to orthodoxy. Finally, the 1916 General Council passed a declaration of principles, only after vigorous debate, that placed the Assemblies firmly on the side of orthodox Trinitarianism. Over one-fourth of the Assemblies of God ministers withdrew over the issue.

The Pentecostal Assemblies of the World. The ministers who withdrew tried to remain together, but racial divisions eventually led to a separation. Two principal denominations emerged from the Oneness controversy. The central personality in the first was G. T. Haywood, a prominent African-American Pentecostal in Indianapolis. It took the name Pentecostal Assemblies of the World and today reports an estimated inclusive membership of 1 million in the United States.[11]

The United Pentecostal Church International. The second major Oneness body was the United Pentecostal Church, formed in 1945 by the merger of two smaller Oneness groups. It currently claims a worldwide membership of over 2.3 million, of whom an estimated 600,000 are in the United States and Canada. Its polity blends congregational and presbyterian elements. The denomination

- affirms a strict view of biblical inerrancy;
- believes the doctrine of the Trinity to be "inadequate and a departure from the consistent and emphatic biblical revelation of God being one";
- states that its overall doctrines "reflect most of the beliefs of the Holiness-Pentecostal movement, with the exception of the 'second work of grace,' the historic doctrine of the Trinity, and the traditional Trinitarian formula in water baptism."[12]

---

10. United Pentecostal Church International home page, <http://www.upci.org/main/about/>, April 1, 1997.

11. Bedell, *Yearbook of Churches, 1996*, 255. This figure of 1 million seems unlikely, however, for the church reports only 1,760 congregations in the United States. This would put the average size of a Pentecostal Assemblies of the World congregation at over 550.

12. See note 10 above.

Interpreting Pentecostal Origins

The baptism of the Holy Spirit and tongues are dominant characteristics of Pentecostalism, but were they its essence? Some analysts say no. In *Vision of the Disinherited,* social historian Robert Mapes Anderson argues that Pentecostalism arose as a millennial (or Second Coming) movement in which tongues and other spiritual gifts were regarded as signs of the Holy Spirit's outpouring just before the end of history. When Jesus did not return immediately and the white-hot millennial fervor cooled, Anderson says Pentecostals shifted their primary emphasis from the end times to the gifts.

But James Goff Jr. argues that Pentecostalism is essentially a missionary movement. He stresses that Charles F. Parham and his associates believed that their "unknown tongues" were human languages, given to evangelize the world, while the "baptism of the Holy Spirit" was understood as the power given to accomplish that task. A strong millennial hope was part of their context, but Goff understands the world mission—not the millennium or the gifts of the Spirit—as their central concern. As Goff sees it, early Pentecostals regarded the "gifts of the Spirit" as tools for world evangelization "in the last days."

Old Bottles, New Wine

Although American Pentecostals settled into three main camps, other forces worked to further diversify the tradition and perpetuate it as a revival movement. Evangelists played an important role in this development, promoting new emphases when older ones began losing their popular appeal. Several of these emphases shaped contemporary Pentecostal/Charismatic life.

The New Order of the Latter Rain. Not all Pentecostals welcomed the stability that Pentecostal denominations offered. The Assemblies of God was shaken in the 1940s by a movement called the New Order of the Latter Rain, which asserted that denominations impeded the Holy Spirit. Latter Rain revivalists influenced pastors and congregations to withdraw from the Assemblies. Other denominations were also affected to a lesser degree. Evangelist William Branham was an influential force in the Latter Rain movement, even after he veered off into Oneness doctrine late in life. The Latter Rain movement emphasized in a new way the "gift of prophecy" within the church. In this, and to the extent that it undermined loyalty to established Pentecostal churches, it helped prepare the way for the Charismatic Movement of the 1960s.

The Healing Revival. An emphasis on divine healing was part of the 19th-century American Holiness Movement, associated largely (but not exclusively) with the non-Wesleyan wings. In the Keswick Holiness camp, for instance, divine healing was a major emphasis in the ministry of A. B. Simpson, founder of the Christian and Missionary Alliance. In the 20th century, the healing revival became a main current in Pentecostal life and enjoyed a dramatic rebirth in the 1950s through the ministries of Oral Roberts, Jack Coe, A. A. Allen, and others. Gordon Lindsay's periodical *Leaves of Healing* was a major link in the healing campaign.

Today, the Word of Faith movement, represented by evangelists Kenneth Hagin, Kenneth and Gloria Copeland, and at times Benny Hinn, combine divine healing revivalism with a gospel of prosperity and riches.

The Full Gospel Business Men's Association. In the 1950s Pentecostals began reaching out in new ways. Dairy farmer Demos Shakarian's Full Gospel Business Men's Association, founded in 1952, met in restaurants and hotel ballrooms. It brought Pentecostalism into mainstream society by creating an atmosphere in which Pentecostal businessmen could invite coworkers and friends. C. Douglas Weaver notes that Shakarian's group also "represented a subtle laymen's rebellion by a new elite of young entrepreneurs who were excluded from denomination decision making."[13]

The Charismatic Movement

These strands all played a part in the Charismatic Movement, which began (by most reckonings) with Episcopal priest Dennis Bennett's acceptance of the Pentecostal experience in 1959. Instead of joining a Pentecostal denomination, Bennett remained at St. Mark's Episcopal Church in Van Nuys, California, and led a Pentecostal revival there. Eventually opponents forced him out, but Bennett simply took his Pentecostal ministry to another Episcopal parish. The pattern was repeated by clergy in Lutheran, Methodist, Presbyterian, and Roman Catholic churches, among others. The neo-Pentecostal revival was on.

Neo-Pentecostal magazines appeared, like *New Wine Magazine* and *Charisma*. Charismatic Bible studies and prayer groups formed, bringing together folks from many denominations. A host of new gurus also arose. Charismatics and old-line Pentecostals took important roles in the Jesus People Movement of the 1960s and 1970s as Evangelicals reached out to the alienated youth culture. Charismatic campus ministries also developed, with names like Mustard Seed and Cornerstone.

To outsiders the most surprising result was the Charismatic Movement's presence in the Roman Catholic Church. Catholic colleges and universities became centers of a new Pentecostalism faithful to church dogma but free in worship style and firm in its belief in the baptism in the Holy Spirit and the restoration of Charismatic gifts to the Church. Catholic theologians, including Notre Dame University's Edward O'Connor and Josephine Massingberd Ford (a noted New Testament scholar), were active in the Charismatic revival. Several large Charismatic communities were formed, and Catholic Ralph Martin headed the Word of God Community, an interdenominational community centered in Ann Arbor, Michigan.

By 1990 an estimated 50 to 65 million Catholics worldwide had been touched by the Charismatic renewal movement. This included about 10 million American Catholics who were active in the Charismatic renewal at some point. About one-half million were still active in 1992, gathered into some 5,000 prayer and Bible study cells. To some in the Catholic Charismatic renewal movement, their chief failure has been the inability to inspire widespread reform of parish worship. Moreover, splits within key Catholic Charismatic organizations have alienated some. Others have joined Pentecostal denominations.[14]

---

13. C. Douglas Weaver, "Full Gospel Business Men's Fellowship International" and "Demos Shakarian," in Reid et al., *Dictionary of Christianity in America*, 459-60, 1078-79.

14. Julia Duin, "Charismatics, After 25 Years, Seek New Spark," *National Catholic Reporter*, June 19, 1992, 5.

New Charismatic Denominations

The Charismatic revival has spawned new denominations, just as the early 20th-century Pentecostal revival did.

Calvary Chapel. Calvary Chapel began in 1965 through the ministry of Chuck Smith, former Foursquare Gospel preacher, whose effective outreach to hippies propelled him to a leadership position in the Jesus Movement on the West Coast. Calvary Chapel has strongly influenced contemporary Christian music through its Marantha! Music company. Larry Taylor, a teacher in the church, states that Calvary Chapel takes the middle ground between Fundamentalism and Pentecostalism, emphasizing the gifts of the Spirit but moderating their use by adhering to scriptural restrictions on their use. By 1997 there were about 700 congregations worldwide, nearly 600 of them in North America.

Vineyard Christian Fellowship. The Vineyard began in 1973 through the ministry of Kenn Gullikson, a Jesus Movement pastor. In the early 1980s John Wimber led a large congregation once affiliated with Calvary Chapel into the Vineyard fellowship and with Gullikson's blessing became the movement's primary leader. The Vineyard emphasizes "signs and wonders"—miraculous elements that include divine healings, exorcisms, and prophecy. In 1991 there were about 330 churches, mostly in North America.[15] Wimber ambitiously hoped to see that number reach 10,000 but died before that could occur.

Charismatic Episcopal Church. The Charismatic Episcopal Church represents a growing phenomenon: churches seeking to recover a broad catholic tradition while remaining attuned to the Holy Spirit. This denomination was founded at a conference of independent churches held in Kansas City in 1992 and had about 200 congregations by 1997. It is episcopally governed, and churches typically follow the Episcopal Church's 1928 or 1979 editions of the *Book of Common Prayer,* but churches are free to adopt another ancient rite of worship if they choose. At the same time, the Charismatic Episcopal Church emphasizes divine healing and spiritual gifts.[16]

The Fanatical Fringe

The solid, middle-of-the-road Christians in Pentecostal and Charismatic denominations and churches have been embarrassed by the fanatical fringe of the movement. Scores of independent churches, clusters of churches, small denominations, television evangelists, and certain specialized ministries have heaped shame on the movement. Most are led by powerful persons with giant egos. They head up ministries that often make their leaders tremendously wealthy. Even worse, they make slaves and spiritual basket cases of their followers.

For example, the Shepherding Movement, launched in the 1960s by Bob Mumford and three associates, appears to have deeply damaged many sincere believers. The Shepherding Movement grew quickly to about 100,000 adherents. Its *New Wine Magazine* had a circulation of 90,000 (larger than *Christianity Today* at the time) and was mailed to 120 countries. Up to a half-million audio-

---

15. Les Parrott III and Robin D. Perrin, "The New Denominations," *Christianity Today,* March 11, 1991, 30.
16. Charismatic Episcopal Church home page, <http://www.iccec.org/info.htm>, March 26, 1997.

tapes were marketed per year during the 1970s and 1980s. Its dramatic evangelistic and church growth methods were soon aped by other Charismatic groups such as Crossroads, Maranatha Christian Churches, the Set Free Christian Fellowship, and others. That the Shepherding Movement made slaves and robots of its disciples—especially women—was seldom noticed at first.

But Shepherding Movement victims began to fill the counselors' schedules all over the country. Deeply troubled, unable to trust anyone, void of self-esteem, and deeply wounded, these people, according to David Seamands, "needed help sorting the true from the false. . . . I have seen serious psychological damage caused by these movements. . . . The repressive relationships and . . . giving up personal autonomy to a pastor/leader can result in a loss of identity."[17]

Jack Hayford, a respected mainstream Pentecostal pastor, said, "Multiplied thousands of pastors, like myself, have spent large amounts of time over the last 15 years picking up the pieces of broken lives that resulted from distortion of truth by extreme teachings and destructive applications on discipleship, authority, and shepherding."[18]

Pastors and counselors have spent considerable time repairing the broken lives shattered by the Shepherding Movement.

Tales of spiritual horror and abuse abound from the fanatical fringe of the Charismatic Movement. They are under no denominational oversight.

Dozens of examples of disciple abuse are documented in Ronald Enroth's study, *Churches That Abuse*. Most of the abuse Enroth found was in the radical fringe of the Charismatic Movement.[19]

What Pentecostals Want You to Know

In 1981 the late Thomas F. Zimmerman, then the highest official in the Assemblies of God, addressed other Christians on the topic of Pentecostalism's priorities and beliefs. At the time, it was estimated that there were over 50 million Pentecostals worldwide. But Pentecostals, Zimmerman said, cannot be judged successful because they are numerous; groups teaching heresy have also grown numerous. Rather, Pentecostals can be judged successful because they, by and large, have remained faithful to these characteristics:

- They hold a high view of Scripture.
- They hold to the great central convictions of the Christian tradition.
- They "honor the Father, Son, and Holy Spirit equally."
- They take seriously the Great Commission.
- They seek to be responsive to the Holy Spirit in their worship.
- They maintain a spirit of cooperation with other Evangelicals and helped to found the National Association of Evangelicals.

---

17. Ron and Vicki Burks, *Damaged Disciples* (Grand Rapids: Zondervan Publishing House, 1992), 7-8.
18. Robert Digitale, "An Idea Whose Time Has Gone?" *Christianity Today* 34, No. 5 (March 1990): 40.
19. Ronald M. Enroth, *Churches That Abuse* (Grand Rapids: Zondervan Publishing House, 1992), 161. See also Wesley D. Tracy, "Abused Believers," *Herald of Holiness*, August 1992, 8.

Some people "believe that the main message of Pentecostalism is the baptism of the Holy Spirit and speaking in tongues," but that is not the case, according to Zimmerman. Pentecostalism's principal message is that the gospel of Jesus Christ can save us from our sins. Zimmerman also noted that "almost all Pentecostals today believe that a person who has accepted Christ is indwelt by the Spirit. . . . Pentecostals differentiate between the Holy Spirit baptizing believers into the body of Christ (1 Cor. 12:13) and Christ baptizing them in the Holy Spirit (Matt. 3:11-12; Acts 1:5)."[20]

The American Holiness Movement and the early Pentecostal Movement sprang from the same social milieu. But they have gone different directions in important matters. Along with other denominations that have watched the Pentecostal/Charismatic Movement, the Church of the Nazarene has resisted many of its claims. To those concerns we turn in the next chapter.

Review and Reflection

1. Checking Ties and Connections

   a. Review the origins of the Pentecostal Movement, noting its connections with the early American Holiness Movement.

   b. Review also the connections between the Pentecostal Movement and the Charismatic Movement of the 1960s.

2. Identify the following:

   a. Word of Faith movement

   b. Charismatic Episcopal Church

   c. Shepherding Movement

   d. The healing revival

3. All faith traditions have strengths and vulnerabilities. Which of the following do you think are strengths or vulnerabilities of the Pentecostal/Charismatic Movement?

   a. Critical thought

   b. Church growth and evangelism

   c. Worship

   d. Stewardship and fund-raising

   e. Discipline of clergy

   f. Anti-intellectualism

---

20. Thomas F. Zimmerman, "Priorities and Beliefs of Pentecostals," *Christianity Today,* September 4, 1981, 36-37.

g. Upbeat worship

h. Liturgies

4. Which of the following do you think the Pentecostal/Charismatic way of doing religion is based most on?

a. The Bible

b. Systematic theology

c. Personal religious experience

d. Historic Christian tradition

NAZARENES IN DIALOGUE WITH PENTECOSTALS AND CHARISMATICS

Historical Background

Nazarenes and Pentecostals have had a tense dialogue since the early days of both movements. Early Nazarenes felt that the emotionalism, tongues-speaking, and doctrine of the Pentecostals were destructive to the Nazarene vision and mission.

The birth of the Charismatic Movement in the 1960s did little to ease tensions. In recent years, however, serious efforts at dialogue—though not close union—have been made.

Core Beliefs of Pentecostals and Charismatics

The extreme diversity of these movements makes generalizing hazardous, but most Pentecostal/Charismatic groups adhere to these beliefs:

1. The authority of Scripture
2. Salvation by grace through faith
3. Born-again conversion
4. The baptism with the Holy Spirit
5. Speaking in tongues as evidence of baptism with the Spirit and as a prayer language
6. Denial of the Trinity by some
7. Theology of prosperity (preached by many Pentecostals/Charismatics)

Agreement and Differences

Nazarenes share common ground on some of these core beliefs but strenuously reject beliefs 5, 6, and 7. They also question the preparation of clergy and the lack of the discipline of clergy as practiced in some wings of the Pentecostal/Charismatic Movement.

Wesleyan-Holiness and Pentecostal/Charismatic Dialogue Today

Pastors report that many former Pentecostals/Charismatics are joining Nazarene churches. In many cases they are willing to give up or refrain from teaching the practice of tongues-speaking.

In 1998 the Wesleyan Theological Society and the Association for Pentecostal Studies held a joint meeting. Scholars from both sides explored the commonalities and differences of the two traditions. It is too early to tell to what extent this meeting will determine how well these parties can walk and work together.

If these people are right in their teachings, the holiness movement, and all the great teachers of the past, including the apostles and prophets, were wrong.

—Isaiah Martin

15

NAZARENES IN DIALOGUE WITH PENTECOSTALS AND CHARISMATICS

ONE THING IS FOR CERTAIN—Evangelicals can learn much from the Pentecostal/Charismatic (P/C) Movement. They wrote the book on church growth—metaphorically and literally. About 60 percent of all Christian books sold are bought by Pentecostals and Charismatics. They can also coach other churches on fervent evangelism. And does any group make religion more direct and personal than the P/Cs? They have connected with the man and woman on the street in making religious experience relevant to felt needs.

Our P/C brothers and sisters in Christ have often modeled exemplary consecration. They have taught everyone how to make worship warmhearted and celebrative. Further, they have carried the banner in seeking to let the Holy Spirit lead in worship and in life.

Yet for all this, a number of things in P/C theology and practice are troublesome. Nazarenes, with believers in other denominations, have watched the P/C Movement emerge and grow and have rejected many of its claims.

Early Nazarene Evaluations

The first generation of Nazarenes witnessed Pentecostalism's rise. R. L. Averill, a Southern revivalist, published an early account of the Apostolic Faith Movement in the Houston area, which he began observing in 1906:

> We have a new movement in our midst. . . . Doctrinally they have as yet no well defined statement, for while some say we must be converted and sanctified and afterwards receive the baptism of the Holy Ghost, which is always evidenced by speaking with other tongues; yet others are claiming that a sinner may at one and the same time get pardoned, sanctified wholly and baptised [with the Holy Spirit] and speak with tongues. I saw this at Oxford. . . . Truly we are in a fast age.

Averill noted "good consecrated, conscientious people among them" but concluded that others "are not so," adding, "I don't know a more divided discordant people. There seemed to be only one point of agreement among them, and that is every one should speak in tongues." His verdict: "The work does not bear the stamp of deep spirituality to my mind."[1]

That assessment was shared by others. The Holiness Church of Christ, a Nazarene parent body, expelled its congregation in Beulah, Oklahoma, after it accepted Pentecostal beliefs. The Holiness Church of Christ was clear: if "at any time they see the error of their teachings, we will gladly restore them." But the Beulah church remained Pentecostal and became a base for early Assemblies of God development in that area.[2]

The division in Holiness ranks proceeded apace as Southern Pentecostalism expanded. In 1909 General Superintendent H. F. Reynolds reported that "the so-called Tongues Movement has swept all of our churches into its fanatical belief in Florida, except one." The Abilene District complained that "in some places our churches have suffered inroads made upon us by the Apostolic Faith Movement. We believe this to be the most blighting and damning heresy that we have ever had to face." In 1910 the Arkansas District reported that "the Tongues Movement has destroyed three of our churches on this district."[3]

Similarly, Nazarenes in Los Angeles had occasion to witness the Apostolic Faith Movement on the West Coast. Isaiah Martin, ordained by the Church of the Nazarene in 1903, left this early account:

A meeting usually takes on the name of whatever subject is stressed or made prominent. . . . In this instance [the Azusa Street revival] is called the "tongues meeting," because they make prominent the speaking with tongues. We found on investigation that there were already divisions among them, and that one meeting had become three meetings. For, while some were saying, "We are with Seymour," others were saying, "We are with Parham," and still others, "We are with Bartleman." Now, who is Seymour, and who is Parham, and who is Bartleman? . . . We do not feel called upon to sit in judgment on them or anyone else. One thing is certain, if these people are right in their teachings, the holiness movement, and all the great teachers of the past, including the apostles and prophets, were wrong.[4]

Although common soil and kinship surrounded the Holiness and Pentecostal Movements, sharply divergent views about the nature of the Holy Spirit's work separated the two traditions. The early Nazarenes rejected the Pentecostal-Holiness message because it

- taught that the baptism of the Holy Spirit is completely separate from entire sanctification and is a third work of grace;
- focused on the gifts of the Spirit rather than the fruit of the Spirit, around which entire sanctification is chiefly oriented;

1. *Holiness Evangel,* January 1, 1907, 1; and November 15, 1907, 4. Also see the *Pentecostal Advocate,* April 8, 1909, 10.

2. *Holiness Evangel,* January 1, 1907, 1; and November 15, 1907, 4.

3. Abilene District Journal, 1909, and Arkansas District Journal, 1910.

4. Isaiah Martin, "Los Angeles Letter," *Pentecostal Herald,* December 12, 1906.

- emphasized speaking in tongues as the "initial evidence" of Holy Spirit baptism.

Thoroughly Wesleyan, the early Nazarenes believed in the inner and outer witness of God's Spirit to conversion and entire sanctification. The inner witness: a quiet but sure confidence in God's grace. The outer witness: not tongues or any other phenomena, but the actual life of holiness as a certain witness to others.

There was one other reason for the Nazarene rejection of Pentecostalism: early Nazarenes were unafraid of emotion in religion, but they regarded the distinctive forms of Pentecostal religion as errant and humanistic emotionalism. They often referred to Pentecostal tongues-speaking, prophecies, and "interpretation of tongues" as "delusions."

Contemporary Dialogue

There can be no doubt that the Holiness Movement (including the Nazarenes) and the P/C Movement have not always treated each other as brothers and sisters in Christ. Sometimes the interchanges—like a family feud—were harsh and vindictive. We're doing better these days, but the two movements, like brothers who have gone their separate ways, are far apart on some issues.

Doctrinal Differences

At least seven significant doctrinal differences loom between Nazarenes and all or part of the P/C Movement.

1. **The Trinity.** "Jesus Only" or "Oneness" Pentecostals deny the Holy Trinity. Nothing could be more heterodox as far as orthodox Christians, including Nazarenes, are concerned.

2. **Baptism.** Our primary problem here is with Oneness Pentecostals who teach that converts are to be baptized in the name of "Jesus only." Those who are baptized "in the name of the Father, and of the Son, and of the Holy Spirit" (the standard Christian formula for nearly 2,000 years) are not Christians at all, according to Oneness Pentecostals.

> *The giving of the gift of languages at Pentecost signaled the Holy Spirit's acceptance of all nations and races in the new Christian Church.*

3. **Entire Sanctification.** Finished Work and Oneness Pentecostals teach a second work of grace in which Christians are empowered by the Spirit for service, but they deny that inbred sin is cleansed. The new Charismatic denominations also deny the possibility of entire sanctification.

The Pentecostal Holiness churches—who agree with us (and disagree with other Pentecostals) about entire sanctification—separate baptism with the Holy Spirit from entire sanctification. They make Spirit baptism a third work of grace. We teach that the baptism with the Holy Spirit is part and parcel of entire sanctification, not a third work of grace.

4. **Speaking in Tongues.** A consistent thread in Nazarene teaching on the gifts of the Spirit is that speaking in tongues, as recorded in Acts and elsewhere

in the New Testament, was the supernatural gift of speaking known languages. This is evident in the Pentecost narrative (Acts 2) and in subsequent passages in Acts in which "speaking in tongues" is referenced. The earliest Pentecostals held this view until they realized their inability to communicate with those of other languages through their "gift of tongues."

The instances where speaking in tongues occurs in Acts are associated with the giving of the Holy Spirit to a new group of people: to Jewish followers of Jesus (chap. 2), to the household of the Roman soldier Cornelius (chap. 10), and to the Ephesians (chap. 19). In the most fundamental sense, the giving of the gift of languages at Pentecost signaled powerfully the Holy Spirit's acceptance of all nations and races in the new Christian Church. Subsequent instances in Acts in which languages were given drive home this point: they re-create the first Pentecost among different groups of people previously separated from Jewish Christians by the Law.

Nazarenes teach that "the gift of tongues is related to the miraculous gift of many languages on the Day of Pentecost. On that great day the Church was enabled to cross language barriers. The people present were astonished because each one heard the gospel being preached in his own native dialect (Acts 2:6, 8). This special miracle was an expression of God's desire to reach every [person] everywhere through the spoken and written word. Language is the vehicle of God's truth."[5]

Only in Corinthians is "tongues" mentioned as a feature in worship. The Charismatic Movement, picking up on this, made speaking in tongues a personal prayer language.

But did Paul mean to promote tongues as a spiritual gift, or did he try to restrict it? Christians can disagree reasonably with one another over how to interpret Paul, but Nazarene teaching on this matter has been clear: Paul says that although he speaks in tongues more than any of the Corinthians, he would rather speak 5 words in a known language than 10,000 words in a language unintelligible to hearers (1 Cor. 14:18-19). And why? Because clarity promotes the gospel of Jesus Christ, while confusion hinders its spread.

It is difficult to know, let alone prove, exactly what the gift of tongues in New Testament times really was. It was divinely bestowed. Was it a grace that enabled people to witness across language barriers? Was it gibberish like that practiced in Greek mystery cults? Was it a supernatural gift of a divine language understood only by superhuman entities or spirits?

No one can prove what it was. Its practice, essence, and significance are shrouded in mystery. Since tongues-speaking is so vaporescent, so miasmatic, so hard to pin down, it seems prudent not to make it the cornerstone or even a major plank in one's theological platform.

Nazarenes patently reject the P/C insistence that tongues-speaking is *the* evidence of the baptism with the Holy Spirit. The *Manual* states,

The Church of the Nazarene believes that the Holy Spirit bears witness to

---

5. Board of General Superintendents, "The Position of the Church of the Nazarene on Speaking in Tongues," *Herald of Holiness,* October 15, 1976, 5.

the new birth and to the subsequent work of heart cleansing, or entire sanctification, through the infilling of the Holy Spirit.

We affirm that the one biblical evidence of entire sanctification, or the infilling of the Holy Spirit, is the cleansing of the heart by faith from original sin as stated in Acts 15:8-9: "God, who knows the heart, showed them that he accepted them by giving the Holy Spirit to them, just as he did to us. He made no distinction between us and them, for he purified their hearts by faith." And this cleansing is manifested by the fruit of the Spirit in a holy life. . . .

To affirm that even a special or any alleged physical evidence, or "prayer language," is evidence of the baptism with the Spirit is contrary to the biblical and historic position of the church.[6]

5. Doctrine of the Holy Spirit. The Church of the Nazarene witnessed Pentecostalism's emergence and, with other classically Wesleyan churches, rejected many of its claims about the nature of the Spirit's role in salvation. What, then, do we teach about the Holy Spirit? A good summary is found in H. Ray Dunning's *Grace, Faith, and Holiness.* We believe that

- to each person the Holy Spirit restores a measure of the free will lost through original sin.
- the Holy Spirit prepares each of us for salvation by awakening us to an awareness of our sin before God.
- the Holy Spirit is the Creator and Dispenser of faith, who gives justifying faith at the moment of conversion and throughout the Christian walk.
- the Holy Spirit renews us inwardly at conversion through the new birth, or regeneration, by planting a new spiritual life within.
- the Holy Spirit assures us that our sins are forgiven and that we are God's children.
- the Holy Spirit is the active Agent in progressive sanctification, or growth in holiness, as God renews us continually in His own image.
- the Holy Spirit is the active Agent in the entire sanctification of believers as our hearts are filled with divine love.
- the Holy Spirit in us is the basis of our hope of resurrection (Rom. 8:11).[7]

Dunning notes two errors about the Holy Spirit that Christian groups often make. One is to retreat into legalism and freeze out the Holy Spirit. Paul opposed that error among the churches of Galatia. The other error is to fall into libertinism—to carry freedom in the Spirit to an extreme. This was the error Paul opposed in the Corinthian church. He listed the spiritual gifts that the Corinthians claimed to enjoy—speaking and interpretation of tongues, prophecy, and spiritual discernment—and still said that they had missed the main point: the divine love in one's heart and life, which is the most important and enduring of the Spirit's gifts.

6. Signs, Wonders, and Healing Miracles. Some Pentecostal and Charismatic groups promote signs and wonders. This leads to sensationalism, pseudomiracles, and in the end, disillusionment of believers. Overemphasis on

---

6. *Manual, Church of the Nazarene, 1997—2001,* par. 904.10, 349-50.

7. H. Ray Dunning, *Grace, Faith, and Holiness: A Wesleyan Systematic Theology* (Kansas City: Beacon Hill Press of Kansas City, 1988), 429-77.

healing often leads to excluding proper medical care. Some groups declare that God is obligated to heal every sick person if the victim's faith is genuine. One Indiana sect has fostered "one preventable death per month" for 15 years by forbidding members to seek medical treatment.[8] Prayer is all they need, they say. This is an independent church led by a renegade preacher, whose abuse cannot be charged to any denomination.

The Nazarene article of faith on divine healing came about during the healing revival, and it lets everyone know that Nazarenes are to seek medical treatment as well as using prayer in times of illness.

7. **Theology of Prosperity.** Some P/C groups and preachers, especially televangelists, preach that financial prosperity lies ahead for all God's children—especially if they'll mail a check today! We believe that following God with all one's heart does not necessarily make the believer wealthy. Also, a huge bank account is no testimony at all to God's blessing or to the advanced spiritual standing of the person whose name is on the account ledger. How wealthy was Jesus, Paul, Brother Lawrence, or Mother Teresa?

Differences of Practice and Philosophy

Every faith tradition has vulnerabilities. Nazarenes, as we saw in chapter 1, know that they need to guard against legalism and the loss of proper confession of sin. A number of vulnerabilities mark the P/C Movement as well.

"The only theological education permitted for those called to ministry is to be done by the head pastor or his inner circle of 'clones.'"

1. **Anti-intellectualism.** "The only thing worse than an old [experienced] Christian is an educated one," declared Charismatic pastor Phil Aguilar of the Set Free Christian Fellowship.[9] A young disciple with an intellectual bent at Wayland Mitchell's church was declared an "educated idiot with a high IQ" by his pastor.[10]

Nazarenes have their own problems with anti-intellectualism. As the young denomination was forming, the world as they knew it was shattered by German biblical criticism, Darwin's evolutionary theory, Dewey's philosophical pragmatism ("Truth is what works"), and theological modernism. As Nazarene pioneers surveyed this battlefield, they noticed that the ones who had destroyed what they had always believed about the origin, nature, and destiny of the Bible, Christianity, and the human race were folks who could read Greek and Latin, people with university degrees. Part of their reaction was a predictable anti-intellectualism. They distrusted education not done under the supervision of the church. The tendency to anti-intellectualism is a vulnerability we share with our P/C friends.

---

8. Enroth, *Churches That Abuse,* 169-72. Enroth refers to Hobart Freeman's Faith Assembly (not associated with the Assemblies of God) in Indiana.

9. Ibid., 26.

10. Ibid., 198.

2. Religious Experience at the Expense of Careful Thought. The strong emphasis on religious experience among P/C groups creates a vulnerability that can result in a definite lack of critical thinking. "You get the experience," some say, "and the doctrine won't bother you."

Nazarenes, too, have coped with this vulnerability but seem to have made more progress toward balancing critical thought and religious experience than some of the P/C groups. When ecstatic experience, high emotion, and speaking in tongues are the principal focus of religion, critical thinking just weighs less.

3. Clergy Preparation and Discipline. The anti-intellectual climate appears to have resulted in inadequate ministerial education. Enroth's study of abusive churches in the Charismatic Movement showed that their pastors had very little formal education for ministry. In many such churches, "the only theological education permitted for those called to ministry is to be done by the head pastor or his inner circle of 'clones.'"[11]

Christianity Today noted that the Charismatic revival in South America had produced 175,000 pastors without one day of ministerial education.[12] This could produce serious problems a decade hence. We are quite sure that the 21st century will require better-educated pastors, not barely educated pastors.

For some reason, the P/C Movement has produced a bumper crop of bully pastors who are answerable to no one. "It's my way or the highway," one pastor announced.[13] "God wants you to do what I ask you to do. . . . If you don't, you are going against God himself," declared Don Barnett of Seattle's Community Chapel.[14] The pastor of the Church of Our First Love proclaimed that "anyone who hinders the work I do, God will remove him."[15]

No one can discipline these bully preachers, it seems. And while their antics cannot be charged to the good rank-and-file members of P/C churches, observers raise the question: Is there something in the movement's message or method that makes such abuse possible by the misguided, the manipulative, or the unscrupulous? Enroth apparently thinks so. For example, while he does not charge the Vineyard Fellowship with abuse, he notes that its structures, procedures, and emphasis on power and signs and wonders make it vulnerable to manipulative abuse.

Among those who seem to go discipline-free are several P/C televangelists whose sexual and financial transgressions and multiple marriages and divorces scandalize the gospel and the Church.

4. Concerns About Pentecostal Worship. Pentecostals have helped millions of Christians rediscover heartfelt religion. Spontaneity in worship—long ago lost to prescribed liturgy or pious lethargy—has been reinstated in many churches through P/C influence. There are, however, some genuine concerns that must be raised about some styles of Pentecostal worship.

---

11. Tracy, "Abused Believers," 10.
12. Ibid., 11.
13. Enroth, *Churches That Abuse,* 196. Phil Aguilar is the pastor quoted.
14. Ibid., 89-90.
15. Ibid., 203.

P/C worship styles major, by and large, on the subjective side of worship, almost to the exclusion of objective worship practices. Some styles do this by:

- Stressing the venting of emotions.
- Neglecting the public reading of the Scripture.
- Reducing the sacraments to mere ordinances.
- Nearly excluding the Trinitarian creeds (the Apostles' Creed, the Nicene Creed, etc.).
- Separating preaching from worship in many cases. This is the first time in Christian history that a major worship style has made preaching less than a part of the worship experience.

In some quarters of Pentecostalism, worship has been reduced to praise, prayer, and song. These follow a predetermined sequence of *invitation, engagement, exaltation,* and *intimacy* (or, if you prefer biblical imagery: *outside the court, in the outer court, in the inner court, holy of holies*). When the peak of *intimacy* or *holy of holies* is reached (usually with the worship leader or others speaking in tongues), a "close-out" song brings everyone back to earth. For all practical purposes, worship is now over. Later, perhaps after a coffee and doughnut break, a "teaching pastor" (not preacher) or several teaching pastors in various rooms, will speak. But this comes after "worship" is over. Thus, the objective elements of worship (public Bible reading, sacraments, and preaching) are diminished or dismissed in favor of the subjective elements. Many worship leaders appear more concerned with the "techniques of rapture" than with the worship of God.

In *Fire from Heaven* (1995), Harvey Cox, a theological liberal at Harvard, celebrates Pentecostalism's sweeping success throughout the developing world. There, he believes, the worship style of Pentecostalism is blending with shamanism and animism, putting people in touch with a universal human primitivism. Cox believes that this blending can lead to a new religion that reaches beyond the narrow-mindedness of traditional Christianity. He thinks this would be good. What do you think?

5. Divisiveness. The P/C Movement has been extraordinarily fractious among themselves. But the divisiveness they often bring to other fellowships is also unsettling. When a cluster of Charismatics move into a non-Charismatic church, there is more than a little fear and trembling about church unity. Often those with the gift of tongues feel so strongly about it that they cannot keep from sharing it with everyone else in the church. Neither Nazarenes nor any other group have generally felt it their duty to infiltrate the Pentecostal ranks and change their doctrine. But the reverse has not always been the case. Even at the 1997 General Assembly, pro-tongues persons tried hard to "evangelize" the 1,100 delegates on the point of "baptizing" several kinds of tongues-speaking.[16]

There is evidence that this problem may be lessening. A number of Nazarene pastors report that many former P/C church members have come to the Church of the Nazarene. Many of them still believe in tongues or practice a "prayer language" or both, but they prudently refrain from making an issue of these matters and faithfully support the pastor and the church.

---

16. See "The Question Box," *Herald of Holiness,* October 1997, 34.

In exploring the areas in which we disagree with our P/C friends, to quote the Board of General Superintendents, "We do not wish to reflect on the sincerity or integrity of those who differ with us on these matters. We recognize as fellow members of His universal body all who are in Christ and extend to them the right hand of Christian fellowship."[17]

Review and Reflection

1. In the ideas or practices listed below, Wesleyan-Holiness churches differ with many Pentecostal or Charismatic churches. Which of these differences trouble you the least? The most?

    a. Doctrine of the Trinity

    b. Speaking in tongues

    c. Education of clergy

    d. Discipline of clergy

    e. Emotional worship

    f. Three works of grace

    g. Entire sanctification

    h. Pastoral authority

    i. Divine healing

    j. Signs and wonders

2. What kinds of things need to happen in order for the Wesleyan-Holiness and Pentecostal/Charismatic churches to be able to work together more closely?

---

17. "The Position . . . ," 5.

PART VII

UNITING AND INDEPENDENT CHURCHES AND ORGANIZATIONS

- The Uniting Churches
- Community Churches
- Parachurch Organizations

THE UNITING CHURCHES

Overview

A sentiment to overcome the splintering of Christian bodies characterizes many Protestants today. Lutherans, Presbyterians, and Episcopalians are seeking closer union. In Australia, Methodists and Presbyterians have merged to become the Uniting Church. Wesleyan and Holiness churches continue a long history of mergers. In this chapter we examine the two churches that have led the way in this area, the United Church of Canada (1925) and the United Church of Christ (1957). Though it does not have a strong connection with the uniting churches, the Unitarian Universalist Association (UUA) is also treated.

Core Beliefs

The uniting churches claim the classic Christian confessions of faith as guidelines for today's church. Their specific teachings, however, are not binding on pastors, teachers, and members. Generally liberal in theology, these churches stress social service much more than doctrinal purity or theological orthodoxy. The slogan "Doctrine divides; service unites" seems to fit.

Agreements and Differences

Nazarenes share the classic confessions of faith with the uniting churches. However, we hold that orthodox teachings about Christ, the Bible, the Trinity, salvation, sanctification, and so on are binding on our pastors, teachers, and members. We, too, are energetically concerned with social justice. But our central concern is soteriological: that is, the salvation of sinners and the sanctification of believers.

Nazarenes have almost no common ground with the Unitarian Universalist Association, which renounces the Trinity, the deity and atonement of Christ, and most other basic Christian doctrines.

Uniting Churches Today

The United Church of Canada ministers to 3.5 million members. Twenty percent of the church's ministers are women. The United Church of Christ has 1.47 million members.

The UUA (which has only a faint historical connection with the uniting churches) reports 204,000 adherents.

I ask . . . that they may all be one.
—Jesus of Nazareth

16 ~ THE UNITING CHURCHES

By THE 19TH CENTURY, America had become a religious free enterprise zone. With nothing like a state church, no tax money, and impatience with the patriarchal bossing of the old denominations, ecclesiastical huckstering flourished like wisteria on the sunny side of the barn. Every local prophet was free to establish a new church, new school, or new religion. Plenty did.

The fragmentation of the Body of Christ became an American scandal. By the 20th century, a number of groups in America and worldwide led the way toward ecumenism. The last half of the 20th century has seen a boom of ecumenical affairs, producing what some call a revolution that equals the power of the Protestant Reformation 500 years ago.

The list starts with the work of the World Council of Churches, the National Council of Churches, Vatican II, the Toronto Statement, and the Institute of Ecumenical and Cultural Research. In June 1995 Pope John Paul II and Eastern Orthodox patriarch Bartholomew conducted a joint service of worship and together blessed the gathered congregation.

For more than 20 years now, nine denominations have been meeting in the Consultation on Church Union to develop a plan for *covenanting*. These people are saying to each other, "We recognize your ordained people as ordained for us too, your table and our table as equally the Lord's table."[1]

A number of Holiness denominations have merged during this century. The Wesleyan Church was born from a union of the Pilgrim Holiness Church and the Wesleyan Methodist Church. For a time The Wesleyan Church and the Church of the Nazarene even conversed about greater cooperation and possible merger.

A dramatic event occurred in 1998. Lutherans and Roman Catholics declared that the mutual condemnations of the 16th century no longer apply. By this action, they basically are saying that "their ancestors were not wrong but recognizing that new occasions teach new duties and indicating that the intention to stay together is more powerful than the pious clinging to divided and divisive tradition."[2]

---

1. Patrick Henry, "New Geometries of Ecumenism," *Theology Today,* January 1997, 494.
2. Ibid.

Many ecumenical efforts start as compassionate ministry service projects. Even when creeds cannot be harmonized, acts of mercy in Jesus' name often can be. For example, the South Albuquerque Cooperative Ministry that works in an impoverished part of the city is a coalition of Mennonite, Presbyterian, Methodist, and United Church of Christ parishes.[3]

If there was a Presbyterian church on one corner, there was no reason to build a Methodist one across the street in a spirit of competition.

Some ecumenical efforts are born of scant resources as well as stewardship—that is, if there's a Presbyterian church on one corner, there's no reason to build a United Methodist one across the street. Duplication of staff, buildings, and publications is seen as a violation of good stewardship and a sign of sinful disunity. Could not what we have in common in Christ become more important than sectarian distinctions?

Some groups of Christians have tried hard to become part of the answer to Jesus' prayer: "I ask . . . that they may all be one" (John 17:20-21, NRSV).

The United Church of Canada

The United Church of Canada was born in June 1925. Four churches merged to form what is now the largest Protestant denomination in Canada. The four who came together were the Congregational Union of Canada; the Methodist Church, Canada; the General Council of Union Churches; and 70 percent of the Presbyterian Church in Canada. This was "the first union of churches in the world to cross historical denominational lines and hence received international acclaim."[4]

The Presbyterians in Canada came primarily from Irish and Scottish immigrants who came to Nova Scotia in the 18th century. French immigrants with the Huguenot Reformed heritage and Dutch Reformed settlers joined with Scottish and Irish Presbyterians to form the Presbyterian Church of Canada in 1875.

Methodism in Canada is traced to Lawrence Coughlan, an Irish Methodist preacher who came to Newfoundland in 1765. In 1779 19-year-old William Black Jr. helped bring about a spiritual awakening. The young Irishman preached throughout Nova Scotia, establishing Methodist class meetings everywhere he went. Several mergers of Methodist groups produced the Methodist Church, Canada, in 1884. They then became part of the United Church of Canada at the 1925 union.

The Congregational Union of Canada sprang from the immigration of New Englanders into Nova Scotia. In 1766 the first Congregationalist church was organized at Mungerville, New Brunswick. The first church in Newfoundland was created in 1846. The Quebec Congregationalists came into being as a result

---

3. Ibid., 498-99.
4. "The United Church of Canada: A Brief Summary of Its History, Life, and Work," Internet: <webmaster@uccan.org>. Copyright 1996. The United Church of Canada.

of the work of a British missionary who started his work in 1801. In 1907 the United Brethren in Christ (United States-affiliated group) joined the Congregationalist fold. These various streams produced the Congregational Church of Canada, a partner in the 1925 union.

The General Council of Union Churches in western Canada was the smallest of the uniting partners, but the bearers of the early Plan of Union that eventually came to guide the unification of the four groups into the United Church of Canada.

Beliefs and Practices

The United Church of Canada has suppressed denominational differences and distinctives in favor of the one supreme doctrine—ecumenism. Each of the joining bodies is free to go its own way theologically as long as it does not impose its practices on the rest of the churches, presbyteries, or conferences. The de-emphasis on things theological contributed to two emerging realities. First, since theology is quite relative and pluralistic as opposed to dogmatic and essential, the trend is toward liberal theology. Second, the church finds its unity in errands of mercy and social services. Much more attention is paid to justice for workers, racism, land use, capital punishment, ageism, political affairs, and the ordination of homosexuals than is given to distinct theological concerns. For example, the Internet materials about the United Church of Canada available at this writing contain 14 pages on "Canadian Social Issues" and one paragraph on "What We Believe." That paragraph reads in part,

> The United Church accepts the traditional Christian beliefs, but there is a wide latitude of personal interpretation. . . . As a result there are strongly liberal positions, ultra-conservative beliefs, and many shades in between. The historic creeds formulated by the ancient Christian church are recognized as valuable guides to the understanding of our relationship with God. Membership is not related to the specific acceptance of a catechism or creed but to a general acceptance of the central truths presented in the gospel. The Bible is regarded as the wholly adequate guide or resource for the person who wants to understand Christian faith and life.[5]

The mission of the United Church includes worship, Christian education, and the devotional life. But the emphasis is put upon "speaking out strongly and consistently on highly controversial subjects . . . such . . . as nuclear power, the right of farm labor to organize, abortion, capital punishment, racial injustices, guaranteed annual income, land use, refugees . . . poverty . . . and numerous other issues."[6]

The mission work of the denomination, as described on its home page, stresses humanitarian and compassionate ministries and not matters of evangelism and salvation.

The United Church of Canada operates a publishing house, produces a television program, publishes several periodicals, and "relates to" a number of edu-

---

5. Ibid.
6. Ibid.

cational institutions, including seven theological colleges, four universities, and five secondary schools.

The government of the church is patterned after the "Canadian federal-provincial-municipal system of government. Traditionally, following the Methodist heritage, the United Church has always been highly centralized through its national offices."[7] But decentralization is catching on. One evidence is that in the organizational flowchart, the local congregations are placed at the top. The flow then goes downward to pastor, presbytery, conference, and General Council.

The United Church of Canada ministers to 3.5 million members in 4,100 congregations. It has 13 regional conferences, 94 presbyteries, and 3,965 ordained ministers, of which 831 are women.[8]

The United Church of Christ

In 1957 the United Church of Christ came into being with the merger of the Evangelical Reformed Church and the Congregational Christian Churches. Each of these institutions had been created by former mergers. Thus, the United Church of Christ springs from four historic denominations: the Congregational Churches, the Reformed Church in the United States, the Christian Churches, and the Evangelical Synod of North America.

The Congregational Churches were organized when the Plymouth Pilgrims (1620) and the Puritans of the Massachusetts Bay Colony (1629) declared their essential unity by adopting the Cambridge Platform of 1648.[9] This is the church of Jonathan Edwards, David Brainerd, and Cotton Mather. This is also the church that arrested Baptists, exiled Roger Williams, and hung Quakers on Boston Commons.

This is the church that by 1674 had 4,000 "praying Indians" and 24 Native American pastors. This is the church that established Harvard (1636), Yale (1707), and Dartmouth (1769). By the 1957 merger, there were 48 colleges and 10 theological seminaries with Congregational origins.[10]

The Reformed Church in the United States sprang up in Pennsylvania among Reformed Christian immigrants from Germany, Switzerland, and other countries. The Reformed believers sent missionaries into North Carolina and Ohio and established a number of colleges. A theological seminary was opened in Carlisle, Pennsylvania. This church was German and Calvinistic, looking to the Heidelberg Catechism, the Augsburg Confession, and Luther's Catechism for theological guidance. It brought 810,000 members in 2,740 churches, eight colleges, and three theological schools to the merger that created the United Church of Christ.[11]

The Christian Churches emerged near the turn of the 19th century, as we have seen in an earlier chapter, in response to the "organizational rigidity of the Methodist, Presbyterian and Baptist churches of the time."[12]

7. Ibid.
8. "Quick Fact Sheet," Internet: <webmaster@uccan.org>.
9. "United Church of Christ," Internet: <http://www.ucc.org> (hereafter: UCC, www).
10. Mead and Hill, *Handbook of Denominations*, 293-94.
11. Ibid., 299.
12. UCC, www.

The Evangelical Synod of North America reflected the work of six Evangelical Lutheran pastors in the St. Louis area. Their churches, through a series of small mergers, grew to 281,598 members when they became part of the Reformed Church in the United States.[13]

The United Church of Christ has welcomed persons and congregations representing Native Americans, Asians, Americans, African-Americans, Pacific Islanders, Volga Germans, Armenians, Hungarians, and Hispanic Americans. Today the United Church of Christ has 1.6 million members worshiping in more than 6,000 congregations.

Characteristics of the United Church of Christ

The United Church of Christ cites on its Internet home page the four key names that formed their union as the marks that characterize their church:

> *Christian*—By our very name, the United Church of Christ, we declare ourselves to be part of the Body of Christ. . . . We continue the witness of the early disciples to the reality and power of the crucified and risen Christ, Jesus of Nazareth.

> *Reformed*—All four denominations arose from the tradition of the Protestant Reformers. We confess the authority of one God. We affirm the primacy of the scriptures . . . justification by faith, the priesthood of all believers, and the principles of Christian freedom [liberty].

> *Congregational*—The basic unit . . . is the congregation. Members of each congregation covenant with one another and with God . . . [and] exist in covenantal relationships with one another to form larger structures for more effective work. Our covenanting emphasizes trustful relationships rather than legal agreements.

> *Evangelical*—The primary task of the church is the proclamation of the gospel—the good news of God's love revealed with power in Jesus Christ. We proclaim this gospel by word and deed. . . . We gather each Sunday for the worship of God, and through each week, we engage in the service of humankind.[14]

What the United Church of Christ Believes

In 1959 the newly formed United Church of Christ announced a statement of faith. It cites affirmations of faith in the Trinity, God as Creator, and humanity as created in His image. It cites the love of God, which aims "to save all people from aimlessness and sin." The incarnation, life, death, and resurrection of Jesus are affirmed, though the Virgin Birth is not cited. The Holy Spirit is bestowed by Christ, and the Spirit creates, renews, and unifies the Church. Believers are to celebrate both the joy and cost of discipleship. Christ promises to all who trust in Him "forgiveness of sin and fullness of grace, courage in the struggle for justice and peace . . . and eternal life in his kingdom which has no end."[15]

The document, according to the church, is a *testimony* of faith, not a *test* of faith. It does not set forth doctrinal positions and is not intended to replace any of the historic confessions or creeds. The theology of each of the merging

---

13. Mead and Hill, *Handbook of Denominations*, 297.
14. UCC, www.
15. Mead and Hill, *Handbook of Denominations*, 289. Mead and Hill print the entire declaration of faith.

churches remains unchanged. The statement of faith is not binding on any local congregation. It does not stand as a guardian of orthodoxy but "does stand for the faith, charity, and understanding of merging groups."[16] Local churches, associations of churches, conferences, national boards and agencies, and the General Synod are free to act in their particular spheres in light of the Scriptures, the guidance of the Spirit, and the mutual commitment to covenantal life.

The calling and challenge of the United Church of Christ is to live in this world—

Ministering to its needs.

Being enriched by those aspects of culture that help make human life more human.

Working through institutions and supporting laws that reflect God's just and loving purposes for the world.

Seeking justice and liberation for all.[17]

The Church of the Nazarene can find common ground with the core beliefs of the uniting churches described in this chapter. However, we look at articles of faith about Christ, the Bible, the Trinity, and so on as binding upon our teachers, pastors, and members. While we share with them a concern for Christian unity, we also affirm that the theological foundations really matter. We believe that we were raised up by God to proclaim the distinctive doctrine of entire sanctification by grace through faith—we just can't be Nazarenes without that belief.

While we share with them a concern for Christian unity, we also affirm that the theological foundations

Further, since they believe that things theological cannot be precisely defined and preached, the uniting churches find an organizing principle in social service. Nazarenes also believe in social service—and our giving and ministries in the central cities of the world prove it—but the Wesleyan heritage is soteriological to the core. That is, salvation, full salvation, is our central concern.

The uniting spirit is strong and getting stronger among mainline Protestants. In Australia, Presbyterians and Methodists have joined to create the Uniting Church. In India, Anglicans, Methodists, and others united to form two indigenous denominations, the Church of South India and the Church of North India. In the United States, the Evangelical Lutheran Church, the Reformed Church in America, the United Church of Christ, and the Presbyterian Church U.S.A. voted in the summer of 1997 to take a giant step toward unity. They have agreed to share clergy, recognize each other's baptism, and permit members to take Communion in each other's churches. This historic move may "refigure the face of American Protestantism," according to Walter Bouman of Trinity Lutheran Seminary.[18] Similar steps to establish mutual recognition between Episcopalians and Lutherans are ongoing.

16. Ibid., 290.

17. United Church of Christ web site, <http://www.ucc.org/who/whatis.htm>.

18. Associated Press, "Church Accepts Plan for Unity," Kansas City Star, August 19, 1997, A-14.

The Unitarian Universalist Association

Nazarenes have even less in common with the Unitarian Universalist Association (UUA)—unless a generic desire for the world to be a better place counts. The UUA is an influential, ultraliberal union of Unitarian and Universalist congregations in the United States and Canada that merged in 1961.

These folks renounce the Trinity, the deity and propitiary atonement of Christ, miracles, original sin, heaven, and hell. They affirm that no minister, congregation, or church member "shall be required to subscribe to any particular interpretation of religion, or to any particular belief or creed."[19]

The UUA has few connections to the other uniting churches treated in this chapter. There is one historical connection. Many of the Congregational churches in Massachusetts went Unitarian in the 19th century. Those who did not lived on to become part of the Congregational Christian Churches who participated in the merger that created the United Church of Christ. In spite of some common historical roots, the affinity between the United Church of Christ and the UUA is slight indeed.

Part of the UUA traces its philosophical roots back to pre-Christian gnosticism, early "Christian" gnostics, and to mysticism, adding the doctrines of universal salvation and a loving God as revealed in the man Jesus. In New England, they sprang up partially as a rebellion against rigid Calvinistic doctrines, particularly the idea of predestination and the notion that salvation is for the elect few. By contrast, they taught that all persons would be saved.

The UUA has been at the forefront of racial and diversity issues, feminism, gay and lesbian rights, and process theology.[20]

The UUA reported 204,000 adherents in 1,020 congregations in 1993. Don't look for uniting talks to bring about a merger of the UUA and the Church of the Nazarene—it would be like oil and water.

In looking at the United Church of Canada and the United Church of Christ, we have gotten a glimpse of ecumenism among mainline Protestant Christians. In the next two chapters, we will observe ecumenism among Evangelical fellowships.

Review and Reflection

1. Vocabulary Test

To properly understand this chapter, you need to understand these key terms. If the authors have done an adequate job, a study of this chapter should at least suggest the meaning. Use a theological dictionary if necessary. Define the term and explain its key function in this chapter.

   a. Soteriology

   b. Ecumenical

   c. Creed

---

19. Mead and Hill, *Handbook of Denominations*, 287.
20. Ibid., 288.

    d. Evangelism

    e. Doctrine

    f. Justice

    g. The elect

2. Priority Setting

If you were to establish a church in your community this year, which of the following would be at the top of your priority list?

    Social justice for the poor

    Bringing persons to a saving encounter with Christ

    Helping people live a holy life as taught in the Bible

    Having a growing church

    Raising money to pay off bills

    Teaching the gospel and the Bible

    Practicing appropriate worship of God

    Other: _____

3. If a visitor observed what was happening at the church you attend now, which of the above would he or she say is at the top of your congregation's list?

Thumbnail Sketch

COMMUNITY CHURCHES

What Are Community Churches?

By "community churches" we mean independent congregations that have no official affiliation with any denomination or national or international church. Many of them, however, belong to a "fellowship" of like-minded independent churches. In this chapter, two such associations are explored: the International Council of Community Churches (ICCC) and the Willow Creek Association (WCA).

Core Beliefs

Though the independent nature of community churches permits a broad theological spectrum, most of the congregations in the two associations of this chapter hold mainstream Protestant Evangelical beliefs. They embrace the inspiration of the Bible; the deity, resurrection, and atonement of Christ; baptism and Communion; the sinfulness of humanity; conversion; eternal rewards and punishments; and so on.

Agreements and Differences

Nazarenes share several basic beliefs with this group. Nazarenes hold a different doctrine of the Church and its administration and a view of sanctification different from that of typical community churches.

Community Churches Today

The ICCC serves 1,200 churches in 17 countries. The WCA serves 1,200 churches from 70 denominations in 19 countries.

Willow Creek Community Church's mission is "to turn irreligious people into fully devoted followers of Jesus Christ."
—"What We're Doing," Willow Creek Community Church

17

COMMUNITY CHURCHE*J*

A LOT OF INDEPENDENT AND EVEN DENOMINATIONAL local churches include the words "Community Church" on their stationery and church signs. For some, it means that this church is congregational in government, and the local community of faith makes all the decisions from the color of the choir robes to the syncopation of the music to how the offerings are spent.

For another church it may simply mean that this church operates "independent" of any denomination. For denominational congregations who call themselves "Community Church," it may mean that they wish to hide their denominational affiliation lest it put off prospective members who may hold some prejudice against the parent organization.

Through the years, clusters of independent Evangelical churches have organized "fellowships" to unite their witness and mission. The avoidance of over-churching, solving the duplication of staffing and services, and the search for self-determination rather than coping with denominational restrictions are among the motivations for such fellowships.

In this chapter we will explore just two organizations as representing the Community Church Movement: the International Council of Community Churches and the Willow Creek Association. In one sense, they represent the ecumenical movement among Evangelicals just as the United Church of Christ and the United Church of Canada represent the ecumenical movement among mainline Protestants.

The International Council of Community Churches (ICCC)

In 1950 two fellowships within the Community Church Movement came together in a historic merger. One represented mostly Black African-American congregations and the other predominantly White Evangelical congregations. "At the time, their joining represented the largest interracial merger of religious bodies in America."[1] The new body of affiliated churches called itself the

---

1. "The International Council of Community Churches" (ICCC) (Internet document, February 8, 1997), 1.

International Council of Community Churches. To this day the affiliated churches are, according to Executive Director Jeffrey Newhall, about half African-American congregations and half Caucasian congregations. The merging groups cited their aim as becoming a fellowship of ecumenically minded, freedom-loving churches cooperating in fulfilling the mission of the Church in the world.

The ICCC now provides services for 1,200 community churches representing all 50 states and 17 countries of the world. Some 406 affiliated churches with 251,000 members provide the financial support for the council.[2]

Currently the organization defines itself as a "post-denominational movement" that has been around for more than 40 years. The ICCC's Internet home page states its purpose:

- To be an answer to Christ's prayer: *"That they may all be one"* (John 17).
- To affirm the worth and dignity of every person.
- To attend to human need and suffering throughout the world.
- To seek and share the truth.
- To build toward a new world of peace.[3]

The group's "vision" document cites individual freedom of conscience, local church self-determination, and support of the worldwide ecumenical movement, and proclaims that the love of God can overcome any division among Christians.[4]

In the ICCC's statement of history, purpose, vision, organization, administration, and the services it offers, no mention is made of specific doctrines such as the primacy of Scripture, belief in the Trinity, the atonement of Christ, or the salvation of souls. It's not fair to say, however, that when it comes to specific theological matters, the various congregations are on their own. In 1989, in order to align itself with orthodox Christianity as opposed to the heretical sects that had sprung up virtually everywhere, the Annual Conference added to its lone affirmation of faith, "Jesus is Lord," a statement of belief in the Nicene Creed and the Apostles' Creed.[5]

The ICCC's dedication to ecumenicity tends to diminish the importance of theology and doctrinal distinctives. The ICCC folks will be quick to say that all member affiliates are free to proclaim and enforce their own theological beliefs as dogmatically as they please. But the ICCC is about unity, not doctrine. That, of course, sends things theological to the end of the line to make room for "more important" matters. Most of the churches, however, that have affiliated with ICCC are Evangelical in aim and purpose.

That, of course, sends things theological to the end of the line to make room for "more important" matters.

---

2. Telephone interview, February 11, 1997.
3. "ICCC" (Internet document, February 8, 1997).
4. Ibid.
5. Telephone interview with Jeffrey Newhall, February 11, 1997.

In many ways the ICCC functions very much like a denomination. It has a central headquarters in Frankfort, Illinois. It conducts an Annual Conference to which each congregation can send two voting delegates—one clergy and one layperson. The Conference elects a slate of general officers to oversee the council's business. In the United States the council is subdivided into regions and areas not unlike Methodist conferences and districts.

The ICCC also offers services much like those that denominations offer. For example, a number of services are offered to clergy, including placement of pastors and chaplains, continuing education, a periodical for clergy (*The Pastor's Journal*), and confidential counseling. The ICCC also assists by way of recommendation (or lack thereof) in the ordination of clergy. It can also recommend discipline or dismissal of clergy guilty of misconduct. Other services include consulting functions for churches in transition or trouble, shared giving to the needy, joint mission projects, a college scholarship program, and a newspaper, *The Christian Community*.

In other ways the ICCC does not operate as a denomination. First, there are no articles of faith to which members or clergy are bound. Second, the role of the ICCC is strictly advisory in setting standards for ordination and for the discipline of clergy. And there are no assessments or required levels of financial support. Each congregation determines the amount it will give for the cooperative budget. The Church of the Nazarene, by contrast, has rigorous prescriptions in these areas.

Further, the ICCC is a member of the Consultation On Church Union (COCU), the National Council of Churches, and the World Council of Churches. The Church of the Nazarene is not a member of any of those groups. Its General Board, General Assembly, and Board of General Superintendents have expressly forbidden membership in the National Council of Churches because this organization is influenced by theological liberalism.

The Willow Creek Association

The Willow Creek Community Church of South Barrington, Illinois, near Chicago, has become a powerful force for Evangelical cooperation and ecumenism. The church was started in 1975 with 125 people and Pastor Bill Hybels in a rented movie theater. From the beginning it was an interdenominational, Evangelical church. Now the church is located on a 140-acre campus and attracts approximately 15,000 people per week.

Willow Creek is the quintessential full-service church, offering ministries for all age-groups. It ministers to identity groups, such as single adults, teens, and so on. Willow Creek also operates sports and fitness programs, men's and women's ministries, and community service outreach, such as food distribution, nursing home care, unemployment programs, 12-step groups, marriage workshops, divorce recovery, unplanned pregnancy counsel, and family finance. A whole raft of small-group ministries take this as their mission: "to connect people relationally in groups for the purpose of growing in Christ-likeness, loving one another, and contributing to the work of the church, in order to glorify God and make disciples of all nations."[6]

---

6. "A Closer Look at Willow Creek Community Church" (Internet: WCCC home page, February 8, 1997), 2.

On Willow Creek's Internet home page the statement of belief is short but important: "We may use up-to-date language, music, and drama to communicate God's Word for today's culture, but our message is as old as the Bible itself. We embrace historic Christian teaching on all doctrines, emphasizing Jesus Christ's atoning death; salvation through repentance and faith as a work of divine grace; and the authority of the unique, God-inspired Bible."[7]

Willow Creek's mission statement ("What We're Doing") is "to turn irreligious people into fully devoted followers of Jesus Christ." Their vision ("What We're Becoming") is "to be a biblically functioning community of believers so that Christ's redemptive purposes can be accomplished in the world."[8]

> *"We may use up-to-date language, music, and drama to communicate God's Word for today's culture, but our message is as old as the Bible itself."*

Pastor Hybels and four helpers hammered out the "10 core values" that guide the local church and the worldwide Willow Creek Association. An abbreviated version of these follows. The church believes that

1. anointed teaching is the catalyst for transformation in individuals;
2. lost people matter to God and therefore ought to matter to the church;
3. the church should be culturally relevant while remaining doctrinally pure. This includes sensitively relating to our culture through our facility, printed materials, and the use of the arts (1 Cor. 9:19-23).
4. Christ-followers should manifest authenticity and yearn for continuous growth;
5. a church should operate as a unified community of servants with men and women stewarding the spiritual gifts—including ministry callings;
6. loving relationships should permeate every aspect of church life;
7. life change happens best in small groups;
8. excellence honors God and inspires people;
9. churches should be led by men and women with leadership gifts;
10. the pursuit of full devotion to Christ and His cause is normal for every believer.[9]

The Willow Creek miracle has attracted much attention. Many churches have patterned themselves after this community church. Some have made their affiliation official by joining the Willow Creek Association (WCA). About 1,200 churches from 19 countries and 70 denominations have signed on. All the churches admitted to the association have professed Evangelical faith and purpose.

The various national chapters of the WCA have modeled their organizations after the mission, vision, and core values of Willow Creek in Illinois. For example, the mission statement of the WCA of Australia is "to assist churches in re-establishing the priority and practice of reaching lost people for Christ

---

7. Ibid.
8. "Welcome to Willow Creek Community Church," ibid., 6.
9. Ibid.

through churches that are culturally relevant."[10] The mission of the WCA of New Zealand is "to help New Zealand local churches reach unchurched people and enable them to become fully devoted followers of Jesus Christ."[11]

Nazarenes will resonate with Willow Creek theology, aims, and methods far more than they will with those of the International Council of Community Churches. Nazarenes share the evangelistic (soteriological) aim of the WCA. From John Wesley on, the Wesleyan-Holiness people have made the salvation of the lost the primary aim—just as it was with the One who gave us the Great Commission.

Further, the emphasis of the WCA on small groups reminds one that John Wesley changed the world through the use of societies, classes, bands, select societies, and mentoring pairs. In this regard, Hybels and Company have been more Wesleyan than some Nazarenes. Again, the WCA has creatively learned to communicate with the unchurched culture just as Wesley used field preaching, popular tunes, and the vernacular vocabulary to capture the attention and hearts of the masses of his day.

There is also resonance between the combination of community service and evangelism modeled by Willow Creek and the perfect marriage between personal religion and social responsibility that John Wesley taught to the world. Again, there is some correlation between the Willow Creek emphasis on every believer seeking continual growth and becoming "fully devoted" to Christ and the Wesleyan and Nazarene doctrines of entire sanctification that is available to every Christian, bringing the believer "into a state of entire devotement," as our *Manual* states.[12]

Thus, it is not surprising that, though some pastors have tried to import precipitously the Willow Creek culture with infelicitous results, most Nazarenes admire much that Willow Creek has achieved. Indeed, we can learn important lessons from them. But there are some things that Willow Creek cannot do for us. It cannot treasure and teach our heritage of faith—that's our job. It cannot stress our distinctive doctrine—community churches cannot be very precise and definitive when it comes to authoritative theology. Nor can a loosely organized association like the WCA (or the ICCC) hold lay and clergy leaders accountable through reporting to denominational agencies and boards or managing such things as qualifying ministerial candidates, disciplining clergy, administering our colleges, taking care of retirement and pension concerns, and carrying on a large worldwide missionary program.

Review and Reflection

1. State in your own words the reasons independent community churches exist and join together in associations.

---

10. "Willow Creek Association Australia Ministries, Inc.," ibid., 1.
11. "Willow Creek Association New Zealand," ibid., 1.
12. Article X, *Manual, Church of the Nazarene, 1997—2001,* 30.

2. What advantages and disadvantages do you see in churches being part of a denomination or being independent? Include in your consideration such matters as missionary outreach, freedom of the congregation, financial accountability, preparation and discipline of clergy, and so on.

3. Compare the Willow Creek statement of belief, mission, vision, and values with the Nazarene Agreed Statement of Belief (par. 26, pp. 35-36, *Manual, Church of the Nazarene, 1997—2001*) and with the summary of the Church of the Nazarene's purpose and mission, found at the end of chapter 2 in this book.

PARACHURCH ORGANIZATIONS

Overview

When denominations, for complicated reasons, became unwilling or unable to resource local churches, parachurch organizations (PCOs) stepped up. Narrow focus enabled PCOs to fill a ministry or market gap more quickly than a lumbering denomination. The acceptance of PCOs across denominational lines has produced a sort of ecumenical movement among Evangelicals. This brings both blessings and hazards.

In this chapter we call on seven of the best PCOs to represent the movement. There are many other worthy PCOs, and some infamous ones. Examined here are Youth for Christ, Navigators, Inter-Varsity, Campus Crusade for Christ, Promise Keepers, and two guided by Nazarenes—Compassion International and Focus on the Family.

Core Beliefs and Practices

The seven PCOs in this chapter are soundly Evangelical and basically orthodox. They accept the Trinity; the deity, atonement, and resurrection of Christ; the Protestant principles of the priesthood of believers; the authority of the Bible; and salvation by grace through faith.

Agreement and Differences

The Church of the Nazarene shares many basic beliefs with the PCOs of this chapter. We have ministered in teamwork with several of them. At best, denominations and local churches and PCOs work to *complement* rather than compete with each other. We must remember, however, that the theology of most PCOs has to be marketable across denominational lines and is thus generic. PCOs cannot properly provide the resources that a local church needs to teach its denomination's heritage. Also, only so many dollars are available to support the work of local churches and denominational ministries on the one hand and PCOs on the other. Church members and local churches are depended on to support both. Funding competition can be a problem.

Parachurch organizations have stepped forward and filled certain needs of the Church of Christ when the denominations seemed unable or unwilling to do so.

18 ~ PARACHURCH ORGANIZATIONS

BY THE LATE 1960S MANY CHURCHES in mainline denominations had gotten out of the habit of looking to their headquarters and central agencies for resourcing. By the mid-1970s, most Evangelical denominations had developed the same tendency.

The pattern, now a mere matter of record, developed along these lines: As the populist rebellion against national and international institutions began to spread like a Kansas prairie fire, grassroots people and local churches came to disrespect and distrust their central agencies. In many cases, the positions of denominational leaders violated grassroots conservatism. The more the local churches "loved to hate" their own hierarchical systems, boards, and leaders, the more reluctant they became to fund them. The more reluctant the people became to fund the denominational agencies, the harder it became for denominational leaders to create and pay for programs to resource their local churches.

Into this resource vacuum of the last third of the 20th century have stepped three kinds of agencies offering exciting new programs to service both individuals and congregations. First, a few aggressive seminaries have stepped up to fill a ministry and training gap. Second, some two dozen teaching churches or megachurches now operate extensive programs complete with seminars, internships, books, and videotapes that tell other congregations and pastors "how we did it."

But the resourcing explosion came from a third group: parachurch organizations (PCOs) who stepped up to fill a ministry, or at least a market, gap. Organizations like Focus on the Family, Youth for Christ, Navigators, Compassion International, Campus Crusade for Christ, Inter-Varsity Fellowship, and Promise Keepers burst into bloom. They operate on billions of dollars raised from church members and congregations of those denominations who decided that they could not resource their local churches. They offer services in the form of books, magazines, training courses, seminars, videotapes—and they give all those church members on their lists repeated chances to donate to their ministries. It has been a sort of Evangelical ecumenism.

The parachurch organizations have some advantages over denominations. First, they specialize on a market niche. Denominations have to be full-service organizations. But Focus on the Family can, well—focus on the family, while Promise Keepers proves that male bonding can cross denominational lines. Further, the parachurch organizations are often run by entrepreneurial leaders with boards ready to approve what the boss wants. Thus, they can spot a market niche or ministry opportunity and move into it at once. A denomination, on the other hand, must wade through a formidable array of committees and boards en route to a General Assembly or Annual Conference, which may debate a ministry move for years.

A Theology of the Marketplace

Parachurch organizations have become a powerful theological force. They have carved out a theology of generic Evangelicalism. Every one of them must market across denominational lines. Thus, they must emphasize the few core beliefs that almost all Christians hold. Denominational distinctives must be minimized. The very beliefs around which some denominations were formed —baptism by immersion, speaking in tongues, entire sanctification, regenerative baptism—must be trivialized because of marketplace demands.

One result of this is that after a few decades of resourcing by generic, consumer-tolerant PCOs, denominational distinctives fade in the minds of church members. Even among the leaders, the denomination's heritage dims into a nebulous cloud haunting their dreams like the memory of a guilty romance. Again, we're speaking about history, not speculation. For three decades several denominations have turned to the three types of agencies mentioned above for resourcing. Today they have an identity crisis. Few really know their denomination's distinctives—and they don't seem to care.

While this may seem like an indictment of parachurch organizations, it is not. They have stepped forward and filled certain needs of the Church when the denominations seemed unable or unwilling to do so.

The theology of generic Evangelicalism marketed across denominational lines by PCOs has these typical tenets:
1. Strong affirmation of the authority of the Bible
2. Jesus Christ as Savior and Lord
3. The deity, virgin birth, death, literal resurrection, and eventual return of Jesus
4. The Triune God—Father, Son, and Spirit
5. Salvation by grace through a conversion experience
6. The need for Christian nurture, training, and growth in grace
7. A strong emphasis on evangelism

Representative Evangelical Parachurch Organizations

1. **Youth for Christ.** One of the oldest and most well-known parachurch organizations is Youth for Christ (YFC), begun in 1944. The first paid employee of Youth for Christ was a young preacher from North Carolina by the name of Billy Graham. Upon the 50th anniversary of YFC, the premier evangelist of our times said, "It was my privilege to be the first full-time employee of Youth for

Christ. After 50 years, Youth for Christ continues to communicate the life-changing message of Jesus Christ to our youth. We all know the problems confronting today's young people are staggering. I can think of no greater cause than to reach our youth for Christ. Let's save our kids."[1]

YFC says that its *mission* is to communicate the life-changing message of Jesus Christ to every young person. Its *purpose* is to participate in the Body of Christ in the responsible evangelism of youth, presenting them with the person, work, and teachings of Jesus Christ, discipling them, and leading them into the local church. The *strategy* of YFC is to mobilize the Christian community to reach lost youth wherever they are and by all responsible means.[2]

Youth for Christ in the United States has 800 full-time employees and 11,000 volunteer workers. About 225 chapters of YFC now operate in the United States, carrying out some 40 min-

> *The first paid employee of Youth for Christ was a young preacher from North Carolina by the name of Billy Graham.*

istry models in schools, institutions, neighborhoods, and local churches. Beyond the typical YFC chapters, ministries include campus ministry, programs for at-risk teens, crisis pregnancy centers, AIDS prevention, abstinence education, gang reconciliation, and conflict resolution programs. Some 600,000 United States teens are touched by these ministries. In a recent year YFC reported 31,000 professions of faith among the nation's youth. Youth for Christ/International (YFCI) has work in 127 countries.[3]

2. The Navigators. In the late 1920s a California truck driver named Dawson Trotman developed a set of spiritual disciplines that lifted his Christian life to a higher level. Those disciplines included daily Bible reading, memorizing Scripture, regular prayer times, and faithfully witnessing to others about Jesus. As he grew in his relationship to Christ, he found that many other Christians seeking the deeper life turned to him for guidance. In 1933 Trotman organized the Navigators with the vision "to know Christ and to make Him known," which is still the watchword of the ministry. The work of the first Navigators was among California sailors. The ministry has grown beyond its military mission but still emphasizes ministry to military personnel. Currently, NavMilitary has 226 staff members and more than 1,200 active-duty workers serving American army, navy, air force, Marine Corps, and Coast Guard personnel on 112 United States and overseas military posts.

Based in Colorado Springs, this organization has three principal ministry entities. NavPress creates educational materials and books. The Navigator small-group Bible studies may be the best-known and most widely used ministry of this organization. NavYouth supports a number of national and international programs for students.

---

1. See this Internet address: <http://www.gospelcom.net/yfc/yfc/Guestbook/whoweare.html>.
2. Ibid.
3. Ibid.

Navigators identifies its *vision* as helping "multitudes of diverse people in America and every nation who have a passionate love for Christ, live a lifestyle of sharing Christ's love, and multiply spiritual laborers among those without Christ."[4] The Navigator *values* are

Loving and serving Christ with a passion.

Living and ministering in the power of the Holy Spirit.

Living by faith and obedience to God's Word.

Developing depth in spiritual disciplines.

Imparting a vision for the world.[5]

The Navigators' *mission* is to reach, disciple, and equip people to know Christ and to make Him known through successive generations. This the Navigators hope to achieve by "discipling people *life on life* to trust and obey Jesus Christ."[6]

3. Inter-Varsity. This organization began in 1877 at the University of Cambridge in England as a group of students became very serious about living the Christian life. In 1928 British Inter-Varsity sent Howard Guinness, a medical student, to begin Canadian Inter-Varsity. The movement soon spread to the United States, and in 1941 Inter-Varsity—U.S.A. was officially started. Today there are 700 campus chapters around the United States.

Inter-Varsity—U.S.A. is affiliated with other student groups in more than 100 countries. This larger association is called the International Fellowship of Evangelical Students.

The Inter-Varsity *vision statement* steers the organization toward building college fellowships, developing disciples who embody biblical values, and engaging the campus in all its ethnic diversity with the gospel of Christ. The Inter-Varsity *values* are

Evangelism—every person ought to have an opportunity to respond to Jesus Christ.

Spiritual Formation—teaching and practicing spiritual disciplines as the way to grow in Christlike maturity.

The Church—serving the Church by helping each person to appreciate its purpose and by encouraging their activity as lifelong worshipers and participating members.

Human Relationships—teaching and demonstrating that healthy human relationships are a mark of true discipleship and eventuate in fruitful friendships, marriages, and working partnerships.

Righteousness—awareness of the reality of evil. Teaching and demonstrating repentance and humility and the importance of personal integrity, compassion, and prophetic renunciation and confrontation.

Vocational Stewardship—challenging Christians to acknowledge the stewardship of personal skills and vocational opportunity.

World Evangelization—believing that God has called all Christians to evangelization.

---

4. See Internet address: <http://www.gospelcom.net/navs/>.

5. Ibid.

6. Ibid.

Inter-Varsity bases the above practices on five *theological distinctives:*

a. The unique divine inspiration, entire trustworthiness, and authority of the Bible.

b. The deity of our Lord Jesus Christ.

c. The necessity and the efficacy of the substitutionary death of Jesus Christ for the redemption of the world and the historic fact of His bodily resurrection.

d. The presence and power of the Holy Spirit in the work of regeneration.

e. The expectation of the personal return of our Lord Jesus Christ.[7]

4. Campus Crusade for Christ (CCC). This organization began as an Evangelical ministry to college students in the United States. It still has vital ministries on 400 college and university campuses. But under the leadership of Bill Bright, it has become a wide-scoped, complex institution that seeks to evangelize around the world. CCC defines itself as "an interdenominational ministry committed to helping take the gospel of Jesus Christ to all nations."[8]

The *goal* by the year 2000 for the CCC is to work with other Christians "to help give every man, woman, and child in the entire world an opportunity to find new life in Christ."[9]

The 110,000 staff members and trained volunteers have taken this as their near-term objective.

> *"By the year 2000 we want to help give every man, woman, and child in the entire world an opportunity to find new life in Christ."*

The *financing* of the program includes this policy. CCC is a faith missions organization. All members of the staff (and their spouses) must meet the qualifications for the organization's ministry. Part of the job is raising funds to cover the needs of the ministry. Each staff member—from founder and president Bill Bright to the newest member—is responsible for lining up a team of individuals and local churches who will underwrite as ministry partners the financial needs of his or her ministry.

CCC has a wide variety of ministry programs, including Women Today International, *Worldwide Challenge Magazine,* World Changers Radio, Children of the World, Priority One (aimed at business and professional persons in major United States cities), SOLO Ministries, Student LINC, Family Life Today, CHURCHLIFE, Medical Strategic Network, Athletes in Action, New Life Publications, and the *Jesus* Film Project. CCC has generously helped the Church of the Nazarene in distributing the *Jesus* film on our mission fields.

Currently the organization is building a new $56 million World Center for Discipleship and Evangelism on 285 acres in Orlando, Florida.

5. Promise Keepers. This organization is the dominant voice of the Christian men's movement. A Nazarene district superintendent said, "The

---

7. All data about Inter-Varsity may be found at the Internet address: <http://www.gospelcom.net/iv/general/vision/html>.

8. Internet: <http://www.ccci.org/contchallenge.html>.

9. Ibid.

Promise Keepers phenomenon is the nearest thing to a genuine revival that has happened in my lifetime."

In March 1990 University of Colorado football coach Bill McCartney and his friend Dave Wardell became fascinated by the idea of filling huge stadiums with men not for football games but for Christian discipleship and the glory of God. Later that year, 72 men began to pray and fast about the spiritual needs of men and how to meet them.

In 1991 some 4,200 men attended the first Promise Keepers (PK) meeting. In 1992 more than 22,000 men met at the University of Colorado's Folsom Stadium. In 1993 some 50,000 showed up. By 1996 22 PK conferences drew 1,098,534 men.

Promise Keepers saw a void in Christian resources. The organization moved quickly to supply rallies, seminars, conferences, books, magazines, and other discipleship products. In 1996 they sponsored 450 local and regional seminars, training sessions, and "wake-up calls" in the United States and Canada. The 1996 PK clergy conference attracted 39,024 ministers. PK now operates offices in 38 states, has a radio program on 1,200 stations, and has produced its first television special.

The *mission statement* affirms, "Promise Keepers is a Christ-centered ministry dedicated to uniting men through vital relationships to become godly influences in their world."[10]

In order to carry out this purpose, PK "ambassadors" have recruited thousands of pastors to appoint "key men" in their congregations who are to serve the men of that church and *to represent the needs of those men to Promise Keepers.* Currently some 14,000 key men and ambassadors work in local churches in behalf of the PK ministry.

Promise Keepers admits that they have a patchwork theology that tries to steer clear of "nonessential" doctrines. The seven promises of a Promise Keeper form the constitution of the organization. A PK is committed

1. to honoring Jesus Christ through worship, prayer, and obedience to God's Word in the power of the Holy Spirit.

2. to pursuing vital relationships with a few other men, understanding that he needs brothers to help him keep his promises.

3. to practicing spiritual, moral, ethical, and sexual purity.

4. to building strong marriages and families through love, protection, and biblical values.

5. to supporting the mission of the church by honoring and praying for his pastor and by actively giving his time and resources.

6. to reaching beyond any racial and denominational barriers to demonstrate the power of biblical unity.

7. to influencing his world, being obedient to the Great Commandment (Mark 12:30-31) and the Great Commission (Matt. 28:19-20).[11]

---

10. Internet: <http://www.pknet.org/21ca.htm>.
11. Bill Bright et al., *Seven Promises of a Promise Keeper* (Colorado Springs: Focus on the Family, 1994), 8.

Critics of Promise Keepers have cited concern that some emphases have encouraged certain men (who had tendencies in that direction anyway) to regress to old ideas of male dominance of women. A Nazarene female pastor reported that the men in her church came back from Promise Keepers "so gung ho about 'headship' over their wives that it outweighed the New Testament teaching of mutual submission in marriage." The movement came under sharp criticism when it at first prohibited women pastors from attending the 1996 clergy conference in Atlanta. The organization in the end lifted the ban on women pastors. In fact, PK has announced that interested women are invited to attend any of their conferences. Further, on its World Wide Web page, PK announces that "one of the primary goals . . . is to deepen the commitment of men to respect and honor women."[12]

Though PK requires no dues and is not a membership-driven entity, the organization has also been criticized for its vigorous fund-raising efforts among members of churches from many denominations. PK has made itself accountable to the Evangelical Council for Financial Accountability and makes its annual audit available upon request. Part of the PK commitment to financial integrity is its practice of "encouraging men to tithe to their local church before making contributions to Promise Keepers."[13]

A survey of Nazarene pastors and laypersons conducted by the Church Growth Division in 1996 revealed that Nazarenes ranked the Promise Keepers ministry very high. The women polled ranked the significance of PK even higher than did the men. Ninety-eight percent of the laypersons and 93 percent of the pastors saw the work of Promise Keepers as *complementing* rather than competing with the local church.

6. **Compassion International.** In 1967 Nazarene pastor Wally Erickson left his church in Hammond, Indiana, convinced that God had called him to work with children and youth. He teamed up with a tiny organization in Chicago called Compassion. In 1975 he was made president after he had done excellent work in Korea and Latin America. Compassion International grew steadily under Rev. Erickson's direction and at the time of his retirement had some 420 employees plus hundreds of volunteers and a budget of more than $50 million per year.

Erickson graduated from Olivet Nazarene University and Nazarene Theological Seminary. It's not surprising that he channeled millions of dollars for children's ministries through the Nazarene missionary organization around the world. In a recent year, Nazarene children in Bolivia, Brazil, Colombia, the Dominican Republic, Mexico, Guatemala, Peru, the Philippines, Los Angeles, Arizona, and Haiti were objects of 171 Compassion International projects. More than 14,000 Nazarene kids received the benefit of $2,071,288 that year of Compassion International funds. The money went to support Nazarene schools, student centers, and Family Helper projects. Of course, that was only a small part of Compassion International's support of children connected with many Evangelical churches.[14]

---

12. Internet: <http://www.pknet.org/21ca.htm>.
13. Ibid.
14. Wesley D. Tracy, "Wally's World," *Herald of Holiness*, June 1993, 13.

The *mission* of Compassion International is to minister to needy children, releasing them from poverty and enabling them to become fulfilled adults by nurturing such children through support, education, training, and guidance to be Christians in faith and deed; teaching them how to support themselves and share with others in need.[15]

W. H. Erickson *defines* Compassion International by saying, "We are not a relief agency. We do not plant churches to compete with missionary churches. We support; we don't compete. We designed our ministry to serve children who are already in touch with or can be reached by Evangelical churches and schools. We only work with Evangelicals—those who preach the gospel of Jesus Christ as the answer to our human predicament."[16]

Typically, the *work* of Compassion International in behalf of children in many work areas includes Family Helper projects, Saturday Bible clubs, tutoring in academics, health monitoring, parents' meetings, home visits, and a wide variety of learning opportunities, including field trips, Vacation Bible Schools, sports, and camping.

7. **Focus on the Family** is another parachurch organization founded by a Nazarene. For 14 years Nazarene psychologist James C. Dobson was an associate clinical professor of pediatrics at the University of California School of Medicine. During that time he was also on the attending staff of Children's Hospital of Los Angeles. Dr. Dobson was overwhelmed by the disintegration of American families that left children to suffer many unnecessary traumas. Thus, he started Focus on the Family in 1977. From a two-room suite in Arcadia, California, Dobson began with a weekly radio program on a handful of stations. Since then, Focus on the Family has become an international organization with 50 different ministries requiring 1,300 employees. Dr. Dobson's daily radio broadcast is aired on some 4,000 stations. Other parts of the organization produce six other radio programs, publish 10 magazines sent to 2.3 million persons per month, publish a full line of Christian books, and produce films and videos on Christian themes, family values, and pastoral support.[17]

One of Dobson's first books was *Dare to Discipline,* which has now sold more than 2 million copies. More than 70 million people have viewed the *Focus on the Family* film series. Dobson has served on a number of boards and committees set up by the federal government under United States Presidents Carter, Reagan, and Bush. On matters of public policy regarding family values, public education, teen pregnancy, and abortion, Focus on the Family has become one of the most influential organizations in America.

The core beliefs of Focus on the Family include strong traditional statements on the authority of the Bible; the Holy Trinity; and the deity, virgin birth, life, work, miracles, atoning death, resurrection, and return of Jesus Christ. The organization also affirms that "for the salvation of lost and sinful man, regeneration by the Holy Spirit is absolutely essential." Holiness is also affirmed in this

15. Ibid., 8.
16. Ibid., 11.
17. Internet: <http://www.cs.albany.edu/~ault/fof/fotbegin.html>.

statement: "We believe in the present ministry of the Holy Spirit, by whose indwelling the Christian is enabled to live a godly life." Faith in Christian unity and in eternal rewards and punishments is also affirmed.[18]

These theological declarations support the work of Focus on the Family, which is summarized in the following affirmations:

We believe that:

- the ultimate purpose in living is to know and glorify God and to attain eternal life through Jesus Christ . . . beginning with our own families and then reaching out to a suffering humanity that does not know His love and sacrifice. The institution of marriage was intended by God to be a permanent, lifelong relationship between a man and a woman, regardless of trials, sickness, financial reverses, or emotional stresses that may ensue.
- children are a heritage from God and a blessing from His hand. We are therefore accountable to Him for raising, shaping, and preparing them for a life of service to His kingdom and to humanity.
- human life is of inestimable worth and significance in all its dimensions, including the unborn, the aged, the widowed, the mentally handicapped, the unattractive, the physically challenged, and every other condition in which humanness is expressed from conception to the grave.
- God has ordained three basic institutions—the church, the family, and the government—for the benefit of mankind.[19]

The Church of the Nazarene and Parachurch Organizations

As far as the Church of the Nazarene is concerned, it can share common ground at several points with the parachurch organizations discussed in this chapter. Like the organizations cited above, Nazarenes embrace the authority of the Bible; the Holy Trinity; the deity, resurrection, and atonement of Christ; and the need to be born again. However, there are concerns. Youth for Christ, Navigators, Inter-Varsity, and Campus Crusade for Christ, it is fair to say, represent popular, generic neo-Calvinism. They are more or less Baptistic and spring from the theological fountains of Wheaton, Illinois; *Christianity Today;* Carl F. H. Henry; and so on.

This is not bad or even negative. But it does mean that Nazarenes cannot expect to find any support for some of their most distinctive doctrines in any program that neo-Calvinist organizations provide. For example, the four parachurch organizations named in the preceding paragraph would not even admit the possibility of entire sanctification as a second definite work of grace that cleanses original sin and fills the heart with divine love. Nazarenes will likewise find no special appreciation for the history and heritage of the Wesleyan-Holiness tradition among their friends in Calvinistic PCOs.

---

18. Ibid.
19. Ibid.

Therefore, it would be wrongheaded to allow PCOs to provide all or most of the resourcing for local church teaching no matter how slick their brochures and videotapes. Denominational distinctives and the direction and purpose that they give to a movement simply cannot be provided by parachurch groups who promote a generic, one-size-fits-all belief system.

Nazarenes established two of the PCOs treated in this chapter. Their theological formulations are certainly friendly to Nazarene tenets of faith.

When it comes to Promise Keepers, we're dealing with a group whose founders and principal early leaders came from the Charismatic Movement in general and Vineyard ministries in particular. One would expect that the ideals of the Charismatic Movement would be intrinsic to that organization, even though they make every effort to steer clear of sectarian teachings. One would not expect to have the Nazarene, Baptist, Lutheran, or any other denominational heritage given any particular attention. In fact, the 1996 PK slogan was "Break Down the Walls." One of the "walls" specifically aimed at was denominational walls. The very best parachurch organizations, by their very nature, must diminish denominational distinctives.

Denominations or local churches are not likely in the near future to come up with the funds, agility, or will to provide all the vital programs and services now made available by PCOs. Therefore, the prudent path may be to use the PCOs as they help us all fulfill the mission of the gospel, without neglecting the treasure of our own denominational heritage.

Funding of PCOs is a concern. Money that local church members contribute to parachurch programs certainly cannot be available for the ministries of the local church or the cooperative programs within its denomination. This concern may seem petty to some. But look at it from a pastor's point of view. To begin with, each Nazarene church is expected by its denomination to support general denominational programs for institutions and missions. In addition, the district office and programs must be financed by the local churches. Further, the regional college has a claim on a small percentage of the local church revenues. The support of general, district, and regional cooperative denominational ministries usually takes between 15 and 23 percent of the local church's budget.

Besides this, the pastor knows that many of his members are plied and pressured by the professional fund-raisers of dozens of PCOs. Every parachurch organization from The Gideons International to Jews for Jesus to Save the Children to World Vision is extracting support for their organization from church members everywhere. Many of these pressure laypersons and pastors to put them on the calendar, let their representative speak, take an offering, and most important, come away with a list of names and addresses for future sales and donations.

If a local church member gives a significant donation, say $1,000 or more, he or she will likely be the target of a personal call by a professional fund-raiser who will pry out as large and as many gifts as possible. Every pastor knows that PCOs work overtime at selling his or her church members Bibles, books, magazines, seminars, cassette tapes, videotapes, and a dozen kinds of "pray and give" memberships. After a while, the pastor begins to think that, in spite of the benefits of PCOs, he or she is winning converts so they can become "tax revenue targets" for every organization that wants to harvest in the local pastor's field.

Some parachurch organizations are plainly fraudulent, some quasi-legitimate. A friend reports that a "missionary" outfit where he worked for a short time held annual meetings at which they planned a "crisis offering" for every month of the year. Many parachurch organizations, however, represent good causes—great causes. But a local church cannot die on every cross, cannot give generously to every outfit that comes up with a cute slogan, slick ad, or good cause. Gifts to parachurch organizations that God has raised up should come after the church's denominational ministries have been considered.

Perhaps more than any other force, the vitality of parachurch organizations has made Evangelical religion respected and popular in North America today. Their pragmatic theology and expedient ecumenism based on marketplace demands have demonstrated that what we have in common in Christ just may be more important than many of our denominational differences.

Review and Reflection

1. When I was a teenager, the small Nazarene church that I attended had a limited youth program. A parachurch organization, Youth for Christ, provided valuable opportunities for me. In fact, I preached my first sermon at a Youth for Christ meeting. What parachurch organizations has God used to help you in your spiritual journey?

2. Given the market-driven nature of the theology of parachurch organizations, they cannot provide teaching materials for passing on our denominational treasures and distinctive doctrines. List some Nazarene distinctives, memories, and treasures that must come to the people in your local congregation from Nazarene sources or be forgotten.

3. Talk with your pastor about guidelines for giving to parachurch organizations. Here's a starter list. Modify as you think best.

a. Give to parachurch organizations only after your tithes and offerings are fully paid to and through your local church.

b. Consider the local, district, regional, and general ministries of your denomination and those of the parachurch organization you are thinking about. Establish priorities.

c. Any parachurch organization that does not publish audited financial records or submit records to the Evangelical Council for Financial Accountability does not deserve to be on your donor list.

d. Radically Fundamentalistic, overly political, or single-issue religious right parachurch organizations should be carefully scrutinized.

e. Know how your donation will be spent. One very popular parachurch organization states in the fine print that half of your gift will be spent in promotional advertising. Is that what you want?

PART VIII

THE AMERICAN MELTING POT OF RELIGION

- Mormonism: Mainstream or Extreme?

- Second-Advent Religious Groups

- Health, Harmony, and Happiness: New Thought Religions

- "In the Last Days" . . . Isms Galore

MORMONISM:
MAINSTREAM OR EXTREME?

How Did Mormonism Get Its Start?

Joseph Smith launched Mormonism after he reportedly received a vision at age 14. He had gone into the New York woods to pray about which church to join. God the Father and the Son allegedly appeared and told him that all denominations were corrupt. Further, he was to start the one true Church. Later, it was revealed to him that he was to write a new Bible—the *Book of Mormon*. The movement started in 1830 with a half dozen disciples.

Core Beliefs

God is not a Trinity, nor a Spirit, but a material being of the male gender. God himself is a begotten being. Jesus is not the Second Person of the Trinity but a superlative man. His atonement makes immortality available but does not remove all our sins. Adultery, murder, and other serious sins—these the sinner must pay for himself. There are three heavens, populated mostly by Mormon males. The *Book of Mormon, Pearl of Great Price, Doctrine and Covenants,* all works of Joseph Smith, have as much authority as the Bible. So do certain pronouncements made by the Mormon president. The Mormon Church is the only true Church. The Reorganized Church of Jesus Christ of Latter-day Saints (Missouri) is more liberal and progressive than the Utah Mormons. It has muted some of the fundamental Mormon theological themes.

Agreement and Differences

While Nazarenes sympathize with the persecution endured by the Mormons and respect their hard work and family values, there is almost no common ground in the area of Christian beliefs. The two are worlds apart— even when they use similar terminology. Almost every Mormon doctrine is heretical in comparison to orthodox Christianity.

Mormonism Today

There are 8 million Mormons worldwide. The Reorganized Church of Jesus Christ of Latter-day Saints has 245,000 members. The Utah Mormon Church is the richest religion in America. Widespread investments in agriculture, finance, retailing, real estate, publishing, broadcasting, and insurance produce billions of dollars of income each year.

When cultural confusion starts to tilt toward chaos, prophets and enlightened ones appear on every hand. . . . Joseph Smith was not the first or even the twenty-first American prophet of his day.
—Jan Shipps, *Mormonism*

MORMONIƒM: MAINƒTREAM OR EXTREME?

BOTH MAJOR BRANCHES OF THE MORMON RELIGION now yearn to be regarded as *mainstream* Christians rather than *extreme* sects. This appeal was made directly to the public by Gordon Hinckley, current president of the Utah Mormons (Latter-day Saints), in an interview on the television program *60 Minutes*. Meanwhile, the Missouri Mormons, the Reorganized Church of Jesus Christ of Latter-day Saints (RLDS), have, in their move toward centrism, all but abandoned certain fundamentals of their faith, according to RLDS historian Roger D. Launius. They want to look like a mainstream Protestant church.[1]

This is the first time in the group's 170-year history that the theological children of Joseph Smith have so openly wanted to be accepted. Earlier, they rigorously asserted their separateness as the chosen people of God. The call now to be regarded as mainstream Christians presents certain problems, even in this ecumenically intoxicated age. Mormon holy writings, laws, and special revelations are at odds with most key Christian doctrines, including the Trinity, the nature of Christ, the nature and origins of humanity, salvation, the primacy of the Bible, and eternal rewards and punishment.

Mormon Origins

The Mormon Church was started in 1830 but was officially organized on April 6, 1833, when Joseph Smith and Oliver Cowdery laid hands on each other in mutual ordination as the first "elders."[2] The Mormon movement found its impetus in the visions of the teenage Joseph Smith Jr., the fourth child of farmer

---

1. Roger D. Launius, "The RLDS Church and the Decade of Decision," *Sunstone*, September 1996, 45-46.

2. George A. Mather and Larry A. Nichols, *Dictionary of Cults, Sects, Religions, and the Occult* (Grand Rapids: Zondervan Publishing House, 1993), 189.

Joseph Sr. and Lucy Mack Smith. The Smith family searched for the American dream, but it eluded them. Their farming ventures in Vermont and western New York failed. Their fiscal woes might be related to their fantastical and superstitious religious and magical pursuits. Treasure hunting and "money digging" became the avocation of the two Joseph Smiths. Young Joseph discovered a smooth, egg-shaped "peep stone" that allegedly helped him locate buried treasure. He and his father were arrested and convicted as impostors and frauds for plying this trade in Bainbridge, New York, just one year before Joseph Jr. began writing the *Book of Mormon*.[3]

At age 14, in 1820, young Joseph had a trancelike vision of God while he was praying in the woods. Two divine "personages" appeared to him to answer his prayer about which church he should join. The divine personages identified themselves as God the Heavenly Father and Jesus the Son. They told him to avoid all Christian groups because they were "all wrong . . . their creeds were an abomination in His sight [and their] professors were all corrupt."[4]

In subsequent visions, it was revealed to Smith that he was the chosen one to correct the errors of Christianity and restore apostolic religion. A divine personage called Moroni (said to be the angel of Rev. 14:6) was the messenger of these and other marvelous revelations. Moroni told Smith that some golden plates were buried on a hillside not far from the family farm near Palmyra, New York. At last the childhood dream of finding buried treasure would be realized. The plates, Moroni said, were written in "reformed Egyptian," and from them Smith was to translate a new Bible, the *Book of Mormon*.

After a divinely appointed four-year wait, the newly appointed prophet dug up the plates and began to translate them. Apparently no one saw the plates besides Joseph Smith. Oliver Cowdery and others testified to having seen them in a prayerlike trance. Smith's wife, Emma, and Cowdery, however, both wrote of watching Smith translate the *Book of Mormon*, not by referring directly to the golden plates but by placing a "seer stone" or "peep stone" into his hat. Then, burying his face in the hat, he dictated to them as scribes.[5] The book was a remarkable literary achievement for a young man still in his 20s. It was written in King James English and was then and is still today regarded as equal to the Bible by Mormons.

Smith's parents were once Methodists but then became Presbyterians. The youthful Smith did not join but was told by God that all denominations were wrong. When cultural "confusion starts to tilt toward chaos, prophets and enlightened ones appear on every hand. . . . Joseph Smith was not the first or twenty-first prophet of his day."[6]

In writing the *Book of Mormon* and constructing the other elements of his "restoration" religion, Smith astutely but predictably reflected the ideological

3. Jan Shipps, *Mormonism: The Story of a New Religious Tradition* (Urbana and Chicago: University of Illinois Press, 1987), 11.

4. Joseph Smith, *History of the Church* (Salt Lake City: Deseret Book Co., 1902-12), 1:5-6. Cited by Melton, *Encyclopedia of Religions*, 93.

5. Shipps, *Mormonism*, 14.

6. Ibid., 49.

fevers that burned in his region. The anti-Catholic movement, the Freemasonry debate, the speculation about Native American origins, and spiritual diversity among religions are all dealt with in Smith's writings. Fawn Brodie wrote, "Any theory of the origin of the *Book of Mormon* that spotlights the prophet and blacks out the stage on which he performed is certain to be a distortion. For the book can best be explained . . . by his responsiveness to the provincial opinions of his time. . . . If the book is monotonous today, it is because the frontier fires are long since dead and the burning questions the book answers are ashes."[7]

The Flowering of Mormonism

The *Book of Mormon* was published in 1830, and a group of six believers formed a religious fellowship that would soon become the Mormon Church. Smith wrote two more works considered to be as inspired as the Bible: *The Pearl of Great Price* and *The Doctrine and Covenants*. The public reaction to Smith's declaration to the folks of New York that their religions were all wrong and that only through his new religion could salvation be found was predictable.

Social pressure soon encouraged Mormons to move west. They settled in Kirtland, Ohio (near Cleveland), and built a temple. Their numbers increased even as the resistance to the sect did the same. When the economic panic of 1837 caused the bank that the Mormons established to fail, the community headed west again.

This time they landed in Jackson County, Missouri, and settled at Independence. Smith declared this the new Zion for his nation of saints. The idea that their area had been declared a Zion for outsiders who had strange doctrines

> *Governor Boggs declared that the Mormons had to be expelled or exterminated.*

and practiced polygamy went over with the locals like a tax hike. Smith was yanked out of his own home and tarred and feathered. More violence against the Mormons broke out, and soon the Mormons were returning the favor. The most warlike of the group called themselves the Danite Band and engaged in guerrilla war with the Missourians. The state militia had to intervene.

Promising to wreak vengeance upon his enemies, Smith and several thousand followers moved to Far West, Missouri. On October 26, 1838, Governor Lilburn Boggs declared that the Mormons had to be expelled or exterminated. The next month the Missouri militia plundered the Mormon community at Far West.[8]

The Mormons moved to the Commerce, Illinois, area, purchased a townsite, and renamed the city Nauvoo. Joseph Smith became mayor and commander of the Mormon Militia of Nauvoo. The converts poured in, particularly poor English immigrants looking for a "promised land" in America. By 1840 the Mormons numbered 30,000, and Nauvoo was the largest city in Illinois. Smith was declared "King of the Kingdom of God," and his rule was absolute.

7. Ahlstrom, *Religious History,* 504.
8. Shipps, *Mormonism,* 158-59.

Through a number of new "revelations," Smith introduced many new teachings that had not been part of the 1830 launching of the movement. Many of them
accented the differences between the American Christianity that not only had
rejected his gracious invitation to join his one true Church but also had relent-
lessly persecuted him. "More than ever, Mormons were defined as a people apart."[9]

His megalomania constantly growing, Smith announced his candidacy for
president of the United States in the election of 1844. His opposition, some of
them Mormon backsliders, published both true and manufactured stories in the
Nauvoo Expositor to discredit him. His arrest for his alleged complicity in an
assassination attempt on the life of Missouri governor Boggs two years earlier
was exploited, along with other accusations of lawlessness and corruption.
Mayor/Commander/King Joseph Smith gathered his council and authorized the
destruction of the Nauvoo Expositor. The printing press was smashed and the
building set on fire.

Illinois officials arrested Smith and his brother Hyrum and jailed them in
Carthage. While they were awaiting trial, militiamen broke into the jail and
murdered the two brothers in cold blood. The movement had a martyred leader
in the second decade of its existence.

Smith had often spoken of an empire in the Far West. The group then
decided to seek their promised land in the Rocky Mountains. After a power
struggle, many of them left under the leadership of Brigham Young, a convert
from Methodism.

Many of the Mormons who were left behind in Missouri, Iowa, and Illinois
would one day be organized under the leadership of Joseph Smith's blood
descendants into the Reorganized Church of Jesus Christ of Latter-day Saints.
They clung to Smith's early vision of Mormonism as a restoration of the gospel
of Christ. The group that headed on the journey to the Far West saw their destiny in terms of Israel en route to the Promised Land, where a theocratic government would be set up for the chosen people.

Throughout what is now Utah, Nevada, and California, the Mormons
established their empire. Young was a better administrator than theologian, but
that did not keep him from making binding theological pronouncements. He
declared a revelation in 1852 about the God-ordained Mormon practice of plural
marriage.[10] He himself begat 47 children from 20 wives. Clashes with the United
States government over plural marriage hindered the statehood desires of Utah.
Such things as the Mountain Meadow Massacre in 1857, when a band of Mormons and Indians slaughtered 137 peaceful California-bound travelers, didn't
help either. In 1890 President Woodruff of the Mormon Church announced a
revelation against plural marriage, and in 1896 Utah was admitted to the Union
as a state.

Today the Mormon faith is one of the largest religions born on American
soil. From the modest half-dozen believers in 1830, the movement has grown to

---

9. Ahlstrom, Religious History, 506.
10. Young credited the revelation of Joseph Smith, saying that it had been kept secret until now. Smith's
son denied that his father ever taught plural marriage.

a membership of more than 8 million. It has had a profound influence upon American culture. Numerous groups have Mormon roots. The Utah Mormons are by far the largest. The second largest is the Reorganized Church of Jesus Christ of Latter-day Saints, with 245,000 members in 35 countries.[11]

Basic Mormon Beliefs

The articles of faith as written by Joseph Smith sound Christian—until you start unpacking the statements. These articles of faith were carefully crafted "to present Mormon doctrine in a form acceptable to mainline Christian denominations."[12] Take, for example, the first article. "We Believe in God the Eternal Father, and His Son Jesus Christ, and in the Holy Ghost." A typical Christian might think that this is an orthodox affirmation of belief in the Holy Trinity. In reality, it is very far from that. It is an affirmation of tritheism, three gods. But as we shall see, they are just three of many divine beings in the Mormon cosmology.

1. What Mormons Believe About God

From the day that Joseph Smith had his vision in the woods in which the Father and the Son appeared to him, the Mormon doctrine of God has been in conflict with Christian belief. Young Smith discovered that contrary to the Bible, "God is not a spirit, but a material being of the male gender."[13]

Further, God the Father (Elohim) is the one God of this earth, but other Gods run other planets. No one knows how many Gods there are. Elohim, "our Heavenly Father," as the Mormons usually term Him, was once a man himself. "God himself was once as we are now, and is an exalted man, and sits enthroned in yonder heaven. . . . He was once a man like us, the Father of us all, dwelt on earth," declared Joseph Smith.[14] "As man is, God once was; as God is, man may become" is an oft-repeated Mormon truism.[15] Thus, God himself is a begotten being. Elohim and all angels and human beings came into existence through literal spirit sex between some "god" and mother god. As fantastic as all of this sounds, one of the serious problems with it is that it contends that God came from the universe rather than the universe coming from God, as the Bible teaches.[16]

2. What Mormons Believe About Jesus Christ

Mormons are quick to identify Jesus as the author of the faith. They affirm that He was a "son of God" but forthrightly deny that He was *the* Son of God." In their view, Jesus was Elohim's firstborn, but the Heavenly Father has been begetting children with "mother gods" steadily.[17] Brigham Young even declared that Adam was the one who impregnated the Virgin Mary and was the father of Jesus. He also taught that Adam became Elohim the Heavenly Father. Young's theology has been an embarrassment to thinking Mormons, and most all that he taught is rejected by the Reorganized Church of Jesus Christ of Latter-day Saints.

---

11. Mead and Hill, *Handbook of Denominations*, 173.
12. Melton, *Encyclopedia of Religions*, 95.
13. Shipps, *Mormonism*, 143.
14. Mather and Nichols, *Dictionary of Cults*, 194.
15. Ibid.
16. Francis J. Beckwith, "Philosophical Problems with the Mormon Concept of God," *Christian Research Journal*, spring 1992, 27.
17. Mather and Nichols, *Dictionary of Cults*, 194.

Mormons teach that the resurrection of Christ made immortality available. While repentance and confession of faith in Jesus are necessary, the sacrifice of Christ on the Cross, being involuntary, is not effective for all sins. Good works, and perhaps a term in "Spirit Prison"—a sort of Mormon purgatory—may be required for full salvation.[18]

3. What Mormons Believe About Humanity

Mormons teach that all humans have a premortal state. Each person was procreated through spirit sex and spirit birth by some god couple. In order to qualify for godhood, each spirit baby must take on flesh and become human. One-third of the preexisting spirits chose to rebel and follow Lucifer, and they are not permitted to take on human form but are consigned to the place of banishment.[19]

Those who choose to obey Elohim in their premortal state come to earth as humans to work out their own salvation. Unless they reject the Mormon Church or commit some other unpardonable sin, they will end up in one of three heavens. Only temple-worthy Mormons can achieve the highest heaven, the Celestial. There they will either live with Elohim and Jesus or go off (with their many wives) to populate a barren planet that they will one day rule the way Elohim, our Heavenly Father, rules earth.[20] Only males who achieve the Celestial level will become gods. "Women are subject to the man's calling them out of the grave and if called, they will remain subservient child bearers throughout eternity."[21]

Those who make it only to one of the lesser heavens (the Terrestrial or Telestial) will serve those in the Celestial heaven eternally. Such teachings are unknown to orthodox Christianity.

The Mormon doctrine of salvation produces a sort of universalism. Given the atonement of Christ, good works, baptism for the dead, the teaching that goes on in the purgatorial Spirit Prison after death, and with three levels of heaven available, just about everyone (except apostate Mormons) will make it to some sort of eternal paradise. Is this a message that the world wants to hear?

4. What Mormons Believe About Salvation

As we have seen, belief in Jesus Christ and repentance for sin are required for salvation. In addition, Mormons teach that baptism by immersion is absolutely necessary for salvation. This baptism must occur within the one true Church, the Church of Jesus Christ of Latter-day Saints. Further, good works of obedience and loyalty to God and the Mormon Church are in some way essential to salvation. While the many Mormon writings on this are complicated, it appears that the Mormons regard good works as meritorious—that is, they're needed for salvation in addition to the atonement of Christ. Though Protestant Christians believe in holy living, obedience to the Scriptures, and acts of devotion and service, there is no doubt that such works do not save.

Some Mormon writings clearly teach that for the remission of the most serious sins, more than the blood of Christ is required—only the shedding of

---

18. John Conlon, "Mormonism: Mainstream or Extreme?" MS acquired by the *Herald of Holiness,* June 1996, 1.

19. Ibid.

20. Ibid.

21. Ibid.

one's own blood can pay for some sins. Adultery, murder, stealing, marrying a Black person, or apostasy from the Mormon Church are sins worthy of death.[22] Brigham Young strongly promoted the blood atonement idea, contending that the only way to save an apostate Mormon from eternal damnation was to shed the apostate's blood and take the person's life. In one sermon he declared, "There are sins which men commit for which they cannot receive forgiveness. . . . If they had their eyes open . . . they would be perfectly willing to HAVE THEIR BLOOD SPILT on the ground, that the smoke thereof might rise to heaven as AN OFFERING FOR THEIR SINS" (emphasis in original).[23] The RLDS find this and other Brigham Young teachings abhorrent.

It's not fair to compare Mormonism at its worst with Christianity at its best. Christianity has had its share of abhorrent misdeeds. But it would not be right to omit these doctrinal matters.

5. What Mormons Believe About the Church

Most Christians believe that all those who have savingly believed on Jesus Christ as Savior are members of the universal Church regardless of the denomination to which they may belong. Mormons, from their very beginning, have proclaimed themselves the one true Church; all other churches are apostate and corrupt. Salvation is to be found in Mormonism alone.

Another aspect of the Mormon Church that makes Protestants nervous is that it is overseen by a president with popelike infallibility. The president is prophet, seer, and revelator, and his proclamations are simply not to be questioned.

> *The president is prophet, seer, and revelator, and his proclamations are simply not to be questioned.*

Several other levels of church hierarchy have priestly and prophetic powers. Beneath the president are the 12 apostles, high priests, seventies, bishops, and elders. All males in good standing are priests of some sort. Every husband is priest and revelator for his family. Revelations that he receives for family affairs are not to be questioned.

6. What Mormons Believe About Worship and the Sacraments

Mormons declare that baptism by immersion is necessary for salvation. Since repentance is involved in baptism, infant baptism is not practiced; infants have not sinned and are not capable of repentance. Further, they are not guilty for Adam's transgression, so baptism to remove original sin would be inappropriate.

In addition, the Utah Mormons practice baptism for the dead and condemn RLDS believers for not doing so.

The Lord's Supper is celebrated every week in Mormon churches. After a "revelation" received by Joseph Smith, water is used instead of wine or grape juice.

---

22. Mather and Nichols, *Dictionary of Cults*, 195.

23. Jerald Tanner and Sandra Tanner, *The Changing World of Mormonism* (Chicago: Moody Press, 1979), 398; cited by Mather and Nichols, *Dictionary of Cults*, 195.

Mormon temple rituals are problematic when it comes to the appeal to regard the Latter-day Saints as mainstream Christians. Most Mormon rituals are secretive. This is the opposite of Christian covenants and rituals. Christian baptism, membership rituals, marriage, confirmation, and ordination are all public. Mormon temple rituals are more like the secret ceremonies of the Masonic Lodge than the Christian liturgies. There is a reason for that. In western New York near where Smith grew up, at the very time when Smith was dealing with the angel Moroni, a former Mason named Morgan who had revealed the secret Masonic rituals was murdered. Smith's brother Hyrum joined the Masons. In 1842 Joseph joined, leading some 1,200 other Mormons into Masonry. Smith was fascinated by their rituals. The endowment ceremonies of the Mormon temple are remarkably similar to Masonic ceremonies.[24] The penalties for revealing the secrets in both organizations were also similar. In the 1930s the graphic descriptions of savage revenge to be taken on those who reveal the secret rites were eliminated from most Mormon documents.[25]

7. What Mormons Believe About Revelation

For Christians the final revelation of God is the revelation of Jesus Christ in the Bible. The canon is closed. No new writing can be as authoritative as the Holy Bible. In Mormon tradition, however, the several books of Joseph Smith are equal to the Bible in authority. In addition, the Lord may at any moment give a new revelation to the Mormon president that carries the weight of Scripture. This is in radical conflict with the Protestant dictum of *sola scriptura.*

We have dealt here primarily with the foundational beliefs of the Utah Mormons. On almost every point of doctrine and practice, the RLDS is more progressive and more liberal. They have deliberately de-emphasized many Mormon fundamentals (such as the one true Church claim) and have worked hard to be regarded as a mainline Protestant body. The *Book of Mormon* and other fundamental writings have been demythologized by RLDS theologians, missionary and evangelistic methods have been criticized, and much of Utah Mormonism rejected. When in 1984 the RLDS church's general conference voted to ordain women, many conservative church members saw apostasy written on the doorposts and a sellout to modernity and Protestant pressure.

Though the quarter million Missouri Mormons (RLDS) are the most likely among the dozens of Mormonite bodies to evolve into a mainstream Christian body, the 8 million Utah Mormons are outside mainstream Christianity. The careful scholarship of church historian Jan Shipps seems to properly locate the Mormons in the religious spectrum. Even though the "saints" see themselves as a slightly idiosyncratic form of Christianity, that perception is wrong, says Shipps. "While it perceives of itself as Christian, Mormonism differs from traditional Christianity in much the same fashion that traditional Christianity . . . came to differ from Judaism. . . . It becomes as clear as can be that . . .

24. See Tanner and Tanner, *Changing World of Mormonism,* 485 ff., and Mather and Nichols, *Dictionary of Cults,* 196-97, for specific examples.

25. Mather and Nichols report that ex-Masons and former Mormons say that the oaths sworn promise slashed throats, torn-out tongues, and breasts cut open to the betraying apostate, 196.

Mormonism is a new religious tradition."[26] Thus we conclude that Mormonism in general is a new religious tradition with roots in Judaism, Christianity, and 19th-century cultic primitivism.

The Mormons have built a positive reputation for moral living, thrift, hard work, and family values, and they survived wicked persecution in an admirable way.

The Mormon Church is, per capita, the richest religious organization in America. From tithes, investments, and church-owned businesses such as the Beneficial Insurance Company, radio and television stations, newspapers, hotels, shopping malls, department stores, ranchland and farmland, publishing firms, bookstores, factories, and office buildings, the Utah church receives some $2 billion per year.[27]

There appears to be very little common ground between Mormons and Nazarenes. Nazarenes do appreciate moral living, thrift, hard work, and family values. But the two faith systems are worlds apart—even when they use the same words.

Review and Reflection

1. Compare and contrast the Nazarene and Mormon affirmations of faith about the triune God, Jesus, the Holy Spirit, the Bible, the Atonement, salvation, and heaven and hell. Refer to the Nazarene Articles of Faith 1, 2, 3, 4, 6, 9, and 16.

2. Do you think Mormonism is *mainstream?* Or *extreme?*

3. In what ways can you relate redemptively to your Mormon neighbors, friends, and coworkers?

26. Shipps, *Mormonism*, 148-49.
27. Mather and Nichols, *Dictionary of Cults*, 197.

SECOND-ADVENT RELIGIOUS GROUPS

Historical Roots

The four Advent-oriented groups treated in this chapter were born in a wave of millennial fever that swept the religious scene in the 19th century. Key leaders were Ellen G. White, Charles Taze Russell, John Nelson Darby, and in the 20th century, Herbert W. Armstrong.

Core Beliefs

The one thing that these groups hold in common is some sort of dispensationalism.

The Seventh-Day Adventists hold many orthodox views but teach heterodox views such as soul sleep; disbelief in immortality; Saturday worship; dietary laws; and the veneration of Ellen G. White.

The Worldwide Church of God taught many heretical doctrines during the reign of Herbert W. Armstrong. Now they have purged their creed of his fantastic inventions and have become so doctrinally "straight" that they have been admitted to the National Association of Evangelicals.

The Jehovah's Witnesses remain the most cultlike of this group, embracing such doctrines as denial of the Trinity; refusal to salute the flag; denial of immortality; forbidding to celebrate Christmas, Easter, or birthdays; and no clergy.

Historically, the Plymouth Brethren are the nearest to orthodoxy but are also the fomenters of a Calvinistic-oriented, premillennial dispensationalism that has also spawned the radical creationist movement, the inerrancy debate, and the dominance of premillennialism.

Agreement and Differences

The Church of the Nazarene shares common ground with the Advent churches only at those points at which they happen to hold an orthodox view. In fact, the Wesleyan-Holiness Movement has been (at least in its official doctrines) a persistent pocket of resistance to the rampant dispensationalism that gave birth to the Advent religions.

Adventism Today

The Seventh-Day Adventists have nearly 9 million adherents in 207 countries. The Worldwide Church of God has about 100,000 members, as do the Plymouth Brethren. Jehovah's Witnesses number 4.3 million in 233 countries.

Farmers became theologians, offbeat village youth became bishops, odd girls became prophets.
—Sydney E. Ahlstrom
A Religious History of the American People

20 ~ SECOND-ADVENT RELIGIOUS GROUPS

JESUS IS COMING SOON" was the watchword and song in many quarters of the nation in the first half of the 19th century. He must be, they figured, because things couldn't get any worse. The chaos in religion, government, and education surely were harbingers of the end times.

The population explosion, immigration, exploitation, and industrialization, combined with a do-what-you-wish philosophy of personal freedom, produced a chaotic cultural climate. The yoke of authority was cast off with greedy delight. The spirit of the age did not miss the religious realm but rather engulfed it. The witch-hunt was on against rigid denominations, seminaries, higher education, ordained ministers, and formal worship. "Farmers became theologians, offbeat village youth became bishops, odd girls became prophets."[1]

Part of this scene was what has been called the "Great Second Advent Awakening" that occurred in the first half of the century. This revival of interest in the second coming of Christ spread to America from Europe and soon captured the attention of the simple and the learned. "New Testament eschatology competed with stock market quotations for front-page space, and the 'seventy weeks' . . . and 'the abomination of the desolation' (Daniel 9:27) were common subjects of conversation."[2] From such songbooks as *The Millennial Harp*, the devout sang songs such as

> *Stand up, stand up for Jesus.*
> *The strife will not be long;*
> *This day the noise of battle,*
> *The next, the victor's song.*[3]

---

1. Ahlstrom, *Religious History,* 475.

2. Walter Martin, *The Kingdom of the Cults,* rev. ed. (Minneapolis: Bethany House Publishers, 1985), 411.

3. George Duffield wrote this hymn, "Stand Up, Stand Up for Jesus." He was a preacher's son—his father a "New School" Presbyterian and a vociferous preacher on millennial themes. See Ahlstrom, *Religious History,* 479.

A number of contemporary religious movements sprang from this milieu. In this chapter we will deal with representative, though very different, religious groups.

Seventh-Day Adventists

One of the farmers who turned theologian in upper Vermont in those days was William Miller. For two years between plowing and calving duties, he studied a King James Bible with Archbishop Ussher's time line in the margins. He then announced, "I was thus brought . . . to the solemn conclusion that in about twenty-five years . . . all the affairs of our present state would be wound up."[4]

Miller began to preach at revivals, became an ordained Baptist minister, and published his lectures on the Second Coming. He teamed up with Joshua Himes and made hundreds of appearances announcing the Second Coming would happen in March 1843. But nothing happened. The date was reset: October 1843. Nothing happened. New date: October 1844. Same result. This became known as the "Great Disappointment." Followers fled what seemed to be a sinking ship. Miller retired to Vermont and died five years later, not knowing he had started a movement.

"To the hardcore believers who survived, the 'Great Disappointment' was only a challenge."[5] The recovery began with a vision that came to Hiram Edison in a New York cornfield. Edison announced that the great event prophesied by Miller had indeed happened, but in heaven, not on earth. God now had put things in order for the earthly Second Advent, which they were to proclaim.

Enter Ellen G. Harmon. A frail teenage Methodist girl who had been won to the Millerite notions just a short time before the "Great Disappointment," she began to have visions. Miss Harmon married an Adventist elder, James White, in 1846. Mrs. White's visions and revelations soon became a second Bible for the groups gathered around her. They would one day officially become the Seventh-Day Adventist Church.

Mrs. White, who claimed the title "Spirit of Prophecy," had some 2,000 visions, transports, and revelations. They are recorded in her nine-volume *Testimonies,* still regarded as barely subbiblical by Adventists. The Seventh-Day Adventist home page on the Internet says that Ellen G. White became and would remain "the trusted spiritual counselor of the Adventist family . . . until her death in 1915. Early Adventists came to believe—as have Adventists ever since—that she enjoyed God's special guidance as she wrote her counsels." The same source adds, "As the Lord's messenger, her writings are a continuing and authoritative source of truth which provide the church comfort, guidance, instruction, and correction. They also make clear that the Bible is the standard by which all teaching and experience must be tested."[6]

Part of the instructions from White have to do with health and diet. Many modern Adventists are vegetarians. In 1855 Battle Creek, Michigan, became the

---

4. Ahlstrom, *Religious History,* 479.
5. Ibid.
6. Untitled document, <http://www.adventist.org>, February 1997.

Adventist headquarters, where Mrs. White's fellow vegetarian, John H. Kellogg, made the town the cereal capital of the nation.

Adventist Beliefs and Practices

The mission of the Seventh-Day Adventist Church is "to proclaim the everlasting gospel in the context of the three angels' messages of Revelation 14:6-12, leading them to accept Jesus as personal Savior and to unite with His church, and nurturing them in preparation for His soon return."[7] This statement focuses the church on evangelism that is energized by the belief in the imminent return of Christ to judge the world, particularly the wicked "Babylon" and those who have received the "mark of the beast." This consuming concern about eschatology has made some Christians cautious in extending fellowship to the Adventists.

The Adventists seek to carry out their mission through *preaching* (which emphasizes the return of Christ and keeping the Ten Commandments), *teaching* of spiritual and general knowledge, and *healing* that seeks the well-being of the whole person.[8]

In several important areas of doctrine, orthodox, Evangelical Christians will find nothing objectionable. While not going as far as the verbal inspirationists of Fundamentalism desire, the Adventist belief in the inspiration of the Bible is very close to that of the Church of the Nazarene. The Adventist doctrine of the Trinity is clear and orthodox. The statements of God the Father, Jesus Christ, and the Holy Spirit are consciously stated to be in harmony with the Nicene and Athanasian Creeds. Some condemn the Adventist Christology on the basis of a 1927 heretical article by L. A. Wilcox in the Adventist paper *Signs of the Times*. However, that article has been renounced by Adventist leaders and by the author himself.[9]

The doctrines of the creation, fall, and nature of human beings (including original sin) are models of traditional Christian beliefs. Even the doctrine of the literal, personal, visible return of Christ is acceptable to most Evangelicals. The practice of baptism not as a conversion experience but as a public testimony that the believer has confessed faith in Jesus as Lord and Savior and intends to walk in newness of life resonates with the beliefs of Nazarenes and other Wesleyan-Holiness people. The Adventist requirement of baptism by immersion only does not connect with our belief that a variety of modes are valid. Like other Evangelicals, the Adventists regard the Communion elements as "emblems of the body and blood of Jesus."[10]

Nazarenes will give a nod of recognition to the Adventist article of faith that calls for "the highest standards of Christian taste and beauty" in amusements and entertainments. Adventists are also charged to get "adequate exercise and rest" and to abstain from "alcoholic beverages, tobacco, and the irresponsible use of drugs and narcotics."[11] Doctrines of tithing and strong guidance

---

7. "Name and Mission Statement of the Seventh-Day Adventist Church," ibid.
8. Ibid.
9. See Martin, *Kingdom of the Cults*, 432-33.
10. "Fundamental Beliefs of the Seventh-Day Adventist Church," <http://www.adventist.org>.
11. Ibid.

regarding the sanctity of marriage and the importance of the Christian home are also found in the Adventist creedal statements. With all of these most Evangelicals would agree.

In some matters, however, the Adventist theology is clearly different from that of the classic Christian faith.

1. Saturday Worship. Adventists are quite dogmatic about the necessity for true Christians to worship on the seventh day, not the first day of the week. They say that in the biblical account of creation, God rested on the seventh day, and so should we. They note that the Ten Commandments cite the seventh day and that Jesus kept the Sabbath. That most Christians, beginning with the first-generation believers, kept the first day in commemoration of the Lord's resurrection does not seem to carry any weight with Adventists. They claim that the pope and the Roman emperors set Sunday as the day of worship.

The New Testament clearly condemns being dogmatic about keeping one day over another or legalistically observing the new moons, feasts, food or drink, or Sabbath (Col. 2:13-17; Gal. 4:9-11).

2. Authority and Veneration of Ellen G. White. Adventists regard the writings of Ellen G. White as divine revelation. Many Christian groups view this as idolatry.

3. Atonement. Some have charged that the Adventists have made Christ's sacrifice only a partial atonement. Many of these charges are inappropriate. Nevertheless, a lot of Adventist language that focuses on the Christian's duty to obey every command of Scripture in order to be saved pushes some to conclude that, for Adventists, the atonement of Christ is not enough. Diligent, legalistic effort is required if we are to be saved. Further, the Adventist insistence that Christ began a new and not yet completed stage of His atoning work in 1844 adds fuel to the charges.

4. Legalistic Dietary Laws. The Advent creed calls for Christians to observe the Leviticus laws about abstaining from unclean foods such as pork and shellfish. Most Christians believe that such observances gave way to Christian freedom as described in the New Testament Epistles. But in addition to the Old Testament food laws, Adventists are urged to abide by the Ellen White diet. This seems too much to demand in the light of Christian freedom.

5. Soul Sleep and Eternal Destiny. "We, as Adventists, have reached the definite conclusion that man rests in the tomb until the resurrection morning. Then, at the first resurrection . . . the righteous will come forth immortalized at the call of Christ . . . and *they then enter into life everlasting.*"[12] Human beings are not immortal (even in spirit) but become immortal only when they are called from the grave, Adventists believe. Also, the dead in Christ do not go into the presence of God, even though this is what Jesus promised the repentant thief on the cross—Mrs. White had a different idea. Rather, the dead "sleep" in a state of unconsciousness until Jesus blows the resurrection horn. Those who die in sin are never immortal. They will not spend eternity in any sort of hell, but will be

---

12. *Questions on Doctrine*, cited by Martin, *Kingdom of the Cults*, 448.

annihilated. The righteous eventually go to heaven, which is a redeemed version of earth.

There are a number of other unique aspects to the complex theology of Adventism. Some of them—the Investigative Judgment, the Remnant teaching, the Great Controversy, and Christ's ministry in the Heavenly Sanctuary—seem to have been created to preserve the Millerite and Ellen G. White heritage.

Such unique teachings so permeate and surround the orthodox doctrines of Adventism that it's hard to separate the sound doctrine from the bizarre and pixilated. This makes cooperation between traditional Christian groups and Adventism difficult.

Facts and Figures of Adventism

The Seventh-Day Adventists are one of the largest and fastest-growing religious groups in the world. The following are statistics from the church's home page on the Internet.

> *Unique and esoteric theologies so permeate the orthodox teachings of Adventism that it's hard to separate the sound doctrine from the bizarre and pixilated.*

A convert is won every 44 seconds, and 5 new congregations are organized per day. World membership now stands at over 9 million. Only one-tenth of the membership is in the United States. Adventists meet in over 42,000 congregations in 207 countries, speaking 725 languages and many dialects.

The Adventists around the world operate 615 health-care units, such as clinics, hospitals, medevac planes, and homes for orphans and the elderly. They operate 5,478 elementary and secondary schools, colleges, and universities.

The Adventists have vigorously used the media in carrying out their mission. They have 55 church-owned publishing plants. Among their high-tech ministries are Adventists Online, Adventist News Network (ANN), Adventist Communication Network (ACN), and Adventist World Radio (AWR). Adventist programs are aired over 2,283 radio stations and 1,681 television stations.[13]

The Worldwide Church of God

The Worldwide Church of God (WCG) is a dubious splinter from the Seventh-Day Adventist Church. George Burnside, writing for the Adventists, calls Herbert W. Armstrong, WCG founder, "an off-shoot of an off-shoot of an off-shoot of the Seventh-day Adventist Church."[14]

Herbert W. Armstrong was born in 1892 in Des Moines, Iowa, to Quaker parents. He went into the advertising business in Des Moines. In 1924 he moved to Oregon, entered the advertising trade there, and went broke. In the meantime he got into an argument with his wife, who had been raised a Seventh-Day Adventist, over whether Christians should keep the Jewish Sabbath or the Lord's day (Sunday).

---

13. "A World Church," <http://www.adventist.org>.
14. Martin, *Kingdom of the Cults,* 305.

After studying the Bible to refute his wife, he lost the argument and became a seventh-day believer. He then decided that everything the historic Christian church had taught was fraudulent. Therefore, he invented his own religion. It turned out to be "a smorgasbord of unorthodox doctrines borrowed from the Seventh-day Adventists, Jehovah's Witnesses, Mormons, Christian Scientists, and others."[15]

Armstrong claimed that the WCG began in January 1934 when the Sardis era of the church ended (see Rev. 3). At that point, the era of the Philadelphia church (that was praised for keeping God's Word and not denying His name) began. It was, of course, Armstrong's own flock that had set before it the open door that no one could shut. And Armstrong was selected because of his knowledge of advertising and radio. The first name for Armstrong's church in Eugene, Oregon, was "The Radio Church of God."[16]

That same year Armstrong launched *Plain Truth* magazine with a humble circulation of 106. Since then, the circulation has varied but has been as high as 8 million. A 1995 report cited a distribution of this free magazine at 5 million. *The World Tomorrow* broadcast is currently aired over 148 radio and television stations. The WCG has about 100,000 members today, of which about two-thirds live in the United States.

By deciphering a number of biblical texts and symbols, Armstrong announced that after two 19-year cycles of preaching by him, the true believers of the one true Church (WCG) would alone be raptured to Petra, near Jerusalem, just in time to miss the Battle of Armageddon. This great end-of-the-world battle would occur in 1972, Armstrong declared.

When the prophecy failed—even after the date was shifted to 1975—a period of turmoil rocked the WCG. Garner Ted Armstrong, fourth son and heir apparent to the aging patriarch, became involved in a sex scandal testified to by six church leaders. He was later "disfellowshipped" by his father, not for moral misconduct but for "liberalism." Garner Ted then started his own church in Texas.

Soon afterward, the newly remarried Herbert Armstrong was accused of incest and financial corruption. Herbert divorced his second wife, Ramona (47 years his junior). By the mid-1980s the church was on the grow again.

Herbert Armstrong died in 1986. The WCG has since tried to remove itself from some of the more extreme teachings of its founder. Since many of his teachings have been declared "obsolete" by the new leadership, we will touch only upon some of the most heretical:

1. God is not a Trinity. He is a family. And as part of "the family of God," every believer in the WCG has a chance to grow up and *become* God. God's family now is two: the Father and the Son.

2. The Holy Spirit is not a person and not a member of God's family. "It" is simply a force God uses, as a person uses electricity.

3. The sacrifice of Jesus on the Cross is not nearly enough to get a person

---

15. *The Plain Truth of Herbert W. Armstrong*, Personal Freedom Outreach, P.O. Box 26062, St. Louis, MO 63136; 314-388-2648 (www Internet document, 2).

16. Mather and Nichols, *Dictionary of Cults*, 320.

to heaven. A rigid keeping of all Old Testament laws is required. To those Armstrong added his own rules against cosmetics, interracial marriage, receiving treatment from medical doctors, celebrating Christmas (a pagan holiday), observing any national holidays, or celebrating birthdays. "Those who disobeyed risked being put on trial and perhaps [being] kicked out of the church . . . [which] was tantamount in members' minds to eternal damnation."[17]

4. Saturday is the true day for worship. Armstrong pronounced, "Sunday observance—this is the Mark of the Beast. . . . You shall be tormented by God's plagues without mercy, yes, you!"[18]

5. The bodily resurrection of Jesus did not happen. A spiritual body was "revived."

6. The British people are the lost tribes of Israel (British Israelism). By the most inept interpretation, Armstrong came up with a bizarre doctrine of the white Anglo-Saxons as the chosen people of God. I (Wesley Tracy) myself heard him trace his reasoning. "The lost tribes were sons of Isaac. Drop the 'I,' and we have 'saac,' the sons of 'saac,' or 'Saxons.'" He claimed that the Stone of Scone in Westminster, where Elizabeth II was crowned, "is the very stone that Jacob used for a pillow. It was moved to England by Jeremiah as part of the migration that brought the lost tribes to England to set up David's throne."[19]

7. There is no eternal suffering in hell. The wicked dead shall simply be burned to death once and for all.

Most of the heterodox teaching listed above has been modified or renounced by the current leaders of the WCG. This has caused thousands to leave the church. Some devotees still believe that Herbert W. will be resurrected from the dead to once again lead the faithful to the Rapture before Armageddon. It was prophesied that this would happen in 1988, but the faithful await a new date.

The new pastor general, Joseph W. Tkach, has purposely moved the church toward more orthodox belief. For example, he said, "The Bible teaching is that there is one God, who is the Father, the Son, the Holy Spirit. It is not my idea, nor is it the idea of some fourth-century theologians. It is the plain Bible teaching."[20] The keeping of Levitical dietary laws, objections to observing Christmas and birthdays, and the rule against cosmetics, interracial marriage, and the proscription of medical care have all been jettisoned, along with the notion that believers will "become God as God is God" and that the British are the lost tribes of Israel.[21] Further, Herbert W. Armstrong's "masterpiece," *The Mystery of the Ages,* has been pulled from distribution because of false teachings.

Evangelical scholars applaud the movement of the WCG toward standard Christian doctrine. Yet there is caution about how thorough such quick moves can be. The doctrine of the Trinity, for example, is still quite nebulous in the new creedal statements. One Evangelical scholar noted that the emphasis on

17. "Worldwide Church of God Edges Toward Orthodoxy," *Christianity Today,* November 9, 1992, 57.

18. Herbert W. Armstrong, *The Mark of the Beast* (Pasadena, Calif.: Ambassador College Press, 1957), 10-11. Cited by Josh McDowell and Don Stewart, *Handbook of Today's Religions* (Nashville: Thomas Nelson, 1983), 119.

19. Mather and Nichols, *Dictionary of Cults,* 324.

20. "Mainstream Moves May Split Worldwide Church of God," *Christianity Today,* November 8, 1993, 59.

21. Ibid.

millennial and angelic themes as well as tithing "makes me suspect a group that majors on the minors. That is one characteristic of a cult."[22] Another evaluator cited concerns over the sufficiency of the salvation by grace plank in the WCG doctrinal platform.

The WCG has, however, so sufficiently renounced its heresies that the church has been admitted into the National Association of Evangelicals.

Jehovah's Witnesses

The millennial craze of the 19th century that turned farmers into theologians, offbeat youth into bishops, and odd girls into prophets also turned one haberdasher into a holy man. Charles Taze Russell of Allegheny, Pennsylvania, gave up selling men's hats, shirts, ties, and gloves to establish one of the most aberrant, illogical, unbiblical, and wildly successful religions ever to see the sun. Nearly every doctrine is heterodox—as if no Christian thinkers in history have ever gotten one thing right. The Jehovah's Witnesses (JW) theology specializes in bizarre interpretations of Scripture and baffling leaps of logic.

A big part of the organization's corporate energies must be spent creating schemes to explain away failed prophecies made by its leaders. For example, the end of the world has been prophesied, complete with dates, six times in this century. Russell claimed that God revealed to him that the world would end in 1914. When that did not happen, the message changed to the inspired declaration that the generation that was alive in 1914 would not pass away until all the end-time prophecies were fulfilled. Problem: even the infants of 1914 are now in their mid-80s. The top leader died recently at 99—has that generation passed? Has prophecy failed—again?

To make things worse, the Jehovah's Witnesses leaders announced that the heavenly class of the 144,000 (mentioned in Revelation) was all filled up with Jehovah's Witnesses in 1935. They teach that God speaks and gives the Holy Spirit only to members of the 144,000 ("the anointed") and not to the "great crowd" (ordinary JW believers), who are not permitted to take Communion, are not eligible for heaven, and cannot hold high places of leadership.

Thus, the movement has a leadership problem. The "anointed" class of 1935 is aging and thinning out. Last year, among the nearly 13 million who attended the annual Memorial Communion service in 233 countries, only 8,757 were permitted to take Communion as members of the anointed class. At this rate, the 144,000 will likely all be dead within a decade, leaving the movement with no one saintly enough to receive divine guidance, interpret signs, and serve as leaders.

Charles Taze Russell. The JW founder was raised as a Presbyterian, tried the Congregationalists, but lost interest in religion until 1870. When he was 28, he bumped into a group of Adventists, a splinter group of Millerites who had survived the "Great Disappointment" of 1844. They were predicting that Christ would return in 1873-74, and Russell believed. But when the prophecy failed, he moved on. He soon hooked up with N. H. Barbour, who was the shepherd of an

22. "Worldwide Church of God Edges Toward Orthodoxy," 58.

Adventist group in Rochester, New York. Russell and Barbour "came to realize" that Jesus had actually returned to earth in 1874, but He came in spirit, not in the flesh. They began to preach that Christ had returned, indeed, and the millennium had begun in 1874. They soon parted company over theological differences, but Russell was on his way.

He established what would become the Watch Tower Bible and Tract Society. His first magazine, *Zion's Watchtower and Herald of Christ's Presence,* was followed by the *Millennial Dawn, The Divine Plan of the Ages,* and acres of tracts and sermons. This vigorous program cost money. Russell financed much of it through the haberdashery that he inherited from his father. But more funds were needed. He began to advertise "miracle wheat" for a dollar a pound, which he claimed would grow and produce five times more than conventional wheat. A New York newspaper criticized the ads, and Russell sued for libel. The United States government was brought into the case. The wheat was tested and discovered to be quite ordinary grain, in fact, inferior to most brands being sold.[23]

Russell went to court again six months later. This time he sued a Baptist preacher who had criticized him in print, saying that Russell was not the Greek scholar that he claimed to be, that he had executed frauds, and that he had no clergy credentials whatsoever. Confronted with the Greek alphabet in court, he could not recognize a single letter and had to admit that he did not know New Testament Greek.

Russell died in Pampa, Texas, in 1916 and was replaced at the JW helm by the lawyer who had unsuccessfully represented him in court, Joseph Franklin Rutherford. He democratized the upper levels of leadership within the movement and focused the Witnesses' witnessing on damning Christian denominations, particularly the Roman Catholics. He served until his death in 1942. He was followed by N. H. Knorr, who led the Witnesses to their greatest growth before he died in 1977.

Frederick W. Franz came to the helm and served until his death in 1992. It was Franz who gave the Witnesses their own version of the Bible. Franz was the only one on the Translation Committee who knew the biblical languages, but he himself was not a recognized scholar. Unfortunately, it appears that Witness presuppositions weighed at least as heavily as good scholarship in the creation of the *New World Translation.*[24]

Core Beliefs

1. Jesus Christ: Witnesses believe that Jesus is not part of the Trinity, but the Son of God, the first of God's creation; that He had a prehuman existence and that His life was transferred from heaven to the womb of the Virgin Mary; that His perfect life laid down in sacrifice makes possible salvation to eternal life by those who exercise faith; that Christ is actively ruling as King over all the earth since 1914. There is no Trinity. Jesus did not die on a cross but on a stake. Jesus did not arise bodily from the grave, but as only a spirit.

---

23. Mather and Nichols, *Dictionary of Cults,* 148.
24. Watchman Fellowship, "Crisis of Authority? Watchtower President Franz, Dead at 99" (Arlington, Tex.: www, February 1997), 1.

2. Heaven and shared rule with Christ await the 144,000 Spirit-anointed Christians. Heaven is not the reward of everyone who is "good."

3. The dead are conscious of absolutely nothing. They experience neither pain nor pleasure. They do not exist except in God's memory. Any hope they have for a future life lies in the possibility that God may call them from the grave and let them live on His redeemed earth.

4. Since 1914 we have been living in the last days. God will crush the existing kingdoms and establish His own never-ending reign on earth. The wicked dead will be annihilated, not sent to an eternal hell. The end is near. The kingdoms of this world belong to Satan and represent the evil "triple alliance" among false churches, human governments, and big business. All of these God will crush at the Battle of Armageddon.

5. Witnesses teach that mortal sins include adultery, fornication, homosexual activity, lying, cheating, idolatry, materialism, eating foods with blood in them, and receiving blood transfusions.

6. Witnesses claim that they have no creed. They follow the Bible as interpreted by the Watchtower Society's anointed leaders. The Bible is not to be interpreted personally by ordinary believers of the "great crowd."[25]

Distinctive Practices

1. Separatism. Witnesses are to stay away from people of other faiths, including Christians. They seek no ecumenical unions or cooperation.

2. No clergy are ordained, and no clergy titles are used. Women cannot be elders or overseers.

3. Among forbidden things is the celebration of Christmas, Lent, and Easter.

One's heart goes out to those trapped in the outlandish theology and the enslaving legalism of the Jehovah's Witnesses cult.

4. Witnesses are not permitted to pledge allegiance or to salute the flags of their countries. Nor can they serve in the military, engage in politics, or even vote. They must not celebrate birthdays.

5. Witnessing from door to door is required of all.

6. Witnesses are expected to work as volunteers in the JW printing plants or sell literature locally.[26]

One's heart goes out to those trapped in this irregular system of speculative heresy and legalistic slavery. Most of them are really trying to do right. They seek salvation and have been taught that the Jehovah's Witness outfit is the only shelter from the Battle of Armageddon and other calamities. It is difficult to change a Witness, for he or she has joined one of the most mind-chaining cults

25. The core beliefs are primarily excerpted from "Who Are Jehovah's Witnesses?" and "What Do Jehovah's Witnesses Believe?" (<http://www.usmo.com>, February 7, 1997), 1.

26. Adapted from Terry C. Muck, *Those Other Religions in Your Neighborhood* (Grand Rapids: Zondervan Publishing House, 1992), 202-3.

of our times. M. Kurt Goedelman offers these guidelines for witnessing to a Witness:

1. Witness in love—not to win an argument.

2. Contrast the Watchtower message with that of the Christian gospel. Check out 1 Cor. 15:1-4; 1 Pet. 1:3; Col. 1:22-23; 2 Tim. 2:8; and 1 Cor. 1:23, among other references.

3. Help the JW person to check out the *context* of the scriptures he or she tosses at you. Insist on an accepted version of the Bible. Watchtower's *New World Translation* misrepresents many passages.

4. Point out that Witness prophecies have repeatedly failed.

5. Describe your own new life in Christ.

6. Leave Christian literature with the Jehovah's Witness you are trying to help.

7. Let the person know that you are praying for him or her—and then do it.[27]

The Plymouth Brethren

You may be surprised to see the Plymouth Brethren included in this chapter about largely heterodox groups. The fact is that in some ways they do not belong. They are, after all, orthodox in most teachings. The Brethren are relatively few in number—with some 98,000 members in the United States—but they have had a profound influence on America's Evangelicals. They are included here because of their preoccupation with millennial concerns and dispensationalism, which they successfully made a part of "orthodox" American Evangelicalism. These matters loom large at the beginning of a new millennium.

Beginnings in England

John Nelson Darby (1800-1882) of England became the first of the Plymouth Brethren to gain notoriety. He joined the movement in 1828 and began spreading his "gospel" about the apostate condition of just about all organized Christianity. True believers should depart from the apostate churches, he said, and prepare for the end of the Church Age and the return of Christ, and the Millennial Reign.

Darby made at least seven trips to the United States between 1862 and 1876 to preach the gospel of dispensationalism. Americans of many denominations, tired of dreary old-line churches and thinking that the beginning of the 20th century might be the end of the world, embraced his notions with enthusiasm.

Prominent preachers like D. L. Moody, A. B. Simpson, and James H. Brooks were powerfully influenced by Brethren dispensationalism. No one was more taken with it than a former Confederate soldier-turned-preacher named Cyrus I. Scofield. By 1907 he had established his Correspondence Bible School in Texas, through which he taught dispensationalism. The school later became Dallas Theological Seminary—still the foremost proponent of dispensational ideas.

27. M. Kurt Goedelman, "Jehovah's Witnesses: The View from the Watchtower," in *Misguiding Lights?* ed. Stephen M. Miller (Kansas City: Beacon Hill Press of Kansas City, 1991), 28-29.

In 1909 the Scofield Reference Bible was published. It has been a best-seller throughout this century. This Bible used Archbishop Ussher's time line in the marginal notes, complete with his young earth theory that set creation in the year 4004 B.C. Also in the margins, Scofield printed his Calvinistic, Fundamentalist dispensationalism. Many Christians adopted his views and came to regard the dogmatic and sometimes fanciful marginal notes to be as true as the Bible itself.

Scofield's dispensationalism pertained to the way he believed that God related to humanity in various eras of history. These were important because it showed that "the end is near." His scheme went like this: the dispensation of

1. Innocence (pre-Fall Eden)
2. Conscience (post-Fall Eden)
3. Human Government (Noah, after the Flood)
4. Promise (the Abrahamic covenant)
5. Law (Moses to Jesus)
6. Grace (Church Age, Pentecost to the Second Coming, Daniel's 69th week)
7. The Fullness of Time (millennial reign of Christ)[28]

In the Fundamentalist controversy that raged in the early 20th century, a strange union took place. A marriage of Fundamentalism and Plymouth Brethren dispensationalism came about. The new "orthodoxy" that emerged and came to be taught at such schools as Moody Bible Institute, Dallas Theological Seminary, and R. A. Torrey's Bible Institute of Los Angeles was characterized by

1. Basic Calvinistic doctrine.
2. Total inerrancy of every phrase of the Bible.
3. The Church Age as the soon-to-be-ended dispensation of grace.
4. The eventual failure of the Church to convert the world, thus setting up the Great Tribulation and the millennial reign of Christ.

This theology permeated American Protestantism as few other notions ever had. One bastion of resistance was the Methodist and Wesleyan-Holiness Movements. Their Arminian theology made poor soil for Calvinistic dispensationalism to grow in. The Wesleyans were busy with the Holiness revival that more or less kept their eyes focused on personal holiness rather than dispensational prophecies. The Nazarene periodical *Herald of Holiness* came out with a full-page article opposing the Scofield Bible. Writer A. M. Hills said of Scofield's work, "The doctrines of Calvinism are hostile to the spirit and mission of the Church of the Nazarene. . . . Our theology is that of Methodism, and our mission is that of early Methodists, to spread holiness throughout the world. Let us not be led astray by any fad theologians and their Bible."[29]

But as the century grew older and as some Nazarenes drifted farther from their strictly Wesleyan moorings, Fundamentalism and dispensationalism all but captured certain branches of the Holiness Movement. Eventually even the

---

28. Ahlstrom, *Religious History,* 809.
29. A. M. Hills, "The Scofield Reference Bible Examined for Nazarenes," *Herald of Holiness,* September 19, 1923, 3.

Nazarene Publishing House was selling the Scofield Reference Bible. By the 1950s, dispensationalism was almost a given in some classes. One professor warned us against the Scofield Reference Bible but didn't explain.

In recent decades, as Nazarenes have rediscovered their Wesleyan-Arminian roots, they have found dispensationalism to be "weighed in the balances, and . . . found wanting" (Dan. 5:27, KJV).

Here on the eve of a new millennium the gifts from Fundamentalist/ Brethren dispensationalism are magnified. Some of the key issues we now face relate directly to this ideology:

1. The inerrancy debate. This flourishes in Calvinist/Fundamentalist soil but seems somewhat out of joint with Wesleyans, who are more likely to speak of the sufficiency of Scripture rather than pounding the pulpit over the inerrancy of the King James Version.

2. Creation science. Creationism and the insistence that all true Christians must believe in a young earth and seven solar creation days are rooted in the Fundamentalist/dispensationalist marriage.

3. End-of-the-world and millennial fever. This has made Dallas Seminary teacher Hal Lindsey (*The Late Great Planet Earth* and other books) the best-selling Christian author of the century.

We believe that Nazarenes do better focusing on the Great Commandment, carrying out the Great Commission, and ministering to the bodies and souls of people in need rather than speculating about creation dates, quarreling over Bible translations, or predicting the Second Coming.

Review and Reflection

One thing that helps when dealing with the claims of heretical or unorthodox religions is to know what your own orthodox church teaches on key doctrines. One of the reasons so many Christians fall for the pitch of the cults is that they don't know the valid teachings of their own faith. This would be a good time to review what the Church of the Nazarene believes and teaches about subjects that the Advent-oriented religions push. Start by referring to the Articles of Faith. Read the Bible references offered in support. Check out the teachings about

a. The second coming of Christ

b. Eternal rewards and punishments

c. Salvation through faith by the atonement of Christ

d. The Holy Spirit

e. The authority of Scripture

f. The Trinity

g. Ordination of clergy

h. Immortality

HEALTH, HARMONY, AND HAPPINESS: NEW THOUGHT RELIGIONS

How Did This Get Started?

New Thought sprang up in a cultural and religious vacuum in 19th-century America. Many churches ignored spiritual and psychological healing, health, and peace in favor of heavy-handed Calvinism that stressed acquiescence to a sovereign God who decided everything in advance and needed no input from His creation.

Phineas Quimby, Mary Baker Eddy, and Charles and Myrtle Fillmore came up with alternate forms of religion. They presented to the world Christian Science and the Unity School of Christianity.

Core Beliefs

The heart of New Thought theology is built on the following ideas:

Sin, sickness, pain, and death are phantasms of a mind out of tune with the divine.

The Trinity is a fiction. Jesus is example, not resurrected Savior.

The Bible is a helpful resource but not a law to live by.

Orthodox Christianity has been fouled by popes, councils, priests, and scholars. It does not, therefore, provide the truth, happiness, harmony, or prosperity that God intended.

Neognosticism is openly embraced. The spiritual is so superior to the physical that the latter doesn't really count and may not even be real.

Agreement and Differences

On nearly every major point of traditional Christianity as adhered to by Nazarenes and other Protestant and Catholic Christians, the New Thought practitioners put forth a mostly heretical teaching.

New Thought Today

Christian Science has 2,300 churches and 200,000 members in 60 countries. Unity has 200,000 members but serves millions more across denominational lines through broadcast and publishing ministries.

21 HEALTH, HARMONY, AND HAPPINE/S: NEW THOUGHT RELIGION/

"MY PREACHING MINISTRY IS GOING GREAT," he said. "I throw in a little Norman Vincent Peale, a little *Reader's Digest,* a little *Guideposts,* a little Bob Schuller—and a little Bible, too, of course. The people love it."

This Nazarene pastor testifies to the fact that New Thought spirituality has seeped into American religion across denominational lines. "Mind science" religion was made in America, and it has created a recognizable trait of the American religious experience. The sad part of all this is that many New Thought teachings are quite sub-Christian.

New Thought: Where Did It Come From?

By the mid-19th century, the churches in America had all but abandoned the New Testament teachings about healing. The medical profession didn't do much healing either. Most American doctors were poorly trained, unskilled, and prescientific. With no balm in Gilead for either body or soul and a hunger for spiritual, mental, and physical healing (life expectancy was 40-something), people searched for healing in all the wrong places.

New Thought mind science religion sprang from this soil and has forever marked American religion. Since the world that spreads before us "hath really neither joy, nor love, nor light, / Nor certitude, nor peace, nor help for pain,"[1] one must look within for assistance. The New Thought religions teach a variety of things but most come together at a few basic points:

1. Sin, sickness, pain, and death are not real to New Thought adherents, but mere illusions, phantasms of the mind, that are healed when the mind is properly tuned to the inner divine nature, God, and the universe.

2. New Thought rejects the Trinity, calling Jesus a "superlative man." Usually His divine and human "beings" are separated. Jesus is example rather than Savior.

3. The spiritual realm is so superior to the physical that the latter cannot be considered real.

4. Most New Thought systems claim that they teach what Jesus practiced

---

1. Matthew Arnold, "Dover Beach," in *The Victorian Age,* ed. John Wilson Bowyer and John Lee Brooks, 2nd ed. (New York: Appleton Century Crafts, 1954), 493.

and modeled about the healing of body and soul before the time that kings, popes, councils, and clergy messed up Christianity.

5. Though they claim as their model Jesus, the penniless peasant who had no place even to lay His head, most New Thought creeds hail prosperity as part of the promise of the gospel. "Spiritual composure, physical health, and even economic well-being are understood to flow from a person's rapport with the cosmos."[2]

Many various philosophies became tools in the hands of the New Thought builders. The flow of this stream of American religious history changes and shifts into surprising creek beds, but the stream can be followed with ease.

Phineas Parkhurst Quimby (1802-66) "takes his rightful place as the guru of the mind sciences."[3] He was a New Hampshire blacksmith's son who became a clockmaker. While practicing this trade in Maine, he became fascinated by the possible psychic causes of illness. Quimby soon became a mesmerist. He took his hypnotist act on the road and informed—or at least entertained—a lot of people with his diagnoses and prescriptions for health.

Graduating from the status of road-show hypnotist, he searched for and believed that he found the secret principle that had made his hypnotic healings work. He concluded that sickness was not real but an unfortunate and erroneous state of mind. Quimby then moved to Portland, Maine, and spent the rest of his life treating the sick, recording a number of "miraculous" healings. He called his theories "Science of Christ" and "Christian Science."[4] For all this, Quimby would be all but forgotten today had he not "healed" a remarkable woman in 1862—one Mary Morse Baker Glover Patterson Eddy, the founder of Christian Science.[5]

After Quimby departed the scene, others took up his torch. Notable among them was Warren Felt Evans, who, after he was "healed" by Quimby in 1863, felt compelled to desert his Methodist pulpit and take up the cause of New Thought science. He did much to publicize the movement.

Julius Dresser, his wife, Annetta, and son, Horatio, gave the movement organizational form. They founded the Church of the Higher Life, established the *New Thought* periodical, and formed the Boston Metaphysical Club and the International Metaphysical League. These were precursors to the 1915 International New Thought Alliance, which was organized "to teach the infinitude of the Supreme One, the Divinity of Man and his Infinite possibilities through the creative power of constructive thinking and obedience to the indwelling Presence, which is our source of Inspiration, Power, Health, and Prosperity."[6]

Among those who picked up the banner of New Thought principles, though not affiliated with New Thought organizations, were Emmet Fox and Glenn Clark. Ralph Waldo Trine (who died in 1958) became a leading voice for the movement, writing several best-selling books and declaring that there is one golden thread that runs through all religions; that thread unites us all, he wrote,

2. Ahlstrom, *Religious History*, 1019.
3. Mather and Nichols, *Dictionary of Cults*, 206.
4. Martin, *Kingdom of the Cults*, 128.
5. Ahlstrom, *Religious History*, 1021.
6. Ibid., 1027.

and Buddhists, Jews, and Christians should all be able to worship in each other's temples. Trine proclaimed in his *In Tune with the Infinite:* "Let us not be . . . so dwarfed, so limited, so bigoted as to think that the Infinite God has revealed himself to one little handful of His children in one little quarter of the globe, and at one particular time."[7] Many Americans found themselves in tune with Trine whether or not they were in tune with the Infinite.

No one did more to exploit the New Thought mood than Norman Vincent Peale. He was born in a Methodist parsonage in Ohio. He became a Methodist pastor but gave up Methodism to join the Dutch Reformed Church in order to pastor New York's prestigious Marble Collegiate Church. From this powerful Calvinistic stronghold he preached the power of positive thinking. This was just the opposite of the creeds of the denomination he had joined.

Through his best-seller, *The Power of Positive Thinking,* and through sermons, radio, and television, Peale made New Thought theology a respected household item in America. His magazine based on New Thought principles, *Guideposts,* is the most popular Christian magazine in the nation—and, strangely enough, the favorite magazine among Nazarenes, according to one recent poll.

From the same Calvinistic denomination came Peale's heir apparent to the New Thought throne, Robert Schuller of the Crystal Cathedral in Garden Grove, California. Neither Peale nor Schuller are connected with the New Thought institutions. Rather, they exploited the principles of the movement.

Christian Science

Christian Science is one of the foremost institutionalized forms of New Thought theology. It grew phenomenally during the late 19th century and the early 20th century but seems now to be losing ground. Founder Mary Baker Eddy forbade the reporting of statistics, so membership is not known. However, in 1995 Mead and Hill, in the *Handbook of Denominations in the United States,* reported 2,400 congregations,[8] but in 1997 the Christian Science home page on the Internet reported "approximately 2,300 branch churches in over 60 countries."[9] In 1992 Terry C. Muck reported 200,000 U.S. Christian Science members.[10]

History. Mary Baker Eddy, founder of Christian Science, was born in New Hampshire in 1821. Her parents were staunch Congregationalists. But even as a child, Mary rejected the harsh Calvinism, particularly the idea of election to salvation by God. She went on to spend much of her adult life attacking traditional Christianity as her faithful disciples cheered her on.

Mary was a sickly child, suffering from spinal and nervous disorders that kept her out of school much of the time. "Everything we know about her early years makes them an understandable prelude to an adult life of ceaseless search

7. Ralph Waldo Trine, *In Tune with the Infinite* (New York, 1897), 205-7. Cited by Ahlstrom, *Religious History,* 1030.

8. Mead and Hill, *Handbook of Denominations,* 106.

9. "Visit the First Church of Christ, Scientist, Boston," <http://www.tfccs.com>, 1.

10. Muck, *Those Other Religions,* 196.

for health, religious certainty, and communion with God on the one hand, and for attention and fame on the other."[11]

In 1843 Mary became the bride of George Washington Glover, a neighbor. He died a year later, leaving Mary pregnant. The next nine years were painful for Mary, who was now a penniless and sickly widow. Her nervous disorders, chronic ailments, and infantilism dominated her life. Morphine and mesmerism were among the treatments that gave her temporary relief.[12] She married Daniel Patterson, an itinerant dentist, in 1853 and began a period of 20 years of physical and personal misery. She divorced Patterson (who appears to have been a heartless womanizer) and returned as an invalid to Portland, Maine. She soon sought the service of Phineas Quimby, who in 1862 miraculously "healed" her. She felt so vigorous that she climbed the 182 steps of the city hall tower with ease. Mary wrote to the Portland newspaper, the *Evening Courier,* praising Quimby and comparing him to Jesus Christ.[13]

Life was still unhappy for Mary. Because of her desire to carry on the work of Quimby (who died in 1866), she encountered many difficulties. Ahlstrom says it was a time of "homeless wandering, contention, estrangement, poverty and intermittent exultation, lived out in a religious and cultic subculture" that can hardly be understood today.[14]

But the tide turned for Mary Baker Eddy (she married Asa G. Eddy when she was 56). In 1875 she published her book *Science and Health with Key to the Scriptures*. Over 9 million copies have now been sold in print, audiocassettes, and compact disc.

Mrs. Eddy claimed to have received the required textbook of Christian Science from God. She wrote in the *Christian Science Journal,*

"I should blush to write of *Science and Health with Key to the Scriptures* as I have, were it of human origin and I apart from God its author, but I was only a scribe echoing the harmonies of Heaven in divine metaphysics. I cannot be super-modest of the Christian Science Textbook."[15]

Mrs. Eddy claimed that she copied down what God had said, but research into *Science and Health with Key to the Scriptures* shows that what she copied down, in many instances, was the writings of her "healer," Phineas Quimby, and an 1823 book by Lindley Murray. Whole passages are taken almost word for word from these sources.[16] When charges of plagiarism were raised, Eddy stoutly denied any Quimby influence at all, though her association with him was common knowledge and a matter of public record. Editions of *Science and Health with Key to the Scriptures* now number 382.

In 1879 Eddy founded the First Church of Christ, Scientist, Boston. This became the mother church, and has ever since been the headquarters, of Chris-

---

11. Ahlstrom, *Religious History,* 1021.

12. Ibid.

13. McDowell and Stewart, *Handbook of Today's Religions,* 126.

14. Ahlstrom, *Religious History,* 1022.

15. McDowell and Stewart, *Handbook of Today's Religions,* 123.

16. See the comparative selections of works by these authors and Eddy in Martin, *Kingdom of the Cults,* chapter 5, 128 ff.

tian Science. She started the *Christian Science Journal* in 1883, the *Christian Science Sentinel* in 1898, and the highly respected newspaper *Christian Science Monitor* in 1908.

Mrs. Eddy finally achieved wealth and fame, coming dangerously close to putting herself on par with Jesus more than once. But spiritual and personal peace seemed to have eluded her. She feared evil powers such as "animal magnetism," by which she believed that wicked persons could kill an individual with vicious thoughts. She often went about with bodyguards who, like spiritual Secret Service agents, were to protect her from evil forces. She believed that her husband died in 1877 from arsenic poison spiritually administered by malevolent people. For the last 20 years of her life she lived in seclusion, not even attending the dedication of the mother church building in 1895. In 1910 she died in her secluded mansion in Brookline, Massachusetts.

Core Beliefs and Practices. Mary Baker Eddy became a strong leader and a skillful administrator. To the original freedom of New Thought she brought legalistic management. Early on, many Christian Science churches had preaching pastors. Eddy soon forbade any pastor to preach, commanding instead that in place of the sermon, a lesson from her book *Science and Health with Key to the Scriptures* be read. The office of pastor was abolished, and the office of "reader" replaced it. Eddy did not shrink from excommunicating her opposition.

Preaching is still absent from Christian Science services. The Christian Science home page says that the hour-long Sunday services "are based on weekly Bible Lessons from the *Christian Science Quarterly*. These include readings from the Bible and *Science and Health*. . . . . The Bible Lessons are studied throughout the week . . . and are read as the sermon at Sunday services by two church members."[17] On Wednesday evenings a testimony service is held in which the congregation shares experiences of spiritual healing or insight gained from the practice of Christian Science.

Christian Science operates "reading rooms" as well as churches. These are available for the study of the Bible, Mary Baker Eddy's writings, and current affairs. The international church is run by a five-member board. They have no clergy, no sacraments, no missionaries. Christian Science practitioners are full-time "spiritual healers" who collect fees the way psychologists or medical doctors do. Christian Science has been in the news often because of the belief that disease is a matter of wrong thinking to be healed by mental and spiritual activity.[18] Therefore, some Christian Science members have refused to accept medical treatment for themselves or their children even when facing killer diseases.

Though relations between Christian Science and traditional Christian churches is often cordial, Christian Science beliefs run so counter to orthodox Christianity that there can be no question about the church's heretical stance.

- Christian Science opposes Christianity on the inspiration of Scripture— the Bible is given to us so that we can see how Jesus, a noble man, demonstrates how to live a totally spiritual life.

---

17. "A Word About Church Services . . . ," <http://www.tfccs.com>.
18. Muck, *Those Other Religions,* 197.

- Christian Science denies the Trinity and the virgin birth of Jesus ("Jesus . . . was born of the Virgin Mary's spiritual thoughts of Life").[19]
- Christian Science denies the power of the blood of Jesus to redeem— "The material blood of Jesus was no more efficacious to cleanse from sin when it was shed upon the 'accursed tree' than when it was flowing in His veins."[20]
- Christian Science denies the death and resurrection of Jesus—Mrs. Eddy declares in *Science and Health* that Jesus did not die; therefore, how could there be a resurrection?[21]

"The material blood of Jesus was no more efficacious to cleanse from sin when it was shed upon the 'accursed tree' than when it was flowing in His veins."

- Christian Science denies sin (merely wrong thinking and illusion) and hell (nothing more than the mental anguish of destructive thinking).

There is little to be gained by continuing this list. At every important point of orthodox Christian doctrine, Christian Science has a different idea. There is no significant common ground between Christian Science and the traditional, biblical doctrines of Evangelical Christianity in general and the Church of the Nazarene in particular.

Unity School of Christianity

History. The Unity School of Christianity is the most prosperous of the institutional descendants of the Quimby, Eddy, and New Thought theology. Charles and Myrtle Fillmore founded the movement in 1889 near Kansas City.

Myrtle was a sick woman. She had tuberculosis and malaria. Her doctor told her she would be dead in six months. But in 1886 the Fillmores attended a New Thought lecture that changed their lives. The speaker, one E. B. Weeks, declared, "I am a child of God and therefore I do not inherit sickness."[22] Myrtle believed and started repeating the thought day after day. Sure enough, she was healed. Charles did not believe at first, but his wife's healing made him take a closer look. He had been deep into Hinduism, Buddhism, spiritism, and mind-over-matter science and decided to consider the new meditation through which Myrtle had been healed. Sure enough, his withered leg was healed, and the two of them started what was to become the Unity School of Christianity. Charles was the chief executive officer and Myrtle the teacher.

They based their new religion on the New Thought ideas of Christian Science, Mary Baker Eddy, and the notions of Phineas Quimby. These Myrtle brought to the table. Charles brought his reincarnation theory and other contri-

---

19. *The First Church of Christ, Scientist and Miscellany,* 1913, 1941. Cited by Martin, *Kingdom of the Cults,* 139.

20. Mary Baker Eddy, *Science and Health with Key to the Scriptures.* Cited by Martin, *Kingdom of the Cults,* 139.

21. Martin, *Kingdom of the Cults,* 140.

22. McDowell and Stewart, *Handbook of Today's Religions,* 131.

butions of Swami Vivekanada of India. When the deck was shuffled and dealt, out came a curious self-help religion. Their ideas were promptly published in a new magazine, which was called *Christian Science Thought*—until Mrs. Eddy found out about it and objected to the name. The name was changed to *Modern Thought* and then to *Thought*.

The movement prospered across denominational lines, primarily through a vigorous publishing program of tracts, pamphlets, periodicals, and books, and the Silent Unity prayer request ministry. Then Unity churches and centers began to spring up.

The movement today has about 200,000 members who attend 574 churches and 245 satellite ministries. Beyond their membership, however, Unity serves some 3 million persons per year. According to scholar Terry Muck, many of Unity's "adherents retain membership in the church of their choice while . . . subscribing to Unity publications which gives them [Unity] direct access to many churches . . . where the Unity cult teachings are subtly disseminated under the guise of a higher plane of Christian experience."[23]

Core Beliefs and Practices. Unity is the largest gnostic cult in history— they admit the gnosticism but resist the "cult" label. Unity is also the world's largest mail-order religion. Its publishing and prayer programs produce most of the $30 million budget required to pay the family members and other staff who still run the organization and maintain the 1,400-acre headquarters at Unity Village, near

> *"God does not love anybody or anything. God is the love in everybody and everything."*

Lee's Summit, Missouri. People send prayer requests to Unity at the rate of 7,000 letters and 1,800 phone calls per day. The requests go in the Silent Unity prayer tower where they are prayed for (submitted to "creative thinking"—the Unity doctrine of prayer) in nine languages.[24]

Like Christian Science and other New Thought outfits, Unity is so badly out of joint with historic Christianity that it could be called "Christian" only in a pluralistic society for which theology and orthodoxy have little value. Let's review only a few points of its beliefs and practice.

- Jesus: Unity says that Jesus' life was a parable to show us the stages a person must go through in order to be in total harmony with God. He was a great man but no more divine than anyone else. We can do and become everything that Jesus did and was. It will not be easy—it took Jesus himself several reincarnated lifetimes to achieve His full potential. He came to earth first, according to Charles Fillmore, as Moses, then Elisha, then David, then Jesus of Nazareth.[25]
- God: God is love, and love is God—Unity repeats the basic error of Christian Science. Charles Fillmore wrote, "God does not love anybody

---

23. Martin, *Kingdom of the Cults*, 279.
24. Muck, *Those Other Religions*, 199-200.
25. Stephen M. Miller, "Unity School of Christianity: Mind Power," in Miller, *Misguiding Lights?* 68.

or anything. God is the love in everybody and everything."[26] The personal God is lost here, to say nothing of the Trinity, which Unity interprets heretically.

- The Bible: The final rule for faith and practice to Protestant Christians becomes a mere fallible resource in the hands of Unity practitioners. Stephen Miller, in *Misguiding Lights?* asked a professor at Unity's ministerial school to respond to John 3:16. Unity does not believe in perishing (death), only reincarnation. Further, they do not believe in atonement or in the requirement to believe in Jesus as Savior. The professor said that a Unity version of John 3:16 would go like this: "For God so loved the world that he/she individualized himself/herself in you and in me. Not so that we may gain eternal life, but so that we may enjoy more abundantly the eternal life that we already have."[27]

- Hell: Unity does not believe in hell. Miller asked another Unity professor, Joseph Wolpert, about Luke 12:5 (a strong warning about fearing God, who has the power to cast one into hell). He got this response: "Everybody takes [out of scripture] what they're comfortable with and just ignores what they're not. So that's not a piece of scripture Unity people would even take more than two glances at."[28]

- Salvation: Unity teaches that Christ is in everyone, and that thus everyone will be saved. But saved from what? Not hell. Not sin. "Your own false thinking, that's the only thing to be saved from," claimed Unity teacher Frank Giudici.[29]

There is no need to explore further the gaping canyon between Unity and the belief and practices of historic Christianity. Every major point of Christian doctrine is trivialized or denied by the descendants of Quimby, Eddy, and the Fillmores.

This does not mean that the whole New Thought tradition made no contribution to the times. In the 19th century it came forward against overwhelming Calvinistic doctrines of extreme emphasis on the sovereignty of God, unconditional election, predestination, and the perseverance of the saints. Rather than acquiesce to such creeds, New Thought teachers dared to declare to one and all that God has planted considerable resources in our hearts and minds, including something of His own divine nature. We are to use those resources to our full ability in order to reach health, serenity, and prosperity.

New Thought's contribution in the 20th century is similar. We no longer are overpowered by Calvinism. Rather, we now cope with the predestination (determinism) touted by the priests of the social sciences who tell us we are mere victims of environment. In the face of this new oppression, New Thought teachers declare that we are responsible for our own personal, physical, and economic problems and challenge us to address those problems as spiritual ones.

26. McDowell and Stewart, *Handbook of Today's Religions,* 133.
27. Miller, "Unity School of Christianity," 68-69.
28. Ibid., 71.
29. Ibid., 67.

Review and Reflection

1. John Calvin studied at the University of Paris. Martin Luther studied at Erfurt and Wittenberg. John Wesley was an Oxford graduate and professor. Where did Phineas Quimby study theology, biblical studies, and church history? What prepared him to become a theologian?

2. How do you think Mary Baker Eddy's physical problems when she was young affected her spiritual needs, desires, and goals?

3. How did Mary Baker Eddy's religious upbringing affect her own spiritual pilgrimage? How has your religious upbringing affected your spiritual journey?

4. Unity openly embraces neognosticism. Read 1 John, and see what you think the Bible says about gnosticism. The people who caused the problems to which John was speaking were early gnostics. They were the ones in chapter 1 who were walking in darkness while claiming the Light. In chapter 2, they were the antichrists who deserted the fellowship (vv. 18-19). In chapter 3, they were the devilish deceivers (vv. 7-8). In chapter 4, the early gnostics were the false prophets (v. 1).

"IN THE LAST DAYS" . . . ISMS GALORE

Overview

In this chapter you will be introduced to several "perilous times" outfits with which you may someday collide. Treated in this chapter are the Unification Church, traditional African religion in America, Scientology, the Church Universal and Triumphant, Freemasonry, Christian Identity, and UFO (unidentified flying object) cults.

Core Beliefs

The only thing that this cluster of isms holds in common is that some of their teachings are sub-Christian, non-Christian, or anti-Christian.

They part company with Christianity at a hundred points. Here's a mere starter list:

Unification Church—Rev. Moon's claim that he is the second Messiah; that the first Messiah, Jesus, failed miserably.

Traditional African religion in America—animal sacrifices to gods like Shango and Ogun in worship services.

Scientology—repentance viewed as a despicable evil.

Church Universal and Triumphant—Jesus is just another *avatar* along with St. Germaine, El Morya, and Elizabeth Clare Prophet.

Freemasonry—secret rituals, which violates Christian openness in such rituals as baptism, marriage, ordination, and so on. The Mason is to pray faithfully to whatever god he believes in.

Christian Identity—belief that the white race is the chosen people. Other races are the "beasts of the field" (Black, brown, yellow races) or half human and half demon (the Jews).

UFO cults—Heaven's Gate, led by Marshall Herff Applewhite, is just one of many cults mesmerized by UFOs and extraterrestrials.

Cults Today

Cults are created according to the fears, anxieties, and fantasies of seekers for the unusual and as the monstrous egos of charismatic cult leaders require.

22 — "IN THE LAST DAYS" ... ISMS GALORE

THE BIBLE SAYS THAT "in the last days perilous times shall come. For men shall be lovers of their own selves . . . lovers of pleasures more than lovers of God. . . . They will not endure sound doctrine; but after their own lusts shall they heap to themselves teachers, having itching ears; and they shall turn away their ears from the truth, and shall be turned unto fables" (2 Tim. 3:1-2, 4; 4:3-4, KJV). There seems to be a lot of that going around today, as you will see while reading this chapter.

The Unification Church

Pop Quiz

1. Which of the following owns the influential newspaper *Washington Times*?

    a. J. Pierpont Morgan IV

    b. The Rockefeller family

    c. Rev. Sun Myung Moon

2. Who owns the following businesses? One Up Enterprises, International Oceanic Enterprises, News World Communications, World Media Association, and Free Press International?

    a. Harry K. Vanderbilt III

    b. American Broadcasting Company

    c. Rev. Sun Myung Moon

3. Which of the following says that Jesus failed in His mission and that God has sent him as the "second Messiah" to complete the redemptive task?

    a. Alfred E. Neuman

    b. Jerry Falwell

    c. Rev. Sun Myung Moon

The answer to all the above is *c*—Rev. Sun Myung Moon, the leader of the cult called the "Moonies."[1]

Moon was born in Korea in 1920. When he was 16, he had a vision in which Jesus himself told the young Moon that since Christ had in fact failed, he was to be the Second Messiah, the Third Adam. He would complete the redemption of humanity. Leaving the Presbyterians, Moon "dabbled with an eccentric

---

1. See Mather and Nichols, *Dictionary of Cults,* 282-83; James A. Beverley, "The Unification Church: A New Messiah," in Miller, *Misguiding Lights?* 94-100.

Pentecostal group that taught him that Korea was the new promised land and that the future new Messiah would be Korean-born."[2]

In 1945 Moon started what would become the Unification Church. The purpose of the new church was to unite Christians everywhere under the leadership of Moon, the new Messiah. "With the fullness of time, God has sent his messenger to resolve the fundamental questions of life and the universe. His name is Sun Myung Moon," declared the modest Moon in his book *Divine Principle.*[3]

During the 1950s Moon divorced his first wife, served a prison term in Korea, and published his book *Divine Principle,* which he says supersedes the Bible. In 1971 Moon came to America and launched a number of successful businesses. By this time his church numbered more than a million and would soon reach the 2 million mark. In America his most successful evangelism efforts were among lonely and insecure college students. They were recruited by friendly proselytizers who offered companionship, compassion, and security. This was followed by intense training sessions that often produced radical loyalty.

During the 1980s Moon married his fourth wife, served a tax evasion prison term in the United States, and performed mass marriages of up to 6,500 couples at once. The newlyweds were part of the sinless Moon's program to perfect his disciples and marry them so that they could produce sin-free children as part of the plan for the physical redemption of humankind. This is the part that Jesus failed to do, seeing that He never married, begat no sinless children, and allowed His plan to be interrupted by the Crucifixion.

Many of the American students who joined the Unification Church got their tuition paid by the church or Rev. Moon. The church has also started ballet companies and symphonies, showing support for the artistic side of the culture. It has sponsored international conferences for scientists, religious leaders, and the news media. Moon

Jesus failed in His redemptive mission by allowing the Crucifixion to happen against God's plan, adherents of the Unification Church claim; therefore, God has sent a Second Messiah to complete the job of redemption.

paid about a billion dollars for the *Washington Times* in order "to save America and the world."[4] His church has provided a loving and caring fellowship for students—converts were nurtured and not merely exploited. Moon has spoken out strongly against drug abuse and other social evils. His followers regard him as a sacrificial servant of the human race.

But in spite of his good works, he is a "much mistaken" man. James Beverley of Ontario Theological Seminary has studied the Unification Church

2. Mather and Nichols, *Dictionary of Cults,* 280.
3. McDowell and Stewart, *Handbook of Today's Religions,* 99.
4. Mather and Nichols, *Dictionary of Cults,* 286.

for years. He applauds their good points but offers these charges against this man and his movement:

1. Moon is wrong about God. He denies the Trinity, the deity of Christ, and the personality of the Holy Spirit, whom he says is the female counterpart of God the Father and thus the Perfect Mother, the second Eve.

2. Moon is wrong about the birth of Jesus. He denies the Virgin Birth and teaches that Zechariah was the father of Jesus. This adulterous affair by John the Baptist's father caused severe tension between Joseph and Mary, Moon says. Joseph resented Jesus so much, Moon claims, that he deliberately left the 12-year-old boy at the Jerusalem Temple when it came time to return to Nazareth.

3. He is wrong about the death of Christ. Jesus was supposed to marry and establish the perfect family, Moon says, and this failure is one thing that led to Calvary.

4. Moon is wrong about the resurrection of Christ. Moon denies the bodily resurrection of Jesus and says His body was delivered to the victorious Satan.

5. Moon is wrong about the second coming of Christ. He denies that Jesus will return, saying that God has sent Moon himself as a second Messiah instead.

6. He is wrong about the Bible, giving his own book, *Divine Principle*, preference.

7. Moon is wrong about the Final Judgment. He denies the Bible's teaching about hell and asserts that in the end everyone will be saved—including Satan himself.

8. Moon is wrong about salvation. He denies the full sufficiency of Christ's atoning death. Salvation comes from good works, such as following the sinless Moon and his fourth wife, Hak Ja Kan, as True Parents.[5]

Membership in the Unification Church has apparently dwindled in the 1990s. It is strongest in Korea and Japan, with several hundred thousand members. Today there are about 10,000 disciples of Moon (pejoratively called "Moonies") in the United States.

Primitive African Religion Comes to America

Newark, New Jersey—the remains of 16 sacrificed animals found in a park baffle police.

George Washington University, Washington, D.C.—a theology professor goes through the initiation rites, including a bath in herbal waters and sacrificed blood, to become a

"On the days when Ogun is angered, there is always disaster in the world. . . . With water in the house he washes with blood. . . . I fear . . . my orisha."[6]

joyful "child" of Elleggua, the most popular African god in North America.

Portland, Oregon—Lydia Olurolo goes to court to keep from being deported to her native Nigeria. There she claims the culture and the religion will

---

5. Adapted from Beverley, "Unification Church," 97-98.

6. Sandra T. Barnes, *Africa's Ogun* (Bloomington, Ind.: University of Indiana Press, 1989), 206, 129.

require her daughters to submit to excision and infibulation, the same sexual mutilation that happened to her.[7]

Tucson, Arizona—250 individual Cuban refugees have been arrested for brazen crimes, including ritual killings. Police say that after offering a sacrificial dog to Ogun, they think they are invisible to the police and thus attempt the most daring crimes in broad daylight.

Hialeah, Florida—the 60,000-member Church of Lukimi Babalu carries its case about animal sacrifices as part of the worship service to the United States Supreme Court. The Court agrees with the Santeros, and animal sacrifice continues under the full protection of the law.

Ready or not, traditional African religion is flourishing in North America like algae in a pond in August.

In one of the most sordid chapters of human history, the 18th and 19th centuries, no fewer than 10 million Africans were captured and delivered to slave holders in the Americas. Many of those who were brought to Protestant North America were won to Christ by faithful Baptist and Methodist witnesses. Within a couple of generations, the Christian religion (complete with evangelical conversion experience) all but replaced the African religions they brought with them. But for those who ended up in Cuba and Haiti, another phenomenon occurred. As soon as they left the ship, they were marched into a Catholic church. There, in a language and a ceremony that they could not understand, they were baptized and declared Christians. The Catholicism they encountered was medieval in character.

The new masters forced the slaves to pray to the images of the Catholic saints. But in their hearts the Africans were praying to the gods of their native land. For example, the icon of John soon came to stand for Shango. James or Peter stood in for the bloody war god Ogun, and the statues of Jesus heard the prayers to Elleggua (Legba). Thus, over time one of the most destructive syncretisms in history developed—a mixture of pagan religion and medieval Catholicism. This product has now been imported to North America by way of millions of immigrants from the Caribbean and Latin America.

Santeria Moves North. The Santeria found in the United States comes primarily from Cuba. During the diabolical slave trade, most of the slaves dumped in Cuba came from Yoruba (modern Nigeria). "Santeria" means "worship of the saints." Santeros have developed a religious life around these elements.

1. Initiation. When a new baby arrives, the Santero priest, by way of certain ceremonies, ascertains which god the baby will belong to and serve. There are hundreds of gods to choose from, but Elleggua, Ogun, Shango, and Obatala seem to be the most popular. The child then begins at a very young age to

---

7. Excision is female circumcision. The clitoris is removed with a knife, piece of glass, or, as in the case CNN recently filmed, a pair of scissors will do. Excision is practiced for the girl's own good, they say, so that she will not enjoy sex and therefore will not be tempted to be promiscuous. Infibulation is simply sewing together the vaginal opening to insure that a young girl's virginity will be preserved or to insure the fidelity of a wife during her husband's absence. Doctors report a number of such surgical requests recently in cities from Seattle to Atlanta. It took only 10 minutes to find in a Kansas City popular music store two recordings of music for ritual excision.

absorb and practice the lore and worship of his or her assigned god. When the person has mastered the way of the *orisha,* as a god is called, a celebration of initiation—often a big rite-of-passage party—takes place.

2. **Divination.** Divination directs the life of the Santero from the cradle to the grave. Decisions and problems about love, money, health, and vocation are brought to the priest's divination chamber—fee in hand or on a leash.

3. **Sacrifice.** The idea of professors, bankers, computer scientists, to say nothing of bus drivers, secretaries, and children, gathering to offer (or even drink) the blood of goats and chickens being offered to wooden, iron, or concrete idols is hard for Americans to get used to. But it happens every day. Santeros give their gods herbal water to drink and sacrificial blood for food. If they fail to do this, the gods may become angry and take vengeance—or even worse, the orisha might die and not be able to protect them.

4. **Possession.** The sure sign that the orisha has accepted the sacrifice is for the god or goddess to sweep in upon the worshiper and "possess" the devotee. Ceremonies of hypnotic drumming, chanting, and singing set the tone for possession. During possession, mysterious, unpredictable, and incredible deeds are performed. In a Kansas City public library, it took only about 10 minutes to find sheet music to invoke possession by Elleggua, Ogun, Oshosi, and Obatala.

Voodoo in North America. Voodoo springs primarily from the culture of Haiti. Slaves brought to work the sugar plantations there came mostly from Dahomey, modern Benin. The development of voodoo is similar to that of Santeria. Voodoo is a syncretism of traditional African religion (TAR), pre-Reformation Catholicism, and medieval French witchcraft. It shares many of the same deities and ceremonies with Santeria. It requires a lifetime of appeasing dozens of gods, hundred of ancestors, and a host of evil spirits that hound the steps of everyone alive. Many Americans regard voodoo as a sort of Halloween entertainment, but for millions it is religion heavy to bear. A Haitian truism reveals the burden of voodoo: "After the dance, the drums are heavy."

When Americans encounter Santeria or voodoo, they often respond with fear, sometimes with fascination. But when you recognize TAR for what it is, both fear and fascination are disarmed. It is a simplistic religion that has no real power over anyone except those who subjugate themselves to its bondage. Often a Christian's response is a deep humanitarian pity for the people who labor under this malignant syncretism. Prayer takes the place of fear or fascination.

What shall we do about these people who have brought their strange religions to our communities? Shall we slander them? Shun them? Try to pass laws to make their religion illegal?

Perhaps we should copy the response of the Lord God to the land of Moab. The Moabites had worn themselves out worshiping false gods. Then God said, "My soul moans like a lyre for Moab, . . . He wearies himself upon the high place" (Isa. 16:11-12, RSV).

Can our souls moan with the mournful tones of the lyre for those people who are wearing themselves out seeking to appease the false gods of TAR? Would that do any good? Indeed it might. Did you know that even under the persecution of the Communist Castro government, the Church of the Nazarene is flourishing in Cuba? Did you know that one of the fastest-growing Nazarene fields is Haiti?

There are plenty of people of TAR persuasion to pray for. More than 100 million persons practice some form of TAR. There are more Santeros and voodoo devotees in New York City and New Orleans alone than there are Nazarenes in the entire world.[8]

Scientology: A Religion Created by a Writer of Science Fiction Tales

Scientology was invented in the 1950s by Lafayette Ron Hubbard of Tilden, Nebraska. Sensing the wide-open idea market in post-World War II America, he devised a clever religious scheme. It was a blend of Freudian psychology's dark teachings about the unconscious mind, the ideas of reincarnation of the Eastern religions, and his own science fiction notions that had already proven salable to the American public through his sci-fi novels.

Hubbard claimed to have an engineering degree from George Washington University in Washington, D.C. But campus records say he attended two years, failed physics, and was put on academic probation, never receiving the degree.[9]

If a man really wants to make a million dollars, the best way would be to start his own religion.
—L. Ron Hubbard

Hubbard's son changed his last name, calling his father "one of the biggest con men of the century."[10] Certain other people have a different idea. Hollywood celebrities like John Travolta, Priscilla Presley, Karen Black, Joe Namath, and Kirstie Alley give vigorous support to the man and his 1950 best-seller, *Dianetics: The Modern Science of Mental Health.*[11]

After the first Scientology church was organized in Washington, D.C., in the 1950s, the movement was headquartered in Saint Hill, England, on Hubbard's 300-foot boat, *Appollo.* But since 1975 the church has operated from a luxurious office building on Hollywood Boulevard in Hollywood, California.

The Big Idea. Hundreds of books and pamphlets came from the pen of leader Hubbard before his death in 1986. The movement is complex, but the overarching idea that has appealed to millions is this: human beings are really age-old beings, "thetans," who have lived through hundreds of evolutionary reincarnations. A thetan (person) may very well be 300 trillion years old and have lived on many planets and centuries in many forms of existence—human and otherwise. Because many things in these many lives have been so painful, the *reactive,* subconscious, mind hides these realities from the *analytical* or *conscious* mind. The infelicitous experiences in previous existences attach them-

---

8. For more information on voodoo and Santeria, see Terry Read and Wesley Tracy, "Primitive Religion in America," *Herald of Holiness,* August 1994, 17-29, 40-41.

9. Mather and Nichols, *Dictionary of Cults,* 251.

10. Ibid., 252.

11. Kurt Van Gorden, "Scientology: Trillion-Year-Old Thetans," in Miller, *Misguiding Lights?* 105.

selves to the subconscious like barnacles on a ship's hull. The road to mental health can be found as a "Scientologist auditor" helps you scrape off the barnacles collected in hundreds of previous existences. These barnacles are called "engrams." When the engrams are all cleared away, the person is declared "clear." Until such a transformation occurs, an individual is "preclear." Scientology claims to have a scientific, technological way to make this happen.

How the Church of Scientology Operates. Recruitment often takes the form of handsome young people in malls and busy streets asking passersby if they want a free personality test. The tests, of course, reveal a serious *engram* problem. Follow-up sessions, books, and seminars help the devotee toward peace of mind, self-acceptance, and spiritual health.

To follow the path from preclear to clear is very costly. Tuition, fees, seminars, and the like, which are required, can cost the candidate $100,000 or more before anything like *clear* status or achieving the OT ("operating thetan") level of salvation occurs.

Hubbard came up with a simple electronic machine called the E-meter (engram meter), which he claimed registers the soul's engrams and makes diagnosis accurate. The United States government thought otherwise, calling the E-meter a fraud. It prosecuted, but Hubbard was able to successfully escape on the grounds of religious freedom.[12]

Scientology's Beliefs. Scientology is clearly a non-Christian religion.

God: Scientology claims that there are many gods in the universe, not one God, as Christianity teaches.

Jesus Christ: Hubbard claims that Jesus was "just a shade above clear" and not as spiritually advanced as some Scientologists. The cross of Christ is dismissed as an ancient legend introduced years ago by a bunch of "preclears."[13]

Humanity: People are deities whose godhood has been covered by engrams. They can be gods again. Like a number of pantheistic Eastern religions, Scientology does not distinguish between the Creator and the created world.

Sin: There is no such thing as sin or evil. "It is despicable and utterly beneath contempt to tell a man he must repent, that he is evil," Hubbard declared.[14]

Salvation: Achieving the status of "clear," that is, becoming an OT and thus being freed from the cycle of reincarnation, is salvation. The resources for salvation are to be found within one's own self.

Heaven and Hell: Hubbard said that such Christian ideas as heaven and hell were "corny."[15]

At the time of L. Ron Hubbard's death in 1986, the Church of Scientology numbered some 3 million members, with about 1 million of them in the United States.

Orthodox Christians find no common ground with Scientology.

---

12. Mather and Nichols, *Dictionary of Cults*, 251.
13. Van Gorden, "Scientology: Trillion-Year-Old Thetans," 108-9.
14. Ibid., 109.
15. Ibid., 108.

The Church Universal and Triumphant

The Church Universal and Triumphant is an offshoot of the "I Am" movement that was started in the United States in the 1930s by Guy Ballard. He based the movement on Exod. 3:14, but it was anything but a biblical movement. It combined elements of ancient gnosticism, theosophy, Eastern mysticism, and Christianity. The movement attracted as many as 3.5 million members in the 1930s before the allegedly immortal Ballard died.

Edna Ballard took over from her husband, and though membership shrank drastically, she and her son kept the outfit going until her death in 1971. At that

We are all part of God, as is your rosebush and the cat under it. point, Edna's organist, Frederick Landwehr, and Jerry and Ann Craig took over. A small remnant is headquartered in Schaumburg, Illinois.

One of the several offshoots of the I Am movement that has prospered in recent decades is the Church Universal and Triumphant. Before it took this name, it was known as the "Great White Brotherhood" and was connected with "Summit Lighthouse." It has been headquartered in Washington, D.C.; Colorado Springs; Camelot (a monastery in California); Corwin Springs, Montana (they bought the Malcolm Forbes ranch there); and now operates from a 40,000-acre "inner retreat" center near Gardiner, Montana.

The principal leader of the Church Universal and Triumphant was Mark Prophet. His associates were gathered in anticipation of his ascension into the Godhead, but unceremoniously, he died of a stroke. Again, the followers thinned out, but again, as Mrs. Ballard had done, Elizabeth Clare Prophet took over the reins and the reign. She proved to be an efficient leader in spite of divorcing her second husband, Randall King, for adultery—though King claims that he and Elizabeth had a regular sexual relationship long before her husband died. Elizabeth claimed that King was a reincarnation of a demoniac in the New Testament, and of Francis Joseph I, the Austrian emperor who caused World War I. She soon married again, and the church, which called her "Guru Ma," prospered. The cult has grown so fast that the leaders say they cannot even estimate the number of followers. The cult flourishes in Ghana, Sweden, and the United States.

Core Beliefs

What are the teachings that attract so many people?

1. **Salvation.** Self-realization is the essence of salvation. This is accomplished as the devotee realizes his or her own divinity. This is in harmony with Hindu and New Age notions. The idea of atonement is mildly present—not the atonement wrought by Jesus, but by all the avatars who take upon themselves some of humanity's karma.

2. **Revelation.** Both I Am and the Church Universal and Triumphant hold that revelation comes only through the "ascended masters," those supersaints who have ascended into God and now communicate with humans by way of mystic illumination. The ascended masters are Jesus, St. Germaine (whom Guy

Ballard claims to have met in 1930 on Mount Shasta in California), El Morya, Guy and Edna Ballard, and Mark Prophet. Communications from them rank at least as high as the Bible, in which the church says it also believes.

3. **Doctrine of God.** The Trinity is denied in favor of an Eastern pantheism. There is no distinction between God and His creation. Thus we are all part of God, as is your rosebush and the cat under it. Jesus turns out to be just one of several helpful deities, and the Holy Spirit is a nonpersonal force.

4. **Eschatology.** The end times teachings of the Church Universal and Triumphant are constant and seem to center on fear tactics. They say that Armageddon is imminent, and they hope to escape the holocaust by building bomb shelters in Montana. The church also went into the business of selling survival gear.

Distinctive Practices

1. **Enticement.** Promises of love, harmony, peace, and elite spirituality characterize Church Universal and Triumphant sales pitches. A newspaper ad in a 1996 edition of the *Kansas City Star* picks up the popular angel theme. For $5 one could hear Elizabeth Clare Prophet lecture about how to invoke the healing and protection of angels.

2. **Brainwashing.** Through intensive training by way of tapes, lectures, seminars, books, and small-group meetings, devotees come to reconstruct their value system and to idolize Elizabeth Clare Prophet.

3. **Conditioning.** Converts (after turning over their earthly riches to the church, some ex-members claim) are kept exhausted and emotionally unbalanced by unceasing chants, devotions, and other exercises.

4. **Mind Control.** One's personal relationship with God is replaced with a supervising spiritual counselor. His or her concerns may include the spiritual advancement of the convert but will surely include serving as a spy for the hierarchy.

This outfit is sub-Christian in just about every important area. There is no common ground between Nazarenes (or any other orthodox church) and the Church Universal and Triumphant.[16]

Freemasonry

No doubt there are many good people who are Masons. Their works of charity and philanthropy are well known. But many Christians still have grave concerns about Freemasonry. The Church of the Nazarene joins with other Christian groups who have forbidden their members to become Masons or have gravely warned their people against the Masonic Lodge. Here is a partial list of churches who have done so: The Lutheran Church (Missouri Synod), the Presbyterian Church in America, the Greek Orthodox Church, the Free Presbyterian Church of Scotland, the Church of the Brethren, the Orthodox

---

16. If you want to read more about CUT, see Mather and Nichols, *Dictionary of Cults,* 125-28; or consult *Lambs to the Slaughter: My Fourteen Years with Elizabeth Clare Prophet and CUT,* self-published by John Joseph Pietrangelo Jr. (Tucson, Ariz., 1994).

Presbyterian Church, the Reformed Presbyterian Church, the Assemblies of God, and the Roman Catholic Church.

1. **Secrecy Versus Openness.** There has always been in America a concern, even suspicion, of the secret rites and oaths of Masonry. This became even more pronounced in 1827 when William Morgan of Batavia, New York, was apparently murdered for revealing Masonic secrets. The uproar that followed is mentioned even in the Book of Mormon. Granted, a lot of anti-Masonry talk at that time was fed by rumors, but the caution about secret orders was, many believe, appropriate—for all the rites and ceremonies of Christianity are public. Conversion, baptism, joining the church, ordination, and marriage all involve public promises, commitments, and pledges. The secrecy of Masonism is at odds with the very essence of Christian openness. Christians have nothing to hide. Thus, they have serious misgivings with secrets, blood oaths, and hidden vows. This is one rationale cited in the Nazarene *Manual*: "their secrecy contravenes the Christian's open witness" (par. 34.3).

2. **A Religious Alternative to the Church.** There can be little doubt that for many of the 4 million Masons in the United States, the lodge functions as a religious alternative to the church. And according to historian Sydney Ahlstrom, this has been the case in America for nearly 200 years.[17] Current exponents of Masonry are quick to declare that the lodge is not a religion and not a substitute for religion, but it does function that way for many.

3. **Is Masonry a Religion?** If it is, it would make perfect sense to say that one could not be a Mason and a Lutheran at the same time. One could not be a Lutheran and a Hindu or even a Methodist at the same time. American and British Masons today deny that Masonry is a religion. The problem with this contention is that many of the leading Masonic writers call Masonry a religion. John Weldon, in the *Christian Research Journal,* collects several quotations to that effect. "The religion of Masonry is cosmopolitan, universal," writes Albert G. Mackey. Henry Wilson Coil declares, "Freemasonry is undoubtedly religion. . . . Many Freemasons make this flight [to heaven] with no other guarantee of a safe landing than their belief in the religion of Freemasonry." Albert Pike wrote, "Masonry . . . is the universal, eternal, immutable religion."[18] The Nazarene General Rules cite this concern: "We hold specifically that the following practices should be avoided: . . . Membership in oath-bound secret orders or societies. The quasi-religious nature of such organizations dilutes the Christian's commitment" (*Manual,* pars. 34, 34.3, pp. 45-46).

4. **The Masonic God.** The first requirement of Masonry is to believe in God. But that does not mean that Masons worship the God of the Bible, the Christian God. The God of the Masons is called the Almighty Parent, the Supreme Being, and the Great Architect of the Universe. Masonic documents declare that a Mason's first duty is "to God, by whatever name he is known." A Mason may worship Allah, Shiva, Elleggua, Buddha, or the Great Spirit. The

17. Ahlstrom, *Religious History,* 557.
18. John Weldon, "The Masonic Lodge and the Christian Conscience," *Christian Research Journal,* winter 1994, 37.

Masonic God seems to look down from a superior vantage point on all the gods of the world's religions.

John Weldon, in "The Masonic Lodge and the Christian Conscience," quotes from a Masonic Bible (King James Version with a lengthy introduction about Masonry). He cites "The Great Light in Masonry" by Joseph Fort Newton: "For Masonry knows, what so many forget, that religions are many, but religion is one . . . therefore, it invites to its altar men of all faiths, knowing that, if they use different names for 'the nameless one with a hundred names,' they are yet praying to the one God and Father of all." Weldon asks, "When a Hindu prays to Vishnu or Shiva, is he really praying to Jesus?"[19] A Masonic leaflet says, "Freemasonry does not tell a person which religion he should practice or how he should practice it."[20]

The Southern Baptists debated the Masonic question in lengthy meetings in 1992 and 1993. A Baptist task force pointed out that "the Masonic Great Architect of the Universe appears more like the Aristotelian 'First Cause' than the personal God who has revealed Himself in the Bible."[21]

In this way, Masonry becomes guilty, many believe, of an arrogant theological minimalism. Henry Wilson Coil, in his encyclopedia on Masonry, calls the God of the Bible a mere "partisan, tribal God," implying that He is dramatically inferior to the God of Masonry, which is "a boundless, eternal, universal, undenominational, and international Divine Spirit, so vastly removed from the speck called man, that He cannot be known, named, or approached. . . . As soon as man begins to . . . endow Him with the most perfect human attributes, such as justice, mercy, beneficence, etc., the Divine essence is depreciated and despoiled."[22]

Does this sound more like the "Unmoved Mover" of deism or like Emmanuel, "God with us"?

Coil goes on to condemn monotheism, declaring that the very belief in one God violates the Masonic principles, for it requires belief in a specific kind of supreme deity.

Masonry appears to be connected in some ways with the ancient Egyptian gods Osiris, Isis, Horus, and Anun. Egyptian religion is the ancestor of the pagan traditional African religion followed to some degree by more than 100 million people today. Pro-Masonry individuals should be patient with those Christians who hesitate to bring into their fellowship Masons who embrace the lore of pagan gods.

5. Salvation. Masonry claims to be nondoctrinal. This is part of its appeal to men of all faiths. Here again, it is trapped by theological minimalism. In the final analysis, "Freemasonry strips Christianity *and every other religion* of its distinctiveness." To cite P. T. Forsyth: "Christianity is a theological religion, or it is no religion at all."[23]

---

19. Ibid., 23.
20. "What's a Mason?" (Silver Spring, Md.: Masonic Information Center), 9.
21. Weldon, "Masonic Lodge," 22.
22. Ibid., 36.
23. Stan Ingersol, "Nazarenes and Secret Societies," essay, n.d., 3.

By studying Masonic documents, one never comes to the idea of salvation by grace through faith in Jesus Christ. The Mason doesn't even have to believe in Christ. So how is a Mason to be saved? By serving whatever god he believes in and by good character and good deeds. Even though the Mason claims to be nondoctrinal, it seems to many that Masonic teaching cannot be separated from salvation by works. Certainly, no one would deride Masonry for encouraging good character and acts of charity. But Christians believe even these cannot save.

6. **Racial Integration.** One eminent historian, Carl Bangs, holds that in the United States, though there *are* Black Masons, unscrupulous persons have used the Masonic system to maintain white power structures.

7. **Different Decisions.** Weldon cites a Presbyterian study, which he summarizes as follows:

a. Joining Masonry requires actions and vows out of accord with Scripture.

b. Participation in Masonry seriously compromises the Christian faith and testimony.

c. Membership in Masonry and activity in its ritual leads to a diluting of commitment to Christ and His kingdom.[24]

The Southern Baptists, on the other hand, after an 18-month study and debate, voted that they "could not frankly state that it is wrong for a Christian to join the Masonic Lodge."[25] Thus, one can be a Southern Baptist and a Mason at the same time. Many, however, believe that the decision came because more than half a million Masons were already in Southern Baptist churches, boards, and pulpits. The vote, many fear, was not based on sound biblical or theological judgment but was merely a vote to legitimize what had already taken place. The *Scottish Rite Journal*, August 1993, called the Baptist vote "a historic and positive turning point for Freemasonry."[26]

It cannot be denied that many notable men have been Masons—Ben Franklin, George Washington, and Bob Dole, to name three. Therefore, a vote to exclude Masons from church membership due to their prior allegiance to a quasi-religious system is not the same as saying that Masons are bad people.

Really, the dilemma that one faces in wanting to join the Church of the Nazarene is quite simply solved. The Mason materials studied for this report, received from the Masonic Center in Maryland and the United Grand Lodge in England, declare with one accord the priorities of the Mason. First is duty to God. Second is his duty to his country; third, to his family; and then duty to others. All these come before his duty to Freemasonry, according to the Masonic documents themselves. If allegiance to Masonry is really no more than a fifth-level loyalty, why would not a person wanting to unite with the church simply leave the Masonic Lodge and join the Church of the Nazarene?[27]

---

24. Weldon, "Masonic Lodge," 39.

25. Ibid., 22.

26. Ibid., 20.

27. If you wish to further explore the relationship between Masonry and Christianity, contact the Christian Research Institute, P.O. Box 500—TC, San Juan Capistrano, CA 92693. The telephone number is 714-855-9926.

Christian Identity

If you encounter a church, survivalist group, or fraternal order that calls itself "Church of Israel," "Aryan Nations," "Israel Identity," or "Christian Identity," you have bumped into one of the ugliest counterfeit Christian outfits in the history of America. These groups have roots in Nazism, neo-Nazism, the Ku Klux Klan (KKK), and the notion that the White race forms the 10 lost tribes of Israel.

The groups have many forms and various particular beliefs. However, they read the same books and call the same speakers to their survivalist militia rallies and

This diabolical scheme declares that Eve and Satan had sex and whelped a half-human, half-demon race—the Jews!

conspiracy hunts. The following beliefs and practices characterize the movement:

1. **Anglo-Israelism.** They believe that the German, British, Scandinavian, and white Americans are the 10 lost tribes of Israel. This makes them God's chosen people and heirs of all God's promises. This idea got started in England by Richard Brothers (d. 1824). Later, in 1870, English minister John Wilson began to preach it. The same year, one Edward Hine established the movement in the United States.[28] His book *Identification of the British Nation with Lost Israel* is still used by Identity groups today. Yale professor A. L. Totten seconded the notion with the book *Our Race, Its Origin and Its Destiny.* It is also still on the must-read list of many Identity adherents.[29] The most vocal proponents of Anglo-Israelism in America were James Lovell of Fort Worth and Howard B. Rand of Destiny Publishers.[30]

Wesley Swift was another influential person. He helped to merge the KKK, Nazism, and the Anglo-Israel teachings into the Identity movement. "His connection to the Nazism of Hitler's Germany are unquestionable."[31] Swift teamed up with Gerald L. K. Smith, the notorious activist of the Silver Shirts, who openly supported Hitler. Swift was also a member of the KKK when he organized the Identity Church of Jesus Christ, Christian, in 1946. His tapes and books are studied and hyped by Identity people such as Richard Butler. He inherited Swift's church and founded an Identity compound called the Aryan Nations, which he located near Hayden Lake, Idaho.[32]

2. **Hatred for Jewish People.** It comes as no surprise that the Identity groups are characterized by anti-Semitism. After all, the biblical chosen people stand as a threat to these self-appointed "chosen people." Pastor Arnold Murray, Identity preacher from Gravette, Arkansas, declares that calling the Jews "the chosen people" is the gravest of sins. Some hate-mongering Identity groups pro-

28. Martin, *Kingdom of the Cults*, 306.
29. Viola Larson, "A 'Christian' Religion for White Racists," *Christian Research Journal*, fall 1992, 5. Christian Research Institute Internet file: CR00aJ11.TXT.
30. Martin, *Kingdom of the Cults*, 306.
31. Larson, "'Christian' Religion for White Racists," 6.
32. Ibid.

claim the "serpent seed" gospel. This diabolical teaching says that Eve and Satan
had sex and whelped a half-human, half-demon race, the first of which was
Cain. Somehow they leap from there to declare the whole Jewish race as half-
breed devils.[33]

One Identity preacher wrote of the Jews, "We know that as a race, they have
the sly characteristics of the serpent. . . . We know they have intimidated . . . our
own government and every government . . . through their dominance of finance,
government, church, education, and the media."[34]

But was not Jesus a Jew? How could any group say they believe in Jesus and
in the same breath call Jews half-devil beings? Howard Rand, who first coined the
term "Identity" as the name for the movement, declared that Jesus was not a Jew
from the tribe of Judah as the Bible says. Rather, He was an Aryan from the lost
tribes of Israel and the ancestor of the British, German, and Scandinavian people.[35]

3. White Supremacy. For the Identity zealots, Whites not only are superior
to their archenemy, the Jews, but are superior to all other races as well. They
teach that only the White race descended from Adam. Further, they declare that
when Gen. 1:24 refers to the creation of the "beast[s] of the earth" (KJV), it refers
to the Black, brown, and yellow races. This notion is also the basis for their rant-
ing against interracial marriage. For a White to cohabit with a person of some
"inferior, beastlike" race would diminish the superior race. Among some reli-
giously fervent Identity people, even Christians of different races should not
have fellowship, let alone get married.

Nothing could be more foreign to genuine Christianity, which teaches,
"There is neither Jew nor Greek, there is neither slave nor free, there is neither
male nor female; for you are all one in Christ Jesus" (Gal. 3:28, NKJV).

4. Feeding on Conspiracy. The Identity movement finds the calories to
keep a movement on the march by discovering as regular as mealtime a new
conspiracy to fight. Most of their "conspiracies" are imagined against the Jews.
They believe that the Jews have infiltrated all the modern institutions and are
controlling the world. Their control is aimed at doing away with the "chosen"
White race. The writings of E. Raymond Capt and Lt. Col. Jack Mohr keep the
conspiracy furnace stoked. These documents and other fraudulent sources
rehearse complex theories of how the Jews have seduced the United States government. The real Armageddon will be between the survivalist troops of Identity
and the demonic forces of the Zionist Occupation Government—the subverted
U.S. government.[36] Thus, United States government installations may become
targets in the misguided minds of the survivalist militia Identity devotees.

There is no common ground between the Church of the Nazarene and the
Identity movement. Identity teachings contradict the Bible and Christian orthodoxy at just about every point that matters.

How, then, have some Evangelicals been drawn into friendly association

33. Ibid., 3.
34. Jack Mohr, "Seed of Satan: Literal or Figurative?" (St. Louis, Mich.: n.p., n.d.), 26, cited ibid., 3.
35. Larson, "'Christian' Religion for White Racists," 6.
36. Ibid., 8.

with the Identity zealots? Identity fights abortion strongly. But if you probed the reason why, you might discover that it's not out of a biblical reverence for life but out of a concern that no superior white babies be aborted. Again, Identity opposes AIDS (acquired immune deficiency syndrome)—but if you think it's out of compassion for homosexuals, you had better think again. Prison reform is on the minds of the Aryan Nations. But Christians working for prison reform should examine the foundations of the Aryan campaign. Identity has spoken out against the disappearance of family farms; some Christians have too. But the Identity vocalizers, if you listen closely, are blaming this on the Jews and using it as a podium from which to preach hate. Identity people fought Communism. Christians did too. There are some Christians who love to spy out conspiracies. They can be as addicted to spotting a liberal behind every tree, a conspirator under every rock, a Zionist plot in every newscast. Such Christians often find themselves drawn to the Identity movement.

Genuine Christianity and the racist, violent, self-serving Christian Identity movement do not mix at any level. Pray for their souls, but create no joint endeavors with this counterfeit of Christianity.

UFO Cults

Until the Heaven's Gate incident, UFO (unidentified flying object) cults might have been thought a parlor game that not even the members took seriously. But the Heaven's Gate tragedy was a reality check. Research into these groups reveals that such outfits have been with us for hundreds of years. In the 18th century Emanuel Swedenborg claimed to have talked with aliens from other planets. In the 19th century a number of persons, mostly psychics, claimed such contact.

This "heritage" formed the launching pad for the UFO groups that have emerged in Europe and the United States during the 20th century. *The Encyclopedia of American Religions* traces such early groups as The Heralds of the New Age, the Cosmon Research Foundation, Christ Brotherhood, the Cosmic Circle of Fellowship, Uranus-Science of Life, Cosmic Star Temple, Solar Light Center, White Star, Universarian Foundation, Mark-Age, and others.[37]

Literally hundreds of UFO-type cults have been started. All began with an alleged message from a supra-human being from somewhere in space. "Historically these groups have collapsed in failure, disappointment and dissent. Promises have not been fulfilled, disasters predicted have not occurred, and nobody has been flown away by UFOs."[38]

Most of these groups have not led their disciples to death like more recent cults, such as the Order of the Solar Temple, which produced 74 suicides in 1994 and 1995. Cult members sought to find their way to the star Sirius in order to escape to a new dimension of truth and absolution far from the hypocrisies of this world. Nor have they matched the acts of Marshall Herff Applewhite, who coaxed his disciples to submit to castration and then eat poisoned pudding.

---

37. Melton, *Encyclopedia of Religions*, 559-66.
38. *Phenomenon: 40 Years of Flying Saucers,* ed. John Spencer and Hilary Evans (New York: Avon Books/BUFORA, 1988, extracted as an Internet document <ufocults.txt> by Don Allen, 1997), 4.

Applewhite, like all cult leaders, exercised a deadly power over devotees. He was the son of a Presbyterian preacher, a music teacher at a Catholic college, a song leader for Unitarian and Episcopal churches, and a homosexual. He also claimed to be Jesus, an extraterrestrial from the "Level Above Human," and one of the "Two Witnesses of Revelation" (the other was his female consort, Bonnie Lu Nettles, who died in 1985). Applewhite, it is believed, was himself dying of cancer. No wonder it was time to catch the Hale-Bopp starship.

Characteristics of UFO Cults

The UFO cults are so diverse that they defy generalization. Nevertheless, some notions appear again and again. For example, most interpret many happenings in history as UFO events. Mount Sinai bursting with clouds and smoke and fire was a UFO contact with Moses. His earlier encounter with the burning bush was the same thing. Ezekiel's vision of the wheel within the wheel is universally claimed by UFO cults as a UFO encounter. The dimming of the sun at the Crucifixion and the "dancing sun" at the Fatima shrine in 1917 were too.

Another common denominator among most UFO/New Age cults is a gnosticism that regards the human body as inferior, even despicable. It is regarded as a shell, as a container or "soul holder." They regard the stereotypical space body—scrawny torso, small limbs, large head (signifying a powerful intellect)—as superior to the beastlike human body.

All UFO cults believe that they are in touch with alien beings from somewhere else. Some say the "space brothers" are from distant planets. Others say they spring from a superior race from the inner earth, while others say they are future earthlings with the kind of bodies and brains that the race will have at the peak of evolution.

Basic Kinds of UFO Cults

There seem to be two kinds of UFO groups. The Aquarian/New Age groups tend to see the space visitors as friends come to lead us to a higher level of existence, to salvation. Mixing New Age optimism, Eastern meditation, astral religion, occultism, UFO lore, computer technology, science fiction, and distorted Christianity, they believe that the space brothers are here to help us cleanse our souls in preparation for the next level of life. Such groups as One World Family, The Light Affiliates, Brotherhood of the Seven Rays, Light of the Universe, Understanding, the Association of Sananda, and even Heaven's Gate fit in this category.

On the other hand, some regard the invaders from space as malevolent. Some UFO aficionados claim that the space men have been raping, abducting, and experimenting with humans as if they were mere lab animals. They mean us harm.

The space invaders, they say, are former Masters of this planet. Probably in the form of extremely intelligent dinosaurs, they "bred" the human race the way we breed horses and dogs to be our servants. The former Masters bred humans to be their watchdogs and war dogs. They instilled in them an aggression as fierce as a rottweiler defending its territory. They made mistakes, like giving their "dogs of war" too much intelligence and a maniacal ego. And like the Dobermans of *They Only Kill Their Masters,* the humans turned on their Masters and drove them from (or deep into) the planet. The former Masters want their planet back.[39]

But they are not going to reclaim it by warfare. Rather, they have been trying for 5,000 years to get it back by selling the earthlings a religion that will make them willingly submit to superior beings.

This started, the theory goes, when Moses, a henchman of the former Masters, dished out the Ten Commandments in an attempt to muzzle the race. Then Jesus was sent by the Conspirators to get the rebellious "Luciferian" earthlings to adopt a philosophy of turning the other cheek, walking the second mile, and forgiving enemies. Jesus, however,

> *The Damascus Road experience of Paul was not a conversion experience, but a UFO abduction, according to UFO aficionados.*

failed miserably. No one was more surprised than He when the Masters deserted Him and left Him to die on the Cross. Next the Master Conspirators made a deal with a compulsive Jew to subdue the race with Christianity. The Damascus Road experience of Paul was not a conversion experience, but a UFO abduction. They then set Paul loose in the world.

In 1917 at the Shrine of Fatima in Portugal, the flying saucers put on a dazzling display of lights and laser, smoke, and the dropping of "angel hair." People reported seeing the sun dance, move toward the earth, hover, and spin. One observer described the "sun" as two disks of stainless steel. But most said that what they saw was the Virgin Mary. Again, the former Masters of the earth were out to give religion a boost in order to get humanity to surrender freedom and autonomy.

The former Masters of the earth then became a bit more aggressive, possessing the mind and soul of Adolf Hitler. He was controlled by the Society of Green Men and often had encounters with entities that no one else could see. The little man with green gloves who holds the keys to the Kingdom of Agharti (the inner earth) was said to be his personal contact with the Masters. He was so possessed that even though he lived and died a Catholic, he persecuted the Church almost as viciously as he did its parent, Judaism. When the Russians invaded Berlin, they captured or killed 1,000 space aliens but mistook them for Orientals—or so says David Barclay in *Aliens, the Final Answer?*[40]

The Roman Catholic Church, according to the cultists, knows all about this league with the earth's former Masters. A number of presidents and kings know or have known of it, but the cover-up continues. Several kings, popes, and presidents have been killed, it is claimed, when it looked as if they would reveal the secret conspiracy.

That hundreds, even thousands, of people really believe this sort of fantasy is disturbing. How could such irrational beliefs flourish in our enlightened age?

---

39. David Barclay, *Aliens, the Final Answer?* (London: Blanford Books, 1995), 69.
40. Ibid., 171-72.

For such ideologies to grow, they must have a fertile soil. An article in *Newsweek* said on July 8, 1996, "America is hooked on the paranormal." It appears that most Americans believe in UFOs as alien spacecraft. If you walk down the street today during your lunch break and encounter 100 people, 14 of them will claim to have seen a UFO—according to a 1990 Gallup Poll.

Other than a distortion of a few Christian ideas that are so warped as to be positively unchristian, the UFO cults have no connection with the gospel of Jesus Christ.

Review and Reflection

1. If you were a full-fledged member of one of the religious groups examined in this chapter, and an Evangelical Christian friend witnessed to you, which of the following do you think would have the most positive results?

   a. A forceful and clear theological argument

   b. A testimony of what Christ had done for the Christian friend

   c. Genuine expressions of love and respect

   d. Citing Bible verses that prove the cult is wrong

   e. Other

2. Each of the groups treated in this chapter add something to, subtract something from, or actually replace the classic Christian and biblical teaching that salvation by grace is through faith in God and the atoning work of Jesus Christ. Now is a good time to affirm your faith in how salvation comes to us. In your devotions this week, study these scriptures:

Rom. 10:8-13; Acts 4:12; Rom. 3:21-25; John 3:16

Sing your faith this week. Make these three Charles Wesley hymns, which make the doctrine of redemption very clear, a part of your devotional times:

"Arise, My Soul, Arise"
"O for a Thousand Tongues to Sing"
"And Can It Be?"

In the Nazarene hymnal *Sing to the Lord,* these songs are hymn Nos. 432, 147, and 225.

PART IX
NON-CHRISTIAN RELIGIONS

- Judaism and Islam

- Eastern Religions: Buddhism and Hinduism

- New Age Thought: The South Wind Blew Softly

JUDAISM AND ISLAM

Historical Overview

Judaism, Christianity, and Islam trace their biological and spiritual roots back to Abraham. The Muslims descended from the Abraham-Hagar side of the family by way of Ishmael. Judaism springs from Abraham and Sarah, their son Isaac, grandson Jacob, and his fourth son, Judah, who gave his name to a nation and a faith. Judaism is the oldest of the three religions. Christianity, if dated at the resurrection of Jesus, dates to about A.D. 33. Islam was born in A.D. 570, when Muhammad wove together elements of Judaistic and Christian monotheism with the worship of Allah, one of the 360 deities worshiped in Mecca and the patron god of an Abrahamic cult.

Core Beliefs

All three religions believe in one God (monotheism), the Old Testament scriptures, and moral living. They quickly part company, however, over other extremely critical issues. Judaism adamantly rejects the very heart of the Christian faith by denying that Jesus Christ was divine, born of a virgin, resurrected, or is the Messiah. They also reject the inspiration of the New Testament and deny original sin.

Christianity and Islam part company on the Trinity; the deity, death, and resurrection of Christ; the authority of the Bible (they put the Koran first); salvation by grace through faith; a personal relationship with Christ; the status of women; and the nature of eternal rewards and punishments.

Judaism, Islam, and Christianity Today

The adherents of Judaism today number 20 million, with 3.1 million adult believers in the United States. Globally, there are 1.1 billion Muslims, with 527,000 adult adherents in the United States. Christians number 2 billion worldwide, with American churches reporting 151 million adult adherents.

Similarities, yes. But these religions are different in important ways.

23

Judaism and Islam

CHRISTIANITY, JUDAISM, AND ISLAM all honor the Old Testament, they believe in one God, they all embrace righteous living, and they all trace their roots to Abraham. You would think that, like three brothers, they would have a lot in common—and they do.

But just as brothers grow up and go off in different directions, so have these religions. And just as brothers often fight, these "descendants of Abraham" have struggled for centuries, marking human history powerfully, sometimes for better, sometimes for worse. They share some beliefs and practices, but they are very different in important ways.

Judaism, in Covenant with the God Beyond Gods

The Hebrew people of the ancient period were ahead of their times. They "experienced liberation from the gods, at the call of the very life of Being itself . . . the God beyond gods."[1]

Every Christian should have a deep respect and love for the Jewish people and heritage. These people who discovered the "God beyond gods" were chosen to bring the Savior, Jesus Christ, to the world. In addition, the Old Testament scriptures were handed to us by a rich Jewish tradition. The accounts of creation, of the exploits of the patriarchs, of the Exodus; the beauty of the Psalms; the dire warnings of the prophets; the Ten Commandments; and the promise of the Messiah are all Christian scripture too. Often the thirsty hearts and souls of Jews and Christians drink from the same fountain.

The roots of Judaism reach all the way back to the dawn of history, Adam and Eve in the Garden of Eden, where they fell into sin and receive a promise of redemption. Later, God gives to Noah a covenant rainbow sign. Moses receives the Ten Commandments—the rules of the covenant. And with the pact between God and Abraham, the Hebrew people become truly a covenant people. Still today, every devout Jew understands himself or herself as living in covenant with God.

---

1. Richard E. Wentz, *Religion in the New World* (Minneapolis: Fortress Press, 1990), 233.

A History of Hate—from Herod to Hitler

No evaluation of Judaism can ignore the frightful persecution that the Jewish people have endured. Herod slaughtered Jewish babies, hoping the Christ child would be among them. The Romans destroyed the Temple in A.D. 70 and drove the Jews out of their homeland in A.D. 135. Wherever the Jews of the Diaspora went, bitter persecution followed. James R. Leaman sees the very hand of Satan in this: "The root of anti-Semitism is Satan's hatred for the Jewish people. Satan is the first and foremost anti-Semite."[2]

Leaman goes on to point out that Satan wants to prevent Christians from witnessing to the Jews about Jesus the Savior. The damnation of God's chosen people is a victory for the devil.

How so-called Christians have furthered Satan's design is remarkable. For centuries, rather than witness to Jews, "Christians" have labeled them "Christ killers" and hounded them mercilessly. En route to the Holy Land, the Crusaders plundered Jewish communities. Once in Jerusalem, these warriors with the cross emblazoned on their shields performed "brave" deeds like herding Jews into a synagogue and burning them and their place of worship.

> *Crusaders, with the cross emblazoned on their shields, performed "brave" deeds like herding Jews into a synagogue and burning them and their place of worship.*

In order to rid the church of heretics, the Spanish Inquisition viciously attacked Christianized Jews, whom they called Marranos (swine). Jews were jailed, tortured, and burned in devil costumes.[3]

Jews were blamed for every misfortune from the burning of Rome to the Black Death plague. They were forced to live in ghettos throughout "Christian" Europe. Pope Innocent III (1198—1216) issued a decree forcing every Jew to wear a yellow badge so Christians could avoid them. On Good Friday and Easter in Toulouse, France, a Jewish rabbi was always arrested and beaten in public as punishment for killing Christ. On at least one occasion the rabbi was killed. In 1492, the same year that "Columbus sailed the ocean blue" as commissioned by Ferdinand and Isabella, the same king and queen expelled all Jews from Spain and confiscated their wealth. Actually, the Jews fared better in Muslim countries than in Christian Europe.[4]

In modern times, Hitler carried out the diabolical holocaust, slaughtering millions of Jews, whose only "crime" was their ethnicity. Anti-Semitism is alive and well today, being hawked by Christian Identity groups, skinheads, the Ku Klux Klan, Aryan Nations, and neo-Nazis. "To be a Jew is to inherit a history of

---

2. James R. Leaman, *Faith Roots* (Nappanee, Ind.: Evangel Press, 1993), 86.
3. Ibid., 90.
4. Ibid.

pain, misunderstanding . . . persecution, and martyrdom, often at the hands of Christians."[5]

Judaism in America

The Sephardim were the first Jews to come to America. For the most part, they were highly educated and well-to-do. By the middle of the 19th century only 3,000 Jews lived in the United States. But many thousands immigrated during the last quarter of that century. Many of the new Jewish immigrants were poor people from eastern Europe. They were something of an embarrassment to the Sephardim, who had made fortunes in "St. Brendan's Land Promised to the Saints." To the Polish, Russian, and Ukrainian Jews fresh from the shtetlach (ghettos), the American Jews were not Jews at all.[6] Today Jews in America number more than 7 million.

Protestant Christianity has divided itself into many sects and denominations. Judaism has done the same thing until now Judaism in America defies generalization. What follows is a description of its more traditional branches in America.

1. Theology. Judaism is more a way of life than a belief system. A devout Jew feels that God, rather than a confession of faith, has revealed to him or her how to live.

Richard Wentz illustrates this fact by citing Chaim Potok's novel *The Promise*. There a Jewish philosophy teacher, one Professor Gordon, claims to be an atheist. Still, Gordon observes the high holy days and says his prayers every Sabbath. Hypocritical? No, he shows that "the full meaning of a religious tradition is not always reducible to our ability to believe, to reason, or explain." Perhaps Gordon, weighing the realism of the holocaust, can find no reason to proclaim that he "believes in God." Yet he knows he is a Jew, and Jewish people do certain things like praying certain prayers and keeping certain times holy.[7]

Moses Maimonides, a 12th-century Jewish philosopher and teacher, put Jewish theology into a creed that is still esteemed by traditional Judaism today:

> *I believe with perfect faith that*
> 1. the Creator, blessed be His Name, is the Creator and Guide of everything that has been created; and He alone has made, does make, and will make all things;
> 2. the Creator, blessed be His Name, is One, and that there is no unity in any manner like unto His, and that He alone is our God, who was, and is, and will be;
> 3. the Creator, blessed be His Name, is not a body, and that He is free from all the properties of matter, and that He has not any form whatever;
> 4. the Creator, blessed be His Name, is the first and the last;

---

5. Ibid., 126.
6. Wentz, *Religion in the New World*, 230.
7. Ibid., 238.

5. to the Creator, blessed be His Name, and to Him alone, it is right to pray, and that it is not right to pray to any being besides Him;

6. all the words of the prophets are true;

7. the prophecy of Moses, our teacher, peace be unto him, was true, and that he was the chief of the prophets, both of those who preceded and of those who followed him;

8. the whole *Torah*, now in our possession, is the same that was given to Moses, our teacher, peace be unto him;

9. this *Torah* will not be changed, and there will never be any other Law from the Creator, blessed be His Name;

10. the Creator, blessed be His Name, knows every deed of children and men, and all their thoughts, as it is said. It is He that fashioned the hearts of them all, that gives heed to all their works;

11. the Creator, blessed be His Name, rewards those that keep His commandments and punishes those that transgress them;

12. the Messiah will come, and though he tarry, I will wait daily for his coming;

13. there will be a revival of the dead at the time when it shall please the Creator, blessed be His Name.[8]

2. Sacred Writings. The Torah (first five books of the Bible) is the most cherished writing. In this book the "God beyond gods" has revealed His will and the way to live. Reflections on the Torah (the Law, the Teaching) have produced volumes of commentary. The Mishnah and the Gemara (commentaries on the Torah) form the Talmud.

The Hebrew Bible is composed of the 39 books of the Old Testament. It is called *Tanakh*, derived from the initials TNK, which stand for Torah (Pentateuch), Nevi'im (Prophets), and Ketuvim (Writings).

3. Sabbath. The seventh day is a holy day for Jewish people, commemorating the rest of God after six days of creation and after the glorious work of freeing His children from Egyptian bondage. It is regarded as a precious jewel, a gift from God himself.

It may be a day of rest, relaxation, or recuperation, but that is not its real meaning. Shabbat is something lovely that happens. The tradition says that Sabbath is like a bride who comes to us graciously, elegantly, waiting for our attention. Shabbat is feminine, a queen, coming into creation, hallowing it. This is eternity in time. Six days a week there is little mind for beauty, for the likeness of God. We work under stress, are driven by anxiety and immersed in worry. But the Sabbath will come on the seventh day, like a lover, to remind us that we are more than all this concern with things.[9]

The Sabbath meal is a special occasion in Jewish homes. A celebration of hope and devotion, it is a dress-up meal with candles that is served just before sundown and introduced with the blessing, "Blessed art Thou, Lord our God, King of the Universe, who has sanctified us with His commandments and commanded us to kindle the Sabbath lights."[10]

---

8. Josh McDowell, *A Ready Defense* (San Bernardino, Calif.: Here's Life Publishers, 1990), 297.

9. Wentz, *Religion in the New World,* 240.

10. Ibid., 241.

4. Sacred Feasts and Fasts

Passover is a spring festival held at the beginning of the harvest. It commemorates deliverance from Egyptian slavery.

Shabout, the Feast of Weeks, comes seven weeks after Passover and celebrates the giving of the Ten Commandments. In ancient times, farmers would offer the firstfruits of their harvest at the Temple.

Rosh Hashanah means "head of the year." It is the Jewish New Year, celebrated on the first two days of the month of Tishri (September-October).

Yom Kippur, the Day of Atonement, is the holiest day of the Jewish year. It comes 10 days after Rosh Hashanah and is given to fasting, repentance, and reconciliation with God and one's fellow human beings.

Sukkoth, the Feast of Tabernacles, or Booths, is a harvest festival. In ancient times the people traveled to the Temple, sleeping in makeshift booths on their journey to offer part of the harvest. See Exod. 34:18-26.

Hanukkah commemorates the heroic revolt of the Maccabees (167 B.C.). They took the Temple back from Antiochus Epiphanes, the foreign ruler who tried to dishearten the Jews by performing such blasphemies as offering swine in the holy of holies. The Menorah, the eight-branched candlestick burning for eight days and nights, signaled the cleansing of the Temple.

Purim, celebrated on the 14th day of the month of Adar, commemorates the deliverance of the Jews from the plot of Haman in Esther's time.

All of the feasts and fasts are related to events in history in which the "God beyond gods" acted in redemptive ways. The ritual expressions remind the Jews that they are a covenant people.

Five Varieties of Judaism

There are many expressions of Judaism in America today. Here five principal groups are briefly described.

1. Orthodox Judaism is the oldest form of that religion in America. It teaches adherence to the traditional mode of doing Judaistic religion. It reveres the Scriptures, the Sabbath, and the feasts and fasts described in the foregoing paragraphs. Orthodox schools today include Yeshivos Seminaries of Torah Studies; Yeshiva University; and Hebrew Theological College, Chicago.

2. Reform Judaism represents the most liberal wing of Judaism in America. They have made a distinct effort to fit into the modern Gentile world. They challenged traditional liturgies, ceremonies, feasts and fasts, traditional garb, the idea of "chosenness," and the use of the Hebrew language in worship. They want Jews to become productive participants in the broader society. They seem to have used mainline Protestantism as a model for transforming Jewish life and practice. They are active in such Reform associations as the National Federation of Temple Brotherhoods, National Association of Temple Educators, and the World Union for Progressive Judaism. Hebrew Union College of Cincinnati is its foremost educational institution.

3. Conservative Judaism came about as a middle way between the right (Orthodox) and the left (Reform) Judaism. This movement calls itself the United Synagogue of America. The Hebrew language is retained in worship services, and the kosher dietary laws are preserved. Many Conservatives see the Reform movement as a "sellout to modernity."[11]

4. **Reconstructionist Judaism** follows the dreams of Mordecai Kaplan, a professor at Conservative Jewish Theological Seminary, New York. Kaplan saw Judaism as a civilization, a way of living together in productive harmony rather than a religion. He set out to create a Judaism that was in touch with modern American life. Reconstructionist Rabbinical College of Philadelphia is its most prominent school.

5. **Humanistic Judaism** is comprised mainly of Jewish agnostics—and atheists. It rejects the idea of a transcendent God and focuses religion and morality on the needs and desires of the "becoming" person or self. Sherwin Wine founded the most representative association of this movement in 1969, called the Society for Humanistic Judaism.

Christianity and Judaism

Jewish writer Pinchas Lapide comments:

> We Jews and Christians are joined in brotherhood at the deepest level, so deep in fact that we have overlooked it and missed the forest of brotherhood for the trees of theology. We have an intellectual and spiritual kinship which goes deeper than dogmatics, hermeneutics, and exegesis. We are brothers . . .
> —in the belief of one God our Father.
> —in the hope of His salvation.
> —in humility before His omnipotence.
> —in the knowledge that we belong to Him and He to us.
> —in doubt about our wavering fidelity.
> —in the paradox that we are dust and yet the image of God.
> —in the consciousness that God wants us as partners in the sanctification of the world.
> —in the conviction that love of God is crippled without love of neighbor.[12]

And yet there are significant differences—differences so immense that dialogue and cooperation are difficult. The first is the denial of Judaism that Jesus

was the Messiah,

the Son of God,

the Savior of the world.

Christians everywhere pray for the day when the spiritual eyes of our Jewish friends will be opened and they will embrace the Messiah, their Messiah, Jesus the Christ.

Missing the saving grace of God in Christ, our Jewish friends labor on believing that salvation will come if they keep the holy days and master the 613 *mitzvoth* (commandments) of the Torah. Protestant Christians are quite sure that salvation is by grace alone, through faith in Jesus Christ alone.

Another key point of divergence is that most followers of Judaism deny original sin. They teach that humanity is basically good. Thus, sin is only an *act*

---

11. Ibid., 249.
12. McDowell, *Ready Defense*, 302.

to be forgiven and not a *state* for which cleansing is needed. Christians, particularly Wesleyan-Holiness Christians, believe that original sin is at the root of acts of sin. Our theology and practice aims at holiness of heart and life. We believe the Bible teaches that we are born in sin and need the cleansing that only the Holy Spirit can provide. The Nazarene Articles of Faith cite five Old Testament passages in which we believe the doctrine of original sin is taught.[13]

A third point of disagreement is the Judaistic rejection of the New Testament as the inspired Word of God. If they accepted this, of course, the problems with salvation by works and original sin would quite likely be resolved.

Even given these significant differences, there are several arenas in which Christians, including Nazarene Christians, can work together with Jews for a better world.

In the struggle against the many deities of New Age whimsy, we will find no stronger ally on monotheism than Judaism.

Also, in promoting the sanctity of marriage, the dignity of women and children, and family values, we will find strong partners among our Jewish friends.

Jews and Christians already find themselves in league against social injustice, economic discrimination, violations of human rights, and racial inequality.

Islam

More than 1 billion people on our planet claim a nominal or fanatic allegiance to the Islamic faith. The most populous Islamic nation is Indonesia, where 100 million believers declare, "There is no god but Allah, and Muhammad is his messenger." The Arabic nations, Turkey, Russia, and Africa also claim large numbers of Muslims.

Islam traces its roots to Abraham through Hagar and Ishmael and from them to its founder, Muhammad. He was born in A.D. 570 and was orphaned early and raised by relatives. As a young man, he grew introspective and somber. He was given to visions, dreams, and to seizures that may have been due to religious ecstasy.

He married a woman 15 years his senior, Khadijah. Muhammad's visionary life intensified. One day as he prayed in a cave, he became

> *"There is no god but Allah, and Muhammad is his messenger."*

possessed or filled with a spirit of prophecy, a demon, or an angel of God—he wasn't sure which. But he was ordered to recite the words supernaturally impressed upon his mind. Being illiterate, he could not write them down, so he memorized them.

Distraught, he fled the cave of prayer with thoughts of jumping off a cliff to keep from being possessed by an unknown spirit. He had always despised the Arabic soothsayers who claimed divine visions. Now it had happened to him. He would rather be dead. But as he fled, he was encountered by a divine being

---

13. *Manual, Church of the Nazarene, 1997—2001,* 28.

"astride the horizon" who called him the "Apostle of God."[14] Still, he was not convinced that the new revelations were from God, but his wife, Khadijah, and others soon convinced him that they were indeed from God himself.

More trips to the cave brought more revelations. In his town of Mecca, Muhammad began to preach his doctrines. He insisted that there was only one God. The 360 deities worshiped in Mecca were false—or 359 of them were. One Abrahamic cult that had spread throughout the area worshiped a god called Allah. Perhaps Muhammad believed that these cultists had direct connection to the monotheism of Judaism and Christianity. He believed that their belief in one God was superior to the primitive idol worship of Mecca. It is certain that Muhammad had contact with both the Jews and Christians of his day. He began to preach and teach that Allah was the one true God.

Predictably, he was resisted and persecuted. Some of his followers were put to death. Soon the city of Medina invited Muhammad to make his headquarters there. They offered him a throne and an army. On July 22, A.D. 622, the devotees made their move to Medina (City of the Prophet). All Islamic calendars mark this date as their beginning. It is called the Hegira (the flight).[15]

By the time of his sudden death just 10 years later, Muhammad, as the spiritual and civil leader, had subjected most of the Arab world to Islamic rule. Those who did not convert were driven out or killed. Within a century, Islamic armies had established a huge empire that stretched from Spain in the west to India in the East.

Over time, a number of different sects of Islam developed. The principal ones are the Sunnis, the Sufis, and the Shi'ites.

The Sunnis look to the Koran, the *Sunna* (or practice) of the Prophet, the *hadith* (traditions), Islamic law (*Sharia*), consensus of the community (*Ijma*), and to reason (*O'yas*) as the foundation for making personal and political decisions. The Sunnis appear to be the more moderate group.

The Sufis are those who have added mysticism to the rather legalistic, cold, and formal worship of mainstream Islam.

The Shi'ites form the most radical group. They claim to have descended from Muhammad himself and hold that only a direct heir should be the prime leader of Islam. This group of Islamic fundamentalists have taken power in Iran.

From the Shi'ites, it seems, come many of the extremists, radicals, and terrorists who push to the forefront Muhammad's sayings about jihad, or holy war against the infidels. Jews, capitalists, and Communists are the "great Satans" against which the radical Shi'ites war. Islamic fundamentalists wage terrorist campaigns in many parts of the world. As only one example, *Time* magazine (October 6, 1997, 50) reported the butchering of tens of thousands of Algerians by the Armed Islamic Group and the Islamic Salvation Front.

Most followers of Islam are sincere, peace-loving people. They will let you know that mainstream Muslims are not like the terrorists who use Allah's name to justify their violence.

14. Norman Anderson, *The World's Religions* (Grand Rapids: Wm. B. Eerdmans Publishing Co., 1976), 52.
15. McDowell and Stewart, *Handbook of Today's Religions*, 380.

Core Beliefs of Islam

The Muslim religion is built around five beliefs and five practices.

The Five Doctrines

The five doctrines all Muslims are called upon to believe are:

1. **There Is One True God—Allah.** He is transcendent, so far above us that He is unknowable. To speak of a personal relationship with God or to call Him "Father" is a blasphemy. Allah is sovereign, running the universe as He pleases. Everything that happens is His will. Allah is the Author of both good and evil. He blesses those who obey Him and punishes those who don't. Muhammad was sure that the Christian doctrine of the Trinity was a fantasy. The Koran declares, "Unbelievers are those who say, 'God is one in three'" (Sura 7:73).[16]

The Koran sees Jesus as a prophet—but not as a Savior and not as the Son of God. "Jesus is like Adam in the sight of God. He created him from dust and then said to him, 'Be' and he was" (Sura 3:59). "Jesus is not God's Son, for God has no Son. Jesus . . . was only a messenger of Allah. . . . Far be it removed from His transcendent majesty that He should have a Son" (Sura 4:171; 43:82; 5:116; 19:88).[17]

According to Muslims, Jesus did not die on the Cross. Most Muslims believe that Judas was substituted for Jesus while Jesus was spirited away to heaven. Jesus did not die and was therefore never resurrected. Easter is a farce to Muslims. Jesus did not bring the final revelation from God—Muhammad did that.

2. **Angels.** Angels were created by Allah from light. They do not have what humans call "free will" but obey God instinctively. "Angels protect humans, keep [Allah]'s records, deliver [His] messages, and administer [His] punishment."[18] Two angels are assigned to each person. One writes down every bad deed. The other records good deeds. At the Judgment a good deed outweighs a bad one 10 to 1.

3. **Revelation.** The Muslims believe that four books are inspired by Allah. The first three are: the Torah (the first five books of our Bible), the Psalms of David, the Gospel of Christ. However, the Jews and Christians have allowed their sacred books to be corrupted. Therefore Allah gave one last holy revelation—the Koran. This book is, according to the Islam Internet home page, "a record of the exact words revealed by God through the Angel Gabriel to the Prophet Muhammad. . . . It was memorized by Muhammad . . . and then dictated to his Companions, and written down by scribes. . . . Not one word of its 114 chapters, Suras, has been changed over the centuries, so that the Quran is in every detail the unique and miraculous text which was revealed to Muhammad."[19] Thus, the Koran has precedence over the Bible. "The Quran, the last revealed Word of God, is the prime source of every Muslim's faith and practice."[20]

---

16. John Conlon, "Why Is It So Difficult to Witness to a Muslim?" *Herald of Holiness*, January 1993, 25.
17. Ibid., 26.
18. Matt Zahniser, "Islam: Where God Is Great," in Miller, *Misguiding Lights?* 34.
19. *Understanding Islam and the Muslims*, "What Is the Quran?"
<http://linus.hartford.edu/"grant Islam/unis.html>, April 25, 1997.
20. "What Is the Quran About?" ibid.

4. **Prophets.** Some of the prophets have been Adam, Noah, Abraham, Moses, David, and Jesus. But the greatest of them all was Muhammad.

5. **Judgment.** Those who have obeyed Allah and Muhammad will be rewarded at the Judgment by being sent to the Muslim heaven, called paradise. It is a place of pleasure where men "will recline on soft couches quaffing cups of wine handed to them by Huris, or maidens of Paradise, of whom each man may marry as many as he pleases."[21] Others will be condemned to the torments of hell, though no true Muslim, it seems, will stay there forever.

Muslims do not know whether they are on the road to paradise or hell. They know they must earn their salvation by racking up good deeds aplenty. But in the end Kismet, the doctrine of fate, determines everything. This rigid predestination leads many to shrug, "It is the will of Allah," when challenged by adversity.

The Five Practices

The Muslim is to add to the five doctrines the five observances or practices. They are

1. **The Creed (*Kalima*).** In order to become a Muslim, one must declare publicly, "There is no god but Allah, and Muhammad is his prophet." This is to be repeated many times a day.

2. **Prayer (*Salat*).** At five appointed times during the day, the Muslim is to recite prescribed prayers in a prescribed position (standing, kneeling, face to the ground, and so on), facing Mecca.

3. **Alms for the Poor (*Zakat*).** Muhammad was himself an orphan and thus had sensitivity for the poor. At the end of each year, the devout Muslim is to give 2.5 percent of his wealth in an offering for the poor. This is one way that he earns entry into paradise.

4. **Fasting (*Ramadan*).** During the month of Ramadan, devout Muslims are expected to fast from sunrise to sunset. Most families eat a meal before dawn and another after dark. The fast is aimed at promoting self-control and empathy with the destitute. Eating, drinking, smoking, and sexual comforts are forbidden during this time.

5. **Pilgrimage (*Hajj*).** If physically able, the Muslim is expected to make a pilgrimage to Mecca to worship the Ka'aba shrine. If he or she cannot make the trip, it is wise to send someone in his or her place, because this is important in avoiding hell and achieving paradise.[22]

Other distinctive Muslim practices include avoiding pork, refraining from gambling, and not drinking alcoholic beverages. Males and females have distinct dress codes as well.

Islam and Christianity

As eager as Christians may be to find common ground with Muslims, such a commodity is hard to find. Islam and Christianity share a common thread of history back to Abraham. But footing for ecumenical dialogue and service is dif-

---

21. Anderson, *World's Religions*, 81; cited by McDowell and Stewart, *Handbook of Today's Religions*, 390.
22. McDowell and Stewart, *Handbook of Today's Religions*, 391.

ficult to discover when Islam refutes just about every core doctrine of Christianity. Muslims deny

the authority of the Bible
the existence of the Trinity
the deity of Jesus Christ
the death and resurrection of Christ
salvation by grace through faith
the possibility of a personal relationship with Christ

One other point is troublesome for Christians. The historic status of females in some Islamic nations is a violation of the dignity that the Bible and Christianity give to women. The Koran tells the Muslim that women are "your tillage" (your field to plow and seed). Marriage and sex are for the sole purpose of producing offspring. Children are an important measure of wealth and manhood. Therefore, in the early centuries a man was permitted to have up to four wives, and he was expected to impregnate all the concubines he could. It is true that in the Koran Muhammad urged men to treat their wives kindly, but he also said, "Men have authority over women because God has made the one superior to the other and because they spend their wealth [to maintain them]. So good women are obedient, guarding the unseen [parts] because God has guarded [them]. As for those from whom you fear disobedience, admonish them and banish them to beds apart and beat them" (Sura 4:31). In too many Islamic cultures, the situation has improved little. In some cultures, Islamic women are limited to domestic roles.

Some Islamic countries permit men to divorce a wife for just about any reason, but a woman cannot divorce her husband. Usually a woman's marriage is brokered by her father. In America, Muslims are quick to point out that women are full human persons in their own right and can own property. Further, they say that though parents arrange her marriage, no Muslim girl is forced to marry against her will.

Most Christians (including Nazarenes) and Muslims wish to be at peace with each other. They can respect each other but must, it seems, stop short of embracing each other's core beliefs and must not act as if the differences are trivial.

Mennonite missionary David W. Shenk points out a basic difference between Christianity and Islam. It is the difference between Hegira and the Cross. Jesus reached the peak of His popularity about the time that He fed the 5,000. The Galileans wanted to make Him their king. Jesus had already said no to a similar offer from the devil. Satan took Him to the top of a high mountain and showed Him all the kingdoms of the world. Jesus declined to win His following through political and military power. He chose, rather, the way of the Cross.

On the other hand, when Muhammad encountered persecution in Mecca, the city of Medina offered him a throne, an army, and a kingdom. Muhammad said yes. His flight to Medina (the Hegira) was a "flight from suffering to a triumph assured through political and military power. By contrast, the Cross is a

23. David W. Shenk, "What's the Difference Between a Muslim and a Christian?" *Gospel Herald,* November 20, 1990, 794.

flight from triumphalism to a ministry of suffering and redemptive love."[23] The Cross and the Hegira move in opposite directions. They invite people to very different perceptions of the nature of God and His kingdom. This foundational difference shows up in a hundred aspects of the two religions.

Witnessing to Muslims

Confrontation is not the way for Christians to witness to Muslims. This has failed miserably for 14 centuries. Muslims, like Christians, hold sincere beliefs that are reinforced by culture and a religion that is a way of life. John Conlon gives us a useful clue about witnessing to Muslims. He points out that "people may have opposite views, but they still have similar needs."[24] Islamic faith has vulnerabilities. Its cold legalism, remote God (Allah), and dependence on fate leave the human heart without assurance of salvation, with no relationship with God, no sense of peace, and no idea of a loving God of grace. Conlon invites Christians to so live that these elements that form the very heart of Christian experience are gently seen and noticed. In this way they may want to take a closer look at the Jesus who brings peace, healing, forgiveness, and love.

Perhaps the best hope for meaningful Christian-Islamic theological dialogue will come from listening to the Christians who persevere so admirably in semihostile Islam-dominated countries. Christian communities in Egypt, Armenia, Syria, Lebanon, Ethiopia, and the West Bank have tenaciously preserved their ancient Christian heritage in Muslim states. They have been in limited dialogue with their Muslim neighbors for years, at least at the level needed for survival. Walter J. Harrelson suggests that the dialogue could begin around three concepts: (1) the nature of God's "oneness," since both religions are monotheistic; (2) the role of redemptive suffering in the two religions; and (3) the character of divine revelation in the Scriptures.[25]

When it comes to sharing Christ with our Muslim friends and our Jewish brothers and sisters, we find a model in Paul. Our prayers should be as urgent as his when he wrote, "I tell the truth in Christ, I am not lying. . . . I have great sorrow and continual grief in my heart. For I could wish that I myself were accursed from Christ for my brethren, my kinsmen according to the flesh, who are Israelites, to whom pertain the adoption, the glory, the covenants . . . and the promises" (Rom. 9:1-4, NKJV).

Review and Reflection

1. Distinctive teachings of the Wesleyan heritage of Nazarenes include the following:
   original sin
   salvation by grace alone through faith in Christ
   entire sanctification; holiness
   assurance; the witness of the Spirit

24. Conlon, "Why Is It So Difficult . . . ?" 27.

25. Randal M. Falk and Walter J. Harrelson, Jews and Christians in Pursuit of Social Justice (Nashville: Abingdon, 1996), 134-37.

Compare and contrast these four Wesleyan distinctives with the teachings of Judaism and Islam as found in this chapter.

2. In thinking about relating to your Jewish and Islamic neighbors, ponder the advice of John Conlon: "People may have opposite views, but they still have similar needs." What are the implications of this idea when it comes to

interfaith dialogue?

cooperative community actions?

witnessing for Christ to Jews or Muslims?

EASTERN RELIGIONS:
BUDDHISM AND HINDUISM

Principal Founders or Leaders

Hinduism originated in the Indus Valley about 3000 B.C. Its animistic origins are shrouded in mystery.

Buddhism, sometimes called a reform movement within Hinduism, was started by Siddhartha Gautama (ca. 563-ca. 483 B.C.), a king's son from northern India. He left his wife and children to search for "enlightenment" about the meaning of life.

Core Beliefs and Practices

Human suffering is universal, according to Hinduism and Buddhism. Its root cause is passion or desire. Thus, desire (the lust for better things, sexual expression, achievement, and so on) must be eliminated. This is to be done through strict attention to hundreds of rules. These lead to right thinking in which one realizes that human existence and suffering are unreal.

The path to enlightenment is long, often lasting through thousands of lifetimes. Salvation must be earned. The goal for the Hindu and the Buddhist is to triumph over personal existence and graduate into nirvana, where individuality is lost in the unconscious Over-soul.

The principal religious practices are fasting, deprivation of comforts, and meditation.

Agreements and Differences

There is very little common ground between Hinduism/Buddhism and Christianity in general or the Church of the Nazarene in particular. Rather than trying to destroy personhood, Christians view it as part of the image of God within. Salvation is by grace through faith in Christ, not by humiliating works of degradation. Christians look forward to an eternity in the presence of God, not unconscious oblivion after thousands of agonizing trips around the wheel of life.

Buddhists and Hindus Today

More than a billion people today embrace Hinduism or Buddhism—about 17 percent of the world's population. Hindu philosophy is also the foundation for much of the New Age movement in North America.

24 EAſTERN RELIGIONſ: BUDDHIſM AND HINDUIſM

ABOUT THE TIME THAT THE PROPHET DANIEL'S FAITH in Jehovah was giving those Babylonian lions lockjaw . . .

About the time that Shadrach, Meshach, and Abednego were waltzing with divine delight in the fiery furnace . . .

About the time that Ezekiel was being seized by visions of dry bones and wheels and acting out his sermons to get the attention of the demoralized Israelites now in their third decade of the Babylonian Captivity . . .

About that time, while those Hebrew heroes were becoming the spiritual giants of Judaism, a little farther east, in India, a king's kid was growing up and pondering the riddles of human existence.

After meditating for 49 days and nights under a bo tree, Siddhartha Gautama figured out the mystery of life, achieving "enlightenment." He became known as the Enlightened One. Thus they named after him the religion he founded—"Buddha" means "enlightened."

Today some 320 million people embrace Buddhism. About 2 million make their homes in North America. The first Buddhist temple in the United States was built in San Francisco in 1898. In 1991 Buddhism celebrated its 250th anniversary as an officially recognized religion in Russia.[1]

Just as there are many denominations in Christianity, there are hundreds of sects in Buddhism. In this chapter we will take a look at the two dominant and ancient parties and then view the most prominent branches of Buddhism in North America today.

The Buddhism of the Elders

Ancient Buddhism was based on the teachings of Siddhartha Gautama. He led a sheltered life at first. The story is that a fortune-teller told his father (the ruler of a rice farming area in northern India) that the boy would grow up to become a sage or traveling holy man. Afraid then that he would lose the heir to his throne, he surrounded the young Siddhartha with the best that money could buy, hoping that he would stay home.

It didn't work. Deserting his wife and children, he left his wealthy, sheltered existence, and his encounter with the world's suffering overwhelmed him. Like

---

1. Mather and Nichols, *Dictionary of Cults*, 45, 48.

many others in his part of the world, he responded by becoming a monk or holy man. But six years of depriving himself of all pleasures, sleeping on beds of nails, walking on hot coals, and long, starving fasts convinced Gautama that this was a waste of time. He plopped himself down under the big bo tree (tree of wisdom), vowing that he would not get up until he had meditated his way through the mystery of life. After 49 days he emerged "enlightened" and shared with his disciples the Four Noble Truths and the Eightfold Path.[2]

The Four Noble Truths are as follows:

1. Suffering is universal.
2. Suffering is caused by personal passion and desire.
3. Personal desire and passion, therefore, must be eliminated.
4. A strict path must be followed in order to achieve the victory over personal desire and to achieve the enlightenment that leads to victory over personal existence and absorption into nirvana.

The Eightfold Path is to guide the pilgrim on his way to the dissolution of individuality and absorption into the Great Over-soul.[3]

The eight guidelines are right knowledge or belief, right feelings or attitudes, right speech, right conduct, right occupation, right effort or resolve, right use of the mind (meditation), and right composure or self-control.

To the Four Noble Truths and the Eightfold Path the Buddhists have added 10 commandments, which in some points sound a lot like the biblical Ten Commandments—or the Nazarene Special Rules: no dancing or worldly entertainment of any kind; no alcoholic beverages; no fornication; no murder; no lying; no stealing; no eating during fasting seasons; no sleeping on elevated beds, that is, one must sleep on the floor; no perfume or ornamental clothes; no accepting of offerings of silver or gold.[4]

In addition, there are hundreds of rules for those who are really serious—like monks or nuns. The monks have 250 rules, and the nuns have 500. Females have more rules to follow "because being a woman is considered inferior. . . . A woman, for example, must be reborn as a male before she can progress on to nirvana."[5]

Upon these foundations the two classical Buddhist branches are based. Theravada is the name of the oldest and most conservative stream of Buddhists. This is the Buddhism of Southeast Asia. Mahayana Buddhists broke off from their Theravada brethren sometime after the emperor of India, Asoka, died in 236 B.C. The Mahayana party became the Buddhism of China, Korea, Japan, Taiwan, Hong Kong, and Vietnam.[6]

Core Beliefs

The core beliefs of classical Theravada and Mahayana Buddhism include the following:

---

2. James C. Stephens, "Buddhism: The Enlightened Ones," in Miller, *Misguiding Lights?* 43-44.
3. Martin, *Kingdom of the Cults,* 262.
4. Mather and Nichols, *Dictionary of Cults,* 46.
5. Stephens, "Buddhism: The Enlightened Ones," 44-45.
6. Ibid., 45.

1. Reincarnation. Like the Hindus, Buddhists believe in a long cycle of reincarnation before a person achieves the bliss of personlessness and nirvana. If one lives badly (in terms of the Eightfold Path), he or she reaps the karma of a lower life form in the next life. One may regress from human to bovine to insect level of life. Many Buddhists are vegetarians, for obvious reasons.

2. God. Buddhism is the only world religion that does not teach that there is a living God. Buddha did not say there were no gods, but he ignored them as useless in the struggle to escape the human predicament. The

> *The nearest thing to God is the impersonal, universal Over-soul, the spiritual ocean into which the raindrop of individuality yearns to be lost.*

nearest thing to God is the impersonal, universal Over-soul, the spiritual ocean into which the raindrop of individuality yearns to be lost. Christianity, on the other hand, insists on a personal God who is both transcendent and immanent.

3. Sin. For the Buddhist, all suffering springs from human lust, desire, and passion. Thus desire, lust, and passion are sinful and must be exterminated. Desire is insatiable. When one desire is gratified, another takes its place. The sinful desire that Buddhism seeks to squelch is the constant desire for more. The more people get, the more they want. To the Buddhist, this is the original sin. As a Tibetan Buddhist teacher, Milarepa, put it, "From the very first renounce acquisition and heaping up."[7] Christians also resist the sinful desire to hoard and build "bigger barns." But they confront such temptations through redeeming grace, sanctification, and Christian simplicity. The Bible warns of this temptation: "When your herds and your flocks multiply, and your silver and gold multiply . . . then your heart becomes proud, and you forget the LORD your God" (Deut. 8:13-14, NASB).

4. Salvation. Salvation for the Buddhist is clearly by works. One must purify himself or herself from the lusts of life and must cultivate strong character and ethical behavior. In this there is no redeeming grace, no rescuing Savior. As Buddha said, "By one's self the evil is done; by one's self one suffers; by one's self evil is undone; by one's self one is purified. Lo, no man can purify another."[8]

Through many reincarnations, which may take thousands of years, the struggle for the good life may finally end in dissolution of individuality and the unconscious bliss of nirvana. Thus, on the road to salvation the person declares war on his or her humanity. The aim is to eventually destroy all the characteristics of personhood and seep into the unconscious Over-soul, where there is no more suffering. This is in stark contradiction to Christians, who believe that their personhood is a gift of God, indeed, part of the image of God within. Therefore, it is not to be destroyed, but treasured, developed, and yielded to the God of all comfort.

---

7. Timothy Miller, *How to Want What You Have* (New York: Avon Books, 1995), 31.

8. *Dhammapada: The Sayings of the Buddha*, ed. Thomas Byrom (New York: Alfred A. Knopf, 1976), 365. Cited by Mather and Nichols, *Dictionary of Cults*, 47.

The Mahayana Buddhists, influenced, some say, by the Jesus of Christianity, have come up with a loving grace dimension in their teachings about salvation. The bodhisattva is something like a Christ figure. He is a person who has achieved enlightenment, but instead of fading into the bliss of unconscious nirvana, he chooses out of love to return to earth to help others with the struggle for enlightenment.[9] The noble, loving bodhisattvas have accumulated a sort of treasury of merits (similar to Catholic teaching about Christ and the saints) that can be used to help those who become their disciples.

5. **Worship and Religious Experience.** Worship occurs both in homes and in temples. Images of Buddha assist the worshiper. The principal religious practice (besides keeping all the rules) is meditation and chanting. The aim of worship and religion for the Buddhist is to escape the world with its pain and suffering. The aim of Christian worship and service is to confront and change the world of pain and suffering in the name of Jesus and in the power of the Holy Spirit.

American Buddhism

The influence of Buddhism in America is on the rise. As it is introduced more and more in our centers of learning, it gains in credence. "Though the Asian-Americans comprise only 2.8 percent of the population, Asian-American students make up 12 percent of Harvard's population, 20 percent of Stanford's, and 30 percent of Berkeley's [University of California]."[10] For the most part, Buddhism is a tolerant religion and thus has been quite acceptable to today's North American culture. Buddhism has been treated favorably in the United States' print and broadcast industries.

1. **Classical Buddhism** is represented in America by the Buddhist Vihara Society. It is the American edition of classic Theravada Buddhist thought and practice. The official "bible" for this branch of the religion is the *Tripitaka* ("three baskets"—*Vinaya, Sutta, Abidhamma*) and the commentaries on these works.

2. **Tibetan Buddhists** operate a four-year accredited college in Boulder, Colorado. The school has a fine academic reputation. The Tibetan Buddhists look to the Dalai Lama as their divinized leader.

3. **Sokagakkai, or Nichiren Shoshu Academy,** are often called the materialistic Buddhists. They may be chanting, not for the dissolution of individuality, but for a promotion at work, guidance to the most profitable mutual fund, or a beautiful girlfriend. This movement was founded in Japan in the 13th century by a radical Buddhist monk. Today the movement has more than 20 million adherents in 115 countries.

This American version of Buddhism is not only materialistic but also militaristic and evangelistic. They work hard at making converts and "crushing other faiths." James Stephens, led from Buddhism to Christianity by a Nazarene pastor, writes that during his 14 years in the Nichiren Shoshu Academy he had

---

9. Muck, *Those Other Religions,* 178-79.
10. Ibid., 17.

personally made 54 converts for Buddhism. He now leads a ministry to help people leave Buddhism.[11]

4. Zen Buddhism is another Japanese import. This version of Buddhism originated in the late 12th century with the Rinzai and Soto sects that taught, among other things, emperor worship. Zen has been well accepted in America. Some notables, such as former California governor Jerry Brown and a raft of Hollywood actors, have embraced it.

The goal of Zen is the freeing of the will to rise above the human plight and find fulfillment in higher realms. Zen calls its disciples to allow their ego to be detached until one's real self calmly floats over the world's confusion like a Ping-Pong ball skimming over the rapids of life.[12] In classic Buddhism, enlightenment comes only after many probationary lives. American Zen, in typical Yankee efficiency, has come up with a shorter way. It teaches enlightenment pronto, in the here and now. This produces more customer satisfaction.

Zen's critics see this as perhaps the most selfish religion of man. Love of God and love for one's fellow human being gives way to shutting out others

> *What if John Wesley had taken a Zen approach to the starving masses of 18th-century England?*

so that one's own peace will not be disturbed. What if John Wesley had taken a Zen approach to the starving masses of 18th-century England? He would have simply closed his eyes and tried to rise above the poverty and suffering rather than confronting them and finding ways to conquer them.

This seeming absence of concern for human welfare led Walter Martin in *The Kingdom of the Cults* to urge prospective converts to Buddhism to look at the historical record: "Historically, Buddhism has produced nothing but indescribable conditions under which its subjects live. For in almost every area of the world where Buddhism of almost any form holds sway, there stalks the specter of disease, hunger, and moral and spiritual decay."[13]

Hinduism: Brahman, Karma, Samsara, Atman, and Moksha

Hinduism is 5,000 years old, twice as old as Buddhism. In fact, some students call Buddhism a mere reform movement within Hinduism. Hindus form the third largest religion in the world, behind Christianity and Islam. Today, 700 million Hindus inhabit our planet, 2 million of them in the United States.

Hinduism came to America in the 19th century when Swami Vivekananda established the Vedanta Society in New York. By the 1960s, Americans had become both amused and fascinated with the gurus who were apparently being sent to the West in a missionary program of the World Hindu Organization. Hinduism got a lot of free press when Maharishi Mahesh Yogi taught transcen-

---

11. Stephens, "Buddhism: The Enlightened Ones," 46-47, 42.
12. Martin, *Kingdom of the Cults,* 269.
13. Ibid., 270.

dental meditation to the Beatles. Then Swami Prabhupapda, an aged monk, founded Hare Krishna by hopping and chanting and preaching in New York's Greenwich Village.[14] Now Hinduism supplies some of the philosophical foundation for the New Age movement.

Hinduism was born in the Indus River valley in India. In its formative stages, it was influenced by neighbors and invaders. It seemed to syncretically blend all the deities and practices of the various primitive religions that impacted the culture. Hinduism is amazingly complex, defying generalization at many points. It is paradoxical in nature. For example, it embraces monism, monotheism, and pantheism, while at the same time believing in 3 million gods.

Core Beliefs

Though Hinduism is diverse and complex, the following concepts seem to be characteristic.

1. Brahman is the life force that exists in everything in the universe. It is the Hindu God, impersonal, neuter, unapproachable, and immovable. "God is all, and all is God" is a familiar Hindu maxim. The Hindu idea of God is both monistic (one) and pantheistic.

The needs of the Hindu worshiper, however, called into being a sort of Hindu trinity: Brahma the Creator, Vishnu the Sustainer of Creation, and Shiva the Destroyer. Vishnu has become the deity that communicates with humans. He has done this by way of 10 incarnations. His mission of mercy sent him to earth in the form of a fish, a tortoise, a boar, a man-lion, a dwarf, Rama-with-the-Axe, King Rama, Krishna, and Buddha. The 10th incarnation is called Kalkin and is yet to come.

Among these 9 incarnations, Lord Krishna has become more important in the Hindu pantheon than even Vishnu, who sent him. Krishna is not a historical figure. He is part of the fictional epic the Bhagavad Gita.

Hindus believe that many of the historical leaders have also been incarnations of Vishnu. Mahatma Gandhi was one, as was Jesus of Nazareth and Buddha.

All of these ideas about the nature and person of God are in stark contradiction to the Christian beliefs taught in the Holy Bible.

2. Karma is the law of sowing and reaping. It is the law of justice and retribution from which there is no escape. Good deeds and righteous living result in a better deal in the next life that is sure to come. Bad deeds mean you go down a rung or two on the ladder of enlightenment. You will come back to more suffering, poverty, and degradation. You will keep repeating life until through enlightenment you escape the "wheel of life."

One of the reasons that the horrible plight of the poverty-stricken lower castes in India invoke no sympathetic response from Hindus is that they believe that the leper, beggar, or cripple brought it all on himself or herself by bad karma. Such a person is simply paying his or her dues. To interfere with that would be to conspire against the divine plan and to subvert whatever it is that dharma is trying to teach the wretch.

---

14. Mark Albrecht, "Hinduism and the Hare Krishna: Quest for the End of Reincarnation," in Miller, *Misguiding Lights?* 54.

3. Samsara is the inevitable transmigration of the soul to the next life in an endless succession of rebirths. All must live in samsara. Along the way a few seem to achieve enlightenment and escape the wheel of life. An old Indian folk song laments the hopeless Hindu philosophy:

> *How many births are past, I cannot tell.*
> *How many yet to come no man can say;*
> *But this alone I know, and know full well,*
> *That pain and grief embitter all the way.*[15]

In *Misguiding Lights?* Mark Albrecht tells of his encounter with a loincloth-garbed man in north India. He was painted with Hindu symbols, including three white stripes signifying his devotion to Shiva the Destroyer. On a cold day he sat in the opening of a small cave, shivering behind his matted hair and beard.

"Why are you doing this?" Mark asked.

He smiled only slightly as he replied in excellent English: "You may not understand. I was born to a wealthy family in Bombay and have a university degree. At the age of 30 I realized it was all meaningless."

He went on to say that samsara was escorting him through his 1,742nd lifetime. He had had enough. He said that to keep his comfortable life in Bombay would mean even more lifetimes on the agonizing wheel of existence. So he decided to earn his salvation (enlightenment) by renouncing it all and living as an ascetic holy man.

"This means I meditate eight hours each day and eat only roots, berries, wild grains, and plants. I drink from the holy River Ganges. . . . When I die, I shall not . . . return to this planet of suffering and woe. I have attained enlightenment."[16]

4. Atman is the word for soul. Salvation of the soul comes when the enlightened one realizes that his or her soul is really Brahman—God. God is all, and all is God. That includes your own soul. How could you be sinful when you are God? In the words of Swami Muktananda, a very popular Hindu figure in America with hundreds of thousands of disciples, "Worship your own inner self. God dwells within you as you."[17] The path to salvation has four stages. The soul moves from beginner to spiritual adult to spiritual grandfather and then to the highest spiritual state—a wandering, homeless, penniless enlightened one free from all earthly care and human desire.

5. Moksha refers to the release from the reincarnation cycle (samsara), finally achieved by the devout person who has suffered through enough lifetimes and has meditated his way to the "enlightened" stage. At this point, one sheds all individuality and is absorbed into Brahman. A frequent Hindu metaphor for this is a drop of water falling into the ocean. The drop does not exist as a drop any longer. It is lost in the vast ocean.

---

15. Cited in Mather and Nichols, *Dictionary of Cults,* 120.
16. Mark Albrecht, quoted in *Misguiding Lights?* 61.
17. Ibid., 57.

It is a salvation totally earned by the efforts of the pilgrim. There is no forgiveness, no grace, no Savior who redeems. Hinduism teaches salvation by works,
plain and simple. This is the ultimate hope for the Hindu—to exist no more.

Hinduism and Christianity

Hindu philosophy provides the backbone of the New Age movement that
has so captivated the American fancy. Transcendental meditation (TM) is the
Hindu practice most often found in North America. Though its influence is wan-
ing, TM popularity in the United States soared during the 1970s and 1980s. Its
claims to aid health, blood pressure, tension, employee productivity, and
achievement in school got it a try in the pragmatic American culture.

The dangers of TM should be well known by now. It is a mind-emptying
procedure that leaves the person vulnerable to whatever spirits, principalities,
and powers that may be at the behest of what the Bible calls "the prince of
demons" (Matt. 12:24) and the "prince of the power of the air" (Eph. 2:2, KJV).

Further, the mantras and one-word chants of TM are often the names of
Hindu deities or the cultic term used to invoke their presence. The initiation
songs, usually sung in the Sanskrit language, are often hymns of praise to Hindu
gods. One such song goes:

Guru in the glory of Brahma,
Guru in the glory of Vishnu. . . .
To Shri Guru Dev adorned with glory,
I bow down.[18]

David Haddon compares this secret worship of Hindu gods foisted off onto
students, corporate employees, and others to inviting a guest for a swim in your
pool only to baptize him or her in the name of the Father, Son, and Holy Spirit,
using the Greek language.[19]

Without stopping to recite the Christian doctrines of God, humanity, sin,
salvation, service, the Church, and eternal rewards and punishments, let it suffice to point out the obvious: every important Hindu teaching contradicts basic
Christian doctrine.

Review and Reflection

1. From your study of this chapter, list what you think are the strengths
and weaknesses of Buddhism and Hinduism.

2. Go back to Part I of this book, and note key Nazarene beliefs. Choose
two or three for further study and comparison to Hindu or Buddhist practices.

18. David Haddon, "Transcendental Meditation: It's More than Relaxation," in Miller, *Misguiding Lights?*
91.
    19. Ibid.

3. Evaluate these ideas from this chapter:

   a. Personhood and individuality are part of the image of God in us. Thus, they should be treasured and cultivated, not eliminated.

   b. The way to cope with human passion and desire is to eliminate it.

   c. Women must be reborn as males before they can make it to "heaven," "nirvana," or eternal bliss.

   d. The wretch on the street—beggar, leper, outcast—brought it all on himself or herself. Such a person is just paying his or her dues.

   e. The ultimate hope for the Hindu is to exist no more.

4. As you watch television and read the newspaper this week, collect the references to Buddhist and Hindu ideas and practices.

NEW AGE THOUGHT:
THE SOUTH WIND BLEW SOFTLY

Historical Roots

The New Age movement is not a religion as much as it is a cultural revolution that became visible in the 1960s, rampant in the 1970s, and more or less accepted in the 1980s. It is a rebellion against Enlightenment rationality, the scientific method, Newtonian physics, and the Judeo-Christian tradition. Several Hollywood celebrities have promoted this modern distortion of some Christian ideas mixed with Hindu and Buddhist notions.

Core Beliefs

Adherents of the New Age movement have a pantheistic view of God: God is all, and all is God. Thus human beings are really gods in disguise. Sin, suffering, and evil are unreal distortions. The goal of life is to develop the god within. Reincarnation, contact with the spirit world and with the dead, and mind-emptying meditation are key practices.

Agreement and Differences

By design, New Age thought is quite the opposite of orthodox Christianity. Thus, Nazarenes and New Agers have very little in common.

The New Age Movement Today

The New Age movement has no offices, no formal creed, no firm philosophy, no congregations, no voting assemblies. It is a popular movement that endorses do-it-yourself religion and has made spirituality in general an OK thing today. It infiltrates society through certain business practices (meditation and yoga are purported to make workers more productive and executives more effective), through the educational system at the hands of convinced teachers (centering and relaxation are believed to make kids less of a behavior problem), and through radically ecumenical and pluralistic religious groups, periodicals, and leaders.

The New Age philosophy could be a deceptive south wind. It could so permeate our culture that its assumptions and methods could seep into the church's life and practice.

25 ~ New Age Thought: The South Wind Blew Softly

B E STILL, AND KNOW THAT *YOU* ARE GOD!" This corruption of Ps. 46:10 is one of the favorite slogans of Shirley MacLaine, America's most famous New Age huckster and seminar leader.[1]

Sylvester Stallone, actor turned New Age theologian, declared that reincarnation is true and that he himself was once a monkey hanging by his tail and feasting on bananas in a Central American jungle.[2]

Recently New Agers sponsored a hunger project. They raised $6 million and promptly spent 97 percent of the funds on seminars in which conferees used mantras, tantras, and yantras trying to "think" and "imagine" hunger off the globe. After all, human ills are really misperceptions of reality, so if you can get people to think in harmony with the universe, their stomachs will surely stop growling.

Such shenanigans make New Age thought instantly reprehensible to serious Christians. Nazarenes are not likely to be duped by the blatantly and antibiblical cavorting of New Age propagandists. Nazarenes are not in danger of promoting the midweek prayer meeting as an out-of-body experience. We do not need to worry much about Nazarene small groups engaging in channeling the spirit of some 35,000-year-old Rama. We do not fear that our contributions to Nazarene Compassionate Ministries will be spent on mantras, tantras, or yantras. We wouldn't be likely prospects for such delusions any more than we would be likely to start publishing astrological charts in our Sunday School quarterlies.

No, the New Age will not conquer us with such obvious propaganda. We are way too rationalistic, pragmatic, realistic, and biblical for them to sell us on such balmless Gileads. However, that does *not* mean that the New Age will not do us damage. But first things first.

---

1. Wesley Tracy, "The South Wind Blew Softly," *Herald of Holiness,* January 1991, 24.
2. Albrecht, "Hinduism and the Hare Krishna," 55.

What Is New Age Thought, and Where Did It Come From?

The New Age movement is not an organized religious group. Rather, it is a cultural revolution that emerged in the 1960s, became widespread in the 1970s, and was more or less accepted by the 1980s. It is a resistance movement against Newtonian physics, Enlightenment rationalism (including the scientific method), the industrial-military complex, and the handmaiden of all these—Judeo-Christian tradition.[3] This cluster of villains has put humanity in grave jeopardy. The solution is to change the basic way people think, and then the Aquarian New Age can dawn with all its bliss.

Thus, the New Age movement competes with Christianity on the one hand and secular humanism on the other. New Agers reject the lack of spirituality of the secular humanists but damn Christian spirituality.

When the cultural revolutionists began to reject Enlightenment rationality, Newtonian physics, and the Judeo-Christian tradition, they quickly turned to Eastern religions and the shamanism of primitive or native peoples. Hinduism and Buddhism became dominant influences.

Core Beliefs of the New Age Movement

1. God

The New Age movement teaches impersonal pantheism. God, the aggregate consciousness of all living things, is impersonal. "It" has no purpose, will, values, compassion, holiness, or love and cannot relate to human beings in any personal way.

God is in all of creation—gnats, cows, weeds, rivers, and human beings are all part of God. New Age environmentalists are often motivated to save plants or animals because they believe them to be "divine."

The pantheistic, impersonal force that some call God embraces all that exists and does not discriminate between good and evil. Violating Rom. 1:25, they worship the *created* and not the *Creator.*

For Christians, God is Creator and thus separate from His creation. His creative work testifies to His existence and nature, but nature and God are not the same.

The God of the Bible is personal, has personal attributes of love, anger, will, morality, and holiness. He relates to humans in distinctly interpersonal ways. "The Spirit himself testifies with our spirit that we are God's children" (Rom. 8:16).

2. Jesus Christ

New Agers say Christ was not the Savior but a gifted spiritual luminary from whom we can learn to tap into the divine energy source. Christians believe that Jesus Christ is the Second Person of the Holy Trinity and is the Savior of the world.

---

3. Mark Graham, "New Age—Same Old Story," *Herald of Holiness,* January 1991, 10.

3. The Bible

New Agers see the Bible as a useful book with some helpful insights about spirituality. But it contains many teachings on sin, guilt, repentance, and submission, which must be tossed out in favor of New Age teachings about enlightenment and becoming gods.

Christians believe that the Bible is the inspired, written Word of God, revealing the record of God's dealings with His people and revealing Jesus Christ, the Son of God, our Savior. In the Bible we find all that we must know in order to find salvation.

4. Sin

There is no such thing as sin for New Age devotees. Sin is a concept created by Western thought. The "enlightened" realize that all things, acts, and experiences are part of God and therefore cannot be sinful. Enlightenment can bring a new way of looking at what appears to be sin. When the "illusions" are transcended, one sees that all things and events are made out of God and are thus good.

The Christian faith teaches a twofold doctrine of sin. Sin as state—the sinful condition of the human heart upon arrival in this world, called "original sin"—results from *deprivation* of God's full image since the Fall in Eden, and *depravation,* the corruption of our fallen nature.

Sin as act pertains to the deeds of selfishness, pride, rebellion, and dishonesty performed by sinful human beings.

5. Salvation

Salvation for the New Age devotee is receiving enlightenment regarding one's own "godness" and working to develop his or her own divine nature, more and more eschewing personal pursuits, becoming more and more one with the cosmic energy that is God.

Christians affirm that when the convicted sinner confesses and forsakes sin (repentance) and believes in Jesus Christ as Savior, he or she is saved by grace through faith, is justified freely, is adopted into the family of God, and is born again.

The faithful Holy Spirit will lead the obedient believer into sanctifying grace, continued spiritual growth, and eventually to heaven.

6. Human Destiny

Generally, New Age thinkers teach reincarnation. One may struggle through thousands of life cycles before becoming enlightened and fully absorbed into the great impersonal force that is God. New Agers embrace reincarnation "and the idea of karma—a graceless tenet of Hinduism that teaches that you reap what you sow—if not in this life, in some other life down the road."[4] This life may be either human or subhuman. Does this give any hints about the fanatical "animal rights" fevers of some New Age disciples?

Christians believe in one life on earth followed by a personal life in the world to come. For those saved by grace, an eternity in God's own presence in heaven awaits. Those who are finally impenitent shall suffer eternally in hell.

---

4. Ibid., 11.

South Winds Blowing Softly

The New Age can blow like a soft south wind and deceive us. The "soft . . . south wind" (KJV) figure comes from the nautical story in Acts 27. Paul warned the officers to stay in Fair Havens rather than sail, lest the winter storms destroy the ship. But "when a gentle south wind began to blow, they thought they had obtained what they wanted; so they weighed anchor and sailed" (v. 13). They soon found themselves in the grip of the demon wind "Euroclydon" (v. 14, KJV), which they fought for a fortnight, and then they lost the ship.

They wanted a south wind, they needed a south wind, and when it came, they were sure it meant safe sailing. Similarly, New Age philosophy could be a deceptive south wind. It could so permeate our culture that its assumptions and methods could seep into the Church's life and practice.

The New Age movement takes full advantage of the human thirst for soft south winds that bear perfumed flattery about ourselves. This belief system announces that all of creation is one divine essence. Therefore, as part of creation, we ourselves are divine. Our human task, then, is to become enlightened about our "godness" and exercise our god power.

This sweet and savage lie has worked since Eden. Every generation loves it.

This sweet and savage lie has worked since Eden. Every generation loves it. Since all is a part of God, then distinctions between good and evil disappear; sin does not exist, nor does guilt, for the real self is God, therefore unsullied and taint-proof. We must forget such puritan illusions as sin and guilt, good and evil, and concentrate on becoming even more enlightened, more self-realized, more deified.

To test how the rudiments of this doctrine influence the Church, ask any group of Christians what the purpose of life is, and note the number who answer exclusively in terms of their own self-fulfillment.

The New Age south wind could blow in through the windows of the popular culture and sully the soul of the Church.

The Most Subtle South Wind

There is, however, a more subtle south wind that could do us grave damage. I speak of the warm south breeze that blows as gently as a love song, bringing deep satisfaction and a sense of "duty done" when we have taken up arms against error and stamped it out. When we do this, we are almost always robbed by that error, that heresy; robbed of treasures that we do not even notice have been stolen.

Consider the Augustine-Pelagius controversy. Pelagius began to teach that humans are basically good but are corrupted by environment. Augustine defended the traditional doctrine of inherited depravity. As they debated, they drove each other into more and more extreme positions.

Augustine finally won, according to most scorekeepers. However, he and his theological descendants lost too. They passed on a doctrine of depravity so extreme that not even the atonement of Christ could do more than put a dent in it. The *pessimism of sin* elbowed the *possibilities of grace* right out of the Christian pulpit. This could happen to us again. As we oppose the "no such thing as sin" doctrine of the New Age, we could find ourselves in the position of so emphasizing the depravity of humankind that the possibilities of grace are hardly heard.

Consider Luther and Calvin versus the Roman Catholic Church. Throughout the Middle Ages the Roman church took upon itself the task of declaring who was to be saved and who was to be lost. In the worst of times, salvation could even be bought from the church. Protestant Reformers like Martin Luther and John Calvin began to lay down the law: the church cannot save—only God does that. The church cannot even know who is saved—only God knows that.

So far so good. But the logic went on: not even the individual believer knows whether he or she is saved—only God knows that.

Further, there is nothing any person can do to bring about his or her salvation—we don't choose God, but God chooses us.

Martin and John won the battle. Protestants do not fear that some church bureaucrat can keep them out of heaven. But Martin's and John's theological descendants also lost. In stamping out the doctrine of salvation by church decree, they, in a sort of reverse backlash, gave up the marvelous doctrine of Christian assurance promised in such scriptures as Rom. 8:16: "The Spirit Himself bears witness with our spirit that we are children of God" (NKJV).

Here's an example a little closer to home. Did you know that as late as 1950 many Evangelical groups in Britain (including Nazarenes) were careful not to have any special celebrations at Easter? In fact, Easter weekend was the time chosen for the annual conference or the district assembly. A friend of mine from Scotland explained why. "Celebrate at Easter? That's what the Catholics did! We didn't want to be mistaken for them."

One way the south wind of the New Age can do us in is by baiting us into overreacting. Suppose that we purge from our language any term used by a New Age guru. Suppose we police our thoughts against any idea the New Age thinkers dwell on. Suppose we oppose any political candidate who espouses any New Age doctrine, such as environmental protection. Suppose we excise from our liturgy or daily religious practices anything that New Agers seem to embrace.

If we do that, we'll lose a lot of genuine Christian practices to well-meaning overkill.

Watch Out for South Winds Here

If we purge ourselves from everything the New Age boosts, we will have to be prepared to surrender the following:

1. Appreciation for Nature

Just because the New Age worships nature does not mean that Christians should stop regarding nature as both a gift from and a revelation of God. According to Rom. 1:19-20, unbelievers would be without excuse if nature were the only revelation of God that they had.

2. Concern for the Environment

New Age prophets preach about protecting rather than polluting or exploiting the created world. They regard creation as God or a part of God, which must

then be reverenced. Christians tempted to abandon environmental responsibili-
ties because of a New Age taint should remember that we were appointed by
God to be the caretakers of the earth (Gen. 1:28; 2:15).

3. Meditation

No New Age practice gets slammed harder in the Evangelical press than
meditation. Many Christian writers now indiscriminately condemn it. True, New
Age practices of meditation range from neutral to bizarre to demonic. However,
ever since Isaac "went out to the field one evening to meditate" (Gen. 24:63),
meditation has been a practice of the people of God. We are commanded to *meditate* on the Law of God day and night (Josh. 1:8). We are urged to *meditate* upon
God's wondrous works, His precepts, His "statutes" (KJV), and His promises (Ps.
119:15, 23, 27, 48, 78, 148). The principal difference between New Age meditation and Christian meditation is that Christians are instructed to *fill* the mind
with noble thoughts or Scripture—while New Agers are coached to *empty* the
mind and open it to whatever "spirit" or impulse that is out there. Businesses
and schools sometimes provide training in the "emptying" sort of New Age med-
itation to reduce executive stress, enhance self-accep-tance, or improve test scores. This Christians should avoid. But it would

> *It would be a tragedy to throw out genuine biblical meditation because a bunch of New Age swamis, gurus, or educators abuse it.*

be a tragedy to throw out genuine biblical meditation because New Age gurus or
educators abuse it.

4. Spiritual Experience

New Age abuses of spirituality, such as channeling, seances, and out-of-
body experiences could make us stop talking about valid religious experiences.
Whatever New Agers do, we must not stop cultivating a daily relationship with
God.

5. Psychotherapy

In some Evangelical circles psychotherapy is being hooted down as a sinful
expression of the New Age movement. It is true that the New Age people have
found the work of such psychologists as Jung, Maslow, and Rogers to be friendly
to their worldview. Caution is justified, but tossing out all that 20th-century
existential psychologists have discovered is not. This crew of psychologists did
much to validate John Wesley's doctrine that, despite depravity, there are some
remains of the image of God in the worst of people. Carl Rogers said that he
found his clients had not just a dark side, but something positive at the deepest
level, something that could be counted on to work toward healing and whole-
ness. John Wesley called it the image of God, put there by prevenient grace.

6. Human Potential

The human potential movement, eagerly embraced by New Age proponents, is guilty of many sins, including the deification of humanity. Self-suffi-
ciency is the very essence of sin, according to the Bible. Yet the tom-tom
pounders of the human potential movement, with slogans like "If it's going to

be, it's up to me," have made us all aware of unused human capacities. They remind us that limp acquiescence to life has little to commend it.

God has granted a multitude of gifts and talents to Christians. These need to be aggressively invested for God and good (Matt. 25:14-30). At the Judgment our greatest embarrassment may be the smallness of our trying.

7. Self-esteem

Evangelicals have made important strides in appropriating a Christian approach to self-esteem. Though many Christians have carried this baton too far, it would be tragic to throw it away just because New Age gurus are calling their paying disciples "gods."

8. Christian Education

Since the New Age movement deals with the noumenal and the pseudospiritual to the point of outrage, we could see a reaction in Christian education that would lurch lopsidedly to the rational. All the gains that have been made recently in the noumenal, spiritual, and affective domains could be pitched out in order to avoid the New Age label.

9. Cooperation Rather than Competition

Typically, the New Age movement values cooperation over competition. Christians should, too, not because the New Agers do it, but in spite of the New Age movement's interest.

10. Networking

"When New Agers talk about this, some Christians get nervous and visualize world conspiracy," says Karen Hoyt. "But the truth of the matter is that the most powerful and effective network ever is the Christian Church."[5] We should make this network more effective, rather than scuttle the structure because the New Age movement has tried to copy it.

11. Importance of the Body

Long before the New Age movement opened a health food store, Christians were reminded to honor their bodies as the *naos,* the very temple of God.

12. Peacemaking

Long before the New Age movement could invent a peace symbol or spell "peacenik," Jesus himself called His followers to be radical peacemakers (Matt. 5:9, 38-44).

The point is this: We must not give up good Christian beliefs and practices just because some segment of the New Age movement picks it up. Just because a practice is adopted by New Agers does not mean that anyone who engages in that practice is a New Ager. As Robert J. L. Burrows notes, "Marx and Jesus were both concerned with the poor. That does not make Marx a Christian or Jesus a Communist."[6]

We could make war on the New Age movement and drive from our sacred precincts anything and any person who sympathizes with anything touted by any New Ager anywhere. We could forsake any practice or idea upon which the

---

5. Karen Hoyt and the Spiritual Counterfeits Project, *The New Age Rage* (Old Tappan, N.J.: Fleming H. Revell, 1987), 12.

6. Robert J. L. Burrows in *The New Age Rage,* 48.

New Age movement has trod. But what would we have left to offer a hungry world dying of spiritual starvation?

We would be on the sidelines holding our dust-dry catechism. Christianity would be a set of beliefs to which coldhearted rationalists could pledge knee-jerk allegiance. Spontaneous spirituality would be scarce, and frigid formalism would characterize worship. Christian nurture would amount to mental mastery of facts, memorizing lists, and answering fact questions in workbooks. And in the end, no one would be more vulnerable to New Age error than our rigid, parched spirits. Then the subtle south wind of the New Age movement would have won the day and carried us into Euroclydon's trap.

Review and Reflection

1. Review the elements of New Age thought and practice. Then examine your own heart and life. At what points have you been influenced by New Age ideas? How did this happen? What correctives come to mind?

2. Think of your church, its music, its preaching, its worship, its fellowship activities. Considering the "south wind" metaphor in this chapter, list methods and practices that people avoid because of fear of the New Age label. On the other hand, what New Ageisms are now such a part of the culture that they have crept into your church's worship and practices?

3. As you read newspapers and magazines and watch television this week, build a file of clippings and notes on New Age concerns. No witch-hunting—just research.

4. Suppose you were going to teach this chapter and decided to aid learning by mounting a half dozen felt-tipped marker "quote posters" on the walls and bulletin boards. What quotes from this chapter would you select? You could start with "Marx and Jesus were both concerned with the poor. That does not make Marx a Christian or Jesus a Communist."

Appendix 1

Articles of Faith

I. The Triune God

1. We believe in one eternally existent, infinite God, Sovereign of the universe; that He only is God, creative and administrative, holy in nature, attributes, and purpose; that He, as God, is Triune in essential being, revealed as Father, Son, and Holy Spirit.

II. Jesus Christ

2. We believe in Jesus Christ, the Second Person of the Triune Godhead; that He was eternally one with the Father; that He became incarnate by the Holy Spirit and was born of the Virgin Mary, so that two whole and perfect natures, that is to say the Godhead and manhood, are thus united in one Person very God and very man, the God-man.

We believe that Jesus Christ died for our sins, and that He truly arose from the dead and took again His body, together with all things appertaining to the perfection of man's nature, wherewith He ascended into heaven and is there engaged in intercession for us.

III. The Holy Spirit

3. We believe in the Holy Spirit, the Third Person of the Triune Godhead, that He is ever present and efficiently active in and with the Church of Christ, convincing the world of sin, regenerating those who repent and believe, sanctifying believers, and guiding into all truth as it is in Jesus.

IV. The Holy Scriptures

4. We believe in the plenary inspiration of the Holy Scriptures, by which we understand the 66 books of the Old and New Testaments, given by divine inspiration, inerrantly revealing the will of God concerning us in all things necessary to our salvation, so that whatever is not contained therein is not to be enjoined as an article of faith.

V. Sin, Original and Personal

5. We believe that sin came into the world through the disobedience of our first parents, and death by sin. We believe that sin is of two kinds: original sin or depravity, and actual or personal sin.

5.1. We believe that original sin, or depravity, is that corruption of the nature of all the offspring of Adam by reason of which everyone is very far gone from original righteousness or the pure state of our first parents at the time of their creation, is averse to God, is without spiritual life, and inclined to evil, and that continually. We further believe that original sin continues to exist with the new life of the regenerate, until eradicated by the baptism with the Holy Spirit.

5.2. We believe that original sin differs from actual sin in that it constitutes an inherited propensity to actual sin for which no one is accountable until its divinely provided remedy is neglected or rejected.

5.3. We believe that actual or personal sin is a voluntary violation of a known law of God by a morally responsible person. It is therefore not to be confused with involuntary and inescapable shortcomings, infirmities, faults, mistakes, failures, or other deviations from a standard of perfect conduct that are the residual effects of the Fall. However, such innocent effects do not include attitudes or responses contrary to the spirit of Christ, which may properly be called sins of the spirit. We believe that personal sin is primarily and essentially a violation of the law of love; and that in relation to Christ sin may be defined as unbelief.

VI. Atonement

6. We believe that Jesus Christ, by His sufferings, by the shedding of His own blood, and by His meritorious death on the Cross, made a full atonement for all human sin, and that this Atonement is the only ground of salvation, and that it is sufficient for every individual of Adam's race. The Atonement is graciously efficacious for the salvation of the irresponsible and for the children in innocency but is efficacious for the salvation of those who reach the age of responsibility only when they repent and believe.

VII. Free Agency

7. We believe that the human race's creation in Godlikeness included ability to choose between right and wrong, and that thus human beings were made morally responsible; that through the fall of Adam they became depraved so that they cannot now turn and prepare themselves by their own natural strength and works to faith and calling upon God. But we also believe that the grace of God through Jesus Christ is freely bestowed upon all people, enabling all who will to turn from sin to righteousness, believe on Jesus Christ for pardon and cleansing from sin, and follow good works pleasing and acceptable in His sight.

We believe that all persons, though in the possession of the experience of regeneration and entire sanctification, may fall from grace and apostatize and, unless they repent of their sins, be hopelessly and eternally lost.

VIII. Repentance

8. We believe that repentance, which is a sincere and thorough change of the mind in regard to sin, involving a sense of personal guilt and a voluntary turning away from sin, is demanded of all who have by act or purpose become sinners against God. The Spirit of God gives to all who will repent the gracious help of penitence of heart and hope of mercy, that they may believe unto pardon and spiritual life.

IX. Justification, Regeneration, and Adoption

9. We believe that justification is the gracious and judicial act of God by which He grants full pardon of all guilt and complete release from the penalty of sins committed, and acceptance as righteous, to all who believe on Jesus Christ and receive Him as Lord and Savior.

10. We believe that regeneration, or the new birth, is that gracious work of God whereby the moral nature of the repentant believer is spiritually quickened and given a distinctively spiritual life, capable of faith, love, and obedience.

11. We believe that adoption is that gracious act of God by which the justified and regenerated believer is constituted a son of God.

12. We believe that justification, regeneration, and adoption are simultaneous in the experience of seekers after God and are obtained upon the condition of faith, preceded by repentance; and that to this work and state of grace the Holy Spirit bears witness.

X. Entire Sanctification

13. We believe that entire sanctification is that act of God, subsequent to regeneration, by which believers are made free from original sin, or depravity, and brought into a state of entire devotement to God, and the holy obedience of love made perfect.

It is wrought by the baptism with the Holy Spirit, and comprehends in one experience the cleansing of the heart from sin and the abiding, indwelling presence of the Holy Spirit, empowering the believer for life and service.

Entire sanctification is provided by the blood of Jesus, is wrought instantaneously by faith, preceded by entire consecration; and to this work and state of grace the Holy Spirit bears witness.

This experience is also known by various terms representing its different phases, such as "Christian perfection," "perfect love," "heart purity," "the baptism with the Holy Spirit," "the fullness of the blessing," and "Christian holiness."

14. We believe that there is a marked distinction between a pure heart and a mature character. The former is obtained in an instant, the result of entire sanctification; the latter is the result of growth in grace.

We believe that the grace of entire sanctification includes the impulse to grow in grace. However, this impulse must be consciously nurtured, and careful attention given to the requisites and processes of spiritual development and improvement in Christlikeness of character and personality. Without such purposeful endeavor one's witness may be impaired and the grace itself frustrated and ultimately lost.

XI. The Church

15. We believe in the Church, the community that confesses Jesus Christ as Lord, the covenant people of God made new in Christ, the Body of Christ called together by the Holy Spirit through the Word.

God calls the Church to express its life in the unity and fellowship of the Spirit; in worship through the preaching of the Word, observance of the sacraments, and ministry in His name; by obedience to Christ and mutual accountability.

The mission of the Church in the world is to continue the redemptive work of Christ in the power of the Spirit through holy living, evangelism, discipleship, and service.

The Church is a historical reality, which organizes itself in culturally conditioned forms; exists both as local congregations and as a universal body; sets apart persons called of God for specific ministries. God calls the Church to live under His rule in anticipation of the consummation at the coming of our Lord Jesus Christ.

XII. Baptism

16. We believe that Christian baptism, commanded by our Lord, is a sacrament signifying acceptance of the benefits of the atonement of Jesus Christ, to be administered to believers and declarative of their faith in Jesus Christ as their Savior, and full purpose of obedience in holiness and righteousness.

Baptism being a symbol of the new covenant, young children may be baptized, upon request of parents or guardians who shall give assurance for them of necessary Christian training.

Baptism may be administered by sprinkling, pouring, or immersion, according to the choice of the applicant.

XIII. The Lord's Supper

17. We believe that the Memorial and Communion Supper instituted by our Lord and Savior Jesus Christ is essentially a New Testament sacrament, declarative of His sacrificial death, through the merits of which believers have life and salvation and promise of all spiritual blessings in Christ. It is distinctively for those who are prepared for reverent appreciation of its significance, and by it they show forth the Lord's death till He come again. It being the Communion feast, only those who have faith in Christ and love for the saints should be called to participate therein.

XIV. Divine Healing[2]

18. We believe in the Bible doctrine of divine healing and urge our people to seek to offer the prayer of faith for the healing of the sick. [Providential means and agencies when deemed necessary should not be refused.] *We also believe God heals through the means of medical science.*

XV. Second Coming of Christ

19. We believe that the Lord Jesus Christ will come again; that we who are alive at His coming shall not precede them that are asleep in Christ Jesus; but that, if we are abiding in Him, we shall be caught up with the risen saints to meet the Lord in the air, so that we shall ever be with the Lord.

XVI. Resurrection, Judgment, and Destiny

20. We believe in the resurrection of the dead, that the bodies both of the just and of the unjust shall be raised to life and united with their spirits—"they that have done good, unto the resurrection of life; and they that have done evil, unto the resurrection of damnation."

21. We believe in future judgment in which every person shall appear before God to be judged according to his or her deeds in this life.

22. We believe that glorious and everlasting life is assured to all who savingly believe in, and obediently follow, Jesus Christ our Lord; and that the finally impenitent shall suffer eternally in hell.

THE CHURCH

I. The General Church

23. The Church of God is composed of all spiritually regenerate persons, whose names are written in heaven.

II. The Churches Severally

24. The churches severally are to be composed of such regenerate persons as by providential permission, and by the leadings of the Holy Spirit, become associated together for holy fellowship and ministries.

III. The Church of the Nazarene

25. The Church of the Nazarene is composed of those persons who have voluntarily associated themselves together according to the doctrines and polity of said church, and who seek holy Christian fellowship, the conversion of sinners, the entire sanctification of believers, their upbuilding in holiness, and the simplicity and spiritual power manifest in the primitive New Testament Church, together with the preaching of the gospel to every creature.

IV. Agreed Statement of Belief

26. Recognizing that the right and privilege of persons to church membership rest upon the fact of their being regenerate, we would require only such avowals of belief as are essential to Christian experience. We, therefore, deem belief in the following brief statements to be sufficient. We believe:

---

2. Constitutional changes adopted by the 1997 General Assembly are in the process of ratification by the district assemblies at the time of printing. Where changes are being made, words in italics are new words and words in brackets [ ] are words being deleted.

26.1. In one God—the Father, Son, and Holy Spirit.

26.2. That the Old and New Testament Scriptures, given by plenary inspiration, contain all truth necessary to faith and Christian living.

26.3. That man is born with a fallen nature, and is, therefore, inclined to evil, and that continually.

26.4. That the finally impenitent are hopelessly and eternally lost.

26.5. That the atonement through Jesus Christ is for the whole human race; and that whosoever repents and believes on the Lord Jesus Christ is justified and regenerated and saved from the dominion of sin.

26.6. That believers are to be sanctified wholly, subsequent to regeneration, through faith in the Lord Jesus Christ.

26.7. That the Holy Spirit bears witness to the new birth, and also to the entire sanctification of believers.

26.8. That our Lord will return, the dead will be raised, and the final judgment will take place.

V. The General Rules

27. To be identified with the visible Church is the blessed privilege and sacred duty of all who are saved from their sins and are seeking completeness in Christ Jesus. It is required of all who desire to unite with the Church of the Nazarene, and thus to walk in fellowship with us, that they shall show evidence of salvation from their sins by a godly walk and vital piety; and that they shall be, or earnestly desire to be, cleansed from all indwelling sin. They shall evidence their commitment to God—

27.1. FIRST. By doing that which is enjoined in the Word of God, which is our rule of both faith and practice, including:

(1) Loving God with all the heart, soul, mind, and strength, and one's neighbor as oneself (Exodus 20:3-6; Leviticus 19:17-18; Deuteronomy 5:7-10; 6:4-5; Mark 12:28-31; Romans 13:8-10).

(2) Pressing upon the attention of the unsaved the claims of the gospel, inviting them to the house of the Lord, and trying to compass their salvation (Matthew 28:19-20; Acts 1:8; Romans 1:14-16; 2 Corinthians 5:18-20).

(3) Being courteous to all men (Ephesians 4:32; Titus 3:2; 1 Peter 2:17; 1 John 3:18).

(4) Being helpful to those who are also of the faith, in love forbearing one another (Romans 12:13; Galatians 6:2, 10; Colossians 3:12-14).

(5) Seeking to do good to the bodies and souls of men; feeding the hungry, clothing the naked, visiting the sick and imprisoned, and ministering to the needy, as opportunity and ability are given (Matthew 25:35-36; 2 Corinthians 9:8-10; Galatians 2:10; James 2:15-16; 1 John 3:17-18).

(6) Contributing to the support of the ministry and the church and its work in tithes and offerings (Malachi 3:10; Luke 6:38; 1 Corinthians 9:14; 16:2; 2 Corinthians 9:6-10; Philippians 4:15-19).

(7) Attending faithfully all the ordinances of God, and the means of grace, including the public worship of God (Hebrews 10:25), the ministry of the Word (Acts 2:42), the sacrament of the Lord's Supper (1 Corinthians 11:23-30); searching the Scriptures and meditating thereon (Acts 17:11; 2 Timothy 2:15; 3:14-16); family and private devotions (Deuteronomy 6:6-7; Matthew 6:6).

27.2. SECOND. By avoiding evil of every kind, including:

(1) Taking the name of God in vain (Exodus 20:7; Leviticus 19:12; James 5:12).

(2) Profaning of the Lord's Day by participation in unnecessary secular activities, thereby indulging in practices that deny its sanctity (Exodus 20:8-11; Isaiah 58:13-14; Mark 2:27-28; Acts 20:7; Revelation 1:10).

(3) Sexual immorality, such as premarital or extramarital relations, perversion in any form, or looseness and impropriety of conduct (Exodus 20:14; Matthew 5:27-32; 1 Corinthians 6:9-11; Galatians 5:19; 1 Thessalonians 4:3-7).

(4) Habits or practices known to be destructive of physical and mental well-being. Christians are to regard themselves as temples of the Holy Spirit (Proverbs 20:1; 23:1-3; 1 Corinthians 6:17-20; 2 Corinthians 7:1; Ephesians 5:18).

(5) Quarreling, returning evil for evil, gossiping, slandering, spreading surmises injurious to the good names of others (2 Corinthians 12:20; Galatians 5:15; Ephesians 4:30-32; James 3:5-18; 1 Peter 3:9-10).

(6) Dishonesty, taking advantage in buying and selling, bearing false witness, and like works of darkness (Leviticus 19:10-11; Romans 12:17; 1 Corinthians 6:7-10).

(7) The indulging of pride in dress or behavior. Our people are to dress with the Christian simplicity and modesty that become holiness (Proverbs 29:23; 1 Timothy 2:8-10; James 4:6; 1 Peter 3:3-4; 1 John 2:15-17).

(8) Music, literature, and entertainments that dishonor God (1 Corinthians 10:31; 2 Corinthians 6:14-17; James 4:4).

27.3. THIRD. By abiding in hearty fellowship with the church, not inveighing against but wholly committed to its doctrines and usages and actively involved in its continuing witness and outreach (Ephesians 2:18-22; 4:1-3, 11-16; Philippians 2:1-8; 1 Peter 2:9-10).

APPENDIX 2

A Family Tree of Religious Groups

Used by permission of the Division of Sunday School Ministries. Created 1992 by Randy Cloud, Stan Ingersol, and William Miller.

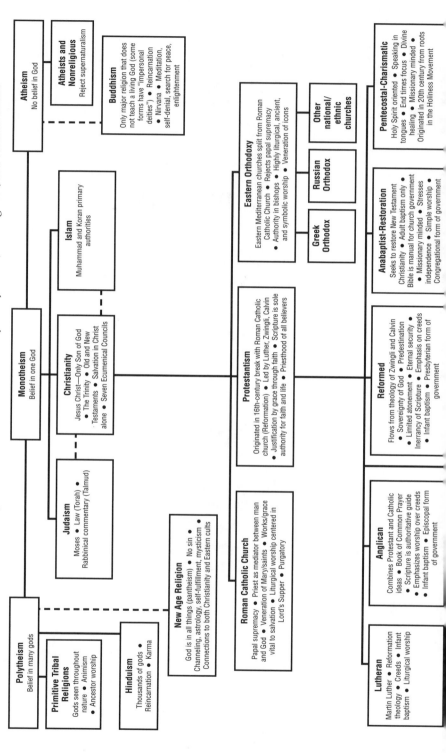

Polytheism
Belief in many gods

Primitive Tribal Religions
Gods seen throughout nature • Animism • Ancestor worship

Hinduism
Thousands of gods • Reincarnation • Karma

New Age Religion
God is in all things (pantheism) • No sin • Channeling, astrology, self-fulfillment, mysticism • Connections to both Christianity and Eastern cults

Monotheism
Belief in one God

Judaism
Moses • Law (Torah) • Rabbinical commentary (Talmud)

Christianity
Jesus Christ—Only Son of God • The Trinity • Old and New Testaments • Salvation in Christ alone • Seven Ecumenical Councils

Islam
Muhammad and Koran primary authorities

Atheism
No belief in God

Atheists and Nonreligious
Reject supernaturalism

Buddhism
Only major religion that does not teach a living God (some forms have "impersonal deities") • Reincarnation • Nirvana • Meditation, self-denial, search for peace, enlightenment

Roman Catholic Church
Papal supremacy • Priest as mediator between man and God • Veneration of Mary/saints • Works/grace vital to salvation • Liturgical worship centered in Lord's Supper • Purgatory

Protestantism
Originated in 16th-century break with Roman Catholic church (Reformation) • Led by Luther, Zwingli, Calvin • Justification by grace through faith • Scripture is sole authority for faith and life • Priesthood of all believers

Eastern Orthodoxy
Eastern Mediterranean churches split from Roman Catholic Church • Rejects papal supremacy • Authority in bishops • Highly liturgical, ancient, and symbolic worship • Veneration of icons

Greek Orthodox

Russian Orthodox

Other national/ethnic churches

Lutheran
Martin Luther • Reformation theology • Creeds • Infant baptism • Liturgical worship

Anglican
Combines Protestant and Catholic ideas • Book of Common Prayer • Scripture is authoritative guide • Emphasizes worship over creeds • Infant baptism • Episcopal form of government

Reformed
Flows from theology of Zwingli and Calvin • Sovereignty of God • Predestination • Limited atonement • Eternal security • Inerrancy of Scripture • Emphasis on creeds • Infant baptism • Presbyterian form of government

Anabaptist-Restoration
Seeks to restore New Testament Christianity • Adult baptism only • Bible is manual for church government • Missionary minded • Stresses independence • Simple worship • Congregational form of government

Pentecostal-Charismatic
Holy Spirit oriented • Speaking in tongues • End times focus • Divine healing • Missionary minded • Originated in 20th century from roots in the Holiness Movement

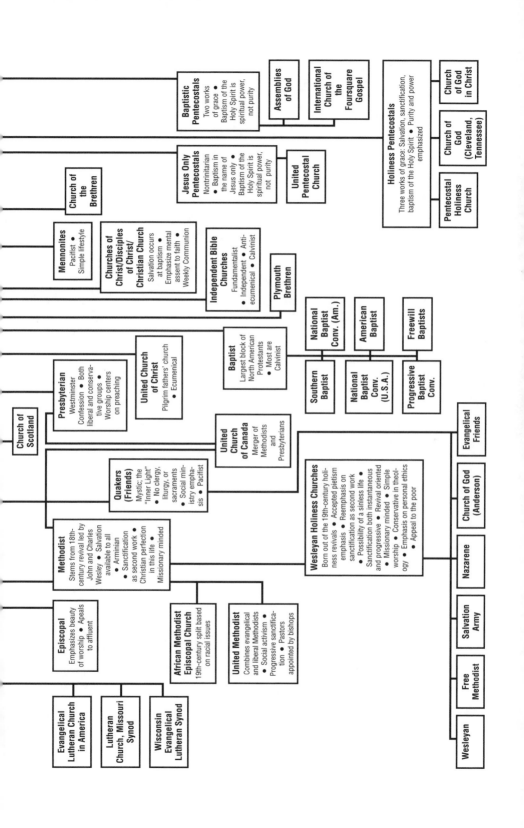

INDEX

343